Caribbean Hideaways

Caribbean Hideaways

Seventh Edition

by IAN KEOWN

Macmillan Travel • USA

MACMILLAN TRAVEL
A Simon & Schuster Macmillan Company
1633 Broadway
New York, NY 10019

First published by Harmony Books, a division of Crown Publishers, Inc., and
represented in Canada by the Canadian MANDA Group

ISBN 0-02-860647-7
ISSN 1069-580X

Editor: Robin Michaelson
Map Editor: Douglas Stallings
Design by Irving Perkins Associates
Maps by John Decamillis
Cover by Lori Singer

Manufactured in the United States of America
10   9   8   7   6   5   4   3   2   1

Contents

The Dutch Windwards 127

The Queen's Leewards 151

The French West Indies 211

Map List

Acknowledgments

As they say in Bonaire, *masha danki* (thank you) to scores of friends and colleagues for tips and suggestions; to readers who took the trouble to send me comments and critiques; to island-hoppers in airports and bars who shared their experiences; to innkeepers who took time, reconfirmed flights, and helped me get to the airport on time.

There are too many friends, colleagues, and correspondents to name individually, but for special efforts beyond the call of duty I'd like to offer a special thank you to the following (in alphabetical order, of course): Alan Bell, Frank Connolly, Dave Fernandez, Sharon Flescher, Gina Henry, Tony Johnson, Richard Kahn, Katherine van Kampen, Monica Leedy, Ralph Locke, Marcella Martinez, Marilyn Marx, Joanie Medhurst, Joe Petrocik, Matt Roberts, and Allison Ross.

Likewise, I herein acknowledge the professionalism and what-would-I-do-without-her dependability of Susan Spencer, who did most of the dirty work—editing, proofreading, keeping track of bits of paper and brochures, and deciphering my scribbles.

Introduction

Introduction

Here is a guide for lovers of all kinds and inclinations—Romeo and Juliet, Romeo and Romeo, Juliet and Juliet, rich lovers, poor lovers, newlyweds and newly unweds, actresses and bodyguards, moms and dads who would still be lovers if only they could get the kids out of their hair for a few days. In other words, it's for anyone who has a yen to slip off for a few days and be alone in the sun with someone he or she fancies, likes, loves, has the hots for, or simply wants to do something nice for.

Whatever your tastes or inclinations, you'll probably find something that appeals to you in these pages. This is a fairly eclectic selection. Some of the resorts are on the beach and others are in the mountains; some are on big islands and some are on islands so small you won't find them on a map; some large resorts are included because there are lovers who prefer the anonymity a large resort affords (but none of them so vast as to be tourist-processing factories); some have nightlife of sorts but most of them don't even have a tape recorder; some are for lovers who want to dress up in the evening and others are for lovers with cutoff jeans and beat-up sandals. But these hotels and resorts all have something special going for them. It may be seclusion (Palm Island Beach Club or Petit St. Vincent Resort, both in the Grenadines), it may be spaciousness (Caneel Bay on St. John, Casa de Campo in the Dominican Republic) or charm (Golden Rock on Nevis, the Golden Lemon on St. Kitts), a sense of the past (the Copper & Lumber Store Hotel on Antigua), or luxury (Malliouhana on Anguilla or Jumby Bay on Antigua). They may be here because they have some of these qualities and are, in the bargain, inexpensive (Frangipani on Bequia or the Hotel Mocking Bird Hill on Jamaica, for example).

In most cases, they're a combination of one or more of these characteristics, and in almost every case they're places where you can avoid neon, plastic, piped music, air-conditioning, casinos, conventions, children, and that peculiar blight of the Caribbean—massed cruise ship passengers.

Above all, none of these hotels try to disguise the fact that they're in the Caribbean; none of them try, the minute you arrive in the Caribbean, to transport you instantly to back-street Hong Kong or ye olde pubbe in Ye Olde Englande (well, one or two of them maybe, but you'll read about their follies so you won't be too startled when you get there). They are hotels that don't make you line up for breakfast in an air-conditioned dining room and then line up immediately afterward to make a reservation for the first

FLORIDA

Gulf of
Mexico

Miami

Straits of Florida

THE BAHAMAS

Havana

Cuba

Little Cayman

Grand Cayman   Cayman Brac

CAYMAN ISLANDS

Montego Bay

Jamaica

Kingston

Haiti

Port-au-Prince

GREATER

Caribbean
Sea

COLOMBIA

The Caribbean Islands

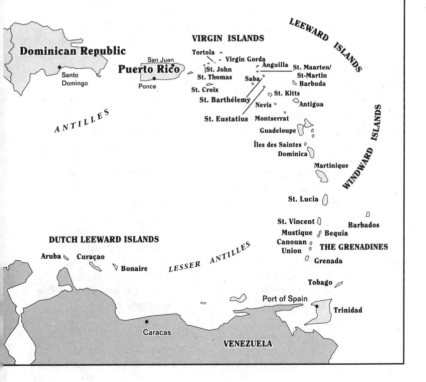

Atlantic Ocean

N W E S

TURKS AND CAICOS ISLANDS

Dominican Republic

Santo Domingo

San Juan

Puerto Rico

Ponce

ANTILLES

VIRGIN ISLANDS

Tortola

Virgin Gorda

St. John

St. Thomas

Saba

St. Croix

St. Barthélemy

St. Eustatius

LEEWARD ISLANDS

Anguilla St. Maarten/ St-Martin

Barbuda

St. Kitts

Nevis Antigua

Montserrat

Guadeloupe

Îles des Saintes

Dominica

Martinique

WINDWARD ISLANDS

St. Lucia

St. Vincent Barbados

Mustique Bequia

Canouan Union THE GRENADINES

Grenada

DUTCH LEEWARD ISLANDS

Aruba Curaçao

Bonaire

LESSER ANTILLES

Tobago

Port of Spain Trinidad

Caracas

VENEZUELA

or second seating at dinner. They're not the sort of hotels that entice you with promises of soft air and trade winds, and then seal you into a box where you're not allowed to leave the balcony door open to let in the promised soft air and trade winds.

PET PEEVES

Curmudgeons of the world unite! There are innkeepers who believe in some of the standards you try to uphold. I quote: "Please do not let your wife wear those ghastly hair curlers out of your room"; or "Tennis whites *does* mean wearing a shirt on court"; or "Transistor radios can be very disturbing to other people. Guests are requested not to play them in public areas"; or "No jeans and tank tops in the dining room."

Air-Conditioning   For me, and I'm sure for a lot of you, louvers and ceiling fans are more romantic than whirring, dripping, throbbing, rusting, shuddering, grinding air-conditioning units, so many of the hotels in this guide either do not have air-conditioning or use it only as a backup system. There is, of course, another side to the air-conditioning debate: In some hotels, the gadget is necessary to block out extraneous noises such as stray dogs, roosters, and roisterers, and on occasion you may welcome the background hum to keep your own noises *in;* moreover, one of my colleagues, who shall remain nameless, claims air-conditioning is a necessity for after-lunch lovemaking in the tropics. Therefore, when a hotel has air-conditioning as a backup system the fact is noted in the listings—but please don't take this as being a commendation at the expense of hotels without air-conditioning. (*Note:* Except for a few weeks in summer, air-conditioning is not as necessary as a lot of vacationers—and travel agents—think it is.)

Cruise Ship Passengers   Presumably you're going to the Caribbean to find a quiet, secluded beach that won't remind you of Coney Island on the Fourth of July, but you can forget that idea if a few hundred old salts arrive in ankle socks and T-shirts. Some hotels encourage these visits because they represent instant profit; others ban them unequivocally, and still others are beginning to learn that after they've cleared up the litter and tallied up the missing souvenirs, cruise ship passengers aren't worth the trouble. ("They buy one Coke, then use the toilet, and the profit on the Coke is less than what I pay for the water.") Most of the hotels in this guide ban cruise ship passengers—or at least limit the numbers.

Piped Music   If you take the trouble to search out a hideaway, as opposed to a big swinging resort, you probably don't want your peace and quiet to be disturbed by piped noise, especially when it's music that has no connection, harmonic or otherwise, with the setting—such as dining by candlelight on the veranda of a centuries-old inn and having to listen to a record of a chanteuse singing, "It's so-o goo-oo-ood."

Other Music Piped noise is not the same thing as discreet background music that's carefully selected by the management to match the mood of the guests or the setting; but any kind of music, taped or live, combo or steel band, should be avoidable (that is, if you don't want to listen, you should be able to go to another lounge or patio where you can't hear it), and it should never keep guests from their sleep. Also, any hotel that plays "Island in the Sun" more than six times in one evening should lose its license. Another ubiquitous blight these days is Bartender's Radio. He's bored, standing around all day serving drinks to a bunch of frolicking foreigners, and he wants his music—usually noisy with an insensate beat. It's a pain for owners, too: "I can see the bartender scurrying to turn down the radio every time he sees me approaching; I agree with you, guests shouldn't have to listen to the bartender's music." The "all" in "getting away from it all" includes other people's radios. That wish should be respected. Worst offense of all, of course, is amplified music—singer, combo, native band, or, horror of horrors, steel band. Quite apart from the fact that the music is often so loud you can't hear yourselves whisper sweet nothings, the sound systems usually distort the music itself—too much *kaBOOM-kaBOOM,* not enough *trala-trala.* Too often, I suspect, loud music is managerial camouflage to distract guests' attention from the wishy-washy food.

In this guidebook, loud music is tolerated (but with the greatest reluctance) only *if* the hotel offers alternative facilities for imbibing and dining away from the noise; but if the kabooming follows guests all the way to their beds or balconies, or lasts beyond, say, 11:00 p.m., that place loses points. Hotel people often boast about the days when their guests were entertained by impromptu performances by a Noël Coward or a Cole Porter, but Coward and Porter never went *kaBOOM-kaBOOM.* Yet presumably people still managed to enjoy their vacations back in the days before combos carted their own power stations around.

Please, please: When you resent the music or the volume of the music, take the manager aside and explain that you paid all that money and took that long journey to get some peace and quiet. Remind him or her, gently, that it's considered bad manners to talk so loudly that people at the next table can't enjoy their own conversation. Ditto a band that plays too loudly.

Television In the following pages, you will come upon several references to television that may at first seem befuddling. The reason is that many innkeepers and thousands of their guests (this one included) feel that television is not compatible with an escapist vacation, that the whole point of a vacation is to get away from television and telephones. For many years, of course, there was no point in TV because no one wanted to watch the local programs. But now with cable and satellite facilities available on most islands, vacationers and islanders can tune in to their daily dose of *Today* and *Tonight* and CNN. Several innkeepers have mentioned that when they considered installing sets to take advantage of these facilities they were overruled by their guests—a typical response being, "This is the one time in the year when I can enjoy his company without competing with baseball/her company without dragging her away from *Oprah*." Etcetera.

Moreover, many resorts are designed to enjoy a natural flow of breezes, encouraging guests to open windows, louvers, and doors and leave the cooling to the ceiling fans. The air of tranquility would be instantly destroyed if the neighbors on the left were watching car chases with sirens and the neighbors on the right were watching the shootout at the OK or any other corral. Television tends to be noisy, hideaways tend to be quiet.

One of the defining moments in this debate came during the Gulf War: People wanted to see what was happening without driving into town to the local bar. Most anti-TV resorts get around this by setting aside special rooms for TV and video, a much better arrangement because major sports events are more enjoyable when watched in the company of fellow enthusiasts rather than sulking companions.

Paging Systems   Even worse than intrusive music is the paging system around the swimming pool and bar; if you're trying to escape telephones and reminders of the office, it doesn't do much for your spirits to know that the people around you are wanted on the phone. Any man or woman who tips a telephone operator to be paged at the pool should be sealed in a phone booth! I can think of only one hotel in this guide with a paging system, and even then it's used sparingly.

Children   Some hotels ban them altogether, as they do cruise ship passengers; others shunt them off to a far corner of the property and feed them separately. It's not really the children who are the problem. It may be the parents, who are trying to have a vacation themselves and have allowed family discipline to break down until it reaches the point where it can be restored only by a public shouting match—usually on the beach or around the pool. As one innkeeper puts it, "Kids around pools mean noise—so we don't allow them at the pool." In any case, many couples in hideaways are parents trying to get away from their own families for a day or two, so they're hardly enchanted to be surrounded by other people's youngsters.

Rowdy families are less of a bother in the Caribbean than they are back home because parents can't just pile everyone into a car and drive off to the islands. Sometimes there's a lot to be said for stiff airfares. However, in recent years, many resorts, even such traditional holdouts as Little Dix Bay in the British Virgins, now accept children. Others, such as Sandy Lane in Barbados and Malliouhana in Anguilla, have created special facilities for kids that tend to keep them under control.

Conventions   The object of a convention or sales conference is to whip people into a frenzy of enthusiasm, but frenzied enthusiasm is something you don't need when you're trying to escape the business or urban world. Very few of the hotels in this guide accept conventions. If they do, the groups are either small enough to be absorbed without a trace, or so large that they have to rent the entire hotel. However, most of the hotels in this guide will accept small, seminar-type groups in the off-season, and in many cases they have to do so to stay in business; but that kind of group shouldn't interfere with your privacy and pleasure. In some cases, it's an advantage: While the group is cooped up studying or discussing its specialty, you have the beach, sailboards, and tennis courts all to yourselves.

SIGNING IN

Some managers prefer that you sign in with your real names, even if they don't match; others prefer you to sign as a couple because it's simpler for the staff. Unless you have strong views one way or another, the simplest procedure is to write the noncommittal M/M—that is, M/M John Smith, M/M Ian Keown, and so on.

However, at least one of you should use your real name. If it's absolutely imperative that you both travel incognito, then at some point you'd better take the manager aside and explain that "Mr. John Smith" will be paying the bill with checks or credit cards in the name of whatever your name is.

Note: If you want to be totally anonymous and don't want anyone to find out where you were even six months later, before you leave the hotel ask the manager to make sure your name does not appear on any mailing lists for Christmas cards, newsletters, and such.

THE RATES

This is the most hazardous chore in putting together a reliable guidebook. Most of the hotels in this guide were visited months before going to press, when many managers or owners had not yet established their rates for winter 1995–1996. Unlike some guidebook writers, however, I feel that rates are indispensable in such a publication; therefore, to simplify the production of the guidebook and ensure that you get the most up-to-date figures possible I've listed all the latest rates in a special section at the end of the guide (except for hotels listed as "Added Attractions," where you'll find the rates at the end of each listing). This way you can scan the list more easily and compare resort A with resort B. Moreover, to give you some indication of what sort of place you're reading about, I've also included, with the description of each hotel, a symbol ($) for *approximate* costs (see page 16).

The symbols (please note this carefully) are based on *high-season MAP (Modified American Plan) rates for two people, with breakfast and dinner*—that is, the cost of room plus breakfast and dinner. They are high-season rather than summer rates because they happened to be the most reliable figures available when the guidebook was compiled. Please remember, the dollar symbols would look much less ominous if they represented summer figures, and if you are considering a summer trip, I suggest that as a rule of thumb you chop off one $, except in the case of the lowest category. For detailed rates, please refer to "The Rates—and How to Figure Them Out" (p. 335).

RESERVATIONS

It's nice to pack a bag and just go on the spur of the moment, and if the moment happens to spur in the off-season, you may be able to drop in on some of these hotels and get the best room without a reservation.

But is it worth the risk? Think of it: You fly down there, take a long, costly taxi ride to the other side of the island, only to discover that by some fluke this happens to be the weekend when a bunch of people have come over from an adjoining island and have filled every room, or that the owners decided to close down for a few weeks because they have some maintenance that needs attention. For the impetuous, I've listed telephone numbers and fax numbers, most of them direct dial (first three digits are area codes for the island). Call ahead at least. In any case, at peak season it's imperative that you also reserve your flight weeks in advance.

For lovers who think ahead, there are several alternatives:

1. Travel Agent The agent who books your flight can also arrange your hotel reservation, probably at no extra charge; he or she will also attend to the business of deposits and confirmations. However, travel agents often have their own favorite islands and resorts, sometimes places involving no complications in terms of flights or reservations. If your agent tries to sell you a bigger island or resort, by all means consider it, but if you feel strongly about your own choice, dig in your heels.

2. Hotel Representative　　You pick up the telephone, call someone such as WIMCO or Ralph Locke Islands, tell them where you want to stay, and they can let you know (often right there and then) if your hotel is full or otherwise; they'll make your reservation, and, if there's time, send you confirmation—at no extra charge, unless they have to fax or telephone. You'll find a list of the leading hotel reps (who handle two or more of the hotels) at the end of this guide; individual hotel representatives and phone numbers are listed under the hotel itself.

3. Fax　　This is now the most efficient way to make a reservation direct, since you will receive your confirmation quickly—and in writing. Most hotels and resorts in the Caribbean now have facsimile equipment, and I have included the numbers where the service is available.

4. Letter　　The least efficient. You could be senile by the time you get a reply.

Whatever method you choose, you must be specific: Know the number of people in your party, date of arrival, time of arrival, and flight number if possible (in peak, peak season, some resorts may not even consider your reservation unless you already have airline seats); number of nights you plan to stay, date of departure; whether you want a double bed or twin beds, bathtub or shower, least expensive or most expensive room or suite, sea view or garden view or whatever; whether you want an EP, MAP, or FAP rate (these terms are explained at the end of this guide). Finally, don't forget your return address or telephone number.

DEPOSITS

Once you get a reply to your request for a reservation, assuming there's time, you'll be expected to make a deposit (usually one, two, or three days, depending on the length of your stay). Of course it's a nuisance—what if you want to change your mind? That's just the point. The smaller hotels can't afford to have reservations for a full house, turn down other reservations in the meantime, only to have half of their expected clientele cancel at the last minute.

From your point of view, the deposit guarantees your reservation. People sometimes make mistakes, especially with reservations, but if you have a written confirmed reservation in your hand *with proof of a deposit* you're not going to be turned away from your hotel.

If you're going in the peak season, you should always allow yourself time to send a deposit and get a *written* confirmed reservation. Again, you're

better off using a fax, which gives you and the hotel a reservation/
confirmation record.

HOW TO LICK HIGH COSTS

So long as people insist on scuttling south to the sun at the first hint of frost
or snow, hotel rates will remain astronomical in the Caribbean during the
winter months. The period from December to April is the island inns'
chance to make a profit and they grab the chance with a vengeance
(remember, the owners have to pay wages and overhead in spring, summer,
and fall, too—even if *you're* in Maine or Europe).

Here are a few suggestions for keeping your budget within bounds:

1. Avoid the Peak Season   Obviously, it's great to get some Caribbean sun when the frost is nipping up north, but March and April are not so
hot in northern climes either, and it's often very pleasant to escape to the
islands in October, November, and early December. Some people head
south in May and June to get an early start on a suntan. Even during
summer, the Caribbean has its attractions, and more and more people are
discovering them. Oddly enough, summer in the Caribbean islands can be
cooler than in stifling northern cities. While northern beaches and facilities
are overcrowded in summer, the beaches in the Caribbean are half empty,
and while the northern resorts are charging peak-season rates, the Caribbean is available at bargain rates. So remember that the peak season lasts
only four months (usually December 15 through April 15), *and for eight
months of the year rates are one-quarter to one-half less.*

2. Choose Your Resort Carefully   Some resorts throw in everything with the rate—sailing, waterskiing, tennis, snorkeling, and so on;
others charge extra for almost everything. Compare, for example, Curtain
Bluff and St. James's Club on Antigua—free scuba diving and waterskiing
at the former; you pay for scuba at the latter. Obviously, if you don't want to
scuba dive or waterski, you may be better off at St. James's Club. But this sort
of situation also occurs with tennis, windsurfing—even with snorkeling
gear.

3. Dodge Taxes   Some islands have no tax on tourists and others, like
the Dominican Republic, are as high as 23%; on a two-week vacation it can
add up to a few hundred dollars. Taxes are listed in the section on rates at
the end of this guide. So are service charges: Read these details carefully for
they can save you a small bundle, not simply because some service charges
are 10% and others are 15%, but because in many cases the service charge
relieves you of the need to tip. For example, this reminder from Antigua's

Curtain Bluff: "A service charge of 10% will be added; please, no tipping." (This does not mean that guests cannot express their appreciation: "Curtain Bluff has a fund for the community of Old Road. If you want to donate funds, please see a member of the management.")

4. Drink Rum   On rum-producing islands, rum is less expensive than scotch or bourbon, and in a thirst-building climate this can make a noticeable difference when the tab is tallied at the end of your stay. However, some island governments clamp such enormous duties on soda or tonic that your rum may cost less than its mixer. In that case, drink the local beer or locally produced mixers.

The best way around big bar tabs is to buy a tax-free bottle of your favorite liquor at the airport before you leave. This may be frowned upon in smaller hotels, but in any case you should never drink from your bottle in public rooms. Several of the hideaways in this guide have a bottle of rum and mixers waiting for you in your room—on the house.

5. Kitchens   No one wants to go off on vacation and spend time cooking, but a small kitchen is useful for preparing between-meal snacks, lunches, and drinks, without running up room service charges. Several of the hotels listed in this guide have refrigerators and/or kitchenettes and/ or fully equipped kitchens, and a few of them have minimarkets on the premises. They can save a lot of dollars without a lot of extra effort.

6. Double Up   Consider the possibility of trotting off to the islands with your favorite couple and sharing a suite or bungalow/cottage/villa. If you do this in a place such as, say, Tryall in Montego Bay, you can enjoy a villa with kitchen, sitting room, and two bedrooms with two complete bathrooms. You'll find many examples of such cost-cutting options in this guide.

7. Packages   These are special rates built around the themes of honeymoons, water sports, tennis, golf. "We have people coming back every year for five or six years on the honeymoon package," sighs one hotel keeper. In fact, some couples have arrived on a honeymoon package with all their children in tow, looking for reduced rates for them, too. Honeymoon packages usually include frills such as a bottle of champagne, flowers for the lady, or a half-day sail up the coast. Check them carefully— you may be better off with a regular rate. Sports packages usually are a good deal. They will probably include free court time (carefully specified) for tennis players, or X number of free rounds for golfers. If you're a sports enthusiast, check with the hotel rep or your travel agent for the nitty-gritty details.

8. Tour Packages   These are dirty words to some people, but they needn't be. A tour package is not the same thing as an escorted tour: It can mean simply that 10 or 20 people will be booked on the same flight to take advantage of a special fare. They may be given their choice of two or three hotels on the island, so you may never see them again until you get to the airport for your return flight. Local sightseeing is sometimes included and sometimes it's an option; some packages include boat trips and barbecues. If you don't feel like taking part in these activities, you may still be ahead of the game because the special rates you will be paying for hotels and flights may be such good deals. The advantages of package tours are that you may qualify for lower airfares (always with conditions, but you can probably live with them), and the tour operator may have negotiated lower hotel rates; in winter, tour operators may have "blocked off" a group of hotel rooms and seats on jets, and package tours may be your only hope of finding reservations.

Few of the hotels in this guide are likely to be overrun with package tours, but some of them do in fact accept small tour groups, a fact that is noted under the P.S. at the end of each hotel listing. Look into the tour brochures of some of the airlines, say, American or Continental, and you may find special packages built around some of these hotels, such as the Half Moon Golf, Tennis & Beach Club in Jamaica, Cobblers Cove and Glitter Bay in Barbados, Casa de Campo in the Dominican Republic, the Grand Palazzo and Point Pleasant on St. Thomas—even the tony Little Dix Bay on Virgin Gorda.

THE RATINGS

All the hotels and resorts in this guide are above average in one way or another, but some obviously are more special than others. To make choosing simpler, I've rated the hotels (using symbols) for romantic atmosphere (stars), food and service (goblets), sports facilities (beach balls), and cost (dollar signs). The ratings are highly personal and subjective—the fun part of compiling the guide, my reward to myself for scurrying around from island to island and hotel to hotel when I could just as easily have been lying on the beach.

Stars   represent the *romantic* atmosphere of a hotel or resort more than the quality or luxury or facilities. Of course, the two go together, and here we're talking also about the setting, decor, size, efficiency, location, personality, welcome—the intangibles.

Goblets   evaluate not just the quality of the food but the overall emphasis and attitude toward dining, the competence of the waiters, the way the food is placed before you. *This is a specifically Caribbean evaluation*—it takes into consideration the special circumstances in the islands. In other words, any hotel that promises "the finest in gourmet dining" or "the ultimate in Continental cuisine" almost certainly gets a low score because this is a vain promise: "The finest Continental cuisine" is something you find at a three-star restaurant in France; Caribbean islands just don't have access to the market gardens and meat markets to match those standards. There are times, in fact, when you get the impression that all the meals in the Caribbean are coming from some giant commissary in Miami (even fish); so hotels that list local dishes, such as conch pie, *keshi yena*, or *colombo de poulet riz* on their menus, even if only occasionally, stand a better chance of getting a higher rating than most hotels trying to emulate Continental cuisine (unless they do it really well).

Any hotel that forces you to dine indoors in an air-conditioned restaurant ranks badly (there are only two or three of them in this guide, and although one of them is Dorado Beach, which gets a three-goblet rating, at least it gives you the option of dining al fresco in a second restaurant, or on your room balcony). It seems to me that one of the great pleasures of dining in the Caribbean is to be in the open air, surrounded by the sounds of the tropical night or the sea, in an atmosphere of palms and stars—not in some third-rate interior designer's concept of an English pub or Manhattan nightspot. Wine does not enter into consideration in this guide. The conditions, usually, are all wrong for storing wine and caring for wine, and by the time it has been shipped three times, it's overpriced. Most of the hotels that rate highly for food have passable to good wine lists; otherwise it's a hit-and-miss affair (except, perhaps, on the French islands, or in special cases such as Curtain Bluff in Antigua, Malliouhana on Anguilla, and Biras Creek on Virgin Gorda).

In the listings following each hotel, you'll occasionally find the term *family style*. This doesn't mean that you all sit down with the kiddies; it means, rather, that you get a fixed menu: You take what's offered, and usually all the guests sit down to dine at the same time, perhaps at communal tables. Sometimes you will be offered a choice of dishes, sometimes not; if you have problems with your diet, check with the manager each morning, and if he or she is planning something you don't fancy, he or she will probably prepare a steak or some other simple alternative. If you're fussy about food, skip places serving family-style meals. Moreover, you may not want to dine with strangers each evening.

While on the subject of dining, please note that under each hotel listing I spell out the evening dress code. I've seen too many hapless vacationers either laden with wardrobes they have no opportunity to show off, or, conversely, the male has to borrow a tie or jacket to get into the dining room. Although most of these hideaways set their code as casual or informal, this does not mean sloppy—and for most places that means no shorts, no tank tops or T-shirts in the evening, cover-ups and no wet swimsuits at lunchtime. My personal preference is to have the option of dressing or not, depending on my mood; I have obviously included some places that expect guests to dress up every evening, but they either have alternative dining areas or can arrange for you to have dinner on your private patio or balcony.

Beach Balls   offer you a quick idea of the availability of sporting facilities, but you'll also find the actual facilities spelled out at the end of each hotel. I tried originally to include prices for each activity, but this became too cumbersome; however, you will learn from the listings whether a particular sport is free or whether you have to pay an additional fee.

Remember, no matter how well endowed the hotel, sports facilities are less crowded in the nonwinter months.

Dollar Signs   should be used as a rough guide only, primarily for comparing one resort with another. For detailed rates, turn to the special chapter at the end of the guide. The $ symbols are based on *winter rates for two people;* since the most accessible rate for comparison between hotels is the *MAP rate,* this is the one that is used (that is, for a room, breakfast, and

Here are the ratings:	
☆	*A port of call*
☆☆	*A long weekend*
☆☆☆	*Time for a suntan*
☆☆☆☆	*A place to linger*
☆☆☆☆☆	*Happily ever after*
♀	*Sustenance*
♀♀	*Good food*
♀♀♀	*Something to look forward to*
♀♀♀♀	*As close to haute cuisine as you can get in the Caribbean*
➊	*Some diversions*
➊➊	*Lots of things to keep your mind off sex*
➊➊➊	*More diversions than you'll have stamina for*
➊➊➊➊	*All that and a spa or horseback riding, too*
$	*$265 or under, MAP for two*
$$	*$265 to $370, MAP for two*
$$$	*$370 to $475, MAP for two*
$$$$	*$475 to $580, MAP for two*
$$$$$	*$580 and above, MAP for two*

dinner). Each $ represents roughly $100 increments; where a hotel over-flows into more than one category, I've used the lower category, assuming that this represents a reasonable proportion of the available rooms. For a quick guide to *summer rates,* you will not be far off the mark if you reduce the higher ratings by one $.

OTHER CHOICES

A special feature in this guide is the "Other Choices" section at the end of the listings for some islands. These are, for the most part, hotels, inns, and resorts that we visited as possibilities but that didn't quite measure up; in some cases they are hotels that were rated in earlier editions of the guide but have since lost some of their appeal or changed management. But they may help fill a few gaps for you, especially since several of them are relatively inexpensive. If you visit any of them and think they deserve to be featured and rated, please let me know.

DOUBLE BEDS

Some Caribbean hoteliers seem to have installed twin beds in most of their rooms. However, most hotels of any size have some rooms with double, queen- or king-size beds, and all but the tiniest hideaways can arrange to push two twins together to make a double—if you give them advance notice. If this is the case, however, check before indulging in any trampolin-ing, because if the beds are pushed together and sheeted lengthwise rather than crosswise, they may part like the Red Sea and you may end up in a voluptuous heap on the floor.

CREEPY-CRAWLIES AND OTHER HAZARDS

Snakes, spiders, and tarantulas are no problem. Mosquitoes, no-see-ums, and sand flies have been sprayed almost to oblivion on most islands; however, they do sometimes appear in certain types of weather, so if you have the sort of skin that can rouse a dying mosquito to deeds of heroism, take along a repellent (or check into a hotel with air-conditioning).

Sea urchins are a hazard on some islands, depending on tides or seasons or something I don't understand. Every hotel seems to have its solution, but, for what it's worth, here is the traditional remedy from the island of Saba: "Count the number of spines sticking in you; then swallow one mouthful of seawater for each spine." Since sea urchin stings are painful, check with the hotel staff before venturing into the sea.

Drinking water is not a problem on most islands, but it is chemically different from what you're accustomed to, so if your system is touchy about such things, ask for bottled water.

Sun is something else altogether. Naturally, you want to get a quick tan, and of course you love lying on the beach—but remember, your reason for slipping off together is love, and love can be a painful affair if you both look like lobsters and feel like barbecues.

Remember, too, the Caribbean sun is particularly intense; one hour a day is enough, unless you already have a hint of tan. Some enthusiasts forget they can get a sunburn while in the water; if you plan to do a lot of snorkeling, wear a T-shirt. If you do get a burn, stand in a lukewarm shower. Some people recommend compresses of really strong tea; one of the beach boys on St. Maarten has quite a sideline going rubbing on the leaf of the aloe plant; the Greeks recommend rubbing on yogurt. For heat prostration, Sabans again seem to have the endearing answer: "Rub the body with rum, particularly around the stomach."

MUGGINGS AND OTHER VEXATIONS

Each time I set out to research this guide, friends keep cautioning me about the horrible things that might happen to me in the Caribbean— robbery, mugging, assault, battery, anti-Americanism, fascism, racism, and other everyday hassles.

Nothing has happened so far. There are probably plenty of statistics around to prove that things can be unpleasant in the Caribbean, but it has never been immediately obvious to me. Nevertheless, travelers should always be alert, keep valuables in a safe place, and listen to any warnings given by hotel personnel or local people. Sad to say, however, some hotels on islands like Barbados now advise guests in ground-floor rooms to keep their doors closed and locked after dark—"for insurance purposes."

PIRACY ON THE HIGH ROADS

Caribbean taxi drivers. Now there's a motley, shameless, scurrilous bunch of brigands! They begin hectoring you, if they can, through customs and immigration, and before they take time to welcome you to their lovely island in the sun they're already trying to make you "reserve" them for sightseeing tours and the trip back to the airport. (There are, of course, exceptions, and I hereby apologize to the one taxi driver in a hundred who is pleasant, courteous, punctual, honest.)

Their gross behavior can get your amorous tryst off to an unpleasant start, and the way around this is to ask your hotel to assign one of its pool of "approved" drivers to meet you at the airport; the hotel will send you his or her name when confirming your reservation, in which case, you simply ask for Sebastian or whatever the name is when you get there. If there's no time to send the name before you arrive, the hotel may post a message for you on the airport notice board, telling you to ask for Sebastian. (This procedure is not the same thing as sending over a hotel limousine; you may still have to pay the regular taxi fare, but at least it will be the official rate and not whatever the driver thinks he or she can get away with.)

Taxis can cost you an arm and a leg in the Caribbean, and the driver may go for the shoulder and thigh too. That's why I've included the cost of the taxi ride from the airport in the list of nitty-gritty details following each hotel.

The drivers' point of view is that their costs are unusually high— imported cars, imported gas, imported parts, highways that knock the hell out of the cars, stiff insurance rates, and so on. Fine. What's not so understandable is why island governments kowtow to the drivers, who won't allow anyone else to operate a bus or limousine service; the result is that you, the visitors, have to pay perhaps $10 to $12 for a taxi ride, when you could be paying only $2 to $3 for a mini-bus or limousine. On some islands authorities quite blatantly post lower rates for residents. In some cases, taxis operate on a "seat available" basis—that is, you pay a share of the cost with other people going in the same direction; but if only six people get off an interisland flight, they may not be going in your direction, and in any case, by the time the immigration officer has finished stamping your passport, all the "seat available" taxis may have mysteriously left. Your best bet, if you have a long taxi ride, is to ask your hotel to have a taxi and driver waiting for you at the airport.

SOME CARIBBEAN COMMENTS

Water   You'll be constantly reminded of the old Caribbean adage— "Water is the gold of the Caribbean," or as it's less eloquently phrased on some signs, "On our island in the sun we don't flush for number one." In deluxe resorts with their own catchments and reverse osmosis plants, the cost to the hotel for one shower may be $5—your two showers each per day account for $30 of your rate; hotels that have to import water will have a still higher bill. Be sparing. Shower together.

Caribbean Service   Don't expect the staff to rush around. It's all right for you—you're there for only a few days, but the people who live there don't find the glaring sun so appealing day after day. They'll operate at a normal Caribbean pace no matter how much you tip, and at a less than normal pace if you shout and snap your fingers and stamp your feet. You just have to learn a few tricks. For example, always *anticipate* your thirst: Order your drinks about 10 minutes before you'll be gasping for them. Also, place your order in simple English; the islanders don't want to figure out what you're trying to say—it's too hot to bother.

ESCAPE ROUTES TO THE CARIBBEAN

There are several hundred flights a week from the North American mainland to the Caribbean islands, and it's about time you were on one of them. But which one? What with deregulation and mergers, it's a hassle trying to keep up with airlines these days. You'll find a quick summary of the major services to the various islands, or groups of islands, at the beginning of each chapter in this guide; please note that this information is based on *winter schedules,* and lists only nonstop or direct (that is, with no change of aircraft) flights from major North American departure points.

The major multidestination carriers to the islands are still *American, Air Canada,* and *British West Indies Airways (BWIA),* but they have been joined by others such as *Delta, United, Continental, TWA,* and a few lesser lines like Carnival, based in Miami. If you live in or transit via the northeast, American and Continental are the carriers with most flights to the islands, and they should be your first choice; most Caribbean flights from Miami are flown by American and BWIA.

But overall, American is now *the* Caribbean carrier, with its major hub at San Juan and interisland services on its offshoot, *American Eagle.* American Eagle, and to a lesser extent *Sunaire* (until the demise of Eastern, it was known as Eastern Metro), are the best things that have happened to the islands in years. They blanket the islands with modern fleets of twin-engined prop or turboprop aircraft, and both have above-average consideration for matters that other Caribbean carriers seem to find tiresome—such as maintaining on-time schedules and honoring confirmed reservations.

Remember (and I've also said this elsewhere because it's important) when using regional services that the smaller aircraft do not have capacious overhead bins or racks for garment bags, so luggage that would normally be considered carry-on will have to be checked. That probably means a little more care in packing.

Of the Caribbean-based carriers, BWIA (known affectionately as Bee-Wee) is a sort of national carrier; it probably has to serve too many islands (and, therefore, too many governments) for its own good—Antigua, St. Lucia, Barbados, Trinidad, and St. Kitts. *Air Jamaica* flies all up and down the eastern states and provinces and sometimes the West Coast, garnering passengers for Montego Bay and Kingston.

AIRLINES WITHIN THE CARIBBEAN

Apart from Sunaire and American Eagle, mentioned above, it may be necessary to finish your trip to your chosen hideaway on a local island-hopper. Here's where the fun begins—if you have a bottomless sense of humor.

Windward Island Airways is my favorite interisland carrier. St. Maarten based, it shuttles between Juliana Airport and Saba, St. Eustatius, St. Kitts, St. Barthélemy, and Anguilla. This very efficient little outfit (36 years old in 1996) operates a complex "bus service" (more than a thousand flights a year to Saba alone) with a few DeHavilland Twin Otters, that short takeoff and landing (STOL) workhorse, the engines of which are washed every morning—inside and out.

The biggest operation in the Caribbean is *Leeward Islands Air Transport (LIAT)*. In terms of departures/arrivals per day it's actually one of the largest airlines *in the world*. It's always been a sort of laughingstock, and in an earlier edition of this guide I quoted some of the scathing comments associated with its acronym—Leave Island Any Time, etc. Truth is, LIAT is a much-improved airline. Serving so many independent islands with the kind of frequency (45,000 takeoffs and landings a year) LIAT has to maintain is a momentous task. LIAT now has a first-rate on-time record (officially), although it's hard to believe when you're on a flight, as I was once, leaving one hour early and heading north instead of south. Moreover, the line has recently introduced new aircraft—updated versions of its warhorse British Aerospace Avro 748s (you no longer feel like you're about to sink through the worn cushions to the floor) and nifty DeHavilland Dash prop jets.

Antigua-based LIAT now finds itself, to the chagrin of many island politicians, confronted with competition from a new carrier called *Caribbean Airways,* which was brought to reality with considerable help from British Airways. The new line is based in Barbados and as of spring 1995 is confined to services to Trinidad, Grenada, and St. Lucia, but it has major plans to expand throughout the region.

Moreover, the airline now flies state-of-the-art aircraft such as the Canadian-built DeHavilland Dash 8 prop jet, a sort of sports car among commuter aircraft, as well as the workhorse Twin Otters and seven-seater Islanders.

For short flights to the smaller islands, it may be smart to charter a small plane. The local hotels will make the arrangements for you, teaming you with other couples to cut costs. These shared charters are common practice in St. Kitts/Nevis and the Grenadines. For St. Kitts/Nevis or other islands around St. Maarten/St. Martin or Antigua, you can arrange to have a Beech-craft or Partenavia of *Carib Aviation* waiting for your jet. From Antigua to

Nevis is a quick flight (10 minutes or so), costs only a few dollars more when shared, and can save hours waiting for a scheduled LIAT flight.

For flights to St. Vincent and its gorgeous Grenadines, you have a choice between LIAT and *Mustique Airways*. LIAT has limited service, whereas Mustique Airways augments its regular scheduled flights with shared charters if there are enough people to get from here to there. "Here" is usually Barbados (although home base is officially St. Vincent), where the line's personnel will meet transferring passengers, and "there" is usually Mustique, Canouan, and Union, with occasional forays to St. Vincent, Bequia, and Carriacou, or even as far distant as San Juan and Caracas. Mustique Airways is now 15 years old; I flew on one of their first flights when they had only two aircraft. Now they have eight—five Britten BN2 Islanders, a Baron, and two Cessna 402Cs—which between them manage to transport something like 120,000 passengers a year. Their U.S. number, by the way, is 800/223-0599.

Caribbean airlines may not have the sophisticated electronic reservations systems, or even the alert staffs of U.S. airlines, so always double-check tickets—date, flight number, check-in times, and so forth.

Even if you're taking a 10-minute flight with only half-a-dozen passengers to be boarded you'll be expected to check in *an hour and a half* before departure. I questioned this with one airline executive, and his disarming reply was: "Because the flight may leave early." He wasn't kidding, either. Moreover, to be sure of your seat, get to the check-in desk as early as possible, even if your ticket is reconfirmed—and make sure the check-in attendant sees it. Don't assume that being *in line* on time is enough to guarantee your seat.

Also, a reconfirmed ticket doesn't mean a thing until it's in the hands of the ticket agent. You can be standing politely in line, ticket in hand, and still lose your seat. The people huddled around the check-in counter may not have tickets—they may be waiting for someone not to show up. You, for example. Push your way to the front—before the ticket agent's cousin displaces you.

Always reconfirm your flight 48 hours before departure. This is very important, because some of the lines have a tendency to overbook, and some passengers have a tendency not to show up; so the airline may simply decide that if you don't reconfirm you're not going to fly and they'll give your seat to someone else. Many hotels will handle your reconfirmations, but there's nothing they can do if you wait until it's too late.

If you're taking along carry-on luggage, remember that what may qualify as carry-on size on a 747 may have to be checked on smaller island-hopping aircraft, so make sure it is locked and labeled. Also, luggage allowances on U.S. carriers may not be acceptable to local carriers, and you may find yourself paying excess baggage charges on some stretches. If you anticipate problems, see your travel agent before you leave.

ISLAND-HOPPING STOPOVERS

This is really something you have to take up with your travel agent, but I mention it here to remind you of some of the possibilities you may be overlooking for visiting several islands for the price of one. A full-revenue ticket from New York to, say, Barbados may entitle you to stop off for a few days in Antigua on the way down, in Martinique or Guadeloupe on the way back. Likewise, with a full-revenue round-trip ticket from New York to Haiti in your pocket you may be able to visit Santo Domingo and/or Puerto Rico, at no extra fare; a round-trip ticket from Miami to Tobago may also take you to St. Lucia and Trinidad. The actual stops will depend on the type of fare, day of week, season, and so on—but the prospect of seeing twice as much Caribbean for the same price is certainly worth the time it will take you to ask about island stopovers.

BOAT TRAVEL

Several of the islands or groups of islands are linked by seagoing ferries.

In the Virgin Islands, the M/V *Bomba Charger,* M/V *Native Son,* and M/V *Speedy's Fantasy* operate 90-passenger, air-conditioned multihulls between Charlotte Amalie in St. Thomas and West End, Road Town, and Virgin Gorda in the British Virgins. Fares are $17 per person each way.

There are also regular services, by powerboat, hydrofoil, or catamaran, between St. Barthélemy and St. Maarten/St. Martin, some departures in the afternoon to connect with flights from New York and other northeastern destinations.

The Cayman Islands

Grand Cayman

Cayman Brac

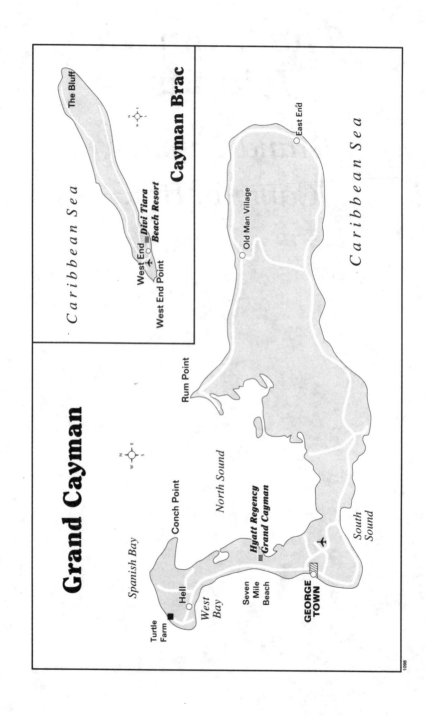

Grand Cayman

Spanish Bay

Conch Point

North Sound

Turtle Farm

Hell

West Bay

Seven Mile Beach

Hyatt Regency Grand Cayman

GEORGE TOWN

South Sound

Rum Point

Old Man Village

East End

Caribbean Sea

Cayman Brac

The Bluff

West End

Divi Tiara Beach Resort

West End Point

Caribbean Sea

1098

The Cayman Islands

There are three of them—Grand Cayman, Little Cayman, Cayman Brac. Together they're a British Crown Colony that will probably remain that way for some time because, as one local taxi driver put it, "If we got independence we'd only end up with a lot of politicians."

Otherwise, the Caymans can't seem to make up their mind what they want to be. On the one hand, the colony claims to be, as the brochures put it, "as unspoiled as it was the day Columbus sailed by"; on the other hand, a banking boom has "transformed George Town from a sleepy village into a dynamic financial capital." At last count there were about 400 banks for a population of less than 20,000 plus who knows how many megabucks wheeler-dealers skulking among the sea-grape trees searching for the perfect offshore banking. The islands are touted as a tax haven, but everyone seems to forget to mention that it's taxless only for people who live there or buy condominiums there; the poor visitors get zapped with a 6% tax on rooms, a $7.50 departure tax (but they *have* fixed up the airport nicely), another fee for a local driver's license, and the aftereffects of an import duty that has sent prices soaring alarmingly ($2.50 for a ginger ale, for example).

All of this would be easier to take if Grand Cayman, the largest of the trio, were something special. But this is no lofty, luxuriant Jamaica or St. Lucia. It's flat, swampy, and characterless (well, what else can you call a place whose prime tourist attraction is a turtle farm?). True, there are lots of beaches, most notably Seven Mile Beach running north from George Town, but they're lined with an uninspired collection of hotels and condominiums (none of them, it should be noted, higher than the palm trees, so no one can accuse the authorities of ruining the place).

What the Caymans do have—in abundance—are miles, fathoms, leagues of coral reefs, with water so clear you can spot an angelfish 200 feet away.

How to Get There Here's an interesting reflection on, I suspect, where the people who keep their money in offshore banks live. There are no nonstops to Grand Cayman from, for example, New York (one-stop on USAir), but there are plenty from Charlotte (USAir), Houston (Cayman Airways), Raleigh-Durham (American), and Miami (Cayman and Northwest). There are also one-stop flights from Memphis (Northwest), Dallas and Hartford (both on American), Boston, Baltimore/Washington,

Cleveland, and New York (all on USAir). Cayman also has nonstop service to Cayman Brac from Miami.

For information on the Cayman Islands, call 212/682-5582.

Hyatt Regency Grand Cayman

Grand Cayman

☆						♀	♀				◑	◑	◑			$	$	$		
Atmosphere						**Dining**					**Sports**					**Rates**				

You won't find many chain hotels represented in these pages, but, like its sister resort at Dorado Beach in Puerto Rico, this $54-million resort eschews the Hyatt formula.

The architecture, described as British colonial, is really more birthday cake colonial, with white iron verandas and decorative trim "icing," a pastel blue facade accented by flower boxes and decorative fanlights. After dark, the *mise-en-scène* becomes positively magical, what with a zillion lights gleaming through French windows, bathing the reflecting pools, spotlighting the fountains, and festooning the ficus trees.

The Hyatt is just one corner of a 90-acre resort development known as Britannia, a tropical conglomerate with 1-, 2-, 3-, and 4-bedroom villas, its own beach club and marina, as well as the current hotel and one-of-a-kind golf course. The hotel itself is comprised of a courtyard of lawns, pools, and fountains surrounded by the seven wings of the hotel, the tallest of which is five stories high. At 235 rooms, it is, for my money, a hundred rooms too big, but it brings to the Caymans a touch of luxury hitherto found only in a few of the island's condominiums. The guest rooms—many newly refurbished—are tastefully designed, as you'd expect from Hyatt, and equipped with all the trimmings, such as mini-bars. Color schemes reflect the aquas and corals of sea and sand, with flashes of lilac and pink tossed in; travertine marble layers the foyers, bathrooms, and oval bathtubs; the custom-designed furniture features mostly upholstered rattan and wicker (the only complaint here is that in the standard rooms a two-seat couch crowds the room without adding much in comfort or convenience, unless you plan to watch hours of television). For a view of the sea (about 300 yards away) you'll have to check into the top two floors; if you want private sunning space, ask for one of the 22 Terrace Rooms. The most attractive accommodations are probably the Deluxe Suites (with sleeping galleries, wet bars, and 1½ baths); but for as much seclusion and privacy as you can muster in a hotel this size, check into the premium Regency Club and ask for a room overlooking the golf course.

Generous in all things, the Hyatt people give you a choice of dining spots—the veranda of the Britannia Golf Club & Grille, another restaurant at the beach club called Hemingways, and the Garden Loggia (the main dining room, where breakfast is served, is stylishly decorated in bleached ash paneling with latticed ceilings and French windows opening to the al fresco garden extension). Menus are hardly predictable Hyatt fare, the Scottish chef producing a masterly combination of Continental, American, and Caribbean dishes—tenderloin of veal with braised bok choy and grilled swordfish with passion-fruit butter. (Remember to make reservations for dinner: The Hyatt is the most stylish dining spot along Seven Mile Beach and popular with nonresident diners.)

Even Hyatt's water-sports facilities are a notch beyond the usual with a flagship 65-foot catamaran designed specifically for cruising around the Caymans and equipped with spacious decks, comfortable seating, stereo, bar, two restrooms, and underwater glass panels for fish watching.

But what heaps most attention on Britannia is its golf course. Jack Nicklaus not only designed the 9-hole links-style course but also designed the special Cayman Ball, a sphere that claims to do something my own tee shots have been doing for years—going half as far as they should. The advantage of the Cayman Ball in a resort like this is that players can get in 18 holes in half the time, on a course that requires space for 9 rather than 18 holes. Figure that out. The links also function as an 18-hole executive course weekday afternoons and as a 9-hole regulation course on weekends. It may not be St. Andrews, but at least it's another reason besides scuba diving for going to the Caymans.

Name: Hyatt Regency Grand Cayman
Manager: Philip Kendall
Address: P.O. Box 1588, Grand Cayman, British West Indies
Location: On the Britannia resort development, across the main road from Seven Mile Beach, 2 miles outside of George Town, 12 minutes and $16.50 from the airport
Telephone: 809/949-1234
Fax: 809/949-8528

Reservations: Hyatt Worldwide, 800/223-1234

Credit Cards: All major cards

Rooms: 235, including 44 Regency Club rooms, 8 Deluxe Suites, 2 Luxurious Suites, some with terraces or patios, some with small verandas, all with ceiling fans and air-conditioning, fully stocked mini-bars (wet bars in suites), satellite TV, clock/radios, direct-dial telephones, and hair dryers; suites are duplexes with sleeping lofts and canopy beds

Meals: Breakfast 7:00–11:30, lunch 11:30–2:30 (everything from sandwiches to complete meals, at any of 3 indoor/outdoor locations), dinner 6:00–10:00, June to November (in the fan-cooled indoor/outdoor Garden Loggia, $60–$85 for 2); Sunday champagne brunch buffet 11:30–2:30; casual resort wear appropriate in all restaurants; no-smoking area in dining room; 24-hour room service

Entertainment: 4 bars, live music all nights except Sunday

Sports: Beach (i.e., a section of the popular Seven Mile Beach across the road), 4 freshwater swimming pools, 1 with swim-up bar, Jacuzzi, tennis (4 Plexipave courts, with lights), croquet—all free; snorkeling gear, catamaran and Sunfish sailing, windsurfing, parasailing, paddleboats, scuba diving, and day sails on the resort's private 65-foot catamaran for a fee; private 9-hole golf course that can be played three ways, including 18 holes with the Cayman Ball

P.S.: At any season you may encounter groups that come perilously close to behaving like conventioneers; open all year

Other Choices

Divi Tiara Beach Resort

Cayman Brac

The brac is the rugged bluff that distinguishes this particular Cayman; the Divi Tiara is just the sort of hotel to help you enjoy the quiet and solitude of this unspoiled island. Because the main attraction of this Divi hotel is the Peter Hughes Dive Center, most of the guests are underwater nuts, and the colorful room decor seems to be trying to outdazzle the reefs. Besides scuba, an underwater photography school, marine ecology classes, paddleboats, a tennis court, beachside pool, snorkeling, and bicycles are available. Even the divers surface for the Sunday buffet brunch, with every dish cooked al fresco beside the pool. A three-story complex with 12 rooms (available for time shares) complements the original 59 air-conditioned, balconied rooms and luxury apartments. 71 rooms. Doubles: $95 to $200. *Divi Tiara Beach Resort, Cayman Islands, British West Indies; reservations via Divi Hotels in Chapel Hill, North Carolina. Telephone: 800/367-3484; fax: 919/419-2075.*

Jamaica

Montego Bay

Falmouth

Ocho Rios

Port Antonio

Kingston

Negril

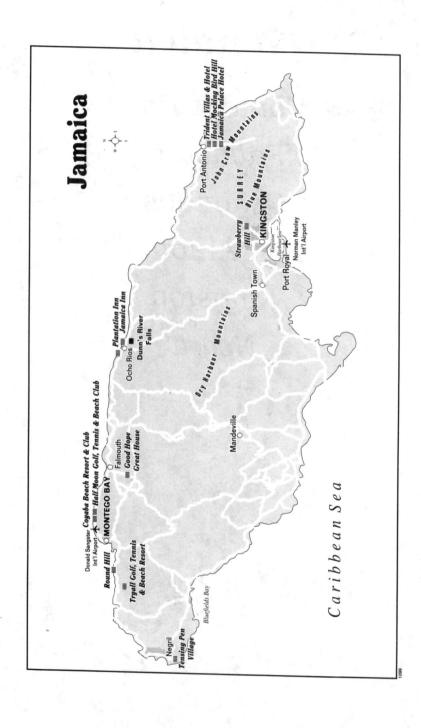

Jamaica

It's the stuff travel posters are made of—rafting down the Rio Grande, frolicking in waterfalls, limbo dancing and reggae, aristocratic plantations, and elegant villas.

Where to go in Jamaica? Most flights from North America touch down in Montego Bay before continuing to Kingston, so MoBay's the place to begin. Once a quiet honeymooners' haven, it's now crowded with tour groups, cruise ship passengers, and honky-tonk. But there's still much to enjoy—in town and in the surroundings—so begin with a few days at one of the three classy resorts just outside town. Two hours east along the north shore, Ocho Rios is a scaled-down version of MoBay, with three more of the island's top resorts and oodles of activities, from scrambling up Dunn's River Falls to touring Prospect Plantation to polo—spectating or playing—at not one but two locations. Port Antonio is the least developed of the three resorts, although visitors drive from all over the island to go rafting down the Rio Grande. You can also go horseback riding on the estate of Patrice Wymore Flynn, the widow of movie star Errol Flynn.

A tip on planning: If you find choosing where to stay as difficult as I do, you might begin with a few days at one of MoBay's top resorts, with a day trip to Negril. Then, I suggest you sightsee your way to Kingston—driving along the north shore, spending a night or two in Ocho Rios and/or Port Antonio on your way to the airport in Kingston, where you can board a flight home (although it may stop in MoBay). If you stop over in the capital itself, be sure to visit the crafts boutiques, café, and restaurants at Devon House.

The selection in these pages begins on the north coast, near Montego Bay, and moves east toward Port Antonio.

How to Get There   Jamaica is now one of the easiest islands to get to from North America. The new, privatized, and much improved Air Jamaica has nonstop or direct flights from Atlanta, Baltimore/Washington, Miami, New York, Philadelphia, and Orlando (not all daily but at least frequently); American and USAir have daily nonstop flights from 14 destinations between them, and Northwest has flights from Minneapolis and Tampa. There's additional service from Toronto, Montreal, and Winnipeg on Air Canada.

For information on Jamaica, call 809/991-9999.

Tryall Golf, Tennis & Beach Resort

Near Montego Bay

Atmosphere

Dining

Sports

Rates

Tryall is 2,200 acres of lush Jamaican plantation that long ago switched from sugar to the sweet life. The 155-year-old Great House is a stylish 47-room inn, perched on a low hill a few hundred yards inland from the beach and surrounded by championship fairways and sumptuous villas (individually owned, uniquely individual, and rentable).

Golfers know Tryall well—they've seen it past winters in live telecasts of the Johnnie Walker World Championship (said to be the top money prize among tournaments). It's an appealing layout: water holes lined with coconut palms, as well as a sixth fairway that skirts a centuries-old, still-turning waterwheel. And there are so many fruit trees lining the course—star apple, orange, breadfruit, mango—that the caddies are not only expert about which clubs to play but also have perfect timing when it comes to knowing which fruits are ripest.

Other guests never leave their knoll top for days on end. Why should they? A few paces from their Great House they have nine well-tended tennis courts. A few steps in the opposite direction, they can plunge into one of the Caribbean's most spectacular swimming pools, complete with waterfall and swim-up bar.

Tryall's guest rooms flank the driveway leading to the Great House, linked by wooden arcades draped with morning glories. The so-called Garden Terrace rooms look out on lawns and fairways; the pricier Junior Suites frame views of seashore, fairways, and the coast all the way to distant Montego Bay—distant enough to preserve Tryall's seclusion, accessible enough for occasional junkets into town to shop, dine, or hit the reggae clubs. Upper-level deluxe rooms have private balconies; lower-level rooms have patios. Just refurbished, all of the rooms are different, yet each is spacious, comfortable, practical. The suites boast marble bathrooms, large sitting areas, king-size beds, and chintz-covered furnishings.

The shingle-roofed, native-stone Great House (designated a national monument in 1989) is Georgian elegant yet comfortable, with chintz-covered furniture, marble floors, and a porte cochere at the end of the elliptical drive. In the formal reception area, guests can relax with a welcome drink as they check in. The Great House dining room was just spruced up, and the al fresco terrace takes advantage of the magnificent view; it abuts a bar room, with stone walls and picture windows. Adjoining the eastern wing of the house, it provides a spectacular, 180-degree view of the coastline.

Guests are so pampered here they don't even have to make a reservation for dinner (villa guests and outsiders most certainly do). Early-bird sunrise watchers find Jamaican Blue Mountain coffee waiting for them on the veranda at 6:30 a.m. And even that lovely championship golf course is now reserved exclusively for villa owners and Tryall guests and the occasional visitor from nearby Round Hill.

Name: Tryall Golf, Tennis & Beach Resort
Manager: Julio C. Melendez
Address: P.O. Box 1206, Montego Bay, Jamaica, West Indies
Location: On the north shore, 12 miles west of Montego Bay, 35 minutes and $35 by taxi from the airport
Telephone: 809/956-5660
Fax: 809/956-5673
Reservations: Icon Hotel Marketing, 800/336-4571
Credit Cards: All major cards
Rooms: 47 Great House rooms, some with balconies or patios, air-conditioning *and* ceiling fans, direct-dial telephones, radios, satellite TV, amenities baskets
Meals: Breakfast 7:00–9:30 (Continental 9:30–10:30), lunch noon–3:30 (in beachside pavilion; salads and sandwiches at Ninth Hole Bar 11:00–5:00, pool or golf clubhouse), afternoon tea 4:00–5:30, cocktails/hors d'oeuvres 6:00–7:30 (Great House), dinner 7:00–9:30 (in the open dining terrace, approx. $80 for 2); Friday evening barbecue on the beach, jackets in the evening in winter; room service during kitchen hours (Great House only); small combo or calypso trio most evenings at the Great House
Entertainment: Lounge/bar, manager's cocktail party on Tuesday (guests and homeowners), music for dancing every evening, TV in meeting room, parlor games, cabaret on some evenings during the winter
Sports: Freshwater pool at Great House, so-so beach across the road, snorkeling, Sunfish sailing, windsurfing, paddleboats, glass-bottom boats, tennis (9 Laykold courts, 5 with lights, pro shop), golf (18 championship holes, full pro facilities—all for a fee); scuba, sport fishing, horseback riding, day cruises to Negril can be arranged

P.S.:   Some children; open all year

P.P.S.:   48 of the resort's 55 villas are available for rent, from 1 to 6 bedrooms, all with a private pool and staff of 3; during the off-season months, twosomes can rent them at special rates

Round Hill

Near Montego Bay

Atmosphere

Dining

Sports

Rates

The sweeping, casuarina-lined driveway says "class." And when you get to the crest of the hill and take in the gardens and the view of coves and mountains, it's easy to understand why this elegant resort has been hosting the rich and famous for 43 winters.

Of all the resorts along Jamaica's fabled north shore this is probably the one that still comes closest to the glory years of everyone's memories. Its villas and servants have beckoned the likes of the Oscar Hammersteins, the Moss Harts, and, in Villa 25, Adele Astaire. As if that weren't cast enough for one resort, Cole Porter and Noël Coward (Villa 3) used to entertain the entertainers. Ever since, the upper crust of show business, high society, and big business has been chauffeured up that driveway in loyal streams, among them Paul McCartney, Harrison Ford, and Diane Sawyer and Mike Nichols. Designer Ralph Lauren spends every other weekend here at his secluded villa (sorry, it's not for rent), and recently redecorated the terrace bar in Laurenesque blue and white.

Many visitors to Round Hill have to bed down in three two-story wings alongside the beach, hitherto known as the Barracks, but now rechristened Pineapple House after what passes in these conservative parts as a major renovation (pencil-post beds handcrafted from local mahogany, pale, cool, green walls, new clay tile floors, bigger windows for better views, newly tiled bathrooms, more space by incorporating the balconies into the rooms). In other resorts, they'd probably be the most desirable rooms because of their beachfront location; but the true Round Hill is to be found on the bosky bowl rising from the beach, what seems to be 28 acres of tropical garden planted with villas rather than the other way around. Each whitewashed,

shingle-roofed villa is privately owned, 17 of them have private pools, many
have recently been outfitted with new kitchens and bathrooms, and each is
designed in such a way that it can be rented as an individual suite, with a
bedroom with louvered shutters opening to a covered outdoor patio
framed by bougainvillea and croton and mahogany trees.

Since they're privately owned, all the villas are different. Unless you book
now for winters two or three years down the line, you will almost certainly
have to settle for whatever is available, but if I were specifying lodgings
these are some of the villas I'd bid for: number 8 (the owners spent a
bundle installing marble floors, silk rugs, walls hand stenciled by a specially
imported Japanese craftsman, a canopy bed with pink chintz); number 13
(these owners have installed a large deck, pool, and the resort's only
Jacuzzi); number 6 (frilly boudoir with chinoiserie living room); number
18 (a particularly attractive high-ceilinged, arched living room, with fabrics
to match the anthurium and elephant ear in the garden).

But what sets Round Hill apart is probably the service. The staff numbers
250. When you rouse yourselves in the morning, your maid sets the terrace
table and prepares breakfast. Your gardener (there are 40 of them!) has
already cleaned the pool and positioned your loungers to catch the morning
sun. If you opt for the cove, each time you paddle into the sea you'll find a
beach boy has edged your chaise around to face the sun. At the lunchtime
buffet, an army of waiters totes your laden plates to your table, whisks away
the empties when you're ready for refills, recharges your water glasses, holds
chairs for the ladies. Laundry? The maid will take care of it. Room service? If
you can't be bothered trotting down the hill, the dining room will send your
dinner up. There are drivers to get you to and from your rooms when you
don't feel like walking, ball boys to retrieve stray serves on the tennis courts.

Many people have misconceptions about Round Hill, so let me correct
three myths: It's not formal; it's not stuffy; it's not prohibitively expensive.
Black tie is requested for some Saturday gala evenings, but only a handful of
men actually dress up; other evenings, dress is informal (but stylishly so, of
course). These rules or suggestions are now in effect all year. Everyone who
wants to mingle, mingles—marquises and marchionesses included, especially at the Monday beach picnic. During the peak season, managing
director Josef Forstmayr makes a point of inviting hotel guests to the
Tuesday evening cocktail parties put on by villa owners. Compare rates
here (and elsewhere in Jamaica, for that matter) with some other islands;
for what some down-island resorts charge for room only, Round Hill throws
in a suite, personal maid, and all meals.

One minor drawback: On weekends in winter regular jet services are
augmented by charter flights that occasionally shatter your sense of seclusion. Luckily, the owners stopped the planes from zooming over the resorts
as frequently as they had.

But that's no reason to forego the lap of luxury, because *once* in a lifetime at least everyone should sample a week in, say, Count Borghese's or Lord Rothermere's newly renovated hillside villa, with its plush outdoor living room, a pool shared only with one other couple, an enormous deck shaded by an even more enormous cotton tree, a gardener to move your lounger around with the sun, a personal maid to bring you afternoon tea.

Name: Round Hill
Managing Director: Josef Forstmayr
Address: P.O. Box 64, Montego Bay, Jamaica, West Indies
Location: On a promontory west of Montego Bay, about 10 miles, 25 minutes, and $35 by taxi from the airport
Telephone: 809/952-5150, 5155
Fax: 809/952-2505
Reservations: Robert Reid Associates or 800/972-2159
Credit Cards: All major cards
Rooms: 101, including 36 rooms in Pineapple House plus 65 suites in 27 villas; rooms in Pineapple House have walls of shutters facing the bay, standing fans or ceiling fans, telephones; villas have maids and gardeners, ceiling fans, air-conditioning, balconies or patios, gardens or lawns, indoor/outdoor living rooms, direct-dial telephones, kitchens (for maids' use), private or shared pools
Meals: Breakfast 7:30–10:30, lunch 12:30–2:30, dinner 7:30–9:30 (on the beachside patio beneath the almond trees, approx. $90 for 2); bonfire beach picnic Monday nights; "Jamaica Night" with local cuisine and calypso music Fridays; dress informal, except jacket and tie after 7:00 p.m. (black tie is "requested" on Saturday nights); room service, no extra charge; music (amplified until 11:00) for dancing most evenings
Entertainment: Local band for beach barbecue, resident jazz band, steel band; library, parlor games, art shows
Sports: Private beach (60 or 90 yards depending on the tides), freshwater pool, 17 villa pools, snorkeling, floats, tennis (5 courts, lights, pro), fitness center—all free; waterskiing, scuba diving, windsurfing, Sunfish sailing, paddleboats from the beach, deep-sea fishing boat charters—at extra charge; golf at Tryall, horseback riding 40 minutes away
P.S.: Some children, some small executive groups; open all year

Half Moon Golf, Tennis & Beach Club

Near Montego Bay

Atmosphere	**Dining**	**Sports**	**Rates**

The beach is indeed an almost perfect half moon, shaded by sea grape onshore, sheltered by a reef offshore, and dotted with tiny black and white shells, like the Half Moon's logo in miniature. The first vacationers settled around their half moon in the fifties in a cluster of private cottages, each one different from its neighbor. Later expansions included undistinguished two-story wings of beachside rooms and suites and the tastefully renovated studios and apartments that were once the neighboring Colony Hotel. The total tally, 220 rooms and suites, plus 20 new 5-, 6-, and 7-bedroom Royal Villas with private pools, is spread along 1½ miles of beach, which in turn is a mere corner of a 400-acre estate that includes riding stables, a working ranch, and a Robert Trent Jones golf course.

That lovely half-moon beach may have been the reason people were first lured to this spot, but the resort's sports facilities have to be a major attraction today. Where else do you get to play a Robert Trent Jones at a 50% discount? And how many resorts that promise free tennis actually give you a chance to get in a game by providing 13 courts? (And with lights, too.) How many resorts that promise horseback riding have a complete equestrian center with 28 horses?

The club has been through several additions and lots of fine tuning recently. The original cottages on the bay are now subdivided into suites—Presidential and Royal—some with private pools (although regulars such as Eddie Murphy frequently rent an entire complex of suites and pools for family and entourage). A new complex of private villas with three, four, and five bedrooms and private staff has been installed in an extension to the eastern end of the estate, alongside a brand new, island-style shopping complex called Half Moon Village, complete with coffee shop, English pub, gourmet takeout, Jamaican and Japanese restaurants. Even the regular dining facilities have been upgraded: The beachside Seagrape Terrace looks lovelier than ever and is still the most popular choice for dinner despite the arrival of the neighboring Il Giardino, serving mostly Italian cuisine.

As if that wasn't enough in the way of choices for a single resort, Half Moon just happens to have one of the best specialty restaurants on the island, the famed Sugar Mill, across the roadway at the golf course and the still-turning waterwheel of the original mill. Swiss chef Hans Schenk is the proprietor here, serving up a menu that is an intriguing blend of Continental and West Indian dishes, served on a bosky terrace beneath trees trimmed with wicker-shaded lights. Now Schenk has opened another specialty restaurant in Half Moon Village, serving mostly native West Indian dishes, at prices noticeably lower than the Sugar Mill's.

Despite the rambling nature of the place, it all seems to hold together architecturally and stylistically, and even with all the additional guests and distractions, the Half Moon staff still manages to offer service in the old Jamaica tradition. Chances are the maître d's and waiters will have your name down pat on your second visit to their breeze-cooled domain, even if it's not George Bush (as in President), Itzhak Perlman, Kiri Te Kanawa, Prince Philip, or Prince Rainier, to name just a few recent, and in some cases, regular guests. This obvious commitment to service comes, of course, right from the top, from Heinz Simonitsch, managing director, part owner, cosmopolite, who has been at the helm here for almost 40 years and knows, I suspect, every flower in the garden and every washer-upper in the scullery.

Which of these varied accommodations you stay in may depend less on the rates than on how you want to fill your days. If you want to step directly from your room into the sea, check into one of the original cottages; the two-story wings of junior and superior suites are closest to the tennis courts; the neo-Georgian villas have private maid service; and kitchens, which can be stocked from the commissary across the driveway, are just a short walk from everything.

The Half Moon is still one of the best values in the Caribbean, given the caliber of the service and the range of sports facilities included in the rate (see below). The lowest category of lodgings, known as Superior Rooms, come with small pantries and patios just a few paces from a coral beach (not the gorgeous half moon itself) and cost much less than you'd pay in lots of more mundane resorts. I stayed in one of these Superior Rooms recently and was surprised to notice that the fellow who comes around in the mornings to tidy up actually turns over the patio chairs to wipe down the undersides. That's what happens when you have a guy like Heinz Simonitsch keeping an eye on things.

Name: Half Moon Golf, Tennis & Beach Club
Managing Director: Heinz Simonitsch

Address: P.O. Box 80, Montego Bay, Jamaica, West Indies

Location: 7 miles from town; 5 miles from the airport, 10 minutes and $12 by taxi

Telephone: 809/953-2211

Fax: 809/953-2731

Reservations: Robert Reid Associates

Credit Cards: All major cards

Rooms: 220, including superior rooms, suites, and 20 villas, all with air-conditioning, some with air-conditioning *and* ceiling fans, satellite TV, balconies or patios, refrigerators or mini-bars, direct-dial telephones, some with kitchens, some with private or semiprivate pools; plus the new complex of 12 villas

Meals: Breakfast 7:30–10:00 (or you can leave your order the night before, wake up, and it's ready on your balcony or patio), Continental breakfast 6:30–noon (in the Cedar Bar or La Baguette snack bar), lunch noon–6:00, dinner 7:00–10:00 (on the open beachside Seagrape Terrace, Il Giardino restaurant, at Half Moon Village, or the Sugar Mill at the golf course, $60–$80 for 2); long-sleeved shirts after 6:00 p.m. in the winter; jacket and tie requested on Saturdays, otherwise informal (but "shorts, T-shirts, and jeans are not allowed" in the evening in the hotel); room service in most rooms, small extra charge

Entertainment: Bar-lounge-terrace, live music every evening for dancing (resident band, calypso, steel band), floor shows, crab races (the profits from the betting go to local charities); new shopping village with 40 stores and 4 restaurants

Sports: Beach, 19 freshwater pools, tennis (13 courts, 7 with lights, pro shop), sauna, croquet, putting green, nature reserve, Nautilus gym, Jacuzzi, squash (4 courts)—all free; golf (18 holes, pro shop), windsurfing, Mistral windsurfing school, Sunfish sailing, scuba, snorkeling, horseback riding (with guide), massage, aerobics, table tennis, bicycles—all at extra charge

P.S.: Children welcome, some seminar groups up to 120; open all year

Good Hope Great House
Near Falmouth

☆					♀					🌑🌑				$				
Atmosphere					**Dining**					**Sports**				**Rates**				

You leave the main road in the middle of Falmouth, then head into the hills and seem to keep going forever until the road gets narrower and more pitted. Finally you crest a hill and there on your right is what looks vaguely like a medieval fortified hill town in Europe, but a closer look reveals flowers rather than cannons, lawns rather than parade grounds. There's a tennis court (well tended, too) and wooden benches where guests can sit and survey the panorama of hills and dales that are typical of the Cockpit Country. Much of what the eye takes in is part of the estate's 2,000 acres, which explains why an inn with just 10 rooms can have stables with 17 horses.

The Great House ruling over this domain is a wonderful 200-year-old Georgian structure, its gray stones accented with shutters and weathered steps leading up to a lounge filled with antiques—including a couple of "toilet" chairs, a trio of thickly padded sofas covered with a red floral print fabric, a pair of crystal chandeliers reflected in old mirrors—and great bouquets of flowers here and there on the broad plank floor. A matching lounge at the other end of a loggia now functions as a homey playroom with card tables, a music center with tapes (jazz, classical, reggae), a wheeled bar cart, and shelves of books and magazines, including *The Sun Also Rises* and the collected works of various no-longer-read writers like John Masefield and Lord Byron.

Each of the inn's 10 guest rooms are different, mostly with cedar plank floors, all furnished with antique beds (mainly four-posters), some with wooden tubs, washbasins, and toilets. The Copper Room, on the other hand, is fitted out with a stone bathtub lined with lead (apparently it was effective in treating a former owner's arthritis) and the original 18th-century canopy beds. The former coach house is now a villa with five bedrooms (with a communal kitchen, sitting room, patio and dining area, it's more suited to a family or group than a couple), but the prime romantic nook is the Counting House. It's located up a few weathered steps (presumably the owner didn't want anyone prying into his books), its big bed angled out from a corner of the room and topped with frilly white canopies;

the tub/shower is tucked into a corner behind a pale green antique screen (well, it was designed as a countinghouse, after all, not a boudoir), with six shuttered windows for cross-ventilation (all the rooms have paddle fans for cooling). It may not be a Ritz-Carlton, but an African head of state bunked down there the night I paid a call.

The Good Hope dining room is simply furnished with wooden-topped tables and cane chairs, its French doors open to the breezes and the passage to the freestanding kitchen, where a team of cooks concocts intriguing menus that mix and match local and Continental—red pea soup, akee triangles with chutney, blackened snapper, gnocchi with sautéed eggplant, grilled lamb with garlic mint butter sauce, plantain pie, and papaya cake. It makes no pretense to haute cuisine—just tasty, wholesome home cooking, as befits an otherworldly Georgian manor on a hilltop in Jamaica.

Name: Good Hope Great House
Owners/Managers: Tony and Sheila Hart
Address: P.O. Box 50, Falmouth, Trelawney, Jamaica, West Indies
Location: About 40 minutes from Montego Bay (at Falmouth, follow the signs for Martha's Brae Rafting)
Telephone: 809/954-3289
Fax: 809/954-3289
Reservations: Island Outpost, Miami, 305/534-2135 (fax 305/531-5543)
Credit Cards: American Express, MasterCard, Visa
Rooms: 10, all different, with ceiling fans, private bathrooms, carafes of ice water
Meals: Breakfast 7:30–anytime, lunch 12:00–2:30, dinner 7:00 on the veranda, the patio, or in the dining room (approx. $30–$40 for 2); casual dress, but sweater or jacket is appropriate in the evening chill; no room service
Entertainment: Tapes from Bach to Marley to Gershwin
Sports: Small pool in the garden, tennis—all free; horseback riding ($25 a ride)
P.S.: Not suitable for children; open all year

Plantation Inn
Ocho Rios

Atmosphere

Dining

Sports

Rates

The white-columned porte cochere may strike you as more Carolinian than Caribbean, the tiny clubby lounge just off reception as more Mayfair than Antillean, but once you step beyond the lobby to the terrace the setting is pure Jamaican. Masses of hibiscus and bougainvillea drape walls and railings. Flights of steps lead to a small swimming pool, then continue down to an expanse of soft, white sand (virtually private because it's surrounded by the hotel). And with the beachside *bohio* bar, you don't even have to come up for lunch and piña coladas.

There are two groups of lodgings here, and all the rooms have been substantially refurbished during the last two years without changing any of their character or charm. The original rooms, in three-story wings, are traditionally tropical—lots of hardwoods and louvers for cooling (they're now air-conditioned as a backup)—and the walk-in closets tell you the oldtime clientele check in for weeks at a time. To the left of the dining terrace, a walkway covered in flowering vines leads to a four-story wing of rooms and suites right on the edge of the beach. This newish wing doesn't do much for the setting when seen from the beach, but from the rooms the views are impressive, east along the bay and coast.

There was a time when Plantation Inn was one of the Big Four on Jamaica's North Shore, a place that attracted English lords and Jamaica lovers like Ian Fleming and Noël Coward on their way east to their homes near Oracabessa. But it has lost some of its glitter, although the rooms are still spotless (upper floors have the best view, fewer distractions) and the staff is welcoming and efficient. Even the dining room, which I always found disappointing, has perked up, but it still lacks the style of its neighbors.

Name: Plantation Inn
Manager: Roderic Crawford
Address: P.O. Box 2, Ocho Rios, Jamaica, West Indies
Location: Just east of town, 1½ hours and $90 by taxi from Montego Bay airport, or $35 per person round-trip by air-conditioned mini-bus, making stops along the way

Telephone: 809/974-5601
Fax: 809/974-5912
Reservations: 800/752-6824
Credit Cards: American Express, Diners Club, MasterCard, Visa
Rooms: 78, in 5 categories including Junior and Deluxe Suites, all with ceiling fans and air-conditioning, balconies overlooking the sea, direct-dial telephones, some with TVs, mini-bars, and refrigerators, 2 with Jacuzzis
Meals: Breakfast 7:30–9:30, consommé on the beach 11:00–12:00, lunch 1:00–2:30 (beach or dining room), afternoon tea 4:00–5:30 (with, alas, occasional fashion shows), dinner 8:00–9:30 (on the terrace, $80 for 2); jackets required Monday through Saturday, "informal elegance" in summer; room service at no extra cost; "breakfast on your private terrace encouraged"
Entertainment: Terrace bar, calypso music, folklore and fashion shows, TV/VCR in main lounge, card room with parlor games, live and amplified music for dancing 6 nights a week
Sports: Beach (reef protected for good swimming and snorkeling), freshwater pool, Sunfish sailing, windsurfing, kayaking, snorkeling, tennis (2 courts, 1 lighted), jungle gym cottage with Nautilus, aerobics, sauna—all free; golf, scuba, horseback riding, glass-bottom boat rides, deep-sea fishing, and polo nearby
P.S.:   Some groups and seminars; open all year

Jamaica Inn

Ocho Rios

Atmosphere

Dining

Sports

Rates

The loggias alone are larger than rooms in most hotels. Better furnished, too, with padded armchairs, ottomans and overstuffed sofas, breakfast tables, desks, desk lamps, fresh flowers, and drying racks for soggy swimsuits and beach towels. Have a swim before lunch and you'll find a fresh supply of big, bulky beach towels waiting for you in your rooms; have a nap or something after lunch, then a dip, and, sure enough, the maid has straightened out your mussed-up bed by the time you get back. Your nap or whatever may take place in a romantic little pencil-post bed, in a tropical boudoir of cool pastel blues and greens and yellows, the sunlight filtered by green and white drapes, the breezes filtered by louvered windows and doors, the terrazzo floors softened by white rugs.

The West Wing is best—with your loggia right on the edge of the water, your front door facing the beach and garden. If you want to be right on the beach, choose the Beach Wing and you can step from your patio over a shin-high balustrade right onto the sand. If you can afford the best, ask for the Blue Suite, a self-contained cottage right on the beach; if the *very* best, then ask for the White Suite, where Winston Churchill stayed in the 1950s—it has its own small pool with a circular ramp, and a path over a private promontory to a very private sun terrace right above the sea.

The inn, once the private hideaway of a Texas millionaire, has two one-story and two two-story wings, all a pretty pastel blue, strung out along a private 700-foot beach, on 6 acres of lawns, wild banana, sea grape, hibiscus and bougainvillea, and very tall coconut palms. The covelike beach (one of the most beautiful on the island), the clear water (as cool and inviting as the bedrooms), the placid tempo and elegance of the place have been attracting devoted fans for more than a quarter of a century. Service is exemplary, mainly because one of the Morrow family, the owners, is sitting right there in the "Morrow Seat" on the terrace, with an uninterrupted view of reception, lounge, bar, dining terrace, and beach.

But ask the resort's fans what they like most about Jamaica Inn and they may well answer, dinner. For a start, it's served in a grand setting like something out of a Busby Berkeley musical—a broad, lamplit terrace with a white ornate balustrade, beside the sea, beneath the palms, beneath the stars. For the past 30-some winters, chef Battista Greco has been flying over from Venice to supervise the kitchen; now he has turned over the reins to his longtime Jamaican assistant, Wilbert Mathison.

But here's the kicker. One of the inn's longtime guests is a partner of the Roux brothers in London, so sous chef Mathison spent a summer slaving over the stoves of Le Gavroche, honing his craft alongside Michelin three-star masters. Now, his own menus in place, Mathison is earning rave reviews from Jamaica Inn's longtime guests for his *magret du canard au cognac* and Jamaican pepperpot soup, veal scallop with cherry brandy sauce, and grilled fillet of yellowtail snapper on a bed of garlic spinach.

With the Jamaica coconut pie and zabaglione comes a trio of musicians for dancing beneath the stars (the strutters come dressed to the Fred Astaire nines on weekends in winter). Some non-fox-trotters mosey over to the croquet lawn for a moonlight duel, while lovers and romantics slip off arm in arm to those tempting loggias with the big, comfy sofas sheltered by wild banana and serenaded by the surf.

Name: Jamaica Inn
Manager: Rudi Schoenbein
Address: P.O. Box 1, Ocho Rios, Jamaica, West Indies
Location: On the eastern edge of town, $80 by taxi from Montego Bay (alert the hotel and they'll have a reliable driver there to meet you)
Telephone: 809/974-2514
Fax: 809/974-2449
Reservations: Caribbean World Resorts, 800/837-4608
Credit Cards: American Express, MasterCard, Visa
Rooms: 45, all with air-conditioning plus fans plus breezes, large loggias, telephones, bathrooms with all the amenities; all facing the ocean
Meals: Breakfast 8:00–10:00, lunch 1:00–2:30, dinner 8:00–9:30 (beneath the stars, approx. $80 for two); jacket and tie (and often, by preference of the guests, black tie) in winter, jackets only in off-season
Entertainment: Dancing to a moderately amplified 4-piece combo every evening, library/lounge with masses of jigsaw puzzles
Sports: Beach (good swimming and snorkeling), freshwater pool, Sunfish sailing, croquet, snorkel equipment, sea kayaks—all free; 1 tennis court (no charge) at adjoining hotel; scuba, boat trips, golf, horseback riding, polo (for players, learners—and sometimes the managers cart all the guests off to a match for a jolly afternoon of spectating) nearby
P.S.: No groups, no conventions ever, no children under 14

Trident Villas & Hotel

Port Antonio

Atmosphere

Dining

Sports

Rates

White breakers come plunging through, under, and over the craggy coral. A winding pathway leads to a gazebo for two that seems to float in the middle of the sea spray. Farther along the coast, scores of waves spume and fume, the Blue Mountains crowd the shore, the narrow road winds among villaed coves and lush green headlands. This is one of the more dramatic corners of Jamaica, and Trident makes the most of its setting. Of all the small luxury hideaways along Jamaica's north shore, here is the one that most magically puts you into another world. Screened from the roadway by garden walls, it's a whitewashed, shingle-roofed enclave of gardens and courtyards, with most of its villas strung out along the edge of the shore, cuddled in bougainvillea and allamanda. At one end of the garden, a big circular swimming pool sits atop the coral; at the other, a columned doorway leads to a secluded cove with private beach and lagoon.

The main lodge has something of the look of one of those whitewashed, black-trimmed staging-post inns in England's Lake District. Even the interiors are more English country house than Antillean resort, the drawing room decked with striped fabrics and wingback armchairs, the dining room with oriental rugs and Baccarat flambeaux. The villas and rooms display many of the grace notes associated with its owner, Jamaican architect Earl Levy—peaked shingle roofs, roughcast stucco, lattice window grills and ornamentation, gazebos, and clay tile patios.

Villa 1 is still my favorite nest here, 20 paces from the lodge, screened from its neighbors by hedgerows and shrubbery. The French doors of the living room open to a patio for wave watching, a dainty gazebo (lovely spot for breakfasts for two), and a patch of lawn separated by a low wall from the coral. In the bedroom, a bay window forms a sunny reading nook with an armchair, footstool, and reading lamp. The living room sports color-coordinated wicker chairs and sofas, tile floors, louvered windows, and an antique desk and end tables, every flat surface a potential setting for vases of fresh tropical flora, plucked that morning by the maids. Colors and furnishings vary from suite to suite, but each is a minor masterpiece, no concessions to untropical carpeting or air-conditioning. On the other hand, I stayed in Villa 14 on my most recent visit and it could easily become my first choice—at the far end of the garden, with one patio facing the cove, another facing the sea. The most impressive accommodation is the Imperial Suite, a 2,000-square-foot duplex in the Tower Wing—dining room and living room downstairs, a twisting white stairway swirling to a capacious bedroom where three more mahogany steps put you onto the mammoth four-poster bed.

In previous editions of this guide I questioned whether vacationers would want to dress up every evening, dine indoors in an air-conditioned, chandeliered salon, consuming seven-course, fixed-menu dinners. Well, apparently they do. The meals are nicely paced, with small portions, classic cuisine accented with local variations such as akee pâté, smoked blue marlin with capers, and red-snapper patties. The menu is posted each morning in the lobby; if you're on a diet you can order substitutes.

Perhaps Trident's distinguished guests enjoy their dinner hours because here's a resort that doesn't feel obliged to regale you with amplified music. A pianist plays in the drawing room; a local trio known as the Jolly Boys—guitar, rumba box, and banjo—plays on the terrace. (They have an amazing repertoire, including their own compositions, which are both jolly *and* wicked. And that's about it as far as nightlife is concerned, unless you trot into town for a night of reggae at the Roof Club.

Whatever you decide to do during the day, be back on the terrace by 4:30, when silver pots, Wedgwood china, finger sandwiches, and home-baked cake are laid out for afternoon tea. Peacocks and peahens preen expectantly—Oscar, Otto, Ophelia, Ozzie, and offspring. It's all very civilized, very garden partyish. Even the breakers seem to calm down at teatime.

Name: Trident Villas & Hotel

Manager: Suzanne Levy

Address: P.O. Box 119, Port Antonio, Jamaica, West Indies

Location: A few miles east of Port Antonio, 2 hours and $84 by taxi from Kingston, 20 minutes by air ($100 per plane, included in the hotel rate if you stay 7 nights or more); the Port Antonio airstrip is about 15 minutes from the hotel

Telephone: 809/993-2602, 2705

Fax: 809/993-2590

Reservations: 800/237-3237 or Robert Reid Associates

Credit Cards: All major cards

Rooms: 30 rooms, including 15 villas, 13 Junior Suites, and 2 Deluxe Suites, all with ceiling fans and louvers, some with air-conditioning, balconies or patios, telephones; all villas have refrigerators and wet bars, some have kitchenettes

Meals: Breakfast "from 7:30 on," lunch "whenever," afternoon tea 4:30–5:30 (all served on the awning-covered terrace), dinner 8:00–10:00 ($80 for 2, in the main dining room, cooled by fans or air-conditioning); Jamaican buffet Thursdays; jackets required, jacket and tie preferred; room service for breakfast and lunch only, no extra charge

Entertainment: Bar/lounge, piano player, calypso trio every evening ("no amplification ever"), occasional folklore shows, parlor games in drawing room

Sports: Small beach, freshwater pool, snorkeling, Sunfish sailing, tennis (2 courts, no lights)—all free; massage, windsurfing, scuba diving, river rafting, horseback riding (with guides) on the Patrice Wymore Flynn Ranch can be arranged

P.S.: "Children any age, anytime," but it's not really suitable for young children; open all year

Hotel Mocking Bird Hill
Port Antonio

☆☆				🍷🍷				🌐				$			
Atmosphere				**Dining**				**Sports**				**Rates**			

Take your favorite small family-owned, family-run inn in New England and set it down on a lush hillside in Jamaica and you have some idea of the charms of the new Mocking Bird Hill. Most hotels around here have a view of the sea, but here's one that with one fell swoop combines the sea and the Blue Mountains—rolling ranges of lush greenery striding upward to forested peaks. Mocking Bird Hill, in a quiet residential quarter 600 feet above town, is basically a split-level villa converted, with the addition of a new bungalow (and another still to come), into a 10-room inn.

You're greeted in the open lobby-lounge, which has walls covered with original art and a figurine of a seated lady crafted from wire and newspapers. They're the work of co-owner Barbara Walker, a Jamaican artist who lived in Germany for several years and established a reputation for her works in places like Düsseldorf and Cologne. Her partner, Shireen Aga, an Indian woman who lived one life as an executive with InterContinental Hotels and now finds herself adapting the methods of big-city hotels to a 10-roomer in the back woods of a Caribbean island. Fairly successfully, I'd say. Given that it will take a few more years to instill competence and confidence in the young, unpolished staff, this is already a place of warmth and tranquility.

The guest rooms come with pretty white on white decor, ceramic tile floors, bamboo furniture, jaunty blue and white striped curtains that match the bedspreads and upholstery. No frills, but very attractive. Committed environmentalists, the owners have banished oversize soaps, paper napkins, and plastic laundry bags, and almost all the furniture and fabrics were produced on the island (the downside to conservation, though, are the eye-straining 40-watt lightbulbs).

Public areas of the Mocking Bird include a spacious sunset viewing deck, the perfect place for a panoramic view of the Blue Mountains, and the 36-seater Mille Fleurs Restaurant, another aptly named terrace with views across the flowers and trees to the sea. Meals focus on island produce and you may find your evening coasting along with a delicious sweet potato and tomato soup, citrus salad with freshly made plantain fritters, plantain stuffed with callaloo, grilled fillet of yellowtail with lime butter in a white-wine sauce, stuffed papaw with minced beef, or local "rundown" in coconut sauce. All but six of the drinks in the bar are produced locally.

Obviously, there's no need for a daily activities bulletin here. That's the attraction. A few steps down from the pool terrace there's a wooden bench beneath the trees. A couple of hammocks. Then there's a pathway leading off through the trees. And by the time you read these words there should be an al fresco massage gazebo under an old fig tree. At some point in the near future there may also be art workshops and field trips. Frenchman's Cove Beach is only 5 minutes away by car, but I suspect that guests are likely to spend most of their sojourn grabbing a book from the library, settling into a hammock, and idling a few hours away until it's time for the next piece of coconut pie with mango ice cream.

Name: Hotel Mocking Bird Hill

Owners/Managers: Barbara Walker and Shireen Aga

Address: P.O. Box 254, Port Antonio, Jamaica, West Indies

Location: A few minutes by car from the center of San Antonio or, for passengers taking the coastal route from Kingston, about $80 by taxi

Telephone: 809/993-3370

Fax: 809/993-7133

Reservations: Unique Destinations, 800/285-2377, or Special Places in Jamaica, 305/430-7227

Rooms: 10 rooms, with ceiling fans, balconies or patios, tiled bathrooms (some with showers only), private safes

Meals: Breakfast 8:30–10:00, lunch noon–6:00, dinner 7:00–9:30 (approx. $60 for 2); casual dress; no room service

Entertainment: TV in lounge, but mostly listening to tree frogs or enjoying the artworks, occasional evenings of folklore by a local "mento" band, art workshops

Sports: Pool, walking trails on the grounds, massage in bamboo gazebo, hiking in the nearby rain forest, beach 5 minutes away

P.S.: Open all year

Strawberry Hill
Kingston

| Atmosphere | Dining | Sports | Rates |

Take the best of native Jamaican architecture, pat and mold it into a collection of little birdhouses, drape them around the crest of a hilltop high above Kingston, add a garden, a sophisticated restaurant, and a few contemporary frills, and you end up with one of the most picturesque, most romantic of the Caribbean's hideaways. All of Kingston at your feet (when the lights twinkle it could almost be Monte Carlo), the sweep of the great estuary, the causeway to Fort Royal, the forested slopes and glens of the Blue Mountains surround you on three sides.

Each of the 12 cottages (with a total of just 18 rooms) is designed by one of the island's leading conservation architects, Ann Hodges, who had a chance here to apply old island theories to the creation of a brand-new inn that appeals to contemporary tastes. Peaked roofs with cedar shake shingles. White clinker-board walls with jalousie louvers where most architects would put glass. Low-slung eaves shading wraparound porches. Broad plank floors of mahogany covered with khuskhus rugs. Fretwork panels set high in the walls to surprise the eye (each one has a different theme) and keep the breezes flowing.

The interiors (by Tanya Melica) are designed with a minimalist elegance—white on white walls and doors accented with period sideboards, cane chairs, sofas, and exotic objects—a coffee table from Indonesia, perhaps, or South American earthenware pots and figurines, wrought-iron lamps crafted specially for the hotel. Some cottages have complete kitchens with yellow and green patterned china, toasters, blenders, microwaves, coffee makers, and family-size refrigerators.

Many of the bedrooms have four-posters draped with wispy mosquito netting and louvered French doors opening to wood-plank verandas with mahogany planters' armchairs. The attractive bathrooms have nice touches such as multihead showers and recessed lighting, closets have heating rods, beds heated mattress pads. Guest rooms are identified by fanciful names—Timbuc Two, Timbuc Three, Mountain View—and I ended up in Birds Hill, a one-bedroom suite with a gazebo at the end of the path. A hot tub sat in the gazebo, screened from the view of every creature except the birds.

But 59 Steps would be another favorite, a studio almost swallowed up by banana plants and ferns, and Mountain View's panorama takes a sweep of the valley to what looks like a romantic little Italian hill town but is, in reality, a boot camp for the Jamaica Defense Force. But don't get bogged down in the subtleties of views and amenities—any of these rooms, studios, or suites is a winner.

The flat top of the 26-acre estate is given over to a lawn that occasionally doubles (but, fortunately, only very occasionally) as a heliport for people who can't wait to get there from the airport, about 50 minutes away by car. Tables and chairs sit beneath eucalyptus and cedar trees. Wooden walkways link three pavilions—the bar (with a fireplace that can be most welcome at this elevation, take it from me), a library-lounge with big-screen TV and an eclectic collection of reading material, and a dining pavilion that must rank as one of the prettiest in the Caribbean, with its double row of fretwork panels, its polished mahogany tables and chairs, sparkling crystal and candles, and four ceiling fans topping off the tropical ambience.

Strawberry Hill's executive chef, Peter Birkheiser, has created what he calls new Jamaican cuisine. It's tempting fare, such as curried pumpkin soup with dried peppered shrimps or flan of ackee, callaloo, and goat cheese for appetizers, main dishes of grilled jack fish with a papaya and cucumber salsa or blackened sirloin steak with a red onion marmalade. I passed them all up for dasheen and sweet potato gnocchi with bok choy, mushrooms, sun-dried tomatoes, and lime in a basil cream sauce followed by jerk roasted lamb loin with a roasted garlic and guava glaze. It was one of the best meals I've had in the Caribbean in months.

This hilltop has led a charmed life. Back in the fifties, a prominent local family, the Blackwells, whose ancestors came over from the U.K. generations ago, used to come here for afternoon tea every weekend. Young Chris Blackwell fell in love with the spot. Years later, after he was the enormously successful founder-impresario of Island Records (Bob Marley, U2, the Cranberries, and others of that ilk), he decided he would like to live on Strawberry Hill, so he bought the entire hilltop, revamped the Great House, added a few cottages for friends, then later still created his small hotel, having caught the innkeeping bug at his famed Deco hotels in South Beach.

Not only did he decide to build in island style, he used local crafters wherever possible. Thus, you sit on cane chairs woven by people at the School for the Blind in Kingston, the frames themselves made to traditional plantation designs and antiqued with shoe polish; the fabrics were sewn by a sewing bee in Irish Town, just up the road; the beautifully framed black and white photographs in the rooms were all taken by local photographers.

Blackwell has done at last what scores of other hoteliers should have done years ago: take the vernacular architecture and adapt it to a contemporary inn. Keep this up, Blackwell, and I may have to stop griping about taped music in restaurants and lounges.

Name: Strawberry Hill

Manager: David Barlyn

Address: Irish Town P.A., St. Andrew, Jamaica, West Indies

Location: 2,800 feet up in the Blue Mountains, near the village of Irish Town, about 20 minutes from downtown Kingston, 50–60 minutes from the airport (let them know when your plane arrives and they'll pick you up free of charge); if you're driving yourself, better call for directions and write down every word

Telephone: 809/944-8400

Fax: 809/944-8408

Reservations: Island Outpost, Miami, 305/534-2135 (fax 305/531-5543)

Credit Cards: American Express, Discovery, MasterCard, Visa

Rooms: 18 rooms, studios, and suites, all with period furniture, direct-dial telephones, radio-cassette players, makeup mirrors, hair dryers, bathrobes, verandas; some with full kitchens; one with private hot tub; TV-VCRs and cassettes on request

Meals: Breakfast 8:00–10:00, lunch 11:30–2:30, dinner 6:00–10:00, all in the hilltop dining pavilion (approx. $60–$80 for 2); casual but stylish dress; room service during dining room hours; afternoon tea Saturday and Sunday

Entertainment: TV lounge, bar lounge, and chatting beside the big wood-burning fire

Sports: None as yet—pool and croquet to come; massage and reflexology by arrangement; guided hikes through the mountains

P.S.:   Open all year

Other Choices

The Jamaica Palace Hotel

Port Antonio

It sounds grand and it looks grand at first sight. Then it turns kind of pompous. The white palatial facade with its porte cochere and two matching *faux* portes cochere lead to a spacious lobby replete with marble floors and white pillars, chandeliers, and gilt-framed portraits. Jamaica, particularly tumbledown Port Antonio, could be on another planet—until you step out onto the big play terrace and discover that the 118-foot swimming pool is shaped to replicate the coastline of Jamaica. The original intention of the European aristocrat who built the place seems to have been a grande luxe hotel to outshine Trident, just down the road (see above), so the guest rooms are quite posh, with lots of marble and ormolu, teardrop chandeliers, and antiques; but somewhere along the way dream turned into reality and the rates and aspirations were toned down. Lucky you—what we have here is a good deal. I can't think of any other hideaway with such lavish marble bathrooms in rooms costing less than $115 in summer. And being only 6 years old, the place is still in tiptop condition.

There's a downside to all this: the service is lackluster; the two (two!) restaurants are gloomy—and the chicken cordon blue [*sic*] hardly compensates for the stygian gloom; and the beds consist of circular or semicircular mattresses on concrete bases (not the last word in comfort).

Although the rates are reasonable, many of the rooms are located off an open passageway that may remind you of a shopping mall. The guest rooms are like tiny boutiques with big windows and everyone looking into someone else's window. Check out your room before you unpack—or splurge on one of the Junior Suites, $55 more. 80 air-conditioned rooms and suites. Doubles $115 to $170, winter 1994–95. *The Jamaica Palace Hotel, P.O. Box 277, Port Antonio, Jamaica, West Indies. Telephone: 800/472-1149 (reservations only) or 809/993-2020; fax: 809/993-3459.*

Coyaba Beach Resort & Club
Montego Bay

Coyaba, according to the brochure, is the Arawak word for a place of peace and rest. That about sums up this friendly, laid-back beachfront hotel. Owner/operators Joanne and Kevin Robertson are newcomers to the hotel business, but they've already racked up some impressive achievements, including membership in the prestigious Elegant Resorts of Jamaica group, along with the likes of Round Hill and Half Moon Golf, Tennis & Beach Club. Three three-story buildings cluster around a verdant courtyard, with views of the garden, the ocean, or the parking lot (not recommended). No shortcuts were taken on the 52 tasteful rooms: The tile floors, classy fabrics, and hand-carved furniture actually look Jamaican, not vaguely European, and the best of them have large sitting areas or bright breakfast nooks and roomy terraces. 52 rooms. Doubles:

$186 to $326, winter 1994–95. *Coyaba Beach Resort & Club, Little River P.O., St. James, Jamaica, West Indies. Telephone: 809/953-9150; fax: 809/953-2244. Reservations: 800/223-9815.*

Tensing Pen Village
Negril

Two words best describe Tensing Pen: rustic and romantic. Imagine staying in a circular thatched-roof treehouse that rises above a jungle of dense island foliage and looks out over a small cove cut out of the cliffs. On a promontory stretching into the ocean, two hammocks (usually occupied) sway in a gazebo. Ten cottages and huts are scattered along 1,700 feet of oceanfront, reached by footpaths that twist throughout the property. The accommodations are open to the breezes, with louvered doors and windows, ceiling fans, tile floors, carved furniture, bathrooms, and in some cases outdoor showers. There's a common kitchen for preparing meals, but most guests seem to prefer to immerse themselves in total privacy. The feeling of seclusion is reinforced by the fact that Tensing Pen is as far west as the West End of Negril will allow; next door (although not in stereo range) is the famous Rick's Beach Bar. 10 rooms. Doubles: $90 to $165, winter 1994–95. *Tensing Pen Village, P.O. Box 13, Negril, Jamaica, West Indies. Telephone and fax: 809/957-4417. Reservations: 216/546-9000.*

Haiti

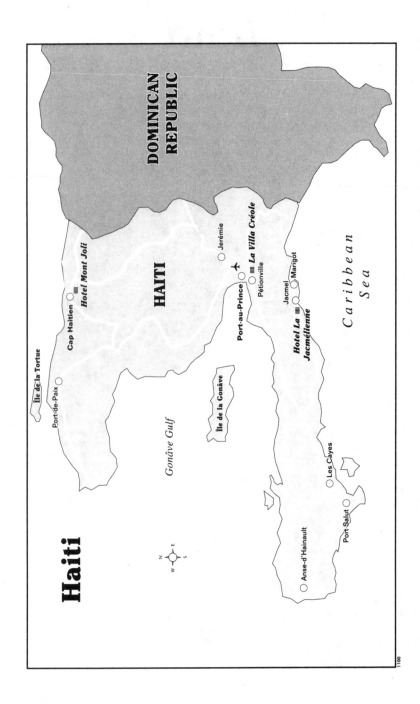

Haiti

I'm a big fan of Haiti. It's everything people say it is. Mysterious. Vibrant. Hot. Spooky. Damp. Poor. Fun loving. Sensual. Edgy.

Haiti, more than any other Caribbean island, is an *experience*. I wish I could exhort you to go there, but because of the unsettled state of the nation, there seems to be little enthusiasm on the part of tourists. (American tourists, that is. Haiti still has a loyal following among Europeans.) Consequently, most (but not all) hotels have been holding back on renovations and refurbishing. Since conditions there can change at any time, for better or worse, I again skipped a research trip to Haiti. What you have in the following pages, therefore, are reminders rather than recommendations, based on previous visits to the island.

Other Choices

Hotel Mont Joli
Cap-Haitien

At its best, the hotel lives up to its name, a pretty mountain setting of gardens and vine-covered terraces overlooking the bay, the town, and the great gleaming dome of the cathedral. The dome was constructed by the father of the Mont Joli's present owner, and Mont Joli was the family home until it became a hotel in 1956. The oldest (and prettiest) of the 30 rooms are furnished with 100-year-old French colonial beds, wardrobes, and chairs, mostly in sturdy mahogany; the remaining 6 rooms are in two-story wings, plus a dozen new minisuites in the terraced garden at the rear. Room 1, in the old wing, is particularly attractive, separated from the others by a porch, with a small terrace overlooking the sea; room 2 sports a canopied bed. All rooms have air-conditioning (rarely necessary at this elevation— 200 to 300 feet above the sea—for cooling but helpful for shutting out the sounds of crowing cocks and barking dogs). 30 rooms. Doubles: $80 to $90, winter 1994–95. *Hotel Mont Joli, P.O. Box 12, Cap-Haitien, Haiti, West Indies. Telephone: 509/620-300.*

Hotel La Jacmélienne

Jacmel

You reach Jacmel from Port-au-Prince by driving south past some of the greenest, lushest scenery in all of Haiti. First, the sugar plantations, then the mountains, with their dizzying, winding roads, clear air, and views that seem to go on forever. Not too long ago the trip took all day, but a superhighway now gets you there in about 2 hours. It's a demanding drive nonetheless, and once in Jacmel, you will probably want to stay a while. The perfect place: La Jacmélienne.

It's a sprawling, contemporary two-story structure directly on the beach at the edge of town. Everything about La Jacmélienne is light and airy and unpretentious—lobby and reception are open to the breezes; a covered dining room, on the second floor, is exposed on two sides; guest rooms are spacious and bright with private terraces facing the water. Even the spirit is open and expansive, due no doubt to the personality of owners/managers Erick and Marlene Danies. Crisply uniformed Jacméliennes take your order and graciously serve you lunch—simple, well-prepared Haitian specialties at reasonable prices.

La Jacmélienne can be a lively place, from the Haitian band that serenades you at dinner nightly and at lunch on weekends to the crowds who linger at the pool and beach. Although there are only 31 rooms, the hotel is a popular spot for day-trippers from Port-au-Prince, with the result that on busy weekends there might be upward of 150 people, including families, enjoying themselves. Beach and pool are both large, however, and there's plenty of room for privacy. In any case, the visitors clear out around sunset and you and the other guests have the place to yourselves.

The Jacmélienne's dark-sand beach is unexceptional, but there are several white-sand beaches nearby, considered to be among the best on the island. You can also explore the town with its colonial architecture (reminiscent of New Orleans) and art galleries. But best of all you can rent a horse, ride into the mountains, and spend an afternoon beside the waterfall of the *bassin bleu* (blue pool) looking for the nymphs who, according to legend, cavort in the mountain grottoes. 31 rooms. *Hotel La Jacmélienne, Rue St. Anne, Jacmel, Haiti, West Indies. Telephone: 509/224-899; fax: 509/465-778.*

La Villa Créole

Pétionville

This is a favorite of many longtime visitors to Haiti. A sprawling (70 rooms) white structure high in the hills of Pétionville (near the deluxe El Rancho, without a harbor view), it has a large swimming pool, attentive staff, and restful atmosphere. The public and private rooms are tastefully decorated. The outdoor dining areas are charming. Guest rooms are a mixed bag. All are air conditioned (necessary), but the hot exhaust ruins too many of the terraces. If you do stay here, I recommend the three "special deluxe" rooms (509, 609, and 710) in the newer wing, decorated with Haitian furniture and marble bathrooms. Each has two terraces to capture the sun at all angles. They're private and quiet. Nelson Rockefeller once stayed in room H in the old wing; its large terrace is, unfortunately, enclosed, but the room is big, comfortable, and quiet, and you can always imagine that the red carpet actually laid down for Rockefeller still leads to the door. 70 rooms. Doubles: $77 to $110, winter 1994–95. *La Villa Créole, P.O. Box 126, Port-au-Prince, Haiti, West Indies. Telephone: 800/223-9815 or 509/571-570; fax 509/574-935.*

The Dominican Republic

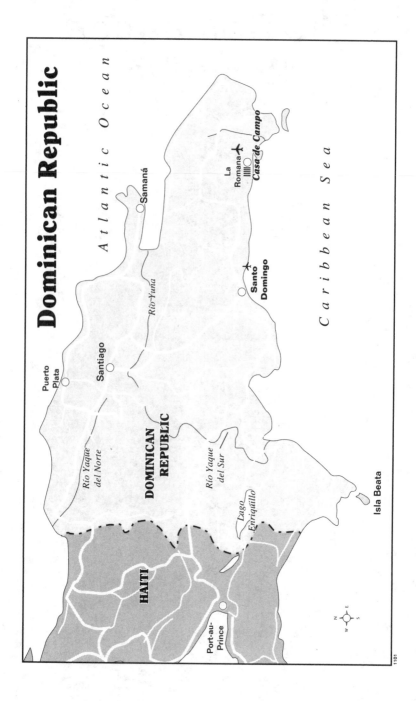

Dominican Republic

Atlantic Ocean

Samaná

Río Yuna

Puerto
Plata

Santiago

Caribbean Sea

La
Romana

Casa de Campo

Santo
Domingo

**DOMINICAN
REPUBLIC**

*Río Yaque
del Norte*

*Río Yaque
del Sur*

*Lago
Enriquillo*

HAÏTI

Port-au-
Prince

Isla Beata

N
W · E
S

The Dominican Republic

It's the other part of Hispaniola, Columbus's favorite *La Isla Española*, which it shares with Haiti. The first permanent European settlement in the Americas was here, in a place called Montecito, founded the year after Columbus arrived in 1492. A few years later, Columbus's brother, Bartolome, founded a city on the banks of the Ozama River and named it New Isabella; we now know it as Santo Domingo. At one time Santo Domingo was the most important city in the Caribbean, and it was from here that renowned conquistadores set forth on their expeditions to colonize the surrounding lands—Diego Velázquez to Cuba, Hernán Cortés to Mexico, and Juan Ponce de León to Puerto Rico, which is less than 60 miles to the east. In recent years, the Dominican government has been forging ahead with an impressive program to preserve and restore the old colonial city. It's well worth a visit.

But Santo Domingo's surprises don't end with the old colonial section; it also has one of the largest botanical parks in the world, a zoological park with 5 miles of pathways and one of the largest birdcages in the world, and somewhere in the city there's a Museum of Miniatures with a fully clothed flea.

How to Get There   From New York, daily nonstops on American, Continental, and Dominicana de Aviacion; from Miami, daily nonstops on American and Dominicana. For vacationers bound for Casa de Campo, the least stressful way to get there may be via San Juan and the American Eagle flights directly into La Romana, the resort's airstrip. This may involve a 1- or 2-hour stopover in San Juan, but it avoids the hassles of Santo Domingo and the long drive east.

For information on the Dominican Republic, call 800/752-1151.

Casa de Campo
La Romana

Atmosphere

Dining

Sports

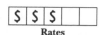
Rates

The original "ambience" here was designed by Oscar de la Renta, and the hotel brochure almost has you thinking that every last guest was designed by de la Renta.

True, many celebrities vacation here and several of them have built private homes on the property, but La Romana's "house in the country" is a pleasant, informal resort with few airs—designed not so much for beautiful people as active people. And how!

Two golf courses (one seaside, one inland) designed by Pete Dye are the pride of the project. With reason. Both are highly rated by pros, but for average duffers they promise more frustration than relaxation. A third Pete Dye course opened in 1989, but this one is reserved for the exclusive use of the homeowners, who were getting peeved because they couldn't get tee times. Tennis facilities are so extensive they get a "village" all to themselves across the main road, where you'll find 13 Har-Tru courts (10 with lights), ball machines—even ball boys. There are, on a casual count, 14 swimming pools, as well as 250 quarter horses and 250 polo ponies in the equestrian center. Even the polo fields come in multiples—two practice fields, two playing fields.

William Cox was the architect who pulled the whole thing together and created a sprawling complex that nevertheless manages to be compatible, more or less, with its Dominican surroundings. Buildings (never higher than three stories, mostly two) are finished in stucco, with red corrugated roofs, native stone, and rough-hewn local hardwoods. Interiors sport floors of hand-fired tile; screened, glazed, and louvered doors; local paintings; and boldly patterned fabrics. Every hotel room has a stocked mini-bar and patio or balcony; villa suites are larger and more luxuriously appointed.

All in all, Casa de Campo doesn't sound like the creation of a big corporate conglomerate, but that's exactly what it is—or was. The Gulf + Western Corporation started the project in a corner of its 7,000-acre sugar plantation, but sold everything—sugar, land, hotel, horses, golf balls—to the Fanjul brothers of Palm Beach, Florida, a family also heavily into sugar plantations. As homeowners themselves on the Casa de Campo estate, they were probably eager to buy up a project 11 times larger than Monaco.

The problem is, Casa de Campo is getting to be more *casa* than *campo*, with new villas going up everywhere. Nowadays, you almost have to plan your travels around this hotel as diligently as you might plan a tour of Caribbean islands: Tennis is here, golf is there, stables thataway, and the closest beach somewhere else. So the first thing guests do when they get here is rent a "villa cart" or moped to avoid standing around waiting for shuttle buses. In fact, smart guests reserve their carts when they reserve their rooms. (Villa guests are provided with a cart.)

The hotel is organized around a handsomely designed core of restaurants, lounges, terraces, patios, courtyards, and a spectacular split-level pool with swim-up bar and thatch-roofed lounge. Grouped around it are the hotel "casitas." Golf villas are half a mile or so east; the equestrian center, polo fields, and tennis courts are across the main island road; Altos de Chavon, the resort's arts and culture village, with a range of restaurants, boutiques, and ateliers, is a few miles farther east. There are private homes on the hill (some for rent, others, like the Pucci place, strictly private) and private homes (like de la Renta's) down by the spectacular shoreline—and adjoining the resort's private international airport. In all, there are more than 750 rooms for rent at Casa de Campo, some in the newly refurbished casitas, some in villas.

To fill all those beds, the resort has to haul in groups and conventions, and since groups and conventions are unwieldy, many of them arrive directly at the airstrip—once the private preserve of corporate mini-jets.

With all those rooms, all those acres, and a staff of 2,000, management obviously can't keep an eye on every detail. Hence, some flaws in basic amenities: The new villas with connecting doors between rooms are not soundproof, and how do you think Oscar de la Renta would feel if a waiter arrived at 6:00 the evening before he checked out to do an inventory of his refrigerator—then locked it? These gripes aside, it should be emphasized that the staff is pleasant even if not always polished, rates are reasonable, and you can eat well at modest prices (there you are, out there in the boonies, miles from the nearest cantina, and they don't try to gouge you— you can have a huge custom-made breakfast for just $14).

And even if you never catch so much as a glimpse of the polo-playing, party-giving, trendsetting socialites who fill the usual glossy articles about Casa de Campo, here's a place where you can never say you're bored. Ever.

Name: Casa de Campo
Manager: Claudio Silvestri
Address: La Romana, Dominican Republic
Location: On the southeast coast, 1½–2 hours from Santo Domingo airport, 2 hours from the capital itself; the resort has an air-conditioned

lounge at the airport and hostesses to escort you to air-conditioned mini-buses for the ride to La Romana ($80 per couple round-trip), but have your travel agent look into the possibility of flying direct to the resort via San Juan on an American Eagle 66-seater turboprop or via Miami on American Airlines

Telephone: 809/523-3333

Fax: 809/523-8548

Reservations: Own Miami Office, toll free 800/877-3643 or 305/856-5405

Credit Cards: American Express, MasterCard, Visa

Rooms: 750, in 300 casitas and 150 villas and homes of various sizes; all casitas have air-conditioning, louvers, wet bars and stocked mini-bars, coffeemakers, hair dryers, balconies or patios, direct-dial telephones; homes and villas have full kitchens

Meals: Breakfast, lunch, and dinner somewhere on the resort or at Altos de Chavon from 7:00 a.m. to midnight in one or another of the 9 restaurants (some with taped or live music; the beachside El Pescador is particularly attractive); dinner for 2 anywhere from $25 to $80; informal dress, but long trousers for men everywhere after 6:00 p.m. and jackets or long-sleeved shirts in the hotel's Tropicana and Casa del Rio restaurants; room service, limited menu, $5 extra per tray

Entertainment: Bars, lounges, taped and live music, dancing, disco, folklore shows, occasional concerts and recitals at Altos de Chavon

Sports: 3 beaches, 14 pools (plus some semiprivate pools, but beware—there's an activities director on the beach with a megaphone); you pay for just about everything else (rates are average)—boat trips to Catalina Island, snorkeling, windsurfing, Hobiecats, Sunfish sailing, scuba, deep-sea fishing, waterskiing, tennis (13 Har-Tru courts, 10 with lights, full pro shop), an enlarged fitness center (squash, racquetball, massage, sauna, whirlpool, exercise equipment), 250-acre trap and skeet shooting club, 110-station shooting center, horseback riding (western and English, with *vaquero* guides only), polo instruction and rentals (winter only), golf (2 superb Pete Dye courses), pheasant hunts

P.S.:   Some kids, some groups—all of which can be avoided most of the time except on the beach; open all year

The U.S. Virgin Islands & Puerto Rico

St. John

St. Thomas

St. Croix

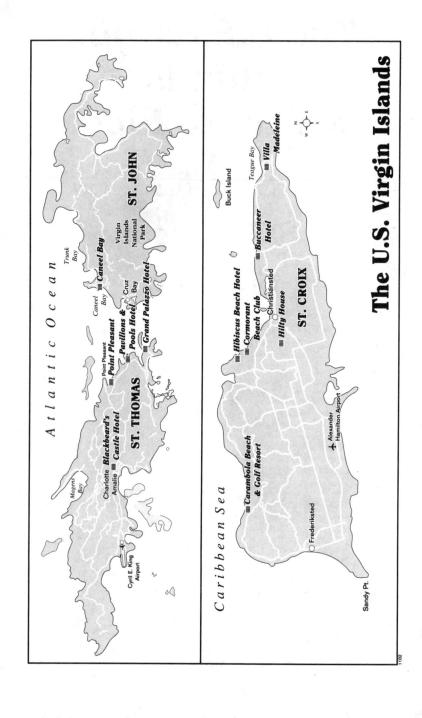

The U.S. Virgin Islands

The U.S. Virgin Islands & Puerto Rico

Suburbia south. With a few delightful exceptions, these islands are just about everything you're trying to escape—shopping centers, real estate billboards, telephone poles, traffic jams, crowded restaurants. However, since they are politically part of the United States, Puerto Rico, St. Thomas, St. Croix, and St. John have their attractions, sometimes bountiful. Not least of these is the fact that you don't have to worry about passports, don't have to fidget in long lines on arrival while some official thumbs his way through immigration formalities, don't have to wait at customs behind returning islanders laden with suitcases and cartons that have to be painstakingly inspected and evaluated. These islands need no introduction, but a few comments might be helpful.

When most people think of Puerto Rico they think of San Juan, which, impressive though it may be from a commercial and political point of view, is no longer a tropical hideaway. But how about *Old* San Juan? The old city, with its narrow streets and fortresses, is still one of the unique places of the Caribbean. Even UNESCO thinks so: It designated six sites in Old San Juan as World Heritage Monuments. Moreover, when you get beyond the city, Puerto Rico can be a stunningly beautiful island. Head for the rain forest. Try a drive along the roadway that runs east to west along the Cordillera Central. And the modern *autopista* from San Juan to Ponce is a spectacular but effortless route across the mountains.

St. Thomas and St. Croix have had more than their share of problems, not least of them Hurricane Hugo and its aftermath. The islanders blame a hostile stateside press for bad publicity, but you should read the lurid headlines in their own local papers. Both islands are low on the list of priorities for this guidebook, not because of any latent unrest but because they are just too overdeveloped for comfort. Charlotte Amalie is an almost constant traffic jam. Poor Christiansted should be one of *the* gems of the Caribbean, but instead its lovely old Danish buildings are almost swamped by masses of power cables and carbuncled telephone poles. Your best bet on either island is to get to your hotel and stay put. Otherwise you'll have to deal with their taxi drivers, who are not the Caribbean's most obliging fellows.

St. John is the delightful, enchanting standout—just 28 square miles, almost half of them national park. Cruz Bay, the main town, looks nothing like a suburb of Florida (or anywhere else, for that matter), and there are more than enough beaches and coves and mountain trails for everyone.

How to Get There   San Juan's Luis Muñoz Marín International Airport is the largest in the Caribbean, (they've spent millions, *millions* in the past few years expanding and improving it); it's served by nonstop flights from almost 20 cities in North America and one-stop direct service from as far away as Los Angeles. From New York alone there are almost 20 scheduled flights every day. American has expanded its activities at the airport, and it's now the hub of interisland services on American Eagle, flying small, efficient aircraft. When using these services, remember that what you consider carry-on luggage may have to be checked for the smaller flight, so pack accordingly.

For St. Thomas, thanks to a longer runway and a larger terminal building, there are more nonstop jet flights than ever, from New York (American, Continental, Delta) and Miami (American), as you would expect, but also Raleigh-Durham (American), and Baltimore/Washington and Philadelphia (USAir). The only nonstop to St. Croix is American from Miami, but since that island is busily, sort of, enhancing its facilities, by the time you read this page there may be more nonstop flights. Otherwise, there are

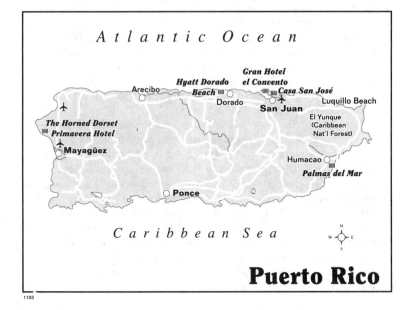

plenty of commuter flights from St. Thomas and San Juan, including a new service by Seabourne Seaplanes, downtown to downtown rather than airport to airport, and Dolphin Airlines.

There's no airport, of course, on St. John, so you get there on ferryboats from Charlotte Amalie or Red Hook on St. Thomas. If you're staying at Caneel Bay, you will be transported in style on one of the resort's private launches.

For information on St. Thomas, St. John, and St. Croix, call 212/332-2222; for information on Puerto Rico, call 800/223-6530.

Hyatt Dorado Beach Resort & Casino

Dorado, Puerto Rico

Atmosphere

Dining

Sports

Rates

Yes, despite the name it's the same classy, elegant Dorado Beach Hotel conjured up by the Rockresort people 37 years ago.

But, it's been fiddled with during those 37 years.

Since it's now coming into its seventh full season under its latest owner (the fourth), perhaps it's more accurate to say it's *almost* the same classy, elegant resort.

The setting is still one of the most majestic of any resort in the Americas: an estate of 1,000 acres and thousands of coconut palms, of winding fairways and manicured lawns, and a pair of crescent beaches. The grounds have been replanted with a botanical bonanza of African tulip and almond trees, sweet immortelle and spice berry, and fiddle-leaf fig.

When I first came here in 1963, a few years after it opened, those crescent beaches were ringed with just 150 guest rooms, in decorous two-story wings hidden among the leafy palms; today, the room count has doubled. The first-rate sports facilities, once the playground of a mere 300, are now shared among all those extra guests *and* a local country club numbering 500-plus members.

Moreover, the 1,000 acres are shared with a sister hotel of more than 500 rooms, a mile down the coast. Nothing very new in that, of course: The eight-story Cerromar has been there for some time now and it, too, has come under the Hyatt banner (it's now the grandly named Hyatt Regency Cerromar Beach Hotel). But since it's given over largely to groups and conventions, whose members have charge privileges at both hotels, the custom-built trolleys that shuttle between the two resorts seem to carry more bodies bound for Dorado than vice versa.

On a recent visit (admittedly out of season) I found the clientele at Dorado Beach was not at all what Laurance Rockefeller had in mind 37 years ago. The guests didn't add anything to the elegance of the original. They cluttered the dining facilities. To keep these guests happy, slot machines have been installed in the casino.

But there certainly are pluses: When you include the sports facilities at Cerromar, you find you now have four championship golf courses (designed by Robert Trent Jones, all four have been rehabilitated). There are 21 tennis courts, a few lit for night play. And it's still a rare pleasure to hop on a tandem and cycle along paths that weave between the fairways and the sea (although you're expected to return the bike to the rental people before 5:00 p.m.—just when the sun and the sea and the palms are at their most ravishing).

What the Hyatt people have also done is lavish millions just on updating and renovating the rooms, and almost everything they've touched is an improvement. Colors are soft and natural. New colonial-style furniture enhances the Caribbean mood. Each room has a mini-bar and a safe, and the centerpiece of guest rooms on the upper floors is a sturdy carved four-poster; beach-level guests have to settle for a pair of queen-size beds. The beachfront patios have dividing walls to maintain a sense of privacy.

The original deluxe beachfront rooms are the favorite of longtime guests, but the top of the line accommodations are actually the Casita Rooms, located between the pool and the beach with split-level layouts and skylights above bath-size shower stalls.

Which room should you choose? The dozen or so "standard" rooms facing the fairways are the least expensive (and perfectly acceptable in terms of facilities); the "superior" rooms are closest to the swimming pool and dining rooms; "deluxe" designates rooms fronting the beach—with those in the East Wing (the originals) closer to the golf and tennis pro shops.

The Dorado kitchens are now in the care of Gino Delillo. His Sunday buffet brunch of local specialties is not only stunningly presented in the classic Dorado manner but at $32.50, it's an outstanding value. Especially good value, I might add, since your $32.50 includes seemingly endless flutes of Domaine Chandon *vin champenois* (the buffet officially lasts until

3:00 p.m., so you have plenty of time for seconds, on your plate and in your flute).

The Surf Room, where dinner is served from 6:30 to 9:30, is hardly the most romantic room in the Caribbean, even with its 3,600 square feet of windows facing the sea. But Su Casa, the original estate house, or *finca*, most certainly is romantic, with its candlelit tables, its cool courtyards, and foliage-draped stairways—a welcome holdover from the original Dorado.

Name: Hyatt Dorado Beach Resort & Casino

Manager: Gary R. McKeighen

Address: Dorado, Puerto Rico, U.S. Virgin Islands 00646

Location: On the island's north shore, 22 miles west of San Juan, about 45 mostly untropical minutes by shuttle van from the airport ($14 per person each way, upon request)

Telephone: 809/796-1234

Fax: 809/796-2022

Reservations: Hyatt Worldwide, 800/233-1234

Credit Cards: All major cards

Rooms: 298 rooms and suites in 2-story and 3-story wings, most of them strung along the beach; each with marble bathroom (bath and shower; bathrobes in the Casita Rooms only), lanai or balcony, air-conditioning and fan, stocked refrigerator, iron, coffeemaker, safe, clock/radio, direct-dial telephone, hair dryer

Meals: Breakfast 7:30–noon, lunch noon–4:00, dinner 6:30–9:30 in any of 4 restaurants—the 400-seat Surf Room, the Ocean Terrace, the Golf Pro Shop (if you don't mind cutely named dishes such as "sandwitches," etc.), and the romantic Su Casa (dinner only)—jackets in the Surf Room and Su Casa; 24-hour room service

Entertainment: Small casino, music for dancing, beach parties, movies, VCR in lounge for special programs, plus the assorted lounges and disco at the nearby Cerromar; live music in the Surf Room and Su Casa (mostly Spanish-style ballads by strolling musicians)

Sports: 2 reef-protected crescent beaches and lagoons (good swimming), 2 pools (plus a children's pool), pedalos, walking/jogging trails, bicycles and tandems—free; at extra charge: tennis (7 courts, 2 with lights, pro shop), golf (36 championship holes, carts obligatory, green fee $40 per day, pro shop), windsurfing, massage, facials, aerobics; the golf and tennis facilities are augmented by additional courses and courts, with lights, at Cerromar; high-tech Spa Caribe at Cerromar

P.S.: In the slack months, the hotel hosts groups up to 300; in summer and during holidays there are lots of children, but youngsters from 3 to 13 have their own day camp; open all year

Palmas del Mar

Humacao, Puerto Rico

			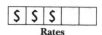
Atmosphere	**Dining**	**Sports**	**Rates**

Cobbled *plazuelas* with splashing fountains. Cupolas and arches. Walls of tiles hand painted by craftspeople in the village across the hill. It may not sound like a big sprawling residential/condominium development but it is—it's just that architect/developer Steve Padilla tried to keep the scale intimate by adding "visual delights" and decreeing that no building go higher than the palm trees. The resort's 2,750 acres are located on a former sugar plantation, in an unhurried and scenic corner of the island, with the island of Vieques offshore and the rain forest an hour's drive up the coast.

This is a place for people seeking the outdoors, lots of sun, lots of play—but with a dash of style and comfort. The 20 tennis courts are grouped in pairs, separated from each other by trees and flowering bushes. Bridle trails and biking trails wind through navelike stands of coconut palms. The fairways are as challenging and sporty as a golfer could hope for. The miles of beach and the marina between them allow for just about every water sport at pretty good values.

Accommodations come in a variety of villas and suites (probably more suited to a family than a couple) and a pair of attractive inns in Mediterranean style—the hilltop Palmas Inn and Casino and the Candelero Hotel (which is also, alas, the core of an executive conference center, but is probably the best bet for one couple). Unlike so many resorts, Palmas del Mar has a room-only rate even in winter, allowing you to take advantage of the resort's varied dining facilities (and varied prices).

I lost track of all the dining spots—stylish French up the hill, Caribbean in the inn, seafood at the marina, Oriental somewhere, burgers and hot dogs by the beach and tennis center.

Twenty-two-year-old Palmas del Mar is now owned by a Houston company, Maxxam, and managed by Club Resorts, whose parent runs such resorts as Pinehurst, North Carolina, and Barton Creek, Texas.

Name: Palmas del Mar
Manager: Shawn Hurwitz
Address: P.O. Box 2020, Humacao, Puerto Rico, U.S. Virgin Islands 00792

Location: On the southeast coast, near the town of Humacao; an hour from the airport by mini-bus ($18 per person when sharing); by car take the autopista to Humacao and Yabucoa, then follow the signposts to the resort

Telephone: 809/852-6000

Fax: 809/850-4445

Reservations: 800/468-3331

Credit Cards: All major cards

Rooms: 290 rooms and suites, in villas, condominiums; including 23 in the Palmas Inn, 102 in the Candelero Hotel; all with air-conditioning (necessary much of the time), direct-dial telephones, stocked mini-bars, radios, and television; apartments and villas also have full kitchens

Meals: Breakfast 7:00–11:00, lunch noon–3:00, dinner 6:00–11:00 in 5 restaurants (up to $80 for 2); more extensive hours elsewhere; informal dress; no room service, except takeout by individual restaurants

Entertainment: Casinos, bars, lounges, live music, depending on the location

Sports: 3 miles of beach and coves, 6 freshwater pools—free; tennis (20 courts, 7 lit, Peter Burwash pro shop), golf (18 holes, designed by Gary Player), fitness center, horseback riding (30-horse equestrian center), snorkeling, scuba diving, windsurfing, waterskiing, paddleboats, deep-sea fishing, sailboat trips, bicycles

P.S.:   Lots of groups and seminars, lots of children (especially on weekends) but there are special playgrounds and pools for youngsters; open all year

The Horned Dorset Primavera Hotel

Rincón, Puerto Rico

| Atmosphere | Dining | Sports | Rates |

Here you are on the unspoiled western coast of Puerto Rico, where the jungly mountains give way to fields of sugarcane, surrounded by 4 acres of tropical lushness dipping gently toward the sea—yet you're staying in a place named after a breed of English sheep? So let's get the ungainly name out of the way.

Owners Harold Davies and Kingsley Wratten own a highly acclaimed restaurant in upstate New York called the Horned Dorset; when they opened a second inn on this island of perpetual spring they decided to retain the goodwill of their Leonardsville original and tack on the Spanish word for spring, *primavera*. At least, I assume that's the reason— and I assume they won't mind if I save paper and refer to it as the Primavera. With that out of the way, let's get back to those four lush seaside acres.

Stateside, the owners have a reputation for meticulous care in preserving old buildings, but here they called in a local architect with the splendid name of Otto Octavio Reyes Casanova. Out of consideration for the set-ting, the inn's 30 rooms and suites are dispersed among two-story villas, all in Spanish-Mediterranean style with stucco walls and red-tiled roofs, lots of polished mahogany with wrought-iron trimmings.

Each room is a gem, decorated with native red-tile floors and fitted with four-poster beds and mahogany furniture custom-designed and hand-crafted in nearby Ponce. Louvered French doors open to balconies and patios facing the sea; the bathrooms are opulent (almost too opulent) with Italian marble and footed bathtubs fitted with brass fixtures from France. Best of all, perhaps, the owners have added eight new suites that are even more sumptuous—four with private plunge pools, four with extralarge sundecks.

The Primavera cultivates an air of relaxation—and unabashed idleness is exactly why you'd want to head out there. Granted, it's an ideal stopover on a round-the-island tour (which I highly recommend), but make sure it's a 2-night stop at least.

By day, the popular agenda seems to be a morning dip in the ocean; lingering breakfast on the terrace—fresh mango and pineapple, fresh coffee from the mountain plantations; an hour or two in one of the bamboo loungers with a good book; light lunch, dip in the pool, siesta; an hour by the pool; a rum punch at sundown.

Evenings begin with tapas at 6:30 in the lounge, followed by leisurely dinners in a salon that has the regal air of a Spanish grandee's manor, surrounded by 14 handsome mahogany doors, decorated with jacquard tapestries and softly glowing sconces and chandeliers. This is just the sort of ambience that caught the attention of the Relais & Châteaux bigwigs, who recently welcomed the Primavera as one of their members. Dinner is a formal (but relaxed) affair beginning at 7:00 and ending, six courses later, with rich desserts. But some guests might prefer a lighter, less ambitious fare, especially if they're staying longer than a weekend.

Sometime during your stay, tell the Messrs. Davies and Wratten you forgive the ungainly name—but thank them profusely for bringing Puerto Rico what it's needed for years: a stylish little inn beside the sea.

Name: The Horned Dorset Primavera
Owners/Managers: Harold Davies and Kingsley Wratten
Address: Apartado 1132, Rincón, Puerto Rico, U.S. Virgin Islands 00743
Location: On Puerto Rico's west coast, just 15 minutes by car north of Mayagüez; you can get there by flying American Eagle from San Juan to Mayagüez (6 flights a day, 30 minutes each way), and from there it's a 15-minute drive to the hotel (you can arrange to be met at the airport); by car from San Juan, it's a 2½-hour drive along the north shore (you might want to consider stopping off at the Hyatt Dorado Beach for lunch) or 3 hours via the more scenic southern route through Ponce
Telephone: 809/823-4030, 4050
Fax: 809/823-5580
Reservations: Direct or Caribbean Inns Ltd.
Credit Cards: American Express, MasterCard, Visa
Rooms: 30, all suites, in 6 2-story Mediterranean-style villas, all with marble bathrooms, ceiling fans, 4-poster beds
Meals: Breakfast 7:00–10:00, lunch noon–2:30 in the open-air terrace of the main house, dinner 7:00 in the formal dining room, breeze-cooled or air-conditioned (6-course dinner, $90 for 2); informal dress ("no shorts or bathing suits in the public rooms after 6:00"); room service for breakfast only
Entertainment: Bar/library, with *tapas* at 6:30 and stacks of vintage *Life* magazines; live classical music or local trio on weeknights; casino nearby
Sports: Freshwater pool, small beach; surfing and water sports at nearby Club Náutico de Rincón (Rincón is the site of world surfing championships); golf 25 minutes away; whale watching, deep-sea fishing, and guided trips to the uninhabited island of Mona can be arranged
P.S.:   No children under 12; no radios or television

Caneel Bay

St. John

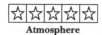
Atmosphere

Dining

Sports

Rates

Where else in the Caribbean, where else in the world, will $580 a day or thereabouts get you a resort with seven beaches (each lovelier than the next), a private peninsula of 170 acres surrounded by 6,500 acres of national park on land and 5,600 acres of national park underwater; where you can hike along paths lined with flamboyant, tamarind, and shower of gold; snorkel among peacock flounders and trumpet fish; spot a yellow-bellied sapsucker or pectoral sandpiper, maybe even a bobolink; build up your strength on a five-course breakfast, buffet lunch, and five-course dinner in some of the best restaurants in the Caribbean, and then bunk down in a double-size love nest open to the breezes and birdsongs?

True, $580-plus a day is the summer rate, but you still get all the attractions that presidents, vice presidents, bank biggies, gospel biggies, French counts, and senators pay almost twice as much for in winter.

Caneel is Caneel 12 months of the year, in season or out of season—just about the ultimate in seclusion, tranquility, a sort of ecological euphoria. You almost have the feeling you're camping out here, but with a roof over your head rather than a tent, a bed under you rather than a sleeping bag, and real china rather than plastic plates.

There are 171 rooms at Caneel Bay (for every room an acre of landscaped parkland!), and most of them are right on beaches, a few are on headlands, 36 hillside rooms are in the Tennis Gardens, the rise behind the courts, with a few bungalows off by themselves on the edge of the national park. A pair of shuttle buses circle the grounds every 15 minutes, but it's still worthwhile to give some thought to *where* you'd like to be. Of the beaches, my preference is leeward Scott (single-story wing), but others prefer the windward Hawksnest (two-story, balconies for morning and afternoon sun) for its views of offshore islands. Rooms at Turtle Bay, perhaps the prettiest beach, are close to the old estate house restaurant (a few are actually in the estate house and may pick up the sounds of what passes as conviviality in these sedate parts, but room number 93 has a particularly bosky balcony).

The most secluded quarters are in the famous Cottage 7, once the home (*a* home) of the Rockefeller family, now the haunt of assorted VIPs who can conveniently park their bodyguards in the attached servants' quarters.

Adjoining Cottage 7, rooms 61 through 66 are on a headland, secluded from the rest of the hotel, with their own patch of sand; on Caneel Bay itself, rooms 26 through 29 are especially popular because they're farthest from the public areas yet close to the main dining room. Up in the Tennis Gardens, rooms 132 and 133 are particularly spacious.

But since Caneel Bay, like its sister resort down the channel, Little Dix Bay, found itself a few years ago about to be managed by Rosewood Hotels of Dallas, many island lovers have been agog to see what would transpire. Not much, as it turns out—at least in the case of Caneel.

Traditionally the exteriors have been painted in colors (variously described as "madonna gray" or "Rockefeller putty") that blend unobtrusively into the surrounding nature, and traditionally the interiors have been only marginally more colorful. Don't knock it—it's always been very soothing even if slightly fuddy-duddy. But now the Rosewood people have installed new fabrics and whatnots to add discreet splashes of color, green decorative tiles in the bathrooms, and two-tone wicker and rattan or cane and bamboo furniture, including a few pieces from the Orient that look good but don't sit well with the old-timers. And for good reason—these people tend to settle in for weeks at a time, travel with an average of five suitcases per couple, and now they find that they have no place to store their fancy togs.

These rooms may surprise some vacationers who think that $580 a night rates include air-conditioning, room phones, and television. Hell, my room didn't even have glass in the window facing the bay, just screens and jalousie louvers, and the wall opposite had only rough-hewn stone and jalousies screened by dense foliage. And that's the way the guests want it; they're the sort of people who could afford to stay anywhere but choose to come back here year after year, in many cases more than 20 years. These are people who can survive happily without TV or radio or room phones—"After all," as one of them remarked, "calm is what we come for in the first place."

Caneel guests have a choice of three dining pavilions: the main one by the beach, one in a former plantation house, another in a former sugar mill. The mill is now known as the Equator ("Whose idea was it to call it the Equator?" harrumphed one old-timer on my shuttle bus. "It's a sugar mill—always was, always will be"), featuring cuisines from those countries circling the middle of the globe. This gives the chefs, taking a little latitude, so to speak, lots of scope—Thai, Indian, Middle Eastern, Mexican, Caribbean. Heaven knows what the carper on the shuttle thought of the bouillabaisse à la Thai with lemongrass, galanga, and coriander or the green curry duck breast with coconut milk and steamed basmati rice, but I found it all very tasty, intriguing, and refreshing for jaded palates.

For active vacationers, there are no fewer than 11 tennis courts (no lights, though, because they'd spoil the magical after-dark atmosphere), a freshwater pool (but no diving, too noisy), Sunfish sailing, snorkeling gear—all included in the rate.

Caneel also has its own fleet of launches plying between the resort and St. Thomas, plus its own air-conditioned lounge at the airport, so guests enjoy VIP treatment even before they set foot on the resort's private dock. But occasionally, just occasionally, the staff falls short: My *Do Not Disturb* sign didn't deter the ice man and the replenisher of the mini-bar; and the porters might have been more efficient about organizing their loading of the luggage—or at least more gracious about keeping guests standing in the sun on the dock while they went about their duties.

These nitpicks apart, Caneel is one of those holdouts that really goes all out to pamper guests with personal attention (staff outnumber guests by a good margin) and cloak them in an atmosphere of calm and serenity. As one lady remarked on the launch, "We've been going there for 20 years and I always think of my 2 weeks there as therapy."

Name: Caneel Bay

Manager: Martin Nicholson

Address: P.O. Box 720, Cruz Bay, St. John, U.S. Virgin Islands 00831-0720

Location: 4 miles across the channel from the tip of St. Thomas; the resort has its own air-conditioned lounge at St. Thomas's airport, and the host there will take charge of your transfer to the resort—by taxi to Charlotte Amalie, where you board a private 58-foot launch, *Caneel Bay Mary II,* for the 45-minute trip direct to the Caneel dock (included in the rates)

Telephone: 809/776-6111

Fax: 809/776-2030

Reservations: U.S. office, 800/928-8889

Credit Cards: All major cards

Rooms: 171 in a variety of 1-story and 2-story wings strategically located around the property, with a few suites in cottage number 7; all with ceiling fans and louvers, balconies or patios, wall safes, mini-bars—but no telephones, no television, no radios

Meals: Continental breakfast 7:00–7:45, full breakfast 7:45–10:00, lunch noon–2:00, afternoon tea 4:00, dinner 7:00–9:00 (approx. $100 for 2), in 3 breeze-cooled dining pavilions, including the lovely hillside Equator Restaurant; jackets for gentlemen after 6:00 p.m. in the Turtle Bay dining room, more casual in the main dining pavilion; "dry bathing suits and beach wraps and sandals at all times, no shorts or blue jeans after 6:00 p.m."; live music in the Turtle Bay dining room, some taped music in the Equator; room service for breakfast only, $2 extra per tray

Entertainment: Live music every evening (guitar, combo, "slightly amplified"), dancing most evenings, movies every evening, nature lectures,
backgammon, Scrabble, chess

Sports: 7 beautiful beaches, good swimming and snorkeling, freshwater
pool behind the tennis courts, Sunfish sailing, windsurfing, nature
trails, tennis (11 courts, Peter Burwash pro shop, no lights)—all free; by
arrangement: scuba (from the dock), sailboat cruises, boat trips to St.
Thomas (popular for shopping) and Little Dix Bay; special package
offering a few days ashore, a few days afloat in a Hinckley

P.S.:   Some children (but on a short leash); open all year

Point Pleasant
St. Thomas

Guest cottages here are so artfully tucked into the crags and cactus gardens
that at first you think you must have blundered onto someone's private
estate. On second glance, a few cedar-shake roofs peek discreetly out of the
greenery. Here and there, you spot a redwood deck, weathered to a sea-
salty silver, jutting from the face of a hill that swoops 200 feet beneath you to
an aquamarine bay.

Although Point Pleasant is around 20 years old, it has the ageless, settled
look of belonging to its surroundings as rightfully as any gnarled old sea
grape or mampoo tree. Colors, materials, designs are all just plain natural,
although a recent sprucing up has lightened up the fabrics and surroundings a tone or two. A bit "condo," maybe, but very comfortable. From a 15-
foot-high redwood ceiling, a paddle fan whirs above your king-size bed.
Walls are mostly windows and glass doors and can stay open to the trade
winds, because there's nothing to screen out. At this height, both humidity
and mosquitoes are conveniently blown out to sea.

Most of Point Pleasant's accommodations, all newly renovated, are in
these airy hillside dwellings, usually two or three to a cottage, with another
18 down by the shore. They range from a single room with either balcony or
sunken garden to a five-room, three-bath villa.

A comfortable, affordable compromise might be what the management calls a "junior" suite—a sleeping-living room plus dining space, kitchen, and a deck with a gull's-eye view of St. John, Tortola, and various other Virgins undulating into infinity. Some of the hilltop rooms, alas, now have their wall to wall views scarred by an ungainly Holiday Inn squatting on the next headland—a decidedly *un*pleasant point.

You, too, can do some interesting undulating—down and around Point Pleasant's boulder preserve. The route you take is a fantastic journey through what must have been a very big bang. In fact, you're standing precisely on the spot where, several billion years ago, a monumental volcanic eruption took place, the results of which look as if some psycho fire god had scooped up an acre of nice, quiet boulders, squeezed premature wrinkles into their skins, and petulantly flung them down like a handful of hot potatoes. And they're still sitting right where they landed, one balanced topsy-turvy on the tip of another, with organ-pipe cacti and century plants sprouting out of them like bizarre hairdos.

Point Pleasant has thoughtfully spiked your route along their half-hour nature trail with some civilized stopping-off places. A woodland glade. A shady gazebo cantilevered over the abyss, where you can catch your breath and sip a planter's punch. Three freshwater swimming pools. A tennis court. A sea deck with comfortable redwood benches and chaises. And finally, at the end of the trail, an immaculate little white-sand beach.

In the bargain, the hotel supplies you with free use of a car for a few hours a day—long enough to take you around the island to other sights, other restaurants, and back again to this very pleasant point.

Name: Point Pleasant

Acting Manager: Mark Kaiser

Address: 6600 Estate Smith Bay #4, St. Thomas, U.S. Virgin Islands 00802

Location: In the northeast of the island, overlooking Pillsbury Bay and the islands of Tortola and St. John, half an hour and about $14 by taxi from the airport

Telephone: 809/775-7200

Fax: 809/776-5694

Reservations: Direct, 800/524-2300 or Robert Reid Associates

Credit Cards: American Express, Diners Club, MasterCard, Visa

Rooms: 134 total, from "junior" to 2-bedroom suites, on the hill or by the beach; all with fully equipped kitchens, direct-dial telephones, breezes, ceiling fans, air-conditioning, and satellite television with remote

Meals: Breakfast 7:00–10:00, lunch noon–2:00, dinner 7:00–10:00 in the hillside Agave Terrace restaurant or Bayside Café (approx. $15 to $50 for 2), informal dress; 2 poolside cafés, open 11:00–6:00

Entertainment: Weekly managers' cocktail parties, island shows, rum tastings, jazz nights, shopping, Magen's Bay and evening shuttle bus service
(small charge)

Sports: Beach, 3 freshwater pools (2 with poolside bars), snorkeling,
Sunfish sailing, windsurfing, scuba lessons, tennis (1 court, lights)—all
free; boat trips, golf nearby; fleet of 15 Corolla Sedans available to guests
for 4-hour tours once a day at no extra charge other than gas and $9.50
insurance charge

P.S.:   Open all year

Pavilions & Pools Hotel
St. Thomas

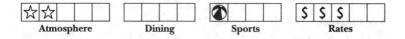

☆ ☆								☎				$ $ $		
Atmosphere			**Dining**				**Sports**			**Rates**		

The genies who designed this place proceeded on the premise that if we all
had three wishes, they would be for (1) a tropical house on a tropical island,
(2) a private swimming pool, and (3) no down payment, no mortgage.
And, sure enough, they've made all three come true. More or less.

The pavilion part of their wish fulfillment consists of a cabana-style suite
(there are two basic designs, one slightly roomier than the other) of big,
open rooms with one long wall of sliding glass doors and new furniture,
kitchens, and tiling. On the other side of the door lies the pool part: a
completely private patio with a completely private swimming pool that's
yours to do whatever you've always wanted to do in a swimming pool. A
stout wall and plenty of tall spiky tropical plantings guarantee Peeping
Toms can't peep.

Unlike most hotels with individual pools, Pavilions & Pools gives you
one big enough (16 by 18 feet or 20 by 14 feet) for something more
athletic than dipping your toes. And with most Caribbean hotels still
frowning on topless tanning, you may be grateful for the chance to color
in your white spaces without causing a riot. The rigorous privacy of the
place, however, extends beyond your doorstep. To some, that's a plus. To
others, a minus.

Because there is no central pool, no beach, and an honor bar with only limited meal service, you're scarcely aware of anybody but the two of you and the friendly people who run the hotel and happily help you arrange side trips, rent cars, call airlines, reserve tables at restaurants, etc. All activities outside your own room are at the hotel next door on Sapphire Beach. That includes tennis, any water sport you can think of, and some meals (unless you prepare them in your own kitchen or drive around sampling the island's varied cooking).

P & P keeps right on being one of the Caribbean's most popular ways of getting away from it all. If you both agree that a king-size bed, a pool of saltwater, and thou are enough, come and join the crowd. Even though you'll never know they're here.

Name: Pavilions & Pools Hotel
Manager: Tammy Waters
Address: 6400 Estate Smith Bay, St. Thomas, U.S. Virgin Islands 00802
Location: In the east, near Sapphire Bay, half an hour and $12 by taxi from the airport
Telephone: 809/775-6110
Fax: 809/775-6110, ext. 251
Reservations: Direct 800/524-2001 or Robert Reid Associates
Credit Cards: American Express, Discover, MasterCard, Visa
Rooms: 25 villas with private pools, king-size beds, kitchen, ceiling fans, hair dryers, safes, air-conditioning, telephones, some with "garden" showers, cable TV, VCRs
Meals: One-entrée dinner served nightly in the bar/café overlooking the garden (approx. $30 for 2)
Entertainment: You; VCR library and 50 U.S. channels; cocktail party Tuesday nights
Sports: Private pools; snorkeling, tennis, golf, and water sports nearby
P.S.:   Open all year

Grand Palazzo Hotel
St. Thomas

Atmosphere	**Dining**	**Sports**	**Rates**

At first sight of the 3-year-old Grand Palazzo you might think that the Caribbean sun has gone to your head: Is that really a Renaissance palace in the U.S. Virgins?

It's not the heat, it's not a mirage, just the upshot of one Englishman's fantasy—Michael Pemberton, the former owner (it's now a Rockresort). He did things with his customary taste and scoured the world to find the best. Hence, mahogany desks and elevator cars hand-carved by Philippine artisans; trompe l'oeils by a muralist flown in from England; antique chandeliers and tapestries imported from Italy; lovely coral-pink marble from Portugal.

This imposing palazzo is merely the centerpiece, with front desk, concierge, boutiques, fitness room. The rest of the hotel, strung out along a more or less private beach, is more down-to-earth. Directly below the lobby is a pink-stucco complex of restaurants, lounges, and bars; pathways of fossil stone lead to a lip-level pool, acres of beautiful gardens, a natural salt pond that's a sort of spa for geese and iguanas. And somewhere behind all those Renaissance-style facades and pink pavilions lurks the state-of-the-art paraphernalia that makes the palazzo self-dependent—reverse osmosis water plant, sewage treatment plant, an "ecologically sound heating system that eliminates boilers burning fossil fuels." That sort of stuff.

The guest rooms are housed in five wings of Mediterranean-style architecture with white stucco, lots of arches, lots of wrought-iron balconies—all facing the beach and sea, each with a balcony framed by a stucco arch or overhung with a tiled ramada. The marble-clad bathrooms come with curtained tubs, separate toilets (with a notepad and pencil conveniently within reach of the extension phone), twin vanities, hair dryers, seersucker lounging robes. Here again, no expense is spared: The towels (10 to a room) are by Fieldcrest, the linens by Lisadell, bedspreads and drapes from an English mercer who outfits Britain's stateliest homes. Well-stocked mini-bars and TV sets (satellite, with remote and Spectravision) are tucked away in custom-designed armoires.

The one-bedroom and two-bedroom suites offer more of the same, with the one-bedroom version clocking in at more than a thousand square feet, not counting the double balcony, which has space for a pair of loungers as well as table and chairs (the Junior Suites get table and chairs only).

All in all, very attractive—and more sumptuous than anything else on the island. But for my money, I would have preferred ceramic tile or wood floors rather than wall to wall carpet, and I would have welcomed louvers in addition to the sliding glass doors so that I could feel the gentle wisp of the trade winds.

Some guests might also grump about too little closet and drawer space (the management says this is being taken care of), and they'd have reason to do so if this were a resort where you had to haul along trunkfuls of your fanciest togs because you were expected to dress up every evening, but it isn't—casual elegance is the order of the day. The dress code requires neither jackets nor ties, although I suspect that during the winter season many guests will, in fact, gussy themselves up since the setting for dinner, the Palm Terrace, is rather posh—a pink-stucco pavilion of exquisite proportions facing the moonlit water of the bay, decorated with fishtail palms and topped with a ceiling of stretched canvas that filters the natural light. Tables are widely spaced, the atmosphere is conducive to leisurely dining, the service attentive and not too pushy.

Since all the entrées look mouthwatering, you might want to choose on the basis of the intriguing sauces: a warm orange-ginger vinaigrette with the fennel-crusted tuna or a brown ale and cumin sauce for the braised breast of pheasant filled with truffles. Dinner in the Palm Terrace, without a wine from the impressive *carte des vins,* will set two people back close to $90 to $100; diners hoping to lop $20 or so off that tab will not be let down by the adjoining Café Vecchio, another breeze-cooled pavilion, which is cooled by a dozen paddle fans. The menu here is lighter, with linguine carbonara and bow-tie pasta with salmon, basil, and tomato interspersed with braised lamb shank and shrimp risotto.

But it doesn't take long to notice that what raises the Grand Palazzo a notch above its neighbors is the service. Certainly there are few places with a more responsive staff: When I pointed out to my server that she had just poured tap water into my almost-finished mineral water she rushed off to the bar and returned with a full bottle, on the house; when I mentioned that I didn't like the way the turndown maid had stacked the bedspread and scatter pillows I returned to my room to find them tucked out of sight.

One reason must surely be that the management has spent more time than usual putting together a handpicked crew of people who are not just unusually congenial, with an enthusiasm as yet unsapped by the tropical sun (or unappreciative guests), but who are also tops in their fields: The chef honed his craft at places like Drouhan in Paris and was personal chef to assorted VIP-hosting sheiks; the resort's dive master has explored reefs with

Jacques Cousteau's team (and runs what is surely the tidiest dive shop in the Virgins); and the skipper of the resort's private 53-foot catamaran is an Olympic sailor. When I posed a few questions about flowers to the young head gardener, she led me off on a tour of every last leaf.

These gardens are one of the most impressive features of the Grand Palazzo—more than 125 species of flowering plants and dozens of types of greenery. Plants climb the walls, rim the balconies, encircle the pond. Shower of gold vies for attention with tree of life, and an expert green thumb could spot close to 20 species of palms and rarities, like the four-sided lucky nut tree.

Maybe it was gardens or the beguiling staff or the spit and polish of the place, but on the ride back to the airport I finally reconciled myself with a Renaissance palace on a Caribbean beach: St. Thomas, with all its shopping malls and condos and traffic, is not really "Caribbean"—and, even if it's a tad pricey (after all, someone has to pay for all those pampering people), Grand Palazzo is just what this island needed.

Name: Grand Palazzo Hotel

Manager: Marston J. Winkles

Address: Great Bay, St. Thomas, U.S. Virgin Islands 00802

Location: On the eastern end of the island, 30 to 40 minutes from the airport, 20 to 30 minutes from Charlotte Amalie; to avoid the usual hassle of waiting for shared taxis to fill up, Grand Palazzo has an airport greeter who will assign you a preselected driver to take you more or less directly to the hotel (fare about $20 per person)

Telephone: 809/775-3333

Fax: 809/775-4444

Reservations: Direct, 800/545-0509

Credit Cards: All major cards

Rooms: 148 Junior Suites, 4 1-bedroom and 2-bedroom suites, all with air-conditioning and ceiling fans, verandas or balconies, direct-dial telephones (3 per room), stocked mini-bars, remote cable TV, bathrobes, and hair dryers

Meals: Breakfast 7:00–10:30, lunch noon–3:00, light snacks throughout the day, afternoon tea 3:30–5:30, dinner 7:00–11:45 (approx. $80–$100 for 2), in 1 of 2 breeze-cooled restaurants—Café Vecchio all day, Palm Terrace in the evening, lunch at the Reef Bar; "casual elegance" for dress—which means shoes and shirts in the lobby (no swimsuits), footwear at all times, while "jeans, T-shirts and sneakers, and rubber flip-flops will not be permitted . . . jackets not required"; piano player in Palm Terrace, room service 24 hours a day, limited menu, extra charge

Entertainment: Bar, some live entertainment on the Café Vecchio terrace with a Caribbean buffet and show on Mondays (sample the buffet, by all means, but skip the show)

Sports: Free-form freshwater pool, tennis (4 courts, lights, Peter Burwash pro shop), sailing, windsurfing, snorkeling gear, fitness center (Lifecycle equipment)—all free; scuba and massage extra; day sails and evening cruises on the 53-foot *Lady Lynsey* catamaran; golf nearby

P.S.:   Some children; open all year

Cormorant Beach Club
St. Croix

☆☆			
Atmosphere			

♀ ♀			
Dining			

◐◐			
Sports			

$ $ $			
Rates			

Hammocks dangle between the tall palms that rise straight from the sandy beach. Gentle trade winds skip ashore from reefs a hundred yards off the beach. Mattresses float guests around the big freshwater pool.

And since there are never more than 76 guests at any time you never feel crowded, never have to "reserve" a hammock, never feel jostled at the breakfast or lunchtime buffet. You just while away your days in an air of total relaxation and contentment.

Cormorant Beach Club is located on 12 quiet acres at the end of a rather domesticated drive from the airport, between a cluster of modest dwellings and a ribbon of beach that runs for probably half a mile in each direction. Not a *great* beach, but with its scores of palm trees and bedazzling background of reefs and multihued waters, it's all very tropical and soothing.

The rather ungainly lines have been softened by trees and bougainvillea; the rooms have been brightened and lightened with floral fabrics and rattan headboards, tables, and chairs; the fitted carpet has been replaced by ceramic tile; and the louvered doors have built-in security bars. Bathrooms have oodles of fluffy towels twice a day, bathrobes, and an amenities basket with shampoo and skin balm; there are fresh flowers in every room. The lobby/bar and restaurant, trimmed with light wood, are open to the breezes and the beach; a tidy little library, just off the lobby, has enough paperbacks and hardcovers to fill a week of lounging in hammocks.

Because *lounging* is what this place is all about. It's a relaxing 12 acres where you can escape *or* mingle with like-minded idlers or find your very own corner or hammock. Apart from the earnest frolickers on the pair of tennis courts, guests move at a very, very lethargic pace; and with sprightly waiters to fetch your piña coladas or whatever, it makes more sense to loaf and lounge at the Cormorant than to go shopping or sightseeing in Christiansted.

The kitchen is thriving under chef Dean Fennessey; the dining room staff has polished its collective skills, but the staff in general seems to have taken its cue from the hardworking, cordial manager, David Balk, so the welcome here is noticeably warm, smiles are genuine, tips are shunned. This is St. Croix? This is the Cormorant.

Name: Cormorant Beach Club

Manager: David S. Balk

Address: 4126 La Grande Princesse, Christiansted, St. Croix, U.S. Virgin Islands 00820

Location: On the north shore, 20 minutes from the airport in one direction, 10 from Christiansted in the other, $10 for 2 sharing a taxi with 2 others to the airport, $6 to town

Telephone: 809/778-8920

Fax: 809/778-9218

Reservations: Direct, 800/548-4460

Credit Cards: American Express, Diners Club, MasterCard, Visa

Rooms: 38, including 4 suites, in 2 2-story beachside wings, all with balconies or patios facing beach, baths and showers, bathrobes, air-conditioning, ceiling fans, wall safes, direct-dial telephones that even dial your own wake-up calls; wet bars in suites

Meals: Breakfast 8:00–10:00, lunch 11:30–2:00, dinner 6:30–9:00 (approx. $76 for 2), all beachside; island casual dress after 6:00; Caribbeau Grill Night on Thursdays; no room service, but tables with coffee and tea are set up in the breezeway of each wing from 7:00 a.m.

Entertainment: Jazz on Fridays, Caribbean Grill with calypso on Thursdays, dance combo on Saturdays (lightly amplified), steel band for Sunday brunch, VCR for new and old movies in meeting room

Sports: Half-mile beach, big hexagonal swimming pool, parcours trail, snorkeling gear, tennis (2 courts, no lights)—all free; scuba diving, sailing, golf, and horseback riding (rain forest or beach) can be arranged

P.S.: No children under 16 from January 7 through Easter Day (at other times, age 5 and up); a few small corporate seminars; the resort also rents 1- to 3-bedroom condos at Cormorant Cove next door; open all year

The Buccaneer Hotel
St. Croix

If setting alone were the deciding factor, the Buccaneer would win hands down as the most attractive resort on St. Croix. Its 300 rolling acres incorporate a challenging but not overwhelming golf course, tidy lawns, the stump of an old sugar mill on the hill, three coves of white sand lined by stands of coconut palms. Tropical flowers vie with the pink and white buildings to splash the hillsides with color. And every way you turn you have another glorious view of sea or bay and Christiansted (from this location, a pretty picture of pastel stucco without the unsightly spaghetti of utility poles and cables).

Guest rooms are deployed around the grounds in a variety of one-, two-, and three-story buildings, some on the crest of the hill, some halfway down the hill, others beside the beach. Which you choose will probably be determined by whether or not you want a steady breeze, whether you want to be closer to the beach than the golf course, and so on; but let me suggest that you consider the Beach Rooms that curve around the point between Cutlass and Beauregard Beach; on the ridge the choice lodgings, apart from room 212 in the main building, are the Ridge Rooms, a parade of little row houses looking across the fairways and sea to St. Thomas, 43 miles away. These rooms have been rejuvenated in recent years with pastel colors, wicker and rattan, Italian marble tiles, and French windows leading to quiet patios shaded by mother-in-law's-tongue trees.

The Armstrong family, owners since the hotel opened in 1988, turned their attention to public spaces in 1992. They called in the acclaimed designer Carleton Varney to restyle the once-stodgy ridge-top lobby and terrace dining room; the air-conditioned Brass Parrot, where guests gather for candlelit dinners, has a more contemporary menu—for example, warm carrot lemongrass broth with lobster wontons and pineapple salsa, island spice crusted swordfish with coconut and plantain ragoût and black pepper crème fraîche.

They're now much jollier environments. Even so, the Buccaneer doesn't set out to attract luminaries and glitterati, and despite the fact that its most secluded beach is named Whistle (as in whistle before you get there to let people know you're coming), the Buccaneer tends to have a fairly conservative clientele. But the real attraction here, besides those beautiful grounds, is the range of sports activities—golf (less expensive by far than at Carambola), eight tennis courts, and water sports on your doorstep.

Name: The Buccaneer Hotel

Manager: Elizabeth Armstrong

Address: P.O. Box 25200, Gallows Bay, St. Croix, U.S. Virgin Islands 00824-5200

Location: On the beach at Gallows Bay, about 10 minutes from Christiansted, $11.50 for 2 by shared taxi from the airport

Telephone: 809/773-2100

Fax: 809/778-8215

Reservations: Direct, 800/255-3881 or Ralph Locke Islands

Credit Cards: All major cards

Rooms: 150, including 13 suites, in 8 categories, each with airconditioning and fan, bathrobes, refrigerator, direct-dial telephone, TV, safe, balcony or patio

Meals: Breakfast 7:30–10:00, lunch 11:30–5:30 in a couple of beachside pavilions, dinner 6:00–9:30 in the beachside Mermaid, or the hilltop Terrace and Brass Parrot dining rooms, the first two cooled by the breezes, the last one by air-conditioning (approx. $75 for 2 in the Brass Parrot), dress casual but "no shorts on the Terrace after 6:00"; room service, all meals, at no extra charge; piano player in the Brass Parrot

Entertainment: 2 movies and live music every evening, including steel bands and guitarists

Sports: 3 beaches, 2 freshwater pools, health spa, new fitness club, snorkeling gear—free; extra charge for tennis (8 championship caliber courts, 2 with lights, pro, $10 per hour), golf (18 holes, pro, $30 per round), windsurfing, rowboats, Sunfish sailing, boat trips, seaweed wraps, and massage; horseback riding on the west end of the island

P.S.:   Lots of families; some business groups in the off-season; open all year

Villa Madeleine
St. Croix

Atmosphere	**Dining**	**Sports**	**Rates**

It's a complex of privately owned villas rather than a hotel, but these 43 hillside suites are among the snazziest and most stylish lodgings on the island. Each is virtually a self-contained cottage (although they're tightly packed in and you might at first glance think they're town houses), with a private 11-by-20-foot plunge pool taking up most of a walled garden. (They range in elevation from 150 feet to 250 feet above the sea, or thereabouts, and although they all have a view, clearly you'll prefer to be near the top, perhaps facing north.)

The interiors, by noted designer Carleton Varney (himself a longtime St. Croix booster), are understated and elegant, with light antiqued woods, subtle pastel colors inspired by the foliage, rattan and wicker furniture. TVs and VCRs are tucked into Henredon armoires; bedrooms are dominated by custom-designed rattan four-posters; the sleek kitchens are fully equipped for occasional snacks or *intime* dinners.

How often the microwave and dishwasher are put to use will probably depend on how often you can resist the temptation to have dinner on the terrace of Café Madeleine, in the "Great House" at the top of the hill. Quote Great House unquote because this two-story manor looks as though it has been sitting here for a couple of centuries, albeit impeccably maintained, but in reality it's less than 6 years old, like the resort itself. The interiors here, too, were decorated by Varney, but in one of his more dashing moods, with look-at-me! colors and a bold mélange of *objets*— Japanese prints, a Shanxi-style chest, hardwood floors, model schooners, and English club chairs. Guests who don't want to sit around a glass and chrome bar can sip their aperitifs in a clublike, mahogany-paneled library or in a lounge featuring a billiard table with blue felt and fringed pockets.

Dinner is served beneath a floral awning on a spacious veranda overlooking Buck Island (which you won't see unless you arrive for cocktails before sunset, since the Buck is uninhabited and without lights). The moderately priced menu changes frequently, but usually features several Italian dishes (pasta pie, maybe, or pesto tortellini) alongside local exotica like marinated chicken and shrimp smoked with cedar and banana leaves and served with an island banana sauce. Since you can walk a few yards rather than drive a few miles before tumbling between the sheets, order the killer dessert known as the Hummer—a goblet of melted ice cream topped with chocolate chips and awash in Kahlúa and rum.

Another reason for walking rather than driving: Café Madeleine's extensive wine list, with a fine selection of Californians and Italians, which will do nicely until it's time to celebrate something, anything, with a rare Bordeaux—from a $70 Château d'Angludet 1978 to a Château Petrus 1975, a cool $600. Come to think of it, the perfect place for sipping rare Bordeaux is not the Café Madeline but beneath the stars, on the secluded terrace beside your very private pool.

Name: Villa Madeleine

Manager: Yanira Melendez

Address: P.O. Box 3109, Christiansted, St. Croix, U.S. Virgin Islands 00822

Location: At Teague Bay, on the eastern end of the island, about 20 minutes by car, up to 40 minutes by taxi, from the airport (ask the airport to select a driver), 10 minutes to Christiansted

Telephone: 809/773-8141

Fax: 809/773-7518

Reservations: Direct, 800/548-4461

Credit Cards: All major cards

Rooms: 43 1-bedroom and 2-bedroom suites, all with air-conditioning and ceiling fans, private patio pools, large shower stalls rather than bathtubs, TV/VCR, direct-dial telephones, kitchens (microwaves, dishwashers, ice makers, coffeemakers)

Meals: Dinner only (approx. $60 for 2), on the terrace of the Café Madeleine; casual but stylish dress; closed Monday and Tuesday

Entertainment: Bar, billiards, some live music (piano, steel band)

Sports: Private pools, tennis (1 court, no lights); 2 beaches, 2 seas 10 minutes down the hill; golf and water sports nearby

P.S.: "We discourage toddlers because of the pools"; open all year

Other Choices

Gran Hotel el Convento

Old San Juan, Puerto Rico

The love nooks here were once the cells of Carmelite nuns, but don't let that inhibit your frolicking. The convent was established 300 years ago, when all those Spanish conquistadores were around and this sanctuary was probably the only place in town where a maiden could remain a maiden. The great mahogany doors of the convent still open onto the same tiny Plaza de las Monjas, which priests and penitents cross before disappearing into the tall blackness of the cathedral, and where old men occasionally play dominoes. This historic convent in Old San Juan actually went through a period of martyrdom as a garage for sanitation trucks, before it was rescued more than 30 years ago by a group of brave and farsighted people, including a Woolworth heir and a pair of local brothers, Ricardo and José Alegría, whose passion it is to restore and preserve all the beautiful buildings of Old San Juan. They decked the halls and galleries with paintings and tapestries, conquistadorean swords and shields, the guest rooms with hand-carved chests and high-backed chairs upholstered in satins and velvets, wrought-iron lamps, elaborate headboards and canopied beds, louvered doors and beamed ceilings (although the rooms were recently refurbished with a somewhat lighter touch—new fabrics, some rattan—to "combine modern comfort with old-world elegance"). The former cells are neatly spaced along graciously arched galleries around a central patio, which now sports a swimming pool and Jacuzzi. Most visitors to Puerto Rico, of course, don't want to spend all their days in Old San Juan, and although El Convento has guest privileges with beachside hotels, it never became the great romantic hideaway it deserved to be. Nevertheless, this is a special place because of its location in miraculous Old San Juan, because of its historic overtones. 100 rooms and suites. Doubles: $150 to $200, winter 1994–95. *Gran Hotel El Convento, 100 Cristo St., Old San Juan, Puerto Rico, U.S. Virgin Islands 00902. Telephone: 809/723-9020; fax: 809/721-2877.*

Casa San José
Puerto Rico

Since the decline and fall of El Convento (above), many travelers like myself have just shied away from staying in Old San Juan, no matter how much we love its narrow, cobbled streets and shaded courtyards. Now we have this charming small inn, basically a swank bed-and-breakfast, in a 300-year-old town house built around an inner courtyard with fountains and marble floors, topped by a skylight and ringed with four floors of dark-railed galleries. Afternoon tea and a sundown glass of wine are served in a 45-foot salon with a grand piano, assorted antiques, and library. Most of the guest rooms are charmingly furnished with (or at least accented with) antiques; a few have four-poster beds, Spanish chests, and island art. They all have air-conditioning, which works so well you may find yourself grateful for the comforter on your four-poster (in some rooms you'll have no choice but to keep the air-conditioning humming, either because of street noise or the lack of cross-ventilation). It is said that $1.5 million was spent to get the inn in shape for its 1991 opening, and it looks top dollar, but some guests may wish the owner had spent a few dollars less on furnishings and a few extra dollars on hiring additional staff, especially at breakfast. Which is not to say that the Casa is unwelcoming—far from it (except for children under 12). 12 rooms (you'll want the top-priced rooms for space, quiet, and ventilation). Doubles: $225–$355, winter 1994–95. *Casa San José, 159 Calle San José, San Juan, Puerto Rico, U.S. Virgin Islands 00901. Telephone: 809/723-1212; fax: 809/723-7620.*

Blackbeard's Castle Hotel
St. Thomas

The sparkling lights of Charlotte Amalie, the harbor, and its cruise ships are spread out at your feet, but up here on the pool deck at Blackbeard's, you're far from the bustle of civilization. The circular watchtower, dating from 1679 or thereabouts, may or may not have been used by the piratical Blackbeard, but over the years the site has been a Danish colonialist's plantation, a home, and, since 1985, a hotel and restaurant (but be sure you don't confuse it with the larger *Blue*beard's Castle Hotel on a nearby hilltop). As of 1995, the inn is now a National Historic Landmark. Guest quarters, in one- and two-story wings around the courtyard, face east or west with some enjoying harbor views; most of the rooms have balconies or patios; all have ceiling fans, air-conditioning, direct-dial telephones, and cable television. Again, the restaurant and bar, both award winners, are prime attractions: Prices are moderate, the food is worth the hike up the hill, and there's live jazz until midnight. 28 rooms. Doubles: $140 to $190, winter 1994–95, including Continental breakfast. *Blackbeard's Castle Hotel, P.O. Box 6041, St. Thomas, U.S. Virgin Islands 08804. Telephone: 800/344-5771 (reservations only) or 809/776-1234; fax: 809/776-4321.*

Hilty House
St. Croix

From the wrought-iron gate, it has the weathered, slightly weary look of a plantation estate just managing to hold its own against the fan palms and breadfruit trees. A huge, 200-year-old rubber tree dominates the front garden, and a long, low ramada-style veranda runs one length of the stone house, with a few guests seated around a circular table enjoying a late breakfast—banana pancakes, fresh-baked muffins with homemade passion-fruit jelly. Hilty House is essentially a bed-and-breakfast inn, opened in 1991, but one with style and flair, starting with the house. It's a former rum factory, its once-gloomy 2,200 square feet enlivened with skylights and big windows, Italian and Portuguese decorative tiles. The old open-spit fireplace is now a conversation area with banquettes and planters. The big open kitchen doubles as an honor bar. Beyond the sliding doors, there's a lap pool, sunning terrace, and 2½ acres of thunbergia and ixorra. Rooms are small but attractive, with ceiling fans and private bathrooms. Although the address is Christiansted, the house is about 10 minutes away in the hills—cool and peaceful and scenic. Hilty House recently started to serve dinner on Monday nights. The $25 prix-fixe dinners focus on a different cuisine every week and are very popular with the locals. 4 rooms and 3 cottages. Doubles: $99 to $165, winter 1994–95 (no credit cards). *Hilty House, 2 Hermon Hill, Christiansted, St. Croix, U.S. Virgin Islands 00824. Telephone and fax: 809/773-2594.*

Hibiscus Beach Hotel
St. Croix

A newcomer in 1992, the Hibiscus offers beachside lodgings for less than $200 in winter. At these rates you can't expect class, but the rooms are really quite pleasant—decorated in island pastels with ceramic-tile floors and pale coral furniture, equipped with balconies, TV, mini-bars, direct-dial telephones, air-conditioning and ceiling fans, clock radios, and showers rather than bathtubs. A beachy but breezy bar/restaurant terrace among the palms is perfect for socializing (except when there's live music and the volume is too loud), and a hundred yards or so down the beach you can sample the bar and restaurant at the Cormorant Beach Club. 38 rooms and suites. Doubles: $180 to $190, winter 1994–95. *Hibiscus Beach Hotel, 4131 La Grande Princesse, St. Croix, U.S. Virgin Islands 00820-4441. Telephone: 800/442-0121 or 809/773-4042; fax: 809/773-7668.*

Carambola Beach & Golf Resort

St. Croix

Tree-clad hillsides plunge into the sea. Reefs and headlands shelter a secluded bay with a curve of white sandy beach. A tiny lighthouse pokes above a distant headland. This is Davis Bay, until the early nineties a "secret" north coast bathing Eden but now the prime attraction of Carambola, a resort that tucks 150 rooms into a narrow 28 acres between hills and beach. The porte cochere sets the architectural tone—steeply pitched, red corrugated roof, hardwood ceiling with sturdy rafters, breezeways leading past the lobby and restaurants to a whimsical gazebo-cum-clock tower beside the beach. By day it's part Danish, part Caribbean, reflecting the island's heritage, but by night it's closer to Disney World. The guest rooms are strung out in 24 two-story cottages among a grove of saman, coconut, and mahogany trees. The interiors feature wooden louvers and screened doors, each 520-square-foot room quartered into tiled bathroom (showers only), sleeping area, sitting area, and porch with padded and cushioned banquettes along two screened walls. The resort's two main dining rooms are imposing, their saman and mahogany rafters supported by massive tree trunks and festooned with scores of paddle fans, their tall windows opening to the sea (when the room isn't being refrigerated). Resort facilities include a beachside swimming pool, water sports, dive shop, and four tennis courts, augmented by guest privileges at the championship golf course just over the brow of the hill. Carambola has had a checkered career since the day it opened, but beginning in April 1995, it will be managed by the Westin people (their first venture in the Caribbean), which bodes well for the resort and St. Croix. 150 rooms. Doubles: $235 and up, winter 1994–95. *Carambola Beach & Golf Resort, P.O. Box 3031, Kingshill, St. Croix, U.S. Virgin Islands 00851-3031. Telephone: 809/778-3800; fax: 809/778-1682.*

The British Virgin Islands

Tortola

Guana Island

Virgin Gorda

Anegada

Jost Van Dyke

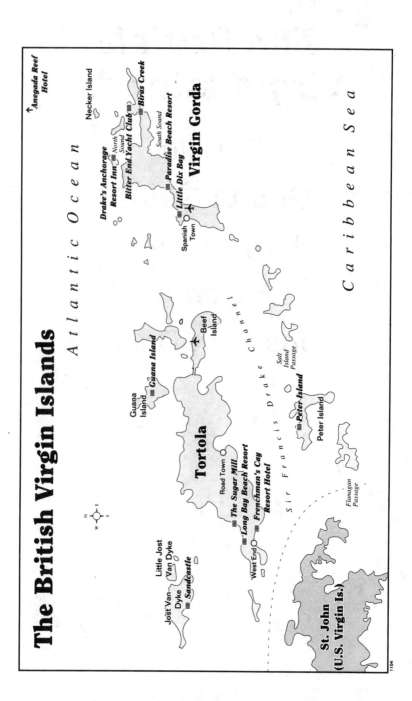

The British Virgin Islands

Atlantic Ocean

Caribbean Sea

Anegada Reef Hotel

Necker Island

Drake's Anchorage Resort Inn

North Sound

Bitter End Yacht Club

Biras Creek

South Sound

Paradise Beach Resort

Little Dix Bay

Virgin Gorda

Spanish Town

Guana Island

Guana Island

Beef Island

Tortola

Road Town

The Sugar Mill

Long Bay Beach Resort

Frenchman's Cay Resort Hotel

West End

Little Jost

Jost Van Dyke

Van Dyke

Sandcastle

N
W · E
S

Sir Francis Drake Channel

Salt Island Passage

Peter Island

Peter Island

Flanagan Passage

St. John (U.S. Virgin Is.)

1104

The British Virgin Islands

Where are they? When Winston Churchill was asked this question in the House of Commons he is said to have replied: "Presumably as far as possible from the Isle of Man." In fact, the British Virgins are more than 3,000 miles from the Isle of Man, but only 60 miles from Puerto Rico and a 20-minute boat ride from St. Thomas. There are 60 of them strung along Sir Francis Drake Channel, where the wily Elizabethan mustered his ships before attacking the Spanish garrison at El Morro in San Juan. The main islands are Tortola (Spanish for turtle dove), Beef, Peter, and Virgin Gorda (the Fat Virgin—named by Columbus, who had obviously been too long at sea by this point); none of them is as big as Manhattan, and if you squeezed them all together, they would still be smaller than, say, Nantucket.

These Virgins have no hangups. They're quite content to lie there drowsing in the sun, loyal outposts of Queen Elizabeth. Britain sends over a governor who nominally attends to matters such as defense and the law courts (which are operated on the British system). Otherwise, the islanders elect their own Executive Council and run their own affairs, such as they are. But they're no dummies, these islanders: Legal tender is the U.S. dollar rather than the British pound sterling.

These are quiet islands for quiet people. There's no swinging nightlife here. No casinos. What little sightseeing exists is usually done by boat rather than car. But what the Virgins dish out in return is glorious sea, glorious scenery, glorious serenity.

How to Get There   Service has greatly improved in recent years with the introduction of dependable flights by American Eagle from San Juan and St. Thomas, two or three times a day each way, getting you to the remotest hideaway in time for a stroll on the beach before dinner. LIAT and Windward also fly to Tortola from St. Croix, St. Maarten, and Antigua.

Two points to remember: Always collect your luggage at San Juan or St. Thomas, rather than checking it through. The American Eagle services have cut down on the delays in transferring baggage, but it's still wise to handle the chore yourself, rather than have to wait for delayed luggage to arrive on the next flight (which may be the next morning).

There's an alternative transfer to the BVI, longer (1 hour) but less expensive (about $19 per person each way): by twin-hulled, air-conditioned ferryboats, each carrying 60 to 80 passengers, leaving from the ferryboat dock in Charlotte Amalie (about 10 minutes by taxi from St. Thomas airport) to West End or Road Town on Tortola, continuing, in some cases, to Virgin Gorda.

> For information on the British Virgin Islands, call 212/696-0400.

Long Bay Beach Resort
Tortola

| ☆☆☆ | | | ♉♉ | | | ◑ | | | $ $ $ | |
| Atmosphere | | | Dining | | | Sports | | | Rates | |

"Long" in this case means 1 mile, give or take a yard or two—1 mile of white sand and glistening sea with sheltering headlands at either end, tucked away on the northwestern corner of the island far from the crowds (not that there are ever real crowds on this friendly little island).

Long Bay, the resort, is really a 52-acre estate, with the ruins of a centuries-old sugar mill beside the beach, rooms and suites strung out along the sea and notched into the leafy hillside, a nine-hole pitch-and-putt golf course weaving through the gardens and lawns between the beach and the hill. The resort has undergone a major transformation in recent years—almost doubling in size to 105 rooms and suites and introducing soothing coral-hued decor with jaunty island fabrics and cane furniture. Some of the rooms have bamboo four-posters and 120-square-foot decks cooled by paddle fans, and the priciest units have full kitchens and microwaves. But all the lodgings come with air-conditioning and ceiling fans, refrigerators, coffeemakers (or, these being British outposts, should it be tea makers?), toasters, clock radios, satellite TV, and direct-dial telephones.

The value-priced lodgings are hillside studios and rooms, totally overhauled for winter 1994–95 to bring them up to par with the newer beachfront quarters. They're 50 to 100 uphill yards from the beach, but the advantage of these lodgings is that guests wake up to a more stunning view—the beach and the breakers, the headlands and offshore islets, scores of scudding sails in the channel between Tortola and the island of Jost Van Dyke.

Much of what makes Long Bay an exceptional value is the sense of space and privacy that comes with all those acres of gardens and lawns and a mile-long stretch of sand. But there's also the fact that guests, no matter how much the room rate, have a choice of sporting activities that come free of charge—pitch and putt, freshwater swimming pool, a brand-new fitness/massage center (opened in 1994–95), with two all-new tennis courts promised for this spring. The beach is one of the best walking and jogging strands in the British Virgins; in winter, it's true, the sea may be more appropriate for board surfing than swimming, but in spring, summer, and fall the water is usually perfect for dipping and dunking. Other water sports (scuba diving, sportfishing, sailing), are available just over the hill in Soper's Hole.

There are also several fine eating places, from beachside shacks to luxury inns, within a 10- to 15-minute drive, but Long Bay itself lays on a couple of fine restaurants. The hillside Garden Restaurant (so popular it was recently enlarged) is set amid masses of flowers and greenery that make a romantic backdrop for candlelight dining. The poolside/beachside Sugar Mill, with tables and sunshades set up on the terrace beneath the sea-grape and almond trees, is open from breakfast (champagne on the house) through daylong lunches to dinners beneath the stars. Prices here are reasonable—about $60 for a three-course dinner for two, without drinks. Despite the classy setting, dress is informal and there's live music two or three evenings a week.

But the best place for a sundown drink or nightcap may well be the terrace of your own hillside room or studio with that great panoramic view.

Name: Long Bay Beach Resort

Manager: James Hawkins

Address: Tortola, British Virgin Islands

Location: On the north shore, 20 minutes and $15 by taxi from Road Town, 40 minutes and $20 from the airport

Telephone: 809/495-4252

Fax: 809/495-4677

Reservations: 800/729-9599 or fax 914/833-3318

Credit Cards: American Express, MasterCard, Visa

Rooms: 105 in 5 categories, all with ceiling fans and air-conditioning, balconies or decks, wet bars, refrigerators (unstocked), coffeemakers, toasters, clock/radios, direct-dial telephones; some with microwaves, some with full kitchen, some with barbecue grills; most with remote-controlled cable TV

Dining: Breakfast 7:30–4:00, lunch 11:00–4:00 (at the beach terrace), dinner 6:30–9:30 at the Sugar Mill or in the Garden Restaurant (approx. $60 for 2); informal dress; no room service

Entertainment: Taped classical music in the bar, live music 2 or 3 evenings a week on the bar deck

Sports: Beach (good for bodysurfing in winter, good for snorkeling in summer, not always great for swimming), 2 freshwater pools, tennis (2 courts with lights), fitness center, 9-hole pitch-and-putt course—all free; snorkeling gear and surfboards for rent; other water sports and horse-back riding nearby

P.S.:   Some children; open all year

The Sugar Mill
Tortola

☆☆					♀♀♀				◑				$ $		
Atmosphere					**Dining**				**Sports**				**Rates**		

You might think that travel writers and food critics, who hear endless accounts of the agonies and travails of innkeepers, would steer firmly clear of such a profession. *No.* Critics Jeff and Jinx Morgan came over from San Francisco in the mid-1980s, plunged into the deep end by acquiring this delightful 20-roomer, and forged ahead upgrading cuisine, service, and ambience. And still, come hurricanes, come hassles, they manage to find time to *write.*

The Sugar Mill is the weathered stone ruins of a 300-year-old mill and distillery set in a hilly garden above the sea, surrounded by flamboyant and wild orchid trees. To this basic setting the Morgans have added three trellised gazebos beside the bar, where most of the evening mixing and chatting takes place, and a beach bar–restaurant called Islands, featuring moderately priced Antillean fare such as rôti and jerk chicken.

No matter where you eat, you don't have far to walk afterward: past the pool and up the hill to cantilevered cottages with traditional island furnishings, or, if you like to be off a little on your own, just across the driveway to room 109.

Guest rooms here are not luxurious by any means, but they're spacious (although the bathrooms are a tad cramped) and each comes with a pantry or kitchen for folks who are checking in for more than a couple of nights. The views from the balconies are almost worth the price of admission. Room 109 is a dinky blue and pink cottage with a few extra square feet of flooring, a couple of wicker armchairs, a small circular dining table, and a big tiled shower stall (although the view is somewhat hemmed in by the bougainvillea and hibiscus that preserve your privacy in the first place, and you may pick up some noise from the roadway beyond the hedgerow).

But it's the reputation of the kitchen that lures vacationers and islanders over to this corner of Tortola. The setting is picture-perfect: candlelight flickering on stone, graystone accented by the colors of Haiti primitives, ceiling fans turning slowly beneath the hip-roof ceiling, tree frogs singing, glasses clinking, and friends exchanging greetings. Dinner is a prix fixe of just three courses, and there must be many diners who wish it would last another course or two—just to sample some of the other dishes from the Morgans's own recipe book. Why settle for West Indian Regimental beef curry and forego snapper with red-pepper relish? Or conch in garden cream instead of tropical game hens with orange-curry butter? The range of desserts makes you wish the Morgans would toss in the towel and start a neighborhood pastry shop: coconut cloud tart, cappuccino mousse with crème de Kahlúa, piña colada cake, and meringue seashells with banana cream.

There may be other fine restaurants on the islands, but few have such a congenial atmosphere. Sugar Mill is sort of the tropical equivalent of one of those tiny auberges in Burgundy, with fine food and a few rooms for staying over. But here you wake up to perfect days and sparkling sea. And no abbeys or châteaux or musty museums that *must* be visited. Here you just slip into days of lazing. Rum French toast on the breakfast terrace, a dip in the garden pool. Read a book and shuffle to the beach bar for a long, boozy lunch that slowly fades into a siesta. Another dip, a walk to the village, a piña colada, and before you know where you are it's time to be thinking about tomato ginger wine soup and grouper in banana leaves with herb butter.

Name: The Sugar Mill
Manager: Patrick Conway
Address: P.O. Box 425, Tortola, British Virgin Islands
Location: On the northwest shore, near Long Bay, about 45 minutes and $30 by taxi from the airport, but only 10 minutes and $6 from the ferry dock at West End
Telephone: 809/495-4355
Fax: 809/495-4696
Reservations: 800/462-8834 or Caribbean Inns Ltd.
Credit Cards: American Express, MasterCard, Visa

Rooms: 21 in various cottages in the garden, all with ceiling fans (4 with air-conditioning), balconies, some with pantries

Meals: Breakfast 8:00–10:00 on the terrace below the bar, lunch noon–2:00 in Islands beach bar, dinner 7:00–9:00 in the main dining room (approx. $80 for 2), 6:30–9:00 in Islands beach bar, January through May (approx. $30 for 2); casual dress, "though a touch of glamour is never out of place"; no room service

Entertainment: Bar, board games, library

Sports: Circular freshwater pool, small beach for sunning, snorkeling gear; other water sports nearby

P.S.:   Closed August and September

Peter Island

Tortola

Atmosphere

Dining

Sports

Rates

Even in the beginning, I never really warmed to this place. It was too much a Norwegian shipowner's dull little Bergen-in-the-sun, so I wrote some unkind comments in an earlier edition of this guidebook.

New owners (the Amway Corporation of Michigan) and several million dollars later, it has seen many changes, even upgradings. But it hasn't quite reached the heights it should have, given, for example, its location—a private 1,800-acre Virgin just across Sir Francis Drake Channel from Tortola. Sun! Breezes! Sailboats! Reefs! Seclusion! It has just about everything going for it. One significant improvement, however, is the staff: Where once there were glowers and ineptness (I remember one lunch with a previous manager when the waiter presented us both with mammoth menus that opened up to two blank pages), there are now competence and confidence. Even smiles. A new restaurant director has livened up the cuisine with more dishes that wed Caribbean with Asian—a recent lunchtime menu gave diners the option of spiced grilled chicken with coconut and plantain or grilled yellowtail with a mango salsa. The wine list, too, now offers a wider range, from an $18 Muscadet Les Ormeaux to a $300 Château Margaux.

But the 30 original A-frame lodgings, stacked on the breakwater beside the eye-catching lip-level pool, still strike me as dull, more suited to northern climes despite all the jazzing up with tropical colors and fabrics. I once raved about the 20 deluxe rooms that were tucked into a corner of Deadman's Bay a few years after the resort opened. Deadman's is one of the most ravishing beaches in the British Virgins and the original bluestone and cedar rooms were designed with one wall of louvered shutters that folded back to bring the view right into the room. Alas, a subsequent restyling substituted glass sliders for the shutters, painted the hardwoods cream to brighten up the interiors, and generally made the place look more Florida Panhandle than Caribbean sophisticate. The original beach rooms also enchanted guests with a wonderful layout that interposed a minigarden atrium between the bedroom and bathroom, with plantings for privacy and dimmer lights for romance. When I did my inspection tour a few months back, the minigarden had been screened behind shutters for the sake of the air-conditioning—and the management type showing me around didn't even know it was there until I unrolled the shutters. Farewell, romance; hail, refrigeration! On the other hand, there are still baskets of Amway toiletries, detergent, and bug spray.

The new Peter Island, of course, still has a lot going for it. The beachside dining pavilion, Deadman's Bay Beach Bar and Grill, is immeasurably more attractive than the meeting-room blandness of the main dining room beside the clubhouse and pool—and is now, praise be, open for dinner as well as lunch. The resort's sense of space and the uncrowded beaches count for a lot, the sports facilities should keep everyone busy for a week or two, and the idea of a picnic for two on a secluded beach, complete with fresh lobster salad and grilled swordfish delivered at the appointed hour, is enticing to more than honeymooners.

But Peter Island just doesn't have that sense of specialness it once had. On the other hand, if someone wants the exclusiveness of an 1,800-acre private island with oodles of toys but doesn't want to pay top-of-the-line rates, then those two-story A-frames may well be the answer. But ask for an upper floor (higher ceilings) as far from the bandshell as possible (for peace and quiet).

Name: Peter Island
Manager: James Holmes
Address: P.O. Box 211, Road Town, Tortola, British Virgin Islands
Location: Across the channel from Road Town on Tortola, a trip of 20 minutes aboard a 46-foot or 65-foot luxury power yacht (regular ferry service 9 times a day between the 2 islands)
Telephone: 809/494-2561
Fax: 809/494-2313

Reservations:　Own U.S. office, 800/346-4451 or 616/776-6456, or Preferred Hotels

Credit Cards:　All major cards

Rooms:　50, including 16 ocean-view rooms overlooking Sprat Bay and Sir Francis Drake Channel and 20 beachfront rooms on Deadman's Bay, plus 3 villas; all rooms have private baths, hair dryers, terry robes, minibars, balconies or patios, ceiling fans and split-unit air conditioning, telephones

Meals:　Breakfast 8:00–10:00, lunch 12:30–3:00, dinner 7:00–9:00 in Tradewinds main pavilion, cooled by the breezes, or Deadman's Bay Beach Bar and Grill (approx. $80 for 2); proper attire required in the dining room after 6:00; complimentary room service 8:00 a.m.–10:00 a.m.

Entertainment:　Bar-lounge, parlor games, live entertainment (amplified) during and after dinner, for listening or dancing

Sports:　Freshwater pool, several beaches (including isolated coves with transportation and picnic baskets supplied), windsurfing, floats, sailing (Hobiecats, Squibs, Sunfishes), snorkeling, tennis (4 Tru-Flex courts, lights on 2), mountain bikes—all free; scuba diving, waterskiing, spa treatments, charter boats for fishing and sailing can be arranged

P.S.:　Some children; open all year

Guana Island
Guana Island

| Atmosphere | Dining | Sports | Rates |

The hotel boatman meets you at the airport, drives you a half mile or so to the jetty, stows your luggage aboard a 28-foot Bertram, then casts off for a 10-minute ride to the island—past the eastern tip of Tortola, past Great Camanoe, around the rock formation that gave the islands its name, and so into White Bay.

There you're greeted by a dazzling sight—glistening water, glistening sand. But instead of the inn being buried among the palm trees, it perches on the hill, in the midday haze, looking for all the world like a hilltop village in the Aegean. As you approach the private dock a Land Rover winds down the hill to meet you. Step ashore and you're in another world: Even the run-of-the-mill Caribbean seems a long way from here.

Guana Island was built in the thirties as a private club on the foundations of a Quaker sugar and cotton plantation. The native stone walls are 2 feet thick, with graying whitewash and green shutters. The rustic library and lounge suggest the country home of a well-bred but overdrawn gentleman farmer; the main dining terrace is a trio of tables beneath a ramada and framed by pomegranate and ginger thomas trees, cape honeysuckle, and white frangipani. From the Sunset Terrace, fragrant with jasmine and carpeted with blossoms from the pink trumpet tree, stone paths and steps wind through archways of trees and off into the hillsides. The loudest sound is a kingbird, perched on the highest bough of the highest tree. The views are stunning—hills and coves, slivers of white sand and polyblue bays, sailboats beating to windward, vistas of distant islands.

Guana Island is not the sort of place you come to for stylish accommodations and luxurious conveniences (for that, head for Little Dix Bay on Virgin Gorda or Grand Palazzo Hotel on St. Thomas). Some people, indeed, may find the lodgings here almost monastic, with their classic simplicity—whitewashed stucco walls, rattan and wicker furniture, rush rugs, handwoven bedspreads in pretty patterns, bathrooms with unusual molded stucco shower stalls. But in their restrained way, these rooms have great refinement—little gems of comfort, charm, and romance.

The most romantic of these rooms may be the Barbados—self-contained, spacious, with a very private balcony overlooking the Atlantic. But I'd happily settle into Fallen Jerusalem, with its mesmerizing views all the way to St. Thomas. Grenada House, with its own pool on the topmost hill, can be reserved in toto—with private access to the pool.

This is a place that either grabs you instantly or leaves you wondering what the fuss is about. It has something of the charm and coziness of the best small inns of New England or Burgundy. Guests mingle on the Sunset Terrace or in the rattan-furnished lounge for cocktails at 7:00; dinner is served by candlelight, everyone gathered around the three tables on the main dining terrace or, by request, at tables for two on nearby tête-à-tête terraces. Dinner is a fixed four-course menu (although guests can request alternatives): "If the cook's husband goes out fishing we may have fish, otherwise roast leg of lamb with fried eggplant or Guana potatoes."

Although dinner has always been a highlight of a day on Guana, new managers Jonathan and Catherine Morley have revamped the menu, so that guests now dine on more varied fare—say, seafood curry with mango chutney, pea and apple soup, fricassee of fish and shrimp flavored with Pernod, and a purée of broccoli flavored with nutmeg. After dinner, the party atmosphere continues in the lounge, where guests reassemble and exchange more travel tales over coffee and cognacs. Or slip into the corner library and browse through the 1933 *Encyclopaedia Britannica*.

By day, Guana Island is 850 acres of ineffable peace. Since the only way to get here is by boat, the island's seven beaches are virtually private, and two of them are so secluded they are accessible only to waterborne castaways. Indeed, so serene is the entire setting that when you finally hoist yourselves from your loungers on White Bay's 600 feet of white sand and peer across the dappled water, all you see is another deserted beach—on the uninhabited side of Tortola. The meadow beside the beach is given over to a croquet court and two tennis courts, one Hydrocourt (similar to clay), the other Omni; the Salt Pond in the center of the island is heaven for bird spotters— a preserve for black-necked stilts and red-billed tropics, plovers, blue herons, and a small flock of flamingos.

The island is, in fact, a designated nature preserve and wildlife sanctuary, with its own ongoing program that brings together scientists of various disciplines for learned networking every October. The director of the project, biologist Dr. James Lazell, says "this island has more species of flora and fauna than any island yet studied in the West Indies and probably in the world." That may be overstating things a little, but it's no exaggeration that people who enjoy a relaxed, soft-spoken, almost genteel atmosphere will love it here.

As we were saying, this is not an everyday Caribbean island.

Name: Guana Island

Manager: Jonathan and Catherine Morley

Address: Guana Island, British Virgin Islands

Location: A private island northeast of Tortola, 10 minutes by taxi and boat ($50 for 2 round-trip) from Beef Island Airport

Telephone: 809/494-2354

Fax: 914/967-8048

Reservations: The inn's stateside office, 914/967-6050, or 800/544-8262

Credit Cards: None

Rooms: 15, cooled by breezes and ceiling fans, all with private bathrooms and terraces; for total seclusion there's North Beach Cottage, built in 1933, with 1 bedroom, living room, and kitchen on its own ⅓-mile-long coral beach

Meals: Breakfast 8:00–10:00, lunch at 1:00, afternoon tea and cookies at 4:00, cocktails at 7:00, dinner at 8:00 (6:45 for children) with a fixed menu; informal (jackets optional, but often worn in January and February); no room service

Entertainment: Library, Scrabble, backgammon, conversation

Sports: 7 beaches (2 accessible by boat only), snorkeling cove (gear available free), tennis, (2 courts, 1 Hydrocourt, 1 Omni, no lights), croquet, walking trails, 14-foot Sunfish and Laser sailboats, kayaks, windsurfing—all free; waterskiing, powerboats for rent (fishing gear available), Bertram cruiser for charter; scuba available

P.S.:   Closed September and October; check with the inn about rules regarding children

P.P.S.:   The entire island can be rented for groups of up to 30

Little Dix Bay
Virgin Gorda

Atmosphere

Dining

Sports

Rates

From the beach, all you can see of Little Dix are the four conical shingled roofs of the main dining pavilion peeking above the palms and casuarina trees. The native stone and hardwood guest cottages, cloaked by seagrape and tamarind trees, are strung out along the beach. And what a beach! A curvaceous half mile of white, powdery sand, sheltered by low headlands at either end and a picturesque reef just offshore. It's the classic beach scene—and Little Dix is still among the classiest of resorts.

Like its sister resort, Caneel Bay, Little Dix is now managed by Rosewood Hotels of Dallas and went through a change of lifestyle a couple of years ago. Most of the guest cottages still feature their trademark louvered walls, but half of them now have air-conditioning (a no-no during the years Little Dix was owned by Laurance Rockefeller) as well as telephones to match other contemporary amenities like stocked refrigerators and wall safes (but anyone wanting to catch up on CNN has to mosey over to the garden pavilion to watch television). Interiors have been spruced up with new fabrics in pastel shades and floral patterns, wicker and rattan chairs with ottomans, and new tiled bathrooms. But the rooms still retain their breezy Caribbean flavor with their native stone walls, shady louvers, and slowly turning paddle fans.

Most distinctive among the resort's 102 rooms and suites are still the 30 beachside hexagonal hives, 15 of them perched on stilts, with patios, hammocks, tables, and chairs at garden level. Of the others, the quietest are rooms 121 and 122 at the Cow Hill end (best vistas) and rooms 77 to 80 at the Savannah Pond end.

Those conical Polynesian-style dining pavilions still create one of the most romantic backdrops for feasting in the Caribbean, but there's also a new chef and new focus in the adjoining Sugar Mill—the lighter Mediterranean cuisines of Italy, the Côte d'Azur, Spain, and Greece.

Little Dix is a place for taking life in nice easy doses (with a staff of more than 300 catering to the whims of just 200 guests, the taking doesn't get easier), but for sports buffs there are seven tennis courts (no lights), snorkeling, waterskiing, small sailboats—all included in the rate. For a really romantic treat, really romantic, book a cruise on Laurance Rockefeller's 49-foot yawl, *Evening Star.* Or simply stroll hand in hand around the grounds, along pathways lined with frangipani and fragrant Jerusalem thorn, admiring the handiwork of the resort's 20 gardeners, who fuss over every blossom as if it were a paying guest.

Little Dix now makes getting there easier than ever with private launch service between the resort and the airport on Tortola—a cool, refreshing trip of 15 to 20 minutes, with tropical drinks on the house to speed the minutes along.

Name:　Little Dix Bay

Manager:　Peter Shaindlin

Address:　P.O. Box 70, Virgin Gorda, British Virgin Islands

Location:　5 minutes from the Virgin Gorda airport (in free shuttle bus), 5 minutes from the marina, light-years from real life

Telephone:　809/495-5555

Fax:　809/495-5083

Reservations:　U.S. office, 800/928-3000

Credit Cards:　American Express, Diners Club, MasterCard, Visa

Rooms:　102 double rooms, various combinations of 1- and 2-story villas, plus 2-bedroom cottages, all breeze cooled, all showers (no baths), all with stocked refrigerator, wall safe, balcony or patio (no radios, no TV, some with telephones and air-conditioning)

Meals:　Breakfast 8:00–9:30, Continental breakfast 7:30–8:00, lunch 12:30–2:00, afternoon tea 4:30, dinner 7:00–9:00 (approx. $65 for 2, in the Polynesian pavilion or the Sugar Mill restaurant, both breeze cooled); jackets no longer required evenings in the pavilion (though this doesn't mean you should wear shorts), informal in the Sugar Mill and for barbecues; room service for Continental breakfast only, no extra charge

Entertainment:　Guitarist, steel band, combo, or dancing 6 nights a week, library, games parlor with VCR; local bars and bands a short taxi ride away

Sports: Half-mile beach, snorkeling gear, small sailboats (and instruction), waterskiing, snorkeling trips, water taxis to adjacent beaches, tennis (7 courts, pro shop, no lights)—all free; day sails on 49-foot Hinckley yawl, *Evening Star* ($95 per person, including lunch and open bar); scuba, Jeep safaris can be arranged

P.S.: Small groups (10–15) for lunch once or twice a week, usually from Little Dix's sister resort, Caneel Bay (a ferry runs between the resorts Mondays, Wednesdays, and Fridays); no children under 5; reservations from December to mid-March are virtually family heirlooms

Biras Creek
Virgin Gorda

Atmosphere	Dining	Sports	Rates
☆☆☆	♀♀	◐◐	$ $ $ $ $

It looks for all the world like a Crusader's castle when you first see it as you cross North Sound: a circular stone fortress with a peaked roof. But when you climb the hill, there's no mistaking it for what it is: a one-of-a-kind luxury hideaway for people who want seclusion without giving up too many comforts. The turretlike structure turns out to be the Clubhouse, bar, and dining room—three shingled roofs over a framework of heavy hewn beams, opulently furnished with custom-designed rattan chairs and tables, boldly patterned Caribbean fabrics, island ceramics, and a huge tile mural.

All the guest rooms are spacious beachside suites, two to a cottage, recently redecorated with expensive-looking furniture indoors and out, bright fabrics, tiled floors, appliqué and ceramic doodads, ceiling fans, big patios, platform rockers, coffeemakers, small refrigerators (stocked with white wine and fresh fruit), private safes (there are no room keys here), and—the nicest touch of all—neat little outdoor shower patios with potted plants and tall walls to hide your hides. Two "grand suites" (their words, not mine) have full walls of glass overlooking the sea and "three-room bathrooms" with sunken tubs.

The surrounding acreage is more than just scenery. It's a living, breathing nature preserve created with equal regard for the animals that live here and the people who come to look at them. Trails wind through a desert landscape so natural you can step right over a 3-foot iguana and it'll never blink. A saltwater lake twitters and flaps with waterfowl and wading birds. Even the docks where Biras Creek's powerboats plow in and out every day are clean enough to support baby lobsters and thousands of delicate tropical fish.

Since the beginning, the Biras Creek kitchen has always ranked among the best in the Caribbean (fresh lobster and a pasta entrée are offered nightly). You'll be expected to make a reservation for a table in the evening, but it's a table for the entire evening. You can turn up whenever you feel like eating, not when they feel like serving. No one will hustle you to finish and make way for other guests, so you can relax and linger lovingly over your Château Montrose or Château Mouton Rothschild. Because what has really distinguished the dining experience here, what has always somehow justified that imposing Crusader's castle setting, is the wine cellar. Your choices are not merely good wines but—even rarer in the islands—good vintages.

Which is all the more remarkable when you see where Biras Creek *is*. Not even the dustiest road leads here. No airplane lands here. And boats are few and far between. So what do you do when you're up this particular creek? Well, you might start by wandering off together over miles of nature trails, by foot or by bike. Visit cactus forests and stands of turpentine trees (locally dubbed "tourist trees," because they're tall, bright red, and peeling). Admire the luxurious gardens, coaxed and cosseted into blooming by a green thumb from the island. There's shell gathering on the long breeze-swept beach outside your cottage and floating, wallowing, or swimming in another sheltered sandy bay. And then there's just winding down and savoring the cherished solitude. Sophisticated solitude.

Name: Biras Creek

Manager: Derek Dunlop

Address: P.O. Box 54, Virgin Gorda, British Virgin Islands

Location: On North Sound, accessible only by boat—usually the *North Sound Express* (see Bitter End Yacht Club, below)

Telephone: 809/494-3555, 3556

Fax: 809/494-3557

Reservations: Ralph Locke Islands

Credit Cards: American Express, Discover, MasterCard, Visa

Rooms: 32, all suites (including 2 "grand suites"), all directly on the bay except for 8 rooms, all with ceiling fans, refrigerators (unstocked), coffeemakers, "garden" showers plus a hillside villa with 2 bedrooms, 2 baths, living area, kitchen, patio

Meals: Breakfast 8:00–10:00, lunch 1:00–2:00, dinner 7:30–8:30 (approx. $80 per person for outside guests), in the hilltop pavilion, except for beachside barbecue lunches 5 times a week; slacks and "shirts with collars" required after 6:00, but no jackets; no room service; live music 3 times a week ("quiet during dinner, louder later")

Entertainment: Mostly yourselves, except for the live music, board games, and a nightly movie

Sports: Virtually private, sandy beach called Deep Bay on leeward side (3 to 4 minutes from rooms by bike, 5 to 8 minutes on foot, with bar service), freshwater pool on windward beach (beside the rooms), tennis (2 courts, with lights), windsurfing, snorkeling, Holders, 26-foot sailboats, motorized dinghies, hiking trails, garden walks, bicycles—all free; scuba diving, waterskiing, deep-sea fishing, and sailing trips can be arranged

P.S.:   "While we welcome families, we regret we cannot accept children under school age"; a popular option is the Sailaway package, which combines a 3-day cruise aboard the resort's 47-foot sloop with a 5-day stay at Biras Creek (rate begins at $3,255 per couple in high season); open all year

Bitter End Yacht Club

Virgin Gorda

☆☆☆			🍷			🌑🌑🌑			$ $ $		
Atmosphere			**Dining**			**Sports**			**Rates**		

The first thing you discover about this wonderfully windblown little place is how apt its name is. To get here from the United States involves two, maybe three, flights, followed by a powerboat ride almost straight to your doorstep.

Well, getting to heaven isn't easy, either.

As for Bitter End, it's worth the trip. How often, after all, do you have a chance to spend your days and nights on land or sea—or both?

Choose sea and you get your own seagoing sailboat—a floating suite, fully equipped and provisioned even if you never leave your mooring. It's a Freedom 30 sloop, easy to handle on voyages to the Baths, Peter, Norman, Treasure, and other nearby cays. Yet whenever you come back, all the landlubber conveniences of the hotel are waiting for you—from hot showers to waiters to live music and movies and camaraderie.

Choose land and you get a room or suite in a big airy guest cottage or chalet, fashioned from fir and topped with an Antillean-style red roof, outfitted in rattan and tile, decorated with serapes and batiks. Ceiling fans cool the interiors (the chalets also have air-conditioning); acres of sliding glass doors open to semiprivate sundecks shaded by Mexican thatch. Some cottages stand on stilts a few paces from the shore; others are perched among hibiscus and hummingbirds on the boulders and have undisturbed views of sea and sails and islets; the chalet suites are two-to-a-bungalow on a hillside dotted with prickly pear and mother-in-law cactus.

Now, what happens if you can't decide between a sea or land vacation? You still get your days afloat because you have at your disposal an entire fleet of sailing craft—all day, every day, and at no extra charge. To Bitter End's credit, when they list windsurfing as an attraction, they don't mean just a couple of boards—they mean top-of-the-line Mistral Sailboards by the dozen. When they say they've added Freedom 30s to the fleet, they mean eight new Freedoms.

Although there are lodgings here for only 200 land-billeted guests, Bitter End is nearly every seasoned sailor's Caribbean itinerary, which means that it's hardly ever a deserted little backwater, even in summer (actually, at times it can be almost raucous). The sea-breezy bars and dining pavilions flutter with hundreds of burgees left behind by the constant tide of salt visitors—from charter yachters lazing their way through the islands on a regimen of Mumm's to flinty Ahabs sailing single-handed around the world with nothing but saltines and a sextant.

If you don't consider yourself especially seaworthy, don't let that keep you away from Bitter End. Take a lesson from the Nick Trotter Sailing School, whose instructors are there for anyone who has never so much as hoisted a jib as well as for old salts who want to learn new tricks at the starting line. Start with a small Sunfish and work up.

Even the scuba diving here ranges from the simple to the serious. There's great coral hopping just about anywhere you stick your mask in the water. Deeper down, Horseshoe Reef is littered with the skeletons of doomed galleons. The resort will set up instruction, trips, and dives (but this you have to pay for).

And don't worry about missing anything when you're underwater. When you go back to the Clubhouse Steak and Seafood Grille, the sea dogs will still be sitting around under the burgees nursing their grog and swapping salty tales.

Name: Bitter End Yacht Club
Manager: Bruce Hearn
Address: P.O. Box 46, Virgin Gorda, British Virgin Islands
Location: At John o'Point, at the east end of North Sound; fly to Tortola,

walk a few paces to the jetty to board the new *North Sound Express,* powerboats with three 225-horsepower engines that carry up to 30 passengers and get you to the resort in about 20 minutes ($18 one-way, last scheduled departure from Tortola at 7:15)

Telephone: 809/494-2745, 2746

Fax: 809/494-4756

Reservations: Own U.S. office, 312/944-5855 or 800/872-2392

Credit Cards: All major cards

Rooms: 100, including 6 suites, in a variety of villas, bungalows, and chalets dotting the hillside on both sides of the dock, each with private bathroom, tiled shower, refrigerator, balcony/deck, ceiling fan; suites, in the former Tradewinds Resort (now called the Chalets), have air-conditioning and especially large bathrooms

Meals: Breakfast 8:00–10:00, lunch 12:30–2:00, dinner 6:30–9:00, in 2 beachside pavilions (approx. $60 for 2); casual dress; no room service; some taped music

Entertainment: Taped music (jazz, pop, modern—sometimes loud), live music 3 nights a week, movies every evening in the Sand Palace

Sports: Beach (not terrific), snorkeling, windsurfing, sailboats (Sunfishes, Lasers, Rhodes 19s, J24s, Vanguard 15s), boat trips on the launch *Prince of Wales* or the *Paranda,* a 48-foot catamaran, to the Isle of Anegada or the Baths (lunch included), skiffs with outboard motors, rowing sculls, ocean kayaks, introductory sailing instruction—all free; Freedom 30 sloops, windsurfing instruction and private sailing lessons, scuba diving with the famed Kilbrides (their base is on the next cay) extra

P.S.:   "We don't encourage preschool children"; open all year

Drake's Anchorage Resort Inn
Virgin Gorda Sound

☆☆☆			♀♀			◑			$ $ $	
Atmosphere			**Dining**			**Sports**			**Rates**	

East-northeast from Tortola there's an island marked Mosquito on the charts—and bliss in the memories of escapists.

Now called Drake's Anchorage, it's all of 126 acres, each and every acre private, the playground of only 24 lucky sandaled sun worshipers. Three wood-frame, gingerbread-trimmed cottages perch on stilts along the shore, three or four rooms in each, all with white walls, tile floors, rattan furniture, wicker lamps, and handmade cotton kimonos for each guest. Bathrooms are strictly functional (although they're currently being enlarged and upgraded); paddle fans and ample louvers take care of ventilation; spacious sundecks overlook the beach (or, at least, *one* of the beaches). The rooms with the best breezes are numbers 10, 11, and 12.

A few shuffling steps away among the casuarina and sea-grape trees you come to the main lodge, a low-slung, timber pavilion where the sea laps at your feet and the trade winds waft through the driftwood decor—turtle shells and fan coral and stuffed snapper and dolphin. Yachters with the foresight to radio ashore for reservations will join you here for drinks and dinner, turning the driftwood pavilion into a merry salon. They've come ashore for the bounty of a menu that's more sophisticated than you might expect in a backwater off a backwater—mahimahi in curry sauce, fillet of beef au poivre. Drake's recipe for chocolate mousse is guarded more zealously than pirate gold, and typical entrées are dolphin in curry sauce with bananas, rack of lamb (for two), and sauté of boneless duck in citrus sauce, served with fried cracklings.

And that's about it. Drake's Anchorage is strictly a place for the Five S's—sunning, snorkeling, snoozing, smooching, sailing. And with only 24 overnight guests there's plenty of room for all five pastimes. Plenty of nature trails lined with frangipani and barrel cactus. Plenty of beach—the one on your doorstep, three more a short walk away. The most idyllic is Honeymoon (10 minutes, over the hill), especially if you don't have to share it with yacht people. Offshore, gardens of staghorn coral and reefs boggle the eyes of snorkelers.

When you amble over to Lime Tree Beach you'll pass the island's big surprise: a pair of villas (belonging to the owners, a Boston University professor and his wife), as stylishly grand as the cottages are plain-Jane—with cathedral ceilings, fieldstone walls, bathrooms with sunken stone tubs, fully equipped kitchens, and stereo. They're rentable by the night or week; weekly rates work out to be *much* less expensive than a mere room in some of the snazzier resorts on bigger islands.

Of course, if all that sand and solitude begin to pall, you can always charter a Boston Whaler and skim across the Sound to Bitter End—Manhattan to Mosquito's Staten Island.

Name: Drake's Anchorage Resort Inn

Managers: Albert and Gloria Wheatley

Address: P.O. Box 2510, Virgin Gorda, British Virgin Islands

Location: On Virgin Gorda Sound. To get there, take the *North Sound Express* from Beef Island to Leverick Bay, where you'll be collected by the resort's launch

Telephone: 809/494-2254

Fax: 809/494-2254 or 617/969-5147 (U.S. office)

Reservations: Own U.S. office, 800/624-6651; 617/969-9913 in Massachusetts

Credit Cards: American Express, MasterCard, Visa

Rooms: 10 (including 2 suites) in 3 cottages, each with shower, ceiling fan, and breezes, terrace, big rechargeable flashlamps for occasions when the lights fail; the suites also have refrigerators (in addition, the resort has 2 deluxe villas with sunken tubs and fully equipped kitchens)

Meals: Breakfast 8:00–10:30, lunch noon–2:30, dinner 7:00 ($60–$70 for 2), all served in a breezy surfside pavilion; informal dress; picnic lunches packed on request; taped background music (classical, jazz, or calypso)

Entertainment: Darts, chess, backgammon, library, VCR, guitarist, occasionally a steel band

Sports: 4 beaches, snorkeling gear, 19-foot Squibb sailboats, motorized dinghies, windsurfing—all free; scuba diving, sailing, and tennis can be arranged

P.S.:   Closed mid-August through September

Other Choices

Anegada Reef Hotel

Anegada

Anegada is the last little speck of the British Virgin Islands before you hit open ocean and, later, Africa. A small plane flies in a couple of times a week, but the thrilling way to get there is by boat—if you can find a skipper foolhardy or skilled enough to get you there. The island is really the top of a reef surrounded by more reef, and since its highest point is the tallest palm tree and there's not a single navigational light, boats are practically on top of the reef before they know the island is there. Hence all the bits of mast and hull popping up from the water—it's said that 200 galleons, caravels, and luxury yachts have gone down on these reefs in the past 300 years. Obviously, then, it's not an overcrowded island, which means that Lowell Wheatley's Anegada Reef Hotel is a far cry from San Juan. The hotel's 16 rooms are simply furnished with wicker and rattan, newly refurbished with sand drift colored walls and bright tropical fabrics. There are no phones, no TV, and you'll have to read your thrillers by the light of 60-watt lamps, but the rooms do have coffeemakers, tiled tubs/showers, and air-conditioning to augment the ceiling fans. Half the rooms face a garden at the rear, the others face the marina up front. It's not exactly the most glorious setting. You have to walk or drive a short distance to the beach (and what beaches once you get there!). But the attractions of such an authentically Caribbean location are beguiling: the lobster is brought in fresh from the boats tied up outside your window, everyone who comes ashore in the pleasure craft sidles up to the bar and sits around sipping tall drinks and swapping tall tales while they wait for their lobsters to be cooked—right there on the beach, on a steel drum over charcoal with a secret barbecue sauce. For guests, there's a small surcharge for the lobster, but otherwise all meals come with the low room rates—enough of a bargain to justify venturing through the coral heads and wrecks to get there. 16 rooms. Doubles: $200 to $230, winter 1994–95, with all meals. *Anegada Reef Hotel, Setting Point, Anegada, British Virgin Islands. Telephone: 809/495-8002; fax: 809/495-9362.*

Sandcastle

Jost Van Dyke

Jost Van Dyke is the island off the northwest corner of Tortola—a Robinson Crusoe place with no airstrip, few inhabitants, and a few restaurants that cater mostly to people stepping ashore from charter yachts. Dinner at Sandcastle is by candlelight, reading is by propane lamps, and water is heated, if at all, by the noonday sun. Which is, for many escapists, what the Caribbean is all about. Sandcastle is right on the beach (a beauty, shared with maybe a couple of private homes that lie empty much of the time). There's no dock. You just roll up your trousers or skirt and wade through the surf to get here, after a choppy ride by water taxi from West End (the hotel will make the arrangements). Activity revolves around the breezy beach bar and the water sports—windsurfing, Sunfish sailing, snorkeling, rafts. But most of the time guests just seem to lounge around in hammocks, wearing to dinner what they wore to breakfast. Menus feature sandwiches at lunch, Continental at dinner. A new owner has made extensive renovations (new floors, new roofs, that sort of thing) and brightened the rooms with new beds, furnishings, and fabrics. 8 rooms in 4 rondavel cottages. Doubles: $325, winter 1994–95, with all meals. *Sandcastle, White Bay, Jost Van Dyke, British Virgin Islands. Mailing address: 6501 Red Hook Plaza, Suite 201, St. Thomas, U.S. Virgin Islands 00802-1306. Telephone: 809/775-5262; fax: 809/775-3590.*

Paradise Beach Resort

Virgin Gorda

It's actually Mango Bay, a half-mile sweep of fine white sand just around the headland from Savannah Bay and screened by a ring of low hills from the occasional vehicles that pass as traffic in these parts. Eight sand-colored contemporary villas hide out in this flowering peaceful garden, but only four belong to Paradise—the others belong to Mango Beach Resort—with only one of them actually on the beach. The owners/managers are friendly and welcoming (they stock your refrigerator with enough provisions to see you through your first supper and breakfast), the furnishings are comfortable, the kitchens are well equipped, and the indoor/outdoor living rooms are generous. 8 studios and suites. Doubles: $155 (studio) to $360 (1-bedroom suite), winter 1995–96, including the use of a Jeep. *Paradise Beach Resort, Virgin Gorda, British Virgin Islands. Telephone: 809/495-5871; fax:*

809/495-5872. U.S. reservations: 800/225-4255 or 212/696-4566; fax: 212/689-1598.

Frenchman's Cay Resort Hotel
Tortola

The cay in question is located at the west end of Tortola, linked to its south shore by a narrow bridge and jutting into the sea so that guests may enjoy ravishing views of sea and islets and the Sir Francis Drake Channel. The villas are sited on the rise above the coral-fringed sea, each with a balcony for sea gazing, kitchen, dining room, sitting room, attractive if undistinguished island furniture (some looking tired and frayed, depending on the villa), and ceiling fan. The 12 acres of relaxing garden incorporate an Omniturf tennis court, six hammocks beneath a cluster of sea-grape trees, a swatch of sand for sunning, a headland for snorkeling around, a swimming pool, and an octagonal pavilion that houses the reception, bar, the Clubhouse Restaurant, and something like 200 paperbacks. Nine one- and two-bedroom villas. Doubles: $200, winter 1995–96. *Frenchman's Cay Resort Hotel, P.O. Box 1054, West End, Tortola, British Virgin Islands. Telephone: 800/235-4077 or 809/495-4844 (for reservations only); fax: 809/495-4056.*

The Dutch Windwards

St. Maarten

St. Martin

Saba

St. Eustatius

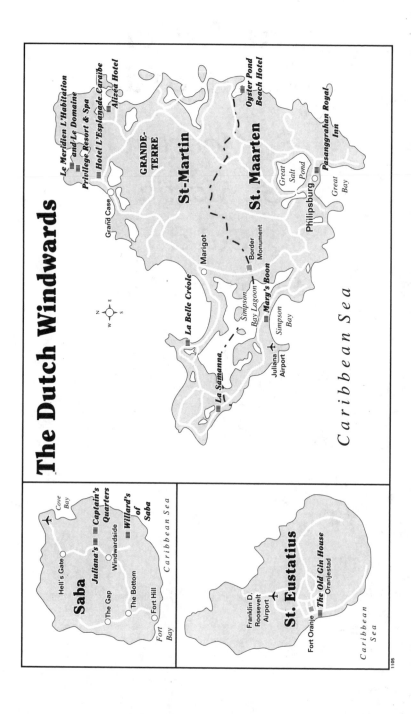

The Dutch Windwards

Le Meridien L'Habitation and Le Domaine
Privilege Resort & Spa
Hotel L'Esplanade Caraïbe
Alizéa Hotel

Oyster Pond Beach Hotel

GRANDE-TERRE

Pasanggrahan Royal Inn

St-Martin

Grand Case

St. Maarten

Great Salt Pond

Marigot

Great Bay

Philipsburg

La Belle Créole

Border Monument

Simpson Bay Lagoon

Mary's Boon

La Samanna

Simpson Bay

Juliana Airport

N
W · E
S

Caribbean Sea

Saba

Cove Bay

Captain's Quarters

Hell's Gate

Juliana's

Windwardside

Willard's of Saba

The Gap

The Bottom

Fort Hill

Fort Bay

Caribbean Sea

St. Eustatius

The Old Gin House

Oranjestad

Franklin D. Roosevelt Airport

Fort Oranje

Caribbean Sea

1105

The Dutch Windwards

The Dutch West India Company that sent Henry Hudson scouting around the northeast coast of America also sent its ships and captains to the Caribbean; and Peter "Pegleg" Stuyvesant, the hobbling Hollander who became governor of New York City, tried to dislodge the Spanish from St. Maarten only to have the Spanish dislodge his leg. What 20th-century lovers will find in this corner of the Dutch Caribbean is a trio of islands—two totally unspoiled and serene (Saba and St. Eustatius), and one (St. Maarten/St. Martin) that offers only pockets of serenity since it tries to be a valid alternative to San Juan and the U.S. Virgins for vacationers who want hamburgers, casinos, and lively, varied nightlife.

Saba is the phantom silhouette you see on the horizon when you're sitting on the waterfront in St. Maarten. It's really the tip of a volcanic cone, a straight-up-and-down island with one roadway and a thousand inhabitants, completely unlike any other island in the Caribbean (it doesn't, for a start, have a beach). What it does have is a haunting, tranquil, otherworldly charm; but it's strictly for lovers who are content to be on their own (or, in recent years, for scuba divers who crave a change of aqueous scenery).

St. Eustatius, likewise, except that you'll find beaches (sort of) here. Statia should be popular with Americans for historic reasons: The Dutch garrison of Fort Oranje fired the first salute to the brand new American flag during the War of Independence. For its pains the island was zapped by England's Admiral Rodney, and Oranjestad, once the busiest harbor in the Indies, is now a half-submerged ghost town—but a treasure trove for snorkelers and scuba divers.

Because the Dutch ended up splitting the island with the French, Sint Maarten is also Saint Martin. When you go from one side to the other (there's no frontier, no customs), you're going from France to Holland— literally, because the French side is part of the Republic of France and the Dutch side is part of the Kingdom of the Netherlands. Between them, they offer you something like three dozen beaches—white, soft, powdery beaches, duty-free shopping, nightlife, scores of interesting restaurants, and more construction and concrete trucks than you probably want to encounter on your vacation.

How to Get There From New York on American (nonstop) and Continental (one stop); nonstops from Miami and Raleigh-Durham

(American), Boston (Northwest), and Baltimore/Washington (USAir). Many of these flights arrive and depart within a short time of each other and the nondescript airport can't cope efficiently. On your return flight, get to the airport early to check in, then go upstairs to the restaurant for something to eat or drink. It's crowded and noisy, just like the departure lounge, but it's air-conditioned, which isn't always the case with the departure lounge, which has only an inadequate counter for drinks and snacks.

Windward (sometimes known as Winair) flies several times a day to Saba and St. Eustatius, each about 20 minutes away unless you stop off at one or the other on the way. Landing in Saba is an experience in itself that's probably worth the $80 round-trip ticket: The only way the Sabans could find a flat surface for the runway was to chop off the top of a hillock beside the sea, so touchdown here is like landing on an aircraft carrier (World War II vintage at that). But it's no problem for such advanced STOL planes as Windward's new Twin Otters (which also, by the way, have picture windows to let you see where you're going—and how you're getting there).

For information on St. Maarten, call 800/786-2278; St. Martin, 900/990-0040 (50 cents a minute); Saba, 800/722-2394; St. Eustatius, 905/803-0131.

The Oyster Pond Beach Hotel, a Colony Resort

St. Maarten

☆☆☆ **Atmosphere**   Ⴘ Ⴘ Ⴘ **Dining**   ● **Sports** $ $ $ **Rates**

To get here, you have to drive all the way over to the other side of the island on a road engineered on the same basic principle as the roller coaster.

The final lurch brings you to the crest of a hill and your first heart-stopping glimpse of the eponymous pond—a circular lagoon with a circular hotel on the point of a promontory.

Until recently, that was about all you saw. That and St. Barthélemy off in the distance. But the island's concept of progress—where there's concrete there's cash—has been catching on even in this remote corner of the island, so there are now more homes, some condos, hotels, and restaurants across the lagoon on the French side. Nevertheless, here at the Oyster Pond Hotel are peace and seclusion in abundance. That hill you've just come over effectively shuts out the casual rubbernecker and bargain-hunting day-tripper. The background distractions of cars, planes, and tour buses are effectively eliminated, and the only distraction is more likely to be the occasional whine of an outboard motor hauling waterskiers around the pond.

Tranquility reigns once you step through the entrance to the hotel (formerly known as the Yacht Club)—a semicircle of natural stone with half a dozen arches, flanked by two square three-story stone towers. Within the arches, planters and white wicker with a scattering of antiques turn the lobby into a conservatory; jaunty sun umbrellas turn the circular courtyard into an al fresco café at lunchtime. Beyond are a plushly cushioned bar-lounge and a breezy candlelit restaurant with arched glass doors opening to the sea—and glimpses of aquamarine and azure every way you turn.

Guest rooms ring the courtyard, all but six of them on the second floor, around a white-walled gallery with dark wooden arches and balustrades, their names on shining brass plates—L'Oiseau des Iles, Passage, Monitor, Nirvana, Tantrum, and so on, echoes of oceangoing ships of bygone times. Decor is more or less identical throughout: Jacques Pergay wicker from France, white on white set against russet tiled floors, Pierre Deux fabrics, the walls decorated with prints by Rothko or Lichtenstein. Variations in rooms are minor—patios on the ground floor, balconies (and higher ceilings) on the upper level, a few extra cubic feet for deluxe rooms. Oddly enough, the duplex suites in the towers have no balcony, and the duplex gallery, accessible by steep wooden steps, is really practical only for reading or siestas. The best views (of the peaks of St. Barthélemy) are framed by the windows of Monitor and Nirvana—but Black Swan and Sea Cloud have practically no view and cost half the price of the Tower Suites.

But it's not just the pond that's expanding: The hotel itself doubled its capacity a few years ago by adding 20 Oceanview Suites, farther out on the bluff. Super location, super views (unobstructed sea and St. Barts), super breezes, boring architecture. The new rooms (or "junior" suites, perhaps, rather than full-scale suites) are larger than those in the main hotel and with more luxurious amenities—cable television, refrigerators, direct-dial telephones, ceiling fans *and* air-conditioning, despite the glorious breezes with sliding glass doors rather than louvers. Decor is stylishly island—clay-tile floors with scatter rugs, blue and coral upholstery on white wicker armchairs, ottomans, sofas, and king-size beds.

Jan Borsje keeps the house running smoothly; the kitchen turns out the kind of cuisine (*soupe aux truffes, médaillons de langouste au gingembre, soufflé aux framboises, marquise aux fraises et bananes*) that has dedicated gourmets scrambling for reservations at one of the 14 Rosenthal-decked tables—even though for outsiders dinner at Oyster Pond involves that helter-skelter ride home on a roller-coaster road.

Name: The Oyster Pond Beach Hotel, a Colony Resort
Manager: Jan Borsje
Address: P.O. Box 239, St. Maarten, Netherlands Antilles
Location: On the southeastern shore, 35 minutes and $22 by taxi from the airport, 15 minutes and $12 from Philipsburg
Telephone: 599/52-2206, 52-3206
Fax: 599/52-5695
Reservations: Own U.S. office, 800/839-3030
Credit Cards: American Express, Diners Club, MasterCard, Visa
Rooms: 40, all with ceiling fans, balconies or patios, showers only in the bathrooms; Oceanview Suites have ceiling fans *and* air conditioners, bathtubs, bathrobes, cable TV, refrigerators, balconies, direct-dial telephones
Meals: Breakfast 8:00–10:00, lunch noon–2:30, dinner 7:00–10:00 (approx. $90 for 2); informal dress ("but no shorts in the evening, proper attire at all times"); room service for Continental breakfast only, extra charge
Entertainment: Bar/lounge with taped music (cool jazz or classical)
Sports: Mile-long beach a 2-minute walk through the gardens, stunning pool carved from coral rocks; water sports across the lagoon
P.S.: Some children; closed September

Mary's Boon

St. Maarten

Atmosphere	Dining	Sports	Rates

The Mary with the boon was the late Mary Pomeroy, one of the Caribbean's legendary innkeepers, but the inn is now owned by Rushton Little, known to many St. Maarten buffs as the long-term manager of Pasanggrahan Royal Inn.

It consists of six white-roofed bungalows with wraparound verandas and gingerbread trim garlanded with hibiscus, in a sandy garden of allamanda and shrubbery. It's right on the beach, practically in the water, on one of the longest stretches of sand on the island, and everything is designed to make the most of the setting. The sea beckons the minute you step through the main gate; lobby, dining room, and bar are all open to the breezes and framed by sea grape, coconut palms, and a wild cotton tree; the murmuring surf is right there all the time.

The rooms are really efficiencies, about half as large again as the average hotel room, fitted out with tile floors, ceiling fans, wicker furniture, a few antiques, original Dutch and Haitian paintings, and a few items that look as though they might have come from a millionaire's yacht. There's a kitchenette in case you feel like rustling up your own breakfasts, but the best feature of all is the bathroom: lots of toweling room, Italian white and sienna floor tiles, and tiled shower stalls.

There's a great atmosphere at Mary's Boon. Pure beachcomber. The setting puts you in the mood for swimming and snorkeling, the exercise puts you in the mood for lunch, and lunch puts you in the mood for a siesta. Before you know where you are you're involved in the favorite pastime at Mary's Boon, sitting around the bar chatting with all sorts of interesting people—a French painter and his mistress; an attractive woman who looks very innocent but happens to work for a think tank in California and knows all about supersonic jets; a few airline people; a few island people, old friends of Rush Little from farther down the islands. The bar is operated on the honor system and drinks (for houseguests) cost only one or two dollars, so most guests are quite happy to have a few before dinner; and since coffee is served in the bar after dinner (damned good food, too), the drinking and conversation continue until the last guest goes home.

Mary's Boon is the almost perfect resort for young lovers except for one drawback—the airport. The runway is a hundred yards away, which means that half a dozen times a day you'll be bombarded by a few seconds of appalling whine, mostly midafternoon, never after 10:00 in the evening. But the agony really lasts for only 60 seconds and only half a dozen times a day, which leaves you another 23 hours and 54 minutes to enjoy all the good things about Mary's Boon.

Name: Mary's Boon
Manager: Rushton Little
Address: Airport P.O. Box 2078, St. Maarten, Netherlands Antilles
Location: On the long, long beach at Simpson Bay, 5 minutes and $5 or more from the airport
Telephone: 599/55-4235
Fax: 599/55-3403

Reservations: International Travel & Resorts or Loews Representation International

Credit Cards: None

Rooms: 12 efficiencies, with showers, ceiling fans, and porches or verandas

Meals: Breakfast 7:30–9:30, lunch at 1:00, dinner at 8:00 ($50–$70 for 2, on the beachside veranda); casual dress

Entertainment: The clientele

Sports: Beach (more than 2 miles of it, one of the finest on the island), good swimming; water sports and tennis nearby

P.S.:   No groups, no children, no cruise ship passengers, no outsiders for meals except by reservation; breakfast is the only meal served in August and October; closed August 15 to October 15

La Samanna

St. Martin

Atmosphere

Dining

Sports

Rates

Step from the patio of your suite and you're right on the beach, surrounded by sea-grape trees, just 20 paces from the sea. You couldn't find a more pristine, beachy location.

Or skip the beach altogether, climb the stucco steps beside your thatched veranda, and head for your own little rooftop sundeck. It's totally secluded up there. Only the frigate birds could be shocked at the goings-on, and they're too busy diving for dinner.

Yet your lodgings are among the swankiest in the Caribbean, and just a few paces away, along paths that wind through hibiscus and bougainvillea and allamanda, you can sit down in style at one of the most sophisticated restaurants in the Caribbean.

I can remember, in fact, the days when there was nothing on this beach. A couple of sun worshipers could have the entire place to themselves, and I was miffed when I learned that a guy, some New York industrialist called James Frankel, was about to build a resort on "my" beach. As it turned out, this James Frankel was a man of refined taste and substantial resources with, we came to learn later, a romantic streak. So he and his architect came up with a Mediterranean-Casablancan mélange of whitewashed stucco with graceful domes and inviting arches, a series of whitewashed villas with bright blue doors and window trim strung out along the beach among the casuarinas and sea grapes, with a two-story main lodge crowning the bluff at one end. Terraces lead down to a large blue-tiled pool, surrounded by colorful blossoms and greenery, the bar is topped by a multicolored Indian wedding tent, and St. Martin disappears, shut off from the resort by 55 acres of grounds.

A few years ago, I had a coffee with Frankel and asked him, as a much-traveled cosmopolite, to describe his favorite hotel. He waved his arm around to embrace his beloved La Samanna and said, "This place, but without the guests." There were times, for sure, when the service could be offhand and irritating for people who weren't insiders like Richard Nixon, Jackie Kennedy, and Billy Graham; but I always admired Frankel and loved the resort, so like many other La Samanna fans I was slightly perturbed to learn, about a year after James Frankel died, that Rosewood Hotels would be running the place. Not that Rosewood stands for the humdrum by any means, but their estimable reputation was made in America, not in the Caribbean. They are a corporation; Frankel was an individual. I was ready for the worst, and it didn't help to learn that Rosewood was planning to install (horrors!) air-conditioning and televisions.

My fears were largely ungrounded. Rosewood has done a first-rate job of rehabbing without altering the basic La Samanna. The air-conditioning is confined to the bedrooms and its split-unit design keeps the hum low; most of the time, we can still get by with the ample louvers and ceiling fans.

"Hah!" cried the skeptics: "If they're putting in air-conditioning they're bound to add television, 50 channels blaring the din of police sirens." Not so. The Rosewood people did some research among longtime guests (smart move) and the message was clear: no TV. (For people who can't live without their CNN, Rosewood has set aside two lounges—one for satellite TV, one for VCR movies.)

The Rosewood decorators, Vision Design, were locked into outmoded bathrooms, which they've upgraded in small ways while retaining the original Portuguese washbasins (chips and all, not surprising after 30 years of use), but elsewhere in the guest quarters there is evidence of too little vision and too much design: The hand-carved spiral standard lamps look good—but someone should have realized that a guest sitting in an armchair might find a reading lamp more welcome than a planter, whereas a planter is more decorative in an unused corner of the room than a reading lamp; and the oversize sofa with natural-finished wood wrapped with hemp is, I suspect, too wide for guests who are not quarterbacks and will probably become an *objet* rather than a functioning piece of furniture. Nevertheless, the lounge chairs in zambale-peel wicker and the hand-carved bedside chests and bamboo dressing bureaus have the right blend of style and tropics; these are beautiful rooms, matched in the Caribbean only by Malliouhana, Cap Juluca, the oceanfront suites at Sandy Lane, and Curtain Bluff (except for those slightly cramped bathrooms). I'd be happy to spend a few days in any one of them, but a few are more romantic than others: the beachside suites with rooftop sundecks; if you want views, the rooms in the main lodge. My previous recommendation was room 110, on the corner of the main lodge with two terraces, one for sunning, one for shade; the Rosewood people, too, realized they had a winner here, so they've jazzed it up, added an al fresco wet bar, and jacked up the tariff—my former best buy is now the resort's showpiece.

There was a time when La Samanna's rates moved in a time frame all their own, which never seemed to deter the celebrities and nouveaux who flocked here in the seventies and eighties; but the new policy is to set the food and wine prices closer to the island's other gourmet restaurants. That doesn't mean cheap eats by any means, but two can now dine for $50 to $60 or thereabouts, without wine.

La Samanna has always been lauded for its restaurant, a romantic *terrasse* shaded by a thatched ramada, on the bluff overlooking the full sweep of Baie Longue. The high-back armchairs of zambale-peel wicker are comfortable, the service is more polished, the walls are decorated with lithos, and the tables are laid with Ricca silverware and Langenthal china.

The kitchen is supervised by Marc Ehrler, who came here from the stoves of Alain Ducasse and Jacques Maximin by way of San Ysidro Ranch in California and a very brief stint at the K Club on Barbuda. That was where I first sampled his dishes, and I was impressed by what he was doing on an island where just about everything except lobster has to come in on single-engine planes. Here, with the resources of Rosewood behind him, on an island with regular jet service direct from Paris, he creates cuisine that ranks up there with the finest in the islands. Try, for example, his thin island crab tarts with Caribbean salsa, or whole roasted grouper with bouillabaisse fumé and pine nuts, or roasted lamb loin with a ragoût of mini-ravioli in lamb juice. Masterpieces all. But I'm sure Ehrler won't be offended if I note that he may be outshone by his pastry chef, whose caramel apple tart with nut cream and lemon tart with coconut shavings will revitalize even the most satiated, Ehrler-indulged palate.

The helm at La Samanna has now passed to Ulrich Krauer, one of those seasoned Swiss, who served as maître d' at government functions when he was a teenaged stripling, a man of such wide-ranging experience that he served a few years in St. Andrew's, Scotland, and learned to play golf on that holy of holies, the Old Course. His roster of languages—English, German, French, Italian—stands him in good stead for hosting the multinationals who check into La Samanna these days (including VIPs in the music business who send their tapes ahead so that the resort will greet them with their own music—"maybe yes, probably no").

Something intangible has probably been lost in the transfer from owner/manager/visionary to safe corporate management (one old Frankel buff claims the sexiness is gone), but La Samanna is still a place of magic.

Name: La Samanna

Manager: Ulrich Krauer

Address: P.O. Box 4077, 97064 St. Martin, French West Indies

Location: On Baie Longue, 10 minutes from Juliana Airport, $15 by taxi (the hotel can also arrange to meet you with a limousine)

Telephone: 590/87-5122

Fax: 590/87-8786

Reservations: Rosewood Hotels, 800/854-2252

Credit Cards: All major cards

Rooms: 80 rooms and suites, all oceanfront, all with verandas, patios, or terraces, ceiling fans and louvers, air-conditioning, direct-dial telephones, stocked refrigerators, hairdryers, bathrobes; some with rooftop sundecks, some with kitchenettes

Meals: Breakfast anytime, lunch noon–5:00, dinner 7:00–11:00 (approx. $50–$60 for 2), in the main restaurant or poolside grill; casual but stylish dress ("no swimsuits"), 24-hour room service

Entertainment: Bar, native bands on weekends, parlor games in lounge-library, 2 video rooms for satellite TV or movies; special theme weeks (e.g., "literature")

Sports: Beach, pool, tennis (3 courts, no lights), fitness pavilion, snorkeling gear, windsurfing, waterskiing—all free; horseback riding, sailing, scuba diving, golf nearby

P.S.: Some children; closed September and October

La Belle Créole
St. Martin

☆					🍷				🌓🌑			$	$	$	$	
Atmosphere					**Dining**				**Sports**			**Rates**				

This is the hotel everyone seems to want to tag with the word *legendary*. The vision of the "legendary" Claude Philippe of the Waldorf-Astoria, we're told. Back in the sixties, Philippe wanted an ultraexclusive resort, in the style of a Mediterranean village, where he could entertain his rich and famous, royal and patrician Waldorf clientele. He finally managed to open the doors for a 1-night stand before running out of money. For the next 20 years or thereabouts, the desolate village/resort squatted on its peninsula, a spectral pink stucco hamlet with a five-story campanile, being ripped off and ravished, waiting for a white knight. Along came Barron Hilton, head of Conrad International Hotels, the overseas division of Hilton USA (not to be confused with Hilton International, if you follow). Finally, La Belle Créole, after countless fits and start-ups, opened in 1988—but alas, the only thing "legendary" about the place is that it may have set the world record for the resort that took the longest to build and the longest to open.

Granted, it has a handsome setting, on the romantically named Pointe des Pierres à Chaux, a 25-acre promontory jutting into Marigot Bay; granted, the pink stucco and native stone buildings echo something of the allure of a Mediterranean village, complete with *plazuelas* and winding cobblestone paths shaded by flamboyant and sea-grape trees. The problem is, it's all so lifeless. Handsome the setting may be, but on an island blessed with beautiful beaches, one of La Belle Créole's is narrow and windswept and unswimmable; the other is an overgrown sandlot alongside an artificial lagoon. And though the guest rooms are more spacious than usual in this part of the world (a minimum of 400 square feet), and the furniture *has* been imported from France, they still look like they've been decorated by committee.

The recently renovated 162 guest rooms and suites are deployed in 22 buildings of one, two, or three stories. They have all the basics (including, I'm happy to say, flow-through ventilation in addition to the ceiling fans and air-conditioning), as well as frills like mini-bars and television to complement the antiqued pine desks and wardrobes, tile floors, and wicker and rattan chairs and sofas. The most inviting quarters are the split-level Loft

Suites, but you want to avoid rooms on the ground floor of buildings 21 through 29; otherwise your patio may be looking directly into someone else's back wall. Next to the Loft Suites, the choice accommodations are the rooms identified as beachfront, in single-story villas lining the windward beach.

It would be gratifying to report that the "legendary" torch had been passed along from the "legendary" Philippe to the present-day staff. It hasn't. They're young and friendly (although not necessarily fluent in English) but decidedly unpolished. New owners, as of 1994, have added a few refinements, such as a "sidewalk" café in the main plaza, but the bartender is still trying too hard to be a celebrity, and with sandwiches at $10 and up, you expect something better than the kind of service you normally get in a corner coffee shop back home.

Although La Belle Créole is now run by Winfair Hospitality Management of Canada, I'd still give this place a few more years to mature.

Name: La Belle Créole
Manager: Jean-Guy Salinesi
Address: P.O. Box 4181, Marigot, 97065 St. Martin, French West Indies
Location: On Marigot Bay, 5 minutes from Marigot, 20 minutes and $15 by taxi from the airport
Telephone: 590/87-6600
Fax: 590/87-5666
Reservations: Robert Reid Associates
Credit Cards: All major cards
Rooms: 162 rooms, including 22 suites in 22 buildings; all with private bathrooms, air-conditioning and ceiling fans, refrigerators/mini-bars, in-room safes, satellite television (6 channels), direct-dial telephones, coffee/tea makers
Meals: Breakfast 7:00–10:30, lunch noon–4:30 in the Pool Bar & Grill, dinner 6:00–10:30 in La Provence indoor/outdoor restaurant ($70–$90 for 2); casual dinners 6:00–10:00 in the Plaza Café ($40–$50 for 2); no room service (not even for breakfast, "but you can always go down to the dining room and take your breakfast back to your room")
Entertainment: Bar/lounge with calypso music several nights a week
Sports: 2 beaches (one a lagoon, neither of them especially inviting compared to their neighbors'), freshwater free-form pool, croquet, fitness room, tennis (4 courts, lit, pro shop)—all free (except lit tennis, $12 per hour); paddleboats, aqua trikes, windsurfers, Sunfishes, floating mats, waterskiing, and other water sports are available at extra charge
P.S.: You may encounter groups of up to 75 participants during the off-season; open all year

Le Meridien L'Habitation and Le Domaine

St. Martin

☆☆				🍷🍷🍷		🌓🌓🌓🌓	S S S	
Atmosphere				**Dining**		**Sports**	**Rates**	

The full name is Le Meridien L'Habitation Lonvilliers, and it's now one part of a complex incorporating a brand-new hotel called Le Meridien Le Domaine. Too many words for a title—especially for a pair of hotels that are not really *that* exceptional.

What they have going for them is a relatively secluded setting on an island that's getting to be uncomfortably congested: an impressive sweep of sand about half a mile long surrounded by sheltering hills. This is a perfect spot for a 200-room, two-story hotel like L'Habitation, even with a marina attached, but it's getting to be a bit *crowded* now that it has a neighbor right next door, another 145 rooms in Le Domaine. I'm told that each hotel has a different owner, although they're both managed by the French chain, Meridien (which in turn is owned by Forte); more ominous, the front desk for both is the lobby of L'Habitation, which seemed overextended even without the extra guests from Le Domaine. The new hotel also brings a new restaurant, in a replica of an old plantation house, with a spacious deck and Italian-oriented menu.

Still, if you want to be on St. Martin, if you want comfortable lodgings, if you want good food and lots of activities, the Meridien hotels have much to commend them. L'Habitation has been rejuvenated by the Meridien people (although the rooms still lack any kind of individuality), and the plantings are flourishing, so you no longer feel as if you're looking directly into the rooms across the garden (ask for a room facing the central garden—the "rear" rooms are dreary).

On the other hand, no one can say that the rooms at the new Le Domaine lack individuality, just a touch of common sense. The designer has managed to avoid the tyranny of four square walls, and the bathtubs are tucked into a corner of the room with a surrounding curtain for the modest bather; but the clothes closets are back at the entrance, so you'd better plan ahead or you may be tracking bathwater all over the white ceramic-tile floor. Utilities like TVs and mini-bars are neatly tucked into a corner cupboard, the sheets are by Porthault, the decor is pleasant enough with antiqued furniture and papier-mâché bananas and fish. The suites on the upper levels have the same eccentric arrangement of tubs, large balconies, and sitting areas with a sofa your back will probably resent after a very short time. Again, all very designy, not very practical.

Some positive notes: The owners of Le Domaine spent $1 million on landscaping, with pretty paths and globe lamps to lead you back to the lobby, and the gardens were beautiful even before the hotel opened; the signature restaurant, La Belle France, is physically attractive, the service is attentive and pleasant, the food well above par for an island hotel. The new La Veranda restaurant, in plantation style, is physically attractive but the service is dotty. The music in the bar is far too loud, even if it does end at 11:00, and I don't appreciate a maid arriving on my doorstep at 8:30 a.m. on departure day insisting on checking a mini-bar that was never stocked in the first place.

Still, by St. Martin standards, the Meridiens are a pretty good value.

Name: Le Meridien L'Habitation and Le Domaine
Manager: Philippe Siegle
Address: B.P. 581, Anse Marcel, 97056 St. Martin, French West Indies
Location: At Marcel Bay, on the northern shore, about 30 minutes and $40 by taxi from Juliana Airport, 15 minutes and $20 by taxi from Marigot (with complimentary shuttle bus to Marigot several times daily)
Telephone: 590/87-3753
Fax: 590/87-3735
Reservations: Meridien Hotels, 800/543-4300
Credit Cards: All major cards
Rooms: 333 in all, plus 51 1-bedroom Marina Suites, all with marble bathrooms, satellite TV with remote, stocked mini-bars/refrigerators, direct-dial telephones, balconies or lanais; Marina Suites have complete kitchens
Meals: Breakfast 7:00–10:30, lunch noon–4:00, dinner 7:00–11:00 in 1 of 4 indoor/outdoor restaurants, plus a café at the marina and another restaurant in the hilltop sports complex; dinner from $55–$100 for 2; informal dress; live music (guitar, piano) in the main restaurant; full room service during dining-room hours, basket service after 11:00, extra charge
Entertainment: Live music every evening, somewhere on the property, disco on the hill
Spots: Lovely sheltered beach, 3 freshwater pools, 2 Jacuzzis, snorkeling gear, paddleboats, canoes, gymnasium, squash, racquetball, tennis (6 courts with lights, pro shop)—all free, except for use of lights on tennis courts; waterskiing, parasailing, wave runners, motorboats, horseback riding at extra charge

P.S.: Some business groups, lots of children at holidays; closed September. Meridien was just acquired by Forte Hotels, so some changes may be anticipated

Captain's Quarters
Saba

☆☆				♀				◑				S			
Atmosphere				**Dining**				**Sports**				**Rates**			

You get a quick tour of this extraordinary island on the way to the inn. Saba is higher than it is long: It goes up, up, and up to 2,900 feet within a sea-level distance of less than a mile. The largest village, Windwardside, is about halfway up, teetering on a ridge between two precipitous flanks of the volcano, one of which drops in a blanket of greenery almost vertically to the sea. It's a hugger-mugger hamlet of whitewashed walls, red tin roofs, cisterns, and family graves in the backyards, a few churches, lots of goats, and an air of charming, total detachment. Back in the 1800s, a retired sea captain (by tradition the Sabans are, not surprisingly, great sailors) built a little square whitewashed cottage with a red tin roof and gingerbread veranda, just as his ancestors and neighbors had done, right on the edge of the ravine. He was joined a few years later by the village doctor, who built yet another small white house next door, practically swamped by hibiscus and orchids and snowflake. Several years ago the two homes were integrated and converted into the Captain's Quarters inn.

Coming upon Captain's Quarters is like discovering a New England inn on top of a magic volcano. All rooms are doubles (some have four-poster beds, some, alas, have a third bed, not at all romantic), with plenty of welcome cross-ventilation, modern tiled bathrooms with hot water, and balconies with great views over the green cliffs to the sea—all renovated in 1994 and upgraded with TVs and mini-bars.

Meals are served in a brand-new cliffside restaurant; there's a pool perched on the edge of the ravine adjoining a sundeck, and a casual, shaded bar close at hand—and that's it. There's nothing to do here but relax and take great chugalugging gulps of fresh air. Maybe you'll hike up Mount Scenery, drive down to the Bottom (Saba's capital), or stroll through the winding streets of Windwardside. Divers have now discovered Saba in a big way, but most of the time you'll eat, have a rum punch in the sun, eat, snooze, take a dip in the pool, eat, make love.

Name: Captain's Quarters
Manager: Calvin Holm
Address: Windwardside, Saba, Netherlands Antilles
Location: At the top of the hill, $8 plus tip from airport or pier
Telephone: 599/46-2201
Fax: 599/46-2377
Reservations: Own U.S. office, 212/289-6031
Credit Cards: American Express, Discover, MasterCard, Visa
Rooms: 12, air-conditioning on request, showers, balconies, mini-bars, cable TV, in-room safes
Meals: Breakfast 7:30–9:30, lunch 11:30–2:00, dinner 6:30–9:00; informal dress (but bring along a jacket or sweater for the evening)
Entertainment: The other guests, library, parlor games, local disco on weekends
Sports: Tiny freshwater pool, tennis, hiking—all free; dive shops nearby
P.S.:   In winter, expect lots of day-trippers around lunchtime; closed in September

Willard's of Saba

Saba

☆☆☆			𝖸𝖸			●			$ $		
Atmosphere			**Dining**			**Sports**			**Rates**		

To find the highest hotel in the Kingdom of the Netherlands, take a Winair Twin Otter on the 20-minute flight from St. Maarten to Saba. The tiny Dutch island of Saba (all of 5 square miles) is that green volcanic peak leaping abruptly from the sea, straight up to 2,855 feet, its precipitous slopes dotted with tiny white cottages with red corrugated roofs. There's one main road—up one side, down the other—plus 1,064 concrete steps up through the ferns and mango trees to the peak of Mt. Scenery. Scuba divers come here for dramatic, uncrowded underwater trips, but regular visitors have been vacationing here for years for total seclusion, tranquility, and a chance to catch up on their reading and thinking.

Saba's brand-new inn, Willard's of Saba, doesn't just have the same name as the Washington, D.C., landmark—it was built by a great-grandson of Henry August Willard, who put his name on what was then the capital's top lodgings (and, in the process, gave us the word "lobbying"). This property comes on a much smaller scale, of course—no more than 14 guests at a time—but it has a more dramatic setting, 2,000 feet up (hence "the highest in the Kingdom of the Netherlands," as owner Will Willard puts it, since no part of Holland is higher than the Empire State Building).

From the hot tub or 20- by 40-foot pool, guests can look directly down the cliffside to the thrashing waters below or across the sea to seven neighboring islands. Three of the rooms (the most spacious, about 400 square feet) are in the main lodge, the remaining four are in cottages notched into the hillside. Surprisingly, given the location, they're among the most stylish lodgings of any small inn in the Caribbean—white on white color schemes, Tennessee ceramic tiles underfoot, furniture of Pacific Northwest cedar and heavy-duty rattan, original island paintings on the walls, ceiling fans overhead (at this altitude, who needs air-conditioning?)—all done with contemporary colors and flair.

Likewise the dining. Manager Corazon de Johnson s [*sic*] doubles as chef and brings the fine touches of her native Philippines to her eclectic cuisine (she happens to have degrees in nutrition, is a champion swimmer, and looks uncannily like diva Kiri Te Kanawa). Lucky guests of Willard's can spend their days lounging on the grand ocean liner–like deck around the pool, playing tennis on the inn's private court, toasting the sunset from the hot tub; then they'll sit down to an evening of Shanghai rolls with zosette sauce or breaded chicken *coujons* with red hot sauce, broiled red snapper with rainbow dressing, or chicken breast baked with a peach sauce and mozzarella cheese, followed by *maruya*—a special dessert of banana and local jackfruit wrapped in a crêpe, which is fried and served with homemade vanilla ice cream. Or, for something really exotic, a special lava-stone grill of shrimp, chicken, or beef cooked right at the table. The house wines are from the Bava vineyards in Italy.

How did all this sophistication happen to come to Saba? Willard, a retired lieutenant general in the Army Corps of Engineers, came to Saba 5 years ago, as so many others do, to dive the virgin waters. He loved the place so much, he bought a vertical acre of land (how they calculate an acre up here is something you can puzzle out in the hot tub) and applied his engineering savvy to constructing his mountain goat of an inn. If you're smart you'll book now before the word gets out and rates go up (inns on neighboring islands get well over $250 for what costs only $175 here).

It may not be appropriate for acrophobes and children, but Willard's of

Saba certainly adds a new dimension to this most unusual up-and-down island.

Name: Willard's of Saba
Manager: Corazon de Johnson s
Address: P.O. Box 515, Windwardside, Saba, Netherlands Antilles
Location: Away up there, about 20 minutes by taxi from the airport
Telephone: 599/46-2498
Fax: 599/46-2482
Reservations: Direct, or through Wilson's Dive at toll free 800/883-7222
Credit Cards: American Express, Discover, MasterCard, Visa
Rooms: 6 rooms and 1 suite, all with ceiling fans, ceramic tile floors, tiled bathrooms (showers only, some with bidets)—no phones, no TV ("but all the wiring's there")
Meals: Breakfast whenever, lunch noon–3:00, dinner 6:00–10:00 (approx. $36–$44 for 2); casual dress but "long trousers after dark—in any case you'd want long trousers and long sleeves at this altitude"); no room service
Entertainment: Taped jazz, conversation, small TV in bar, counting the offshore islands
Sports: Solar-heated lap pool, hot tub, tennis (1 court, no lights), hiking nearby—all free; diving can be arranged
P.S.: "We discourage children under 14 because of the location"; open all year

Other Choices

Alizéa Hotel

St. Martin

Named after the trade winds (*les alizés*) that regularly waft over from the bay, this amiable inn is located in the Mont Vernon section of St. Martin. Small condo complexes and a large first-class hotel are sprouting on the neighboring hillsides, but the shore is nonetheless magnificent—a mile-long curve of white sand abutting a sea that is a dozen shades of blue. Guests have their choice of 26 spacious rooms and apartments, the latter located in bungalows scattered up the hillside. The decor is tropical standard: tiled floors, new rattan furniture, and walls decorated with large, colorful murals. Whirring ceiling fans augment the breezes (air-conditioning is available), and the bathrooms have big shower stalls rather than tubs, but the best feature is the oversized balconies, with views of the seas, and fully equipped kitchenettes.

However, once you've dined in the restaurant you'll be hard-pressed to put your private kitchen to use. It's not the restaurant's setting (a breeze-cooled terrace with a peaked roof hung with eight paddle fans, and coral and canteloupe color scheme) nor the service (friendly but a tad hesitant) that has put Alizéa on the map—it's the food. To work off all those calories, you can sail, horseback ride, snorkel, windsurf, and play tennis or squash at the neighboring Le Meridien L'Habitation (above), a 5-minute taxi ride away. The nearest beach is a 10-minute stroll across a road and through a field—a great way to build an appetite for dinner. 26 rooms. Doubles: $173 to $252, winter 1994–95, including Continental breakfast. *Alizéa Hotel, 25 Mont Vernon, 97150 St. Martin, French West Indies. Telephone: 590/87-3342; fax: 590/87-4115.*

Privilege Resort & Spa

St. Martin

Here's an attractive hilltop alternative to the beachside Meridien complex on Anse Marcel. Privilege, the resort, is a new integral part of Privilege, the sports complex that's been around since the opening of the Meridien—tennis (six lit courts), fitness pavilion open to the breezes, racket ball (four courts), squash (two courts), pool, two restaurants, and a disco. Now there's also a fancy health spa for shiatsu, lymphatic drainage, hydro-jet massage, and various balneotherapy treatments. Crowning it all is this new 40-room hotel in plantation style with broad verandas and hardwood trim. All the rooms face the bay, the sea, and, unfortunately, the mustard-colored rooftops of the Meridiens. Guest rooms, in two two-story wings, are spacious (about 24 by 24 feet) and gracious, with lots of wicker and rattan, mini-bars, TVs, VCR, air-conditioning, ceiling fans, and electric window shutters for contemporary comforts. Verandas are furnished with steamship-style deck chairs that look so inviting I'd be tempted to ignore the spa and sports and just settle in with *Remembrance of Things Past*. The bathrooms come with tiled floors and hair dryers. Breakfast is served either on your veranda or on the terrace beside the small private pool, and there's room service for lunch and dinner, but otherwise you're sharing all the facilities here with guests from the Meridiens. The resort's manager (a charming Frenchwoman with the unlikely name of Scarlett Rac) has arranged beach privileges at a privately owned secluded beach, but to get there you'd need to drive over a dirt track for 10 or 15 minutes. If that sounds like too much trouble, there's also a shuttle bus to and from the Meridiens and their beach on Anse Marcel. But I suspect that most guests will merely think about going to the beach and instead while away their days up on their hilltop aerie. 40 rooms. Doubles: $350 to $530, winter 1994–95, with Continental breakfast. *Privilege Resort & Spa, Anse Marcel, 97150 St. Martin, French West Indies. Telephone: 590/87-3838; fax: 590/87-3838.*

Hotel L'Esplanade Caraïbe
St. Martin

Most of the overbuilding on this island has been churning out undistinguished structures that mar the landscape rather than fit in unobtrusively, but here's an exception. Decked around with hibiscus and bougainvillea just months after its early 1993 opening, L'Esplanade sits on a rise just outside the village of Grand Case, that culinary mecca, within walking distance of half-a-dozen of the island's best beaneries—and one of its prettiest beaches. The white-walled, red-roofed Mediterranean-style structure, all balustrades and pergolas and hardwood trim, houses just 24 rooms and suites, some duplex, all with kitchenettes, satellite TV, direct-dial telephones, air-conditioning and ceiling fans, and hair dryers. (Eleven new deluxe studios are planned for 1995.) Very comfortable. Balconies have stunning views of the sunset—and the new swimming pool with swim-up bar. 24 rooms and suites. Doubles: $190 to $260, winter 1994–95. *Hotel L'Esplanade Caraïbe, P.O. Box 5007, Grand Case, 97150 St. Martin, French West Indies. Telephone: 590/87-0655; fax: 590/87-2915.*

The Pasanggrahan Royal Inn
St. Maarten

There are not many authentic old West Indian guesthouses still in business, but this is one of them—so authentic its very name is Indonesian for "guesthouse." This is the West Indies as they were back in the days when London and Paris and, in this case, the Hague, had to build government lodgings for roving royalty and officials because there was no other place to put them up. Royalty doesn't stay here anymore, but you may find

yourselves downing rum punches in the company of publishers, art directors, executives, professors, and students, all with a common predilection
for a relaxed, informal atmosphere. Pasanggrahan is located on the cluttered main street in Philipsburg, between the street and the beach. It's a
pretty little oasis—with a deep white porch, potted plants, ceiling fans, and
an antique-filled lounge (but the rocking chairs have been replaced by
white plastic). Ahead of you, beyond the Dining Gallery, are the beach, the
bay, and the Garden Café—a cool jungle of knep trees and coconut palms,
almond and avocado trees. This is the most popular spot in the hotel by day,
particularly at teatime; after sundown, imbibers withdraw to the Evening
Bar with its four rattan stools, cowhide chairs, four-bladed fans. The original 12 guest rooms are in a two-story veranda-trimmed wing (known as the
West Wing) next to the Garden Café, screened from the beach by trees and
hanging plants. Probably the most romantic room is the Queen's Room
(21) on the second floor of the main house, up a private spiral stairway
wreathed with bougainvillea, a sort of tree house among the birds. There
are also six efficiency apartments in a two-story wing on the other side of the
Garden Café; these rooms are more comfortable (air-conditioned, too),
but the price you pay for the extra touches is that you're closer to the
garden. Despite the crowds and traffic on Front Street, Pasanggrahan
is quiet and relaxing. 32 rooms. Doubles: $118 to $160, winter 1994–95.
*The Pasanggrahan Royal Inn, P.O. Box 151, Philipsburg, St. Maarten, Nether-
lands Antilles. Telephone: 599/52-3588; fax: 599/52-2885. Reservations:
800/223-9815.*

The Old Gin House

St. Eustatius

"We wanted to build a small inn that had island flavor, but we also wanted
it to have good beds and good plumbing." So you'll find Sealy Pos-
turepedic mattresses, modern bathrooms, and hot water behind the warehouse doors and louver windows (all hand carved on the island). The
bedspreads and curtains were hand stitched by the women of the island,
the armoires hand carved by the men. Everything else is antique, mostly
French or Welsh, mostly 18th century "and violently anti-Victorian"—tea
chests, captain's trunks, and other pieces appropriate to a former trading
post. The first of the two inns, Old Gin House, consists of 6 guest rooms,
sitting directly above the beach and 14 rooms facing the pool and courtyard. All rooms have showers and individual water heaters. (Rooms 22 and
23, by the way, are the favorites of Holland's—and Statia's—Queen Beat-
rix.) Breakfast and lunch are served beachside, on a trellised terrace lined

with ferns and crotons, shaded by palm trees, cooled by the breezes off the beach. This is where *le tout* Statia gather—swimmers, snorkelers, scuba divers, expatriate Americans, crews from the sailboats in the bay. So many visitors gathered here that John May and his late partner, Marty Scofield, decided to produce a second dining room with island flavor, across the street in the tumbledown ruins of an old cotton-gin factory at the foot of the cliff. Evenings are passed in a leisurely, congenial manner in the raftered Publick House, sampling strawberry daiquiris or playing Scrabble in the library on the wooden gallery. Soft candlelight glows on hardwood shutters and sturdy beams and walls of bare brick that once served as ballast on sailing ships. Which is more pleasurable—the setting or the hearty dinner? Both. 20 rooms. Doubles: $115, winter 1994–95. *The Old Gin House, St. Eustatius, Netherlands Antilles. Telephone: 599/38-2319; fax: 559/38-2555.*

Juliana's

Saba

Instead of just trying to imagine what it would be like to snuggle up inside one of those enchanting Saban cottages, check into Flossie's Cottage, a green and white two roomer that's so reasonably priced you won't feel extravagant leaving the second bedroom undisturbed. There's an old stone oven in the master bedroom, and the cottage is full of island charm with latticework indoors and out. Three porches overlook Saban homes, including the Floral Cottage, one of the most painted and photographed places in Windwardside. Flossie's is part of a tiny complex called Juliana's, lovingly managed by its owners, a warmhearted couple who recently expanded their small bed-and-breakfast into 10 comfy, pine-paneled rooms with private balconies (some views are even better than those at Captain's Quarters, one street below). They may not have the charm of Flossie's Cottage, but these guest rooms are comfy, spotless, with contemporary decor and such thoughtful touches as candles and umbrellas. A small pool, light-fare restaurant, and recreation room are the only distractions. On land. Up here, anyway. You may find you have most of the place to yourself since many of the guests to this lofty aerie have come to the island to go diving down the deep spectacular Saba Wall. 10 rooms plus a 2½-room apartment and a 2-bedroom cottage. Doubles: $115 to $135, winter 1995–96. *Juliana's, Windwardside, Saba, Netherlands Antilles. Telephone: 599/46-2269; fax: 599/46-2389.*

The Queen's Leewards

Anguilla

St. Kitts

Nevis

Antigua

Barbuda

Montserrat

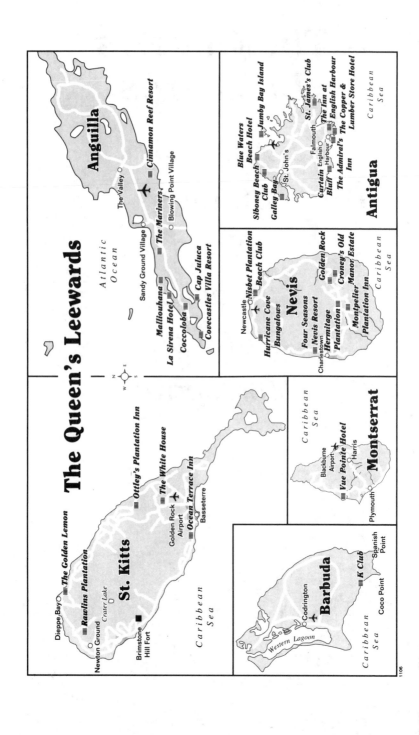

The Queen's Leewards

Anguilla

- Cinnamon Reef Resort
- The Mariners
- Blowing Point Village
- The Valley
- Sandy Ground Village
- Malliouhana
- La Sirena Hotel
- Coccoloba
- Cap Juluca
- Covecastles Villa Resort

Atlantic Ocean

Antigua

- Blue Waters Beach Hotel
- Jumby Bay Island
- St. James's Club
- The Inn at English Harbour
- The Admiral's Inn
- The Copper & Lumber Store Hotel
- Siboney Beach Club
- Galley Bay
- Curtain Bluff
- St. John's
- Falmouth
- English Harbour
- *Caribbean Sea*

St. Kitts

- The Golden Lemon
- Ottley's Plantation Inn
- The White House
- Ocean Terrace Inn
- Rawlins Plantation
- Dieppe Bay
- Newton Ground
- Crater Lake
- Golden Rock Airport
- Basseterre
- Brimstone Hill Fort
- *Caribbean Sea*

N
W—E
S

Nevis

- Nisbet Plantation Beach Club
- Golden Rock
- Croney's Old Manor Estate
- Montpelier Plantation Inn
- Hurricane Cove Bungalows
- Four Seasons Nevis Resort
- Hermitage Plantation
- Newcastle
- Charlestown
- *Caribbean Sea*

Montserrat

- Vue Pointe Hotel
- Blackburne Airport
- Harris
- Plymouth
- *Caribbean Sea*

Barbuda

- K Club
- Spanish Point
- Codrington
- Coco Point
- Western Lagoon
- *Caribbean Sea*

1106

The Queen's Leewards

The six islands that make up this group are, with one exception, former British islands that now owe allegiance to Queen Elizabeth as head of the Commonwealth. The exception is Anguilla, whose citizens decided to secede from the St. Kitts/Nevis partnership and remain a Crown Colony, governed more or less directly by London.

Antigua claims that lovers can spend a year on the island and visit a different beach each day. Maybe so, but once you see the beaches at, say, Half Moon or Curtain Bluff, you'll wave good-bye to the others. Most of the tourist resorts are in the northwest, vaguely between the airport and St. John's, the capital; with the exception of Blue Waters and the offshore Jumby Bay, all the hideaways in this guide are toward the *south* of the island, where the country is lusher, the hills higher (all the way to 1,319 feet at the curiously named Boggy Peak), and picturesque English Harbour fairly oozes with memories of those dashing young 18th-century officers about town, Commander Horatio Nelson and Prince William Henry, duke of Clarence. Apart from Nelson's Dockyard and Shirley Heights, forget the sightseeing; enjoy the beaches, even if you don't make it to all 365 of them.

St. Kitts, alias St. Christopher, may not be the most gorgeous island in the Caribbean and you have probably seen more romantic beaches; the central part has been developed (hotel, condos, golf, casino) for a mass tourism that has yet to mass, but the mountainous western half is authentic Caribbean, with foothills of sugarcane, narrow coast-hugging roads, huddled villages. Two attractions worth the bumpy drives: the spectacular fort perched on Brimstone Hill (take a picnic) and Romney Manor, a batik workshop in a lovely old plantation house.

Nevis—now there's a fabulous little island. Slightly mystical, slightly spooky, with centuries-old plantations, tumbledown hamlets, rain forests, a mountain with its head in the clouds (hence Columbus's designation—*nieves*, or snow). Alexander Hamilton was born here, the illegitimate son of a Scottish planter (his restored home is now a museum); Fanny Nisbet lived here with her husband until he died, and she was later wooed, won, and wed by Nelson in the parish of Fig Tree. If they returned for a reunion, they'd find their island hadn't changed all that much—people still seek solace in the mineral baths where England's aristocracy came to frolic.

Anguilla is set apart from the others by geography as well as politics. It's just to the north of St. Martin, a 20-minute ferryboat ride from Marigot. It's long and flat and physically as undistinguished as the eel for which it's named, but if you want beautiful beaches, here are beautiful beaches. And unaggressive, friendly people. In the past several years, a few new hotels have made people sit up and take notice. But Anguilla is a long, long way from being overdeveloped or crowded or spoiled—although there are now six traffic lights on the island and a smart new bungalow-size terminal at the airport.

Montserrat, 15 minutes by air southwest of Antigua, is one of the least visited of the Antilles—yet it's one of the lushest and prettiest, with its steep hills and dales, glens and glades. Some people compare it to Ireland (early settlers were Irish and the shamrock is the island's emblem). They wish. If Montserrat had beaches as beautiful as those in Ireland, we might have heard more of Montserrat.

How to Get There   For Antigua, American, BWIA, and Continental from New York; by American and LIAT from San Juan; by Air Canada and BWIA from Toronto. For St. Kitts, connecting flights from San Juan (American Eagle and LIAT), St. Maarten (LIAT or Windward), or Antigua (LIAT). For Nevis, the computers will tell you via Antigua and LIAT, but since connecting times are not always convenient it's worthwhile to look at other possibilities from St. Maarten and St. Kitts. Most inns on Nevis will recommend a seat on a shared charter on Carib Aviation. It costs a few dollars more, but it can save a lot of time and anguish, and the inn can probably make all the arrangements. There is also ferryboat service between St. Kitts and Nevis, a 1-hour trip and a lot of fun, but the airline and ferry schedules rarely mesh. Guests of the Four Seasons, of course, have their own luxury launches between St. Kitts and the resort.

For Anguilla, the most convenient way these days seems to be the twice daily nonstop flights (40 minutes) from San Juan on American Eagle; the alternative is St. Maarten, with connecting flights (10 minutes) on Windward or a shared charter on Tyden Airways (your resort can arrange this). There is also ferryboat service 12 times a day between Anguilla and Marigot (on the French side)—again, a fun way to go but inconvenient if you have more than light carry-on luggage.

For information on Antigua and Barbuda, call 212/541-4117; Anguilla, 800/553-4939; St. Kitts and Nevis, 800/582-6208; Montserrat, 516/425-0901.

༺ 𝛼 ༻

Malliouhana

Anguilla

Atmosphere

Dining

Sports

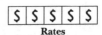
Rates

When I first saw Anguilla's Mead Point in the early 1980s, it was a craggy coral headland flanked by two dream beaches—one a cove, one a ribbon of white sand—where "someone was planning to build a luxury hotel more beautiful than La Samanna." Ho-hum. How many times had we heard that over the years?

The next time I went there, someone was building a hotel. The stark headland was now a stark construction site, and during my tour of the cinder blocks and piled pipes, I met a young couple who had come over for the day from La Samanna just to see this new place they'd heard about. They were so impressed they left behind a $1,000 deposit for the following February, for a room that didn't exist in a hotel yet to be built. I knew then that I was present at the birth of a legend.

From the day it finally formally opened in November 1984, people have clamored to get a room at Malliouhana. And most of the people who go there book on the spot for the following year. And who wouldn't want to return as often as possible to Malliouhana's delights? Thirty flowery acres with royal palms for shade, sea bean for greenery, purple and yellow allamanda for splashes of color, night-blooming jasmine for fragrance. Two beaches, one almost a mile long, the other a secluded cove, both with beach bars and loungers (the hotel assigns eight members of the staff just to look after two beaches!). A 30,000-bottle wine cellar, a kitchen headed by a Michelin two-star chef from Paris. Villas whose bathrooms rival other hotels' *bed*rooms for size and appointments.

Step into the grand open-sided atrium lobby with its arched galleries and imposing paintings by Haiti's Jasmin Joseph and you feel like you're in a sort of Caribbean château. Settle into the plethora of pillows in the lounge's plump banquettes and admire the intricate raw-silk tapestries and hand-carved wooden figurines (mostly lions in honor of owner/manager Leon Roydon). The playground just beyond is a stunning landscape rather than a multi-level swimming pool.

The Roydons, *père et fils*, on the spot day and night keeping an eye on things, have pulled out all the stops for their guests. Guest rooms are a carefree, non-bed-bumping 20 by 18 feet (a couple of feet larger in the villas) with decks only a few feet smaller. Interiors were designed by the esteemed Larry Peabody, with the same sensuous ambience he contrived for the much-lamented Habitation LeClerc in Haiti. Filtered sunbeams dapple hardwood louvers and quarry tile floors. Blossomy vines spill in profusion over balcony balustrades. Soft indirect lighting transforms lush planters and leafy ficus into mini-Edens. It's an atmosphere calculated to induce instant indolence. In addition, each villa comes with its own service pantry, a godsend for those of us who enjoy dawdly bathrobe breakfasts on the balcony, attended by not one but two maids—the first to set up the table and flowers, the other to serve piping hot croissants and pour freshly brewed tea. Granted, such a breakfast will set you back a tidy sum, but think what it does to set you up for another day of dallying.

Interiors are basically the same throughout the hotel, but location may make a minor difference. Assuming you have a choice (which might mean going in, say, June or July), rooms 109, 209, 110, and 210 would be my choices, although Leon Roydon's favorite is 101, above the bar but with a particularly large balcony. The most popular villas are those on the cliff beyond the pool, for the view; room 300 has its own Jacuzzi; the two directly on Mead's Bay are for people who are water sprites. I spent time in a Garden Villa (i.e., looking at the hotel rather than the sea but surrounded by flowers) and didn't feel deprived in the slightest. The newest (1990) accommodations are six enormous two-terrace Junior Suites on the bluff above the cove—quiet and secluded, but that much farther from the dining room and tennis courts ("farther"—all of 3 minutes' stroll).

Many people travel much more than 3 minutes, of course, to dine here (if they can get a reservation), for the terrace restaurant is one of the undoubted lures of Malliouhana. Again, Leon Roydon wanted the best, and since one of his longtime friends was none other than the late Jo Rostang of the Michelin two-star La Bonne Auberge in Antibes, he invited him to direct the Malliouhana kitchen. Now Rostang's son Michel supervises the kitchen and cuisine. Anguilla is no Riviera with an infinite supply of fresh produce, but given the shortcomings of a Caribbean island, the Rostang corps do a commendable job of creating an Antillean Antibes. The setting helps immensely: an open fan-shaped pavilion above a sparkling sea, a hardwood canopy rising over giant ginger and stephanotis trees, with that final touch of civilized well-being—the pleasures of a well-endowed wine list (up to $400, but most are in the $25 to $35 range), the product of Leon Roydon's longstanding oenophilia.

All of which may make dining at Malliouhana sound like a stuffy activity. Far from it. The cuisine may be French, the china Limoges, the crystal French, and the cutlery Christophle, but the guests are as casually, but stylishly, dressed as they would be in St. Tropez. And the resort as a whole is as sports oriented as it now is luxurious—and now almost all the sporting activities are available at no extra charge. A recent addition is a children's playground, complete with seesaw, sandbox, and a one-on-one basketball court. Including the smart new gymnasium/exercise pavilion above the beach, its walls open to the sea and sky. You'd expect to find a place like this on the French Riviera, but on an unspoiled Caribbean backwater such as Anguilla, it's a marvel.

Name: Malliouhana

Owners/Managers: Leon and Nigel Roydon

Address: P.O. Box 173, Anguilla, British West Indies

Location: On Mead's Bay, on the northeast shore of the island, about 10 minutes and $14 by taxi from the airstrip, 6 or 7 minutes and $12 from the ferryboat pier at Blowing Point

Telephone: 809/497-6111

Fax: 809/497-6011

Reservations: Direct, 800/835-0796

Credit Cards: None

Rooms: 34 rooms, plus 18 1- or 2-bedroom suites, in the main building or villas, overlooking beach or garden, all with ceiling fans (all but 3 of the villas have air-conditioning), balconies and/or lanais, stocked mini-bars with ice makers, telephones

Meals: Breakfast anytime in your room, lunch 12:30–3:00, dinner 7:00–10:30 (approx. $90 to $100 for 2), served in the breeze-cooled dining terrace above the sea, also, lunchtime snacks in a new beach bar for hotel guests only; informal but stylish dress; room service 7:30 a.m.–11:00 p.m. (special menu)

Entertainment: Elegant bar/lounge, 2 television rooms (cable and video), library, backgammon, chess, cribbage

Sports: 2 beautiful beaches (1 long and public, 1 virtually private cove, both with beach bars, good swimming and snorkeling), 2 freshwater pools (chlorine free but not for laps), heated Jacuzzi, tennis (4 courts, Peter Burwash pro, lights), Sunfish and catamaran sailing, windsurfing, waterskiing, exercise room (Nautilus devices, Aerobicycles, weights), trips to adjoining islets, supervised children's playground—all free; massage, scuba diving, 35-foot powerboat for fishing available on the premises at extra charge

P.S.: 1-week minimum stay in season; some kids; closed September and October

Cinnamon Reef Resort
Anguilla

Atmosphere

Dining

Sports

Rates

Take your pick: beach or bluff—either way you'll wallow in spacious surroundings at Cinnamon Reef's 40 beachside acres. Most of them in individual bungalows, they're suites rather than rooms, all with big patios and dressing rooms. Half of them are set beside the beach, the remainder on a bluff on the far side of the clubhouse. Otherwise, all the suites are identical, with those lovely big patios, loungers, ceiling fans, sitting areas with sofas and coffee tables, king-size or two double beds, and tiled sunken shower stalls (no baths), all recently redecorated.

Architecturally, the Cinnamon style is eclectic, white poured concrete that falls somewhere between Cinder-block Traditional and Mediterranean Fanciful, all arches and portholes and cathedral doors. Patios are shaded by arbors draped with wood rose and bougainvillea. The "clubhouse" (there's no significance to the word *club*) is a long, white arched temple abutting the bay, open to the trade winds (but with electric-powered windows for those occasions when the breezes are too stiff), Italian tiled floors, pine and wicker and bamboo and canvas furnishings.

Pleasant setting, pleasant dining. Chefs Zeff Bonsey and Vernon Hughes have turned their Palm Court into one of Anguilla's most talked-about restaurants, with their "New Caribbean" cuisine—island grouper with banana rum sauce, breast of duck with pineapple ginger confit, mango puffs with caramel sauce. There's entertainment (delightful, not obtrusive) most evenings by one of several local bands. Across the courtyard, the cavernous but well-disguised cistern provides an elevated foundation for the hotel's playground—a 40-by-60-foot pool, a snack bar, two tennis courts, and a new Jacuzzi in the poolside gazebo.

It's a shame that on an island with so many beautiful beaches, Cinnamon Reef has to make do with a modest curve of sand at the end of a pondlike harbor; on the other hand, the reef creates a lagoon-smooth bay and is one of the safest spots on the island for sailing and windsurfing.

Name: Cinnamon Reef Resort
Owners/Managers: Carol and Richard Hauser

Address: Little Harbour, Anguilla, British West Indies

Location: On the south coast, at Little Harbour, 5 minutes and $8 by taxi from the airstrip and $10 for the ferryboat dock

Telephone: 809/497-2727

Fax: 809/497-2727

Reservations: Direct, 800/346-7084

Credit Cards: American Express, MasterCard, Visa

Rooms: 14 bungalows and 8 suites, all with spacious bathrooms, ceiling fans, stocked mini-bars, telephones, hair dryers, patios, hammocks

Meals: Breakfast 8:00–10:30, lunch noon–2:30 in the main dining room, pool bar, or courtyard, afternoon tea 4:00, dinner 7:00–9:30 (approx. $70–$80 for 2), "long trousers for gentlemen in the dining room" in the evening; room service 8:00 a.m.–11 p.m.

Entertainment: Taped music, live music ("that is, evenings the musicians show up"); backgammon, chess, Scrabble, dominoes, and Chinese checkers

Sports: Beach, 2 Deco-turf tennis courts, freshwater pool, Jacuzzi, windsurfing, Sunfish sailing, sailboats, paddleboats, floats, snorkeling, fishing gear—all free; island tours, sails, and picnic lunches can be arranged

P.S.: No children under 12 during peak season; closed September and October

Cap Juluca

Anguilla

Atmosphere

Dining

Sports

Rates

Let's start with the bathrooms: tubs for two, with headrests and Italian porcelain faucets, separated by a wall of glass from an *intime* sunbathing patio; floors and walls are marble, doors are louvered Brazilian hardwood, the walk-in closets could accommodate Elizabeth Taylor's wardrobe with hangers to spare (well, her swimsuits, anyway); dimmer lights and ceiling fans add just the right romantic touch.

Granted, not all the rooms and suites have the double tubs and patios, but even the few with only showers stand out from the crowd. Just as the resort itself is unique. Cap Juluca is located on the leeward side of the island, on a heart-stoppingly beautiful mile of white sandy beach called Maundys Bay, with Cove Bay, another mile or so of sand, on the other side of a low headland; 179 acres of land and lagoon surround the guests and hold the world at bay. The distinctive architecture is a sort of Moorish-Patmos-Xanadu, a series of whitewashed one-story and two-story villas with domes and cupolas, arches and pseudoparapets peeping through the palms and wispy casuarinas. If you think it's all very beautiful by day, wait until you see how ravishing it can be after dark when soft lights add their flicks of magic. And if you think *that's* ravishing, time your trip to coincide with a full moon and you'll think you've finally escaped this world.

The resort has been abuilding since 1988, but Cap Juluca is finally in its final form, with the addition of six new pool villas (each with three bedrooms or five bedrooms grouped around a walled garden and secluded pool); a beachside playground with swimming pool, bar/café, and shrub-screened tanning areas; and the "great house" with its stunningly hand-decorated media room and library.

Last time around, I stayed in pool villa number 5, or rather one suite thereof, a 1,540-square-foot expanse with a skylighted circular dining nook, a spacious living room with a wall of folding hardwood louvers, an equally spacious bedroom with shuttered doors leading to a large, shaded terrace. I lost track of the light switches. But even if I never stay in anything grander than one of the original rooms (a mere 790 square feet), I'll never feel deprived because they are so exquisitely decorated: banquettes piled high with pillows, antique Moroccan wedding belts, and saddlebags artfully framed. Walls of louvered shutters lead to enormous patios with arches framing a dazzle of flowers and hammocks slung between the sea-grape trees. Each group of rooms and suites comes with its own maids' pantry, where your breakfast is prepared to order every morning, then brought to your room by not one but two maids: one to set the table with linen and silverware, the other to set out the fruits and juices and freshly baked croissants.

Service with a capital S is, of course, a major enticement of a swank resort like Cap Juluca, and with two staffers per room, this one can offer service well above the Caribbean norm. Among the flourishes: having the taxi take you straight to your room (a boon for couples on secret trysts); settling bills in your room rather than in the lobby (this way you can swoon when you read the total without embarrassing everyone); pre-check-in of luggage and tickets at the airports on St. Maarten or Anguilla, which gives you an extra hour of sunning rather than standing in line—and well worth the extra fee; when you're sprawled out on the beach and feel like a drink, just poke a red flag into the sand and a roving bartender will come and take your order.

And just when you think there's nothing else the good people at Cap Juluca can do to fill a vacation with romance, you walk back along the beachside path after dinner at Pimm's, past gardens fragrant with jasmine and frangipani, open the door to your suite, and find that the maid has not only turned down the bed but turned down the lights—*and* lit the candles in the storm lanterns. The world is suffused with magic. Candlelight flickers on red tiles and antiques. Beyond the louvered hardwood shutters, the surf sighs and the moon silvers the sea.

Name: Cap Juluca

Manager: Brian Young

Address: P.O. Box 240, Maundy's Bay, Anguilla, British West Indies

Location: On the leeward coast, about 15 minutes and $18 by taxi from the airport, $16 from the ferryboat dock (the resort has someone at the airport to meet you; on the way out, for a fee, you can have the resort check your bags and get your boarding pass in advance)

Telephone: 809/497-6666

Fax: 809/497-6617

Reservations: Own office, 800/323-0139 or 212/425-4684

Credit Cards: American Express

Rooms: 75 rooms, 13 suites in several 1-story and 2-story villas strung out along the edge of the beach, all with marble bathrooms (some with showers only, hair dryers, bathrobes), covered terraces or patios, hammocks and loungers, stocked refrigerators/ice makers, air-conditioning and ceiling fans, direct-dial telephones; some with kitchens; some suites with private or semiprivate plunge pools

Meals: Breakfast served in villa at any time after 7:30, lunch noon–2:30, snacks 11:00–7:00, dinner 7:30–10:00 in one of 3 restaurants (approx. $70–$80 for 2 in Pimm's); informal dress but generally stylish; some live music for dancing; room service 8:00 a.m.–10:00 p.m., extra charge

Entertainment: Chatterton's Bar, live music several evenings a week, media room, library/games room

Sports: 2 miles of beach, snorkeling gear, windsurfing, waterskiing, sailing, croquet, tennis (3 courts, lights, pro), state-of-the-art fitness center—all free; other water sports nearby

P.S.: Children age 6 and over during high season; open all year

Coccoloba

Anguilla

☆☆				
Atmosphere				

Dining   **Sports**   **Rates**

If what you have in mind is a quiet unspoiled island and a quiet small resort where you can lounge on a patio a few paces from a beautiful beach and a beckoning sea, this may be the answer. It's located on a low coral headland between two postcard-pretty beaches, with the main lodge perched on the promontory and the guest rooms in cottages arranged in a series of Vs stretching along the bluff above the beach.

The peak-roofed main lodge may look more like the chapel in the valley than a rejuvenating resort, but the dining terrace has a superb view of endless sea. The revamped guest rooms have a modified split-level layout, with a sitting area up front, double beds and dresser at the rear. There are lots of nice touches here: bathrooms stacked with fluffy white towels and bathrobes, shower stalls with lots of shelves for soaps and shampoos from the amenities tray, refrigerators stocked with goodies on the house (you pay only to have the items restocked). Because of the V-type setup of the layout, some of the rooms are less desirable than others, as their arbor-decked patios are too close to the footpath. Ask for one of the following rooms: 106 through 111, 115, 117, 121, 122, 124, or 125—all set back from the path but still with sea views. There are also seven rooms in a two-story villa known as the Residence, at the far end of the beach, some with very generous balconies or patios; there's also a second swimming pool here, one floor up.

Name: Coccoloba
Manager: Sergei Terenzi
Address: P.O. Box 332, Barnes Bay, Anguilla, British West Indies
Location: Between Barnes Bay and Meads Bay, 20 minutes from the ferry or airport (by taxi, $10 from ferry and $15 from airport); the hotel will help you arrange flights by small plane to Anguilla from San Juan or St. Maarten
Telephone: 809/497-6871
Fax: 809/497-6332
Reservations: Direct, 800/982-7729

Credit Cards: American Express, MasterCard, Visa

Rooms: 51 rooms, including 2 suites, most of them in beachside cottages, except for 7 in a beachside villa; each with sea view (some more so than others), patio, sitting area, 2 double beds, bathrobes, stocked refrigerator, air-conditioning, direct-dial telephone, ceiling fans, hair dryer, wall safe, walking cane, and umbrella

Meals: Early-morning coffee 7:00–8:00, breakfast 8:00–10:00, poolside lunch 12:30–2:30, afternoon tea 4:00–5:00, dinner 7:00–9:30 ("reservations, please") in the indoor-outdoor pavilion; 4-course dinner (approx. $80 for 2); informal dress; room service for Continental breakfast only; West Indian buffet once a week; some background music (mostly classical tapes)

Entertainment: Live music in the lounge-bar three times a week; library, game room with backgammon, chess, etc.; TV/VCR lounge

Sports: 2 beaches (each about a mile long), large L-shaped pool with swim-up bar (second pool atop the Residence), exercise room, massage, sun floats, tennis (2 lit courts, ball machine), snorkeling and fishing gear, windsurfing, Sunfish sailing—all free; other water sports and sailboat trips to outlying islands can be arranged

P.S.:   Some children; open all year

La Sirena Hotel
Anguilla

☆ ☆		♀		◉		$ $	
Atmosphere		**Dining**		**Sports**		**Rates**	

It may not have the cachet of Malliouhana or Cap Juluca—neighbors that are two of the classiest, most expensive resorts in the Caribbean—but this small, friendly hotel has other charms. First of all, with a room rate of just less than $300 a night, it's much easier on the pocketbook. Second, many couples seeking to get away from it all may actually prefer the casual, more relaxed beach ambience of La Sirena. You don't have to worry about staining the chair cushions with suntan lotion, and the rooms, each with a balcony or patio, are spacious enough to function as comfortable retreats. Best of all, the beach—a mile-long, half-deserted, glistening white strand—

is only a 2-minute stroll away. It's the same beach used by high-paying guests at Malliouhana, and to get to it, all you have to do is stroll a hundred yards down the hill, past a scattering of private homes.

The three-story hotel rises above a spread of lawns, gardens, and a large swimming pool; stone pathways lead through the gardens to the three villas, a Jacuzzi, and a second, more secluded pool. The Spanish-Mediterranean architecture—white walls and arches, wooden balconies, ochre-tiled roofs—is complemented inside by a decorating scheme of wicker and terra-cotta tile floors.

Each of the 20 guest rooms in the hotel has a mini-bar concealed in a light wicker chest, a bed with an arched wicker headboard, and contemporary accoutrements such as a floor lamp and a clock radio. The balcony or patio is furnished with a canvas deck chair and a table. The bathrooms have large tiled showers and fine toiletries. Only the closets are a bit skimpy; the Swiss owners must assume that their guests travel light.

For the best views and highest ceilings, reserve a room on the upper floors; two of the rooms on the third floor have wraparound views and lead to a roof terrace. Those seeking absolute privacy and more space should check out one of the three villas, two with two bedrooms and one with three bedrooms. Each costs about the same as a single room at many of the more exclusive resorts.

True, the dining room is uninspired. However, since meals are optional, if you want to dine in style I suggest you head for the more elegant dining rooms at Malliouhana and Cap Juluca. The lower room rate you're paying at La Sirena will enable you to splurge at the dining table without guilt.

Name: La Sirena Hotel

Manager: Rolf Masshardt

Address: P.O. Box 200, Mead's Bay, Anguilla, British West Indies

Location: On mile-long Mead's Bay, 10 minutes and $15 by taxi from the airport

Telephone: 809/497-6827

Fax: 809/497-6829

Reservations: International Travel & Resorts, Inc.

Credit Cards: American Express, MasterCard, Visa

Rooms: 20, all with balcony with deck chair, tile floors, telephone, clock/radio, ceiling fans, hair dryers, mini-bars; plus 3 villas

Meals: Breakfast, lunch, dinner (in dining room, approx. $70–$80 for 2); casual dress; villas have kitchens and barbecue equipment; no room service

Entertainment: Barbecue dinner with live music on Mondays, local folkloric group on Thursdays, taped music in bar-lounge, cable television, videos for rent

Sports: 2 freshwater pools; tennis, waterskiing, windsurfing, day trips to adjoining islands available

P.S.: Some children, especially on weekends; open all year

The Golden Lemon
St. Kitts

Atmosphere

Dining

Sports

Rates

Take a 17th-century French manor house, in a walled garden beside a grove of coconut palms, and fill it with antiques and bric-a-brac. Paint the exterior a bright lemon yellow, tuck a pool into a corner of the leafy garden, and you'll have a handsome country inn in the tropics.

But you still wouldn't have the legendary Golden Lemon.

The Golden Lemon is, indeed, all of these things—a 17th-century manor of volcanic stone with a wood-framed upper floor, an 18th-century addition, surrounded by a gallery with a wide-plank floor. From the gallery you look out to unspoiled Caribbean—a reef, a lagoon, a beach of black sand, and the palm trees, tall and spindly and well into their second century. In the walled garden, loungers invite guests to relax among the trees, and white tables and chairs set on the arcade beneath the gallery beckon for a punch or lunch. All very romantic for escapists who want to savor authentic Antillean surroundings (the inn is located at the end of a narrow street in a simple fishing village). But there's more to the Golden Lemon than that.

It was the old manor's good fortune to be spotted by a connoisseur with a sharp eye who could recognize the house's thoroughbred qualities in its then dilapidated state. At the time, Arthur Leaman was an editor with *House & Garden* magazine who also happened to be an avid collector with an eclectic array of antiques—four-poster beds, mahogany tables, blue delft tulipieres from Holland, clocks from Italy.

Leaman has an extraordinary and enviable ability of taking a castoff and, by deft juxtaposition or downright alchemy, turning it into an heirloom. Each room at the Lemon is different, each a masterpiece of composition and color (I have a hunch that if you stood on your head in one of the rooms here you'd still have a picture-perfect interior). I can never decide which is my favorite—the Hibiscus Room with its two white canopy beds, the Batik Room with steps up to the big antique double beds, the Victorian Room for its ornamentation, the Turtle Room for its carapaceous doodads. Every detail reflects Leaman's refined sense of style, so much so that you're so busy admiring the grace notes in the bathrooms you don't even notice you're stepping into a prefab plastic shower stall. Rooms on the upper floor, it should be noted, are wood framed and not infallibly soundproof, but your compensation for keeping your voices down or overhearing extraneous sounds is breakfast on the gallery. First the maid announces its arrival by the sounds of a table being set with a trayful of playful lemon-motif mugs and plates; then she returns with pewter dishes of homemade preserves, perfectly browned toast, perfectly timed scrambled eggs, a thermos of coffee—all served course by course. It gets your day off to a very slow, very stylish start—just the way life should be at the Golden Lemon.

For guests who want more substantial accommodations, there are newer wings of duplex one- and two-bedroom villas across the garden, beside the volcanic shore—some with decks overhanging the sea, most of them with small private pools. The interiors, needless to say, are exquisite: some with canopy beds, some with bull's-eye orrery windows that dapple sunlight on the ceramic tile floors. The prices are extravagant at first glance, but, considering the setting and surroundings, not outlandish.

Evenings have always been special at the Golden Lemon. For one thing, the walled garden setting out front and the junglelike garden at the rear become quite magical with soft lighting and soft breezes. The antique-filled dining room sparkles in the soft light of candelabra and chandeliers. Traditionally Arthur Leaman hosts a sort of captain's table, but tables are also set for twos and fours, with guests rotated so that everyone has a chance to mix, if that's what they want. But his patrician presence and wit still turn evenings into house parties. Especially since the guests next to you in the bar may be paying their 20th visit in 20 years. Dinner is a fixed menu, with the inn's cooks always coming up with something to look forward to; but repeat guests know to rev up the taste buds for Sunday brunch and the inn's West Indies rum beef stew, liberally laced with Mount Gay.

The Golden Lemon, let me quickly add, is not for everyone. Its devotees are mostly designers and writers, young Californians, young Washingtonians, people in the theater. Gracious Arthur Leaman may be, but he doesn't want his inn (and the solitude of his guests) disturbed by cruise ship passengers. And because, he claims, "you can take only so much of paradise," no one is allowed to stay longer than 2 weeks.

Name: The Golden Lemon
Owner/Manager: Arthur Leaman

Address: Dieppe Bay Town, St. Kitts, St. Kitts and Nevis, West Indies

Location: In the village of Dieppe Bay Town, on the northeast coast, about 30 minutes and $28 by taxi from the airport (let the hotel know when you're arriving and they'll arrange for a dependable driver to meet you)

Telephone: 809/465-7260, 800/633-7411

Fax: 809/465-4019

Reservations: Caribbean Inns Ltd.

Credit Cards: American Express, Diners Club, MasterCard, Visa (personal checks accepted)

Rooms: 8, in 2 buildings, all with private bathrooms, ceiling fans, balconies or patios; kitchens in the 16 new condo units, 2 sharing 1 pool, the others with private pools

Meals: Breakfast 7:30–10:00, lunch noon–3:00 in the patio, afternoon tea 4:00 ("real tea, *not* bags"), dinner 7:00–9:00 ($50–$70 for 2, in the fan-cooled main dining room); informal dress ("no wet bathing suits at lunch"); room service, no extra charge

Entertainment: The bar (occasionally with live piano music), quiet taped music, backgammon, parlor games

Sports: Beach, 20- by 40-foot freshwater pool (plus private pools in the villas), tennis court, snorkeling gear, "tremendous reef"—free

P.S.:   "No young people under 18"; stays limited to 4-night minimum, 2-week maximum

Rawlins Plantation

St. Kitts

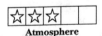
Atmosphere

Dining

Sports

Rates

Don't be put off by the bumpy, hilly dirt road that meanders through the fields of sugarcane. Granted, 260 acres of the sweet stuff are hardly a romantic introduction to a hideaway, but press on up the hill and around one last bend and you arrive at a 12-acre oasis of clipped lawns and clumps of croton, breadfruit, and African tulip trees. Up ahead, the cane fields rise to the foothills of forest-clad Mount Misery; behind you, the fields fall off to the sea and distant views of St. Eustatius.

At 350 feet above the sea, Rawlins is exactly the sort of cool, calm place you relish returning to after a sticky day at the beach or a hike through the rain-forest foothills beneath canopies of trailing vines and wild orchids. Some guests actually make it all the way up to the peak, 4,000 feet above the sea, where Misery must seem like cloud nine. The Rawsons will arrange picnic outings up the mountain, part of the way by Jeep, the rest on foot, fortified by their special rum punch. They've also flattened a corner of their lawn into that rarity—a grass tennis court.

But essentially, this is an inn for relaxing. You'd never get me near the beach or up a hill. Sit on a picket-fenced porch and read a hefty book. Dunk in the spring-fed pool that was once the mill's cistern. Sit on the veranda of the great house at sundown, gin and tonic in hand, and chat with fellow guests or simply dream sundown dreams. Check out the library. Watch the sunset's glow on Statia. Listen to the birds and tree frogs. This is what people have in mind when they dream about a place to unwind, really unwind.

The inn still looks like a gentleman's plantation—white great house at the center, cottages for managers and overseers in the gardens, a white lattice gazebo beside the pool. The circular stone base of the 17th-century windmill is now a duplex suite, much favored by honeymooners—pretty red and white sitting room downstairs, white cast-iron double bed upstairs; another pink and pretty suite has a king-size bed, and semisunken bathroom with semisunken tiled bath. The remaining guest rooms reflect the ambience of colonial times, with mahogany floors and rush rugs rather than fitted carpet, ceiling fans rather than air-conditioning, wicker and rattan rather than leather, mosquito nets for decoration rather than protection. It's very tasteful and low-key. No television, no telephones. Plumbing and electricity are the sole concessions to the 20th century.

The former boiling room, where the cane was converted to molasses, is now a flower-draped, stone-floored patio where guests gather for drinks before moving to the new indoor/outdoor dining salon. Dining has always been especially pleasurable here. Rawlins has never promised "the finest Continental cuisine" or any of the fatuous claims of some island inns. What Claire Rawson and her local cook serve are perfectly prepared local dishes with their own local embellishments and Claire's "lightly French accent." Thus, guests gathered on the veranda can wile away sun-dappled noondays while nibbling on flying-fish fritters, rice with akee and dill, soups (breadfruit, eggplant, or cucumber with fresh mint), curries garnished with garden-fresh avocados and papaws. In the evening, candles sparkle on gold and white Royal Doulton and servings of, say, crab and callaloo soup, St. Kitts shrimp with orange butter, roast lamb with mango sauce, and, for dessert, bananas in puff pastry with local mountain oranges.

Between them, Rawlins and Golden Lemon have created a haven for the lovers of fine food who wend their way to this unspoiled corner of the Caribbean year after year—Rockefellers, Cabots, Rothschilds, peers of the realm, doctors and lawyers and writers.

Name: Rawlins Plantation

Owners/Managers: Paul and Claire Rawson

Address: P.O. Box 340, St. Kitts, West Indies

Location: At Mt. Pleasant Estate, near Dieppe Bay Town; directly across the island from the airport, about 30 minutes and $28 by taxi (let the Rawsons know when you'll arrive and they'll send a driver to meet you, "probably Dash, who'll wait forever in case your flight is late")

Telephone: 809/465-6221

Fax: 809/465-4954

Reservations: JDB Associates

Credit Cards: American Express, MasterCard, Visa

Rooms: 10, in various cottages, including the Sugar Mill Suite and 1 2-bedroom cottage with 2 sitting rooms, all with breezes and ceiling fans, private bathrooms, hair dryers, balconies or patios

Meals: Breakfast from 8:00 on, buffet lunch 1:00–2:00 on the veranda, afternoon tea 4:00, dinner at 8:00 (approx. $70 for 2, fixed menu, in the dining room); informal dress, but no shorts; room service for breakfast only, no extra charge

Entertainment: "Good conversation," parlor games, library with more reading material than you can handle on a single vacation

Sports: Small spring-fed pool, croquet, tennis (1 grass court, cramped, no lights), snorkeling gear—free; full-day cruises on catamaran to Nevis and crater trips by Jeep and foot can be arranged

P.S.:   Children under 13 not encouraged; open all year

Ottley's Plantation Inn
St. Kitts

			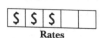
Atmosphere	**Dining**	**Sports**	**Rates**

The Ottley sugar plantation was founded in the early 1700s and the Great House was built in 1832, but its career as an inn didn't begin until 2 years ago. It was bought by the Keusch family, former bookstore owners in New Jersey, who saw the tumbledown estate as the perfect means for fulfilling their dream of becoming Caribbean innkeepers. After a year of scraping paint, hammering, chipping, and (to say nothing of a month or two of renovation after Hurricane Hugo paid a brief call), their fantasy has finally come true.

The Great House, a two-story manor of brimstone walls, has a wraparound veranda, yellow storm shutters with white trim, and Brazilian hardwood doors—features that give the structure the appropriate tropical flavor. It sits on 35 acres of splendid grounds, with a row of coconut palms in the front and a rain forest out back in the foothills that lead to the peak of Mount Liamigua. Stone paths lead past crumbling statuary, allamanda-draped terraces, silk-cotton and cinnamon trees, and massive strangler figs to a mango orchard.

In the inn itself, overstuffed rattan chairs and paisley Sheraton sofas on the veranda and in the Great Room are an invitation for afternoon tea taking or just plain lounging around. Stunning Portuguese rugs accent the hardwood floors, and an antique Chippendale-style bar in the Great Room sets just the right tone for sundown socializing. A small anteroom with a television set and VCR functions as an entertainment center and library.

Ottley's 15 guest rooms are all variations of an overall style that's a cross between English Country and Caribbean colonial, enhanced by wicker and rattan, floral chintz bedspreads and upholstery, antiques, and bric-a-brac. Island prints decorate the white walls, while Portuguese scatter rugs cover the white plank floors. Thoughtful touches include reading lights beside the comfy armchairs (the touch of a former bookseller), gardenia pot-pourri, and plentiful supplies of beach towels. Some of the rooms are quite large for a plantation-style inn, with high-peaked ceilings and floor dimensions of 24 by 24 feet. Several of the bathrooms are also unusually generous, with separate dressing areas and tiled bathtubs and showers. A favorite with privacy seekers is the English Cottage, the former cotton house, which has mullion windows, a separate sitting room, and a small patio looking out to sea. In its former incarnation, Princess Margaret reputedly stayed here. All the rooms are cooled by breezes and ceiling fans (air-conditioning is available as well).

The owners' daughter, Nancy Lowell, and her husband, Martin, run a tight ship with a staff of 40 (a guest-to-staff ratio of almost one to one). The inn's restaurant, the Royal Palm, is popular with Kittitians. Overnight guests have first dibs on the 15 tables, set up beneath ceiling fans and with a folding wall opening on to the swimming pool.

Name: Ottley's Plantation Inn

Managers: Nancy and Martin Lowell

Address: P.O. Box 345, Basseterre, St. Kitts, West Indies

Location: About 15 minutes from Basseterre, 12 minutes and $12 from the airport (let the hotel know your flight number and they'll send a reliable driver to meet you)

Telephone: 809/465-7234

Fax: 809/465-4760

Reservations: 800/772-3039 or International Travel & Resorts, Inc.

Credit cards: All major cards

Rooms: 15, 9 in the guesthouse, 6 in cottages, all with private bathroom, air-conditioning and ceiling fans, balconies or lanais, direct-dial telephone

Meals: Breakfast, lunch, dinner in the pavilion, known as the Royal Palm ($70 for 2); informal dress; Sunday brunch; room service for Continental breakfast only

Entertainment: Bar-lounge, TV room with VCR, parlor games, in-house movies

Sports: 60-foot-long spring-fed pool, hiking trails from the back door through a mango orchard and past allamanda-decked ruins to the rain forest; beaches nearby (transportation daily); tennis, golf, horseback riding, and sailing can be arranged

P.S.: Children not encouraged; closed September and October

The White House
St. Kitts

Atmosphere	Dining	Sports	Rates

With its white-picket fence, broad lawns, and gardens blooming with alla-manda and bougainvillea, this airy, 250-year-old Great House is thoroughly at home on its hill overlooking the capital, Basseterre. There's a swimming pool in the front garden, and somewhere among the mango and bay trees, a grass tennis court and croquet lawn.

But the main attraction here is the galleried, peak-roofed manor house itself, the former home of a colonial plantation owner whose fields of sugarcane once covered the nearby slopes. The house remained in the hands of the original family for more than 200 years before being restored and converted to a country inn by Malcolm and Janice Barber in 1988. They had just finished restoring the house when Hurricane Hugo struck, tearing off part of the roof, uprooting an enormous banyan in the front yard, and delaying the opening until January 1990.

So far, it's been the White House's only snafu. You'd never guess, judging from the style and attention to detail, that the owners are novice inn-keepers (in their former lives, Malcolm was a developer and Janice sold medical supplies). Now they expertly supervise the staff, go to market, drive guests to the beach or shops, and even provide full room service for recluses (let them know in advance, though, since there are no phones in the rooms).

Every last floorboard and panel is scrupulously polished. The cushions are plumped, and vases of fresh flowers and artfully arranged antiques fill the rooms. In each of the 10 guest rooms, a four-poster bed is comple-mented by Laura Ashley fabrics and floor tiles. The bathrooms feature new shower units. The second-story rooms are slightly more spacious, with higher ceilings and better views. But the keynote of all the rooms is a wonderfully refreshing simplicity: There are no radios, televisions, or air-conditioning (with its ceiling fans and 18-inch walls, the house remains cool even at midday).

The original freestanding kitchen, transformed by gleaming 20th-century equipment, is still the place where meals are prepared. On any given night, dinner might be shrimp brûlée, chilled watermelon or orange soup, a choice of filet of beef in rum and black pepper or swordfish in white wine, and mango or coconut ice cream. It's served by candlelight in a dining room dominated by an enormous mahogany table, in a salon at the rear, or in a tented pavilion overlooking the twinkling lights of Basseterre.

The dedication of the Barbers and their staff makes it easy to unwind at the White House. If you could own your second home in the Caribbean, this is probably what it would be like—slow paced, quiet, shaded, comfortable, unmistakably tropical.

Name: The White House

Owners/Managers: Malcolm and Janice Barber

Address: Box 436, St. Peter's, St. Kitts, West Indies

Location: In the foothills above Basseterre, the capital; 10 minutes by car from the airport (the owners provide round-trip transportation)

Telephone: 809/465-8162

Fax: 809/465-8275

Reservations: Direct

Credit Cards: American Express, MasterCard

Rooms: 10, 2 of which are suites, all in the Great House, with private bathrooms, hair dryers, ceiling fans, complimentary laundry service

Meals: Breakfast 8:00–10:00 (on garden terrace), lunch noon–2:00 (on garden terrace), afternoon tea, dinner 8:00–9:30 (in fan-cooled dining room, family style, in the salon, or in tented pavilion, $90 for 2); informal dress; full room service available with advance notice at no extra charge

Entertainment: Taped classical music in evenings

Sports: Pool, grass tennis court, croquet—all free; daily shuttle to nearby beaches; water sports, horseback riding, golf can be arranged

P.S.: Children are not encouraged; open all year

Nisbet Plantation Beach Club

Nevis

Atmosphere

Dining

Sports

Rates

Under current owner David Dodwell of the Reefs resort in Bermuda, this inn has undergone extensive changes in recent years. The first difference returning guests will notice is that the tiny pink cottage with gingerbread trim, called Gingerland, has been turned into a boutique. Next to it is a pavilion housing an airy reception lobby.

But that's just the beginning. A new timbered complex on the beach incorporates a freshwater pool and an open-air restaurant called Coconuts, giving guests the opportunity to dine beneath the stars, with the rumbling of the surf just a few feet away. Then there are the new lodgings. The two-story, pale yellow villas that house the 12 Premier rooms are somewhat obtrusive, given that all the other plantation buildings are one story and half-concealed by the shrubbery. Inside, however, the rooms are large and pleasant, with wet bars and refrigerators, king-size beds on elevated platforms, and sitting areas with comfortable sofas. Each bathroom has a wall of closets and an elevated bathtub. The walls, ceramic floors, rafters, and wicker furniture are white; wooden window louvers and ceiling fans help keep the rooms pleasantly cool.

The Great House, connected to the beach by a 200-foot-long *grande allée* lined with coconut palms, has been rejuvenated, with new shutters around the screened veranda and a bright floral fabric on the sofas and chairs. Thankfully, the atmosphere of a gracious, peaceful, generations-old country house, complete with antique-filled salons that function as dining rooms, has been retained (although I wish they'd revert to the old practice of house wines with dinner—it added a nice house-party touch). The square two-story dwelling is a sterling example of a traditional Nevisian plantation: It's built of native stone with a screened porch reached by an imposing flight of steps. In bygone days, when Nevis was wall-to-wall plantations, this was the estate of a Mr. William Nisbet, who lived here with his lovely young bride, Fanny (a few years later, she was widowed and went on to more universal fame as the wife of Admiral Horatio Nelson). The house is not the one in which the Nisbets lived, but rather an authentic-looking reconstruction.

All of the hotel's original gingerbread cottages, scattered under the coconut palms, have been spruced up with lighter furniture, stocked refrigerators, and bathrobes. The layout in most of these is two rooms per bungalow, arranged so that bathrooms rather than bedrooms abut each other and porches face away from their neighbors. Furnishings are island simple but comfortable and relaxing, and the newer bungalows have screened porches.

Despite the changes, Nisbet, which I first saw some 20-odd years ago, will always have a place in my heart. True, its original 12 rooms have mushroomed to 38 and the inn is no longer quite the same, but first timers seeking a romantic escape will probably not be disappointed.

Name: Nisbet Plantation Beach Club

Manager: Tim Thuell

Address: St. James Parish, Nevis, West Indies

Location: On the northeast coast, just 1 mile from the airstrip, $7 by taxi, and 8 miles and $16 by taxi from Charlestown

Telephone: 809/469-9325

Fax: 809/469-9864

Reservations: Direct, 800/344-2049

Credit Cards: All major cards

Rooms: 38, 12 in new 2-story villas, 26 in cottages and bungalows, all with private bathrooms (some with showers only), ceiling fans, safes, porches

Meals: Breakfast 8:00–10:00 (on the veranda or at the beach bar), lunch 12:30–2:30 (at the beach restaurant; box lunches available with advance notice for those going on an excursion), afternoon tea 4:00–5:00 (in the lounge), dinner 7:30–8:30 (in fan-cooled dining room); informal but stylish dress; taped music; room service for Continental breakfast, no extra charge

Entertainment: Beach bar (open 10:00–5:00), Great House bar (open from 3:00 to late evening), library, backgammon, Scrabble, piano in winter, occasional local bands, TV in lounge (but rarely used)

Sports: Beach, beachside freshwater pool, snorkeling, croquet, tennis (1 court, no lights)—all free; other water sports about 3 miles down the road at Ouali Beach and Newcastle Marina; golf nearby; boat trips, horseback riding, taxi tours, air charters to other islands can be arranged

P.S.: Some children, but not really suitable for the very young; open all year

Four Seasons Nevis Resort

Nevis

Atmosphere

Dining

Sports

Rates

I've been carping about this place ever since I first heard that one of my favorite coconut groves was going to be carved up for a luxury resort (and, of course, it was no fault of Four Seasons that Hurricane Hugo came along in the midst of the construction and did its own thorough job of scything still more trees). Farewell, densely planted grove! What are we left with?

For starters, a breathtaking golf course. Since the surrounding landscape is virtually unspoiled nature, these fairways benefit from the happy confluence of forest and sea and gullies set off by the mystical backdrop of a perfect volcanic cone wreathed in clouds.

Then, too, we have Luxury with a capital L. Four Seasons didn't earn its present preeminence with no-frills lodgings, so here we have the lot—130-square-foot bathrooms with acres of marble, separate showers, and soaking tubs and toilets; closet safes; stocked refrigerators; direct-dial telephones; credenzas with concealed 15-channel television and VCR; ceiling fans and air-conditioning; spacious screened porches. (There are several suites, but given the size and amenities of the regular rooms, I can't see any reason for upgrading.)

The public rooms are just as grand: a soaring lobby/lounge accented with antiques; a wood-paneled library-style lounge/bar; two high-ceilinged, chandelier and crystal dining rooms, each seating about 140 diners indoors and air-conditioned; or outside. The cuisine exceeds island norms, the breakfast and luncheon buffets are diet busters, and the breads and pastries are freshly baked. So what's my problem, then?

For my money, it's all more Four Seasons than Nevis. It just seems such a shame that with all the resources of Four Seasons (the budget for this resort was said to be $75 million), with all their proven good taste, with all that talent at their disposal, they could not have come up with the perfect small resort for a perfect small island. Instead, we have 10 cottages that could be plopped down in Colorado or Maui with only minor adjustments, despite lavish trimming with gingerbread and giving each one an island plantation name. Granted, this is less of a drawback now that the lavish plantings are blooming and sprouting. The interiors seem to have been inspired less by a sense of place than by the corporate manual. No Four Seasons fan will find anything out of place; island lovers may wake up discombobulated, wondering where the hell they are.

The Four Seasons people, to their credit, have been very concerned from the start about fitting into their new surroundings, aware that they were making an unusual impact on the delicate social, professional, and environmental balance of Nevis by moving in, on an island hitherto known only for modest inns, a world-class resort with a guest count that doubled the island's capacity overnight, with a championship golf course on an island that can count players on one hand, and with potential wages beyond the average Nevisian's dreams. So they went to extraordinary expense and care to adapt to Nevis, and mounted an impressive program we needn't consider here, other than noting that they shipped their rookie staff off to learn about luxury service in various Four Seasons hotels in the States.

And service is what Four Seasons is all about, after all, and here it has many refinements: a staff of 450, a golf cart patrolling the fairways with light refreshments, chilled towels for sunbathers and tennis players, an immigration form enclosed with the guests' room confirmations, jogging gear for guests' use, a taproom with darts and billiards for rainy days, a nurse, a nanny, a masseuse, and staff at the airport to meet you.

Accessibility is likely to be a major drawback, I suspect. Nevis is a favorite hideaway for many simply because you have to put in that little extra effort to get there. Here again Four Seasons tackles the problem with thoroughness: Since most guests are likely to be arriving via St. Kitts, Four Seasons people meet their flight there, transfer you by air-conditioned mini-bus to a private waterfront lounge, where you check in, sip a rum punch, and, if you wish, book court time, tee times, and massages; then you board a private 65-foot launch that conveys you directly to the resort's pier, where you are again greeted by staff and escorted directly to your room, with your luggage arriving before you've had a chance to wash your hands. Not just any old launch, of course: This is a custom-designed, rather rakish twin-hulled vessel, with twin GM motors, air-conditioned lounge, open deck, and bar.

Very impressive—and it's a beautiful trip, with volcanic peaks fore and aft, one on St. Kitts, one on Nevis.

Name: Four Seasons Nevis Resort

Manager: Mark Hellrung

Address: P.O. Box 565, Charlestown, Nevis, West Indies

Location: On Pinney's Beach, just outside Charlestown, 15 minutes and $10 by taxi from the airfield, 40 minutes by private launch from St. Kitts

Telephone: 809/469-1111

Reservations: Four Seasons U.S., 800/332-3442; Canada, 800/268-6282

Credit Cards: All major cards

Rooms: 196, including 10 Four Seasons and 2 Presidential Suites, all with screened porches, air-conditioning, ceiling fans, stocked refrigerators, remote cable TV-VCR, direct-dial telephones, closet safes

Meals: From 7:00 a.m. on, in the Dining Room, Cabana, or Clubhouse, dinner 7:00–10:00 in the Dining Room or Grill Room (approx. $90–$100 for 2); "gracious informality . . . after sunset, we would recommend collared, buttoned shirts and closed-in footwear for gentlemen"; 24-hour room service

Entertainment: Lounge-bar, publike Tap Room (billiards, darts), movie library

Sports: 2,000 feet of beach, 2 freshwater pools, croquet, exercise room (Lifecycles, Stairmasters, sauna, whirlpool)—all free; golf (18 holes), tennis (10 courts, clay and all weather, with lights, pro shop), small-boat sailing, pedalos, windsurfing, waterskiing, snorkeling gear, aquacycles, paddle cats, massage—all for a fee; scuba diving by arrangement

P.S.: Some children (they're tucked away in their own game room and have separate dining hours), some executive seminar groups; open all year

P.P.S.: American Airlines, which serves St. Kitts out of San Juan, now has an office on the grounds of the Four Seasons with complete check-in facilities—a godsend. Also available for rental are privately owned 2-, 3-, and 4-bedroom villas at Four Seasons Resorts Estates (many have their own pools). Rates start at $1,450 a night.

Montpelier Plantation Inn

Nevis

| ☆☆☆ | | Atmosphere |

Dining   Sports   Rates

Horatio Nelson married Fanny Nisbet beneath a silk-cotton tree on this hillside plantation, a few miles from Fig Tree Church, where visitors can still see the couple's names in the wedding register. Or so goes tradition, and there's no need to ponder it too deeply as you lounge here, content in the shade of your own silk-cotton tree. The estate now belongs to James and Celia Milnes Gaskell, and it was James who transformed the 100-acre estate and former sugar works into an inn in the early 1960s. "We made our home here and our life in the garden," he writes in his brochure. "We love it and you will, too."

The hub of the inn is the flower-draped gray stone great room, open to the breezes but with a cheery, floral-print clubhouse feel to it. This is the evening social spot; by day, guests tend to gather around the big swimming pool with its tropical murals and landscaping and the attendant bar/lounge/terrace, or they hop on the shuttle bus for a day at Montpelier's beach, beach bar, and sun shelters (toilets available). Dinner is served on a covered, candlelit terrace with views through floodlit palms; the European chefs (three of them!) are classically trained, but favor fresh local produce and recipes.

The 16 guest rooms are comfortable and efficient in a sort of traditional island way, located in 8 cottages angled and staggered in such a way that each patio or terrace has plenty of privacy and views across the estate or the surrounding hills and the sea. Currently the Gaskells are spiffing up the rooms with white ceramic-tile floors and nifty white-tiled bathrooms, which may lose some of the traditional flavor but may add a touch of class. Regular guests (a cross-section of Americans and British) don't come to Montpelier for *HG* chic—they come to enjoy the quiet, courtly tone set by the Gaskells and the calm, unhurried air of bygone days.

Name: Montpelier Plantation Inn
Owners/Managers: James and Celia Milnes Gaskell
Address: P.O. Box 474, Nevis, West Indies
Location: By taxi, 30 minutes and $20 from the airport
Telephone: 809/469-3462
Fax: 809/469-2932
Reservations: E & M Associates
Credit Cards: Discover, MasterCard, Visa
Rooms: 16 in 8 bungalows, some shower only, some tub and shower, ceiling fans, tea- and coffeemakers, patios
Meals: Breakfast 8:00–9:30, lunch 1:00, afternoon tea at 4:00 (not included in rate), dinner at 8:00, on the covered patio (approx. $90 for 2); informal; limited room service
Entertainment: During the winter season, evenings of dancing to the Honey Bees native band; beach barbecues with beach cricket
Sports: Large pool, tennis (1 court, no lights, rackets and balls), free transportation to private beach facility
P.S.:   Children ages 8 and over; closed July 19 to September 11

Golden Rock
Nevis

Atmosphere

Dining

Sports

Rates

Orchids grow in the stone patio; hummingbirds flit from blossom to blossom, from saman tree to saman tree. You're a thousand feet above the sea here, in a flowering 25-acre garden surrounded by 150 private acres of tropical greenery, with a misty rain forest an hour's hike from the pool.

Golden Rock is a 200-year-old sugar estate, its countinghouse converted into a guest cottage, its old stone stable now two guest rooms, its original windmill an unusual duplex suite with stone walls, *three* antique four-posters, and a private sundeck at the rear. The remaining rooms, in pastel-colored bungalows widely spaced among the allamanda and hibiscus, have one-of-a-kind bamboo canopy beds and verandas with views of unspoiled countryside and unending sea. Three newer rooms are located one level down the hill, between the rose garden and the herb garden, but still with that stunning view.

The dining room is a garden porch in the old vaulted "longhouse," where candlelit dinners might include pumpkin soup, lobster on the half shell or curried lamb with hot Nevis sauce, mango mousse or banana cream with meringue.

It's an unhurried life up here, at the end of a long bumpy driveway lined by poinsettia and flamboyant. Unhurried breakfast on your veranda, unhurried lunch on the patio, unhurried drinks in Ralston's bar, unhurried dinner in the garden porch. This is a place for reading (in the "secret garden" orchid courtyard, for example). For backgammon or Scrabble. Maybe a game of tennis, surely a dip in the big spring-fed pool. Twice a day Pam Barry offers her guests a trip to one of two private beaches or town, and twice a day many of them decide not to leave the garden or gazebo. A couple of evenings a week the gardener picks up his bamboo flute and leads his group, the Honey Bees, through their repertoire of local airs.

But most of the time the loudest noise is the sighing of the breeze in the saman trees.

Name: Golden Rock
Owner/Manager: Pam Barry

Address: Box 493, Nevis, West Indies

Location: In the parish of Gingerland, a thousand feet in the hills, give or take an inch or two, about 25 minutes and $22 by taxi from the airfield

Telephone: 809/469-3346

Fax: 809/469-2113

Reservations: Caribbean Inns Ltd., International Travel & Resorts, Inc.

Credit Cards: American Express, Discover, MasterCard, Visa

Rooms: 16, including the Sugar Mill Suite, all with verandas, showers only (limited supplies of hot water), bamboo four-poster beds; the Sugar Mill Suite has an additional sleeping gallery, stone-walled shower, and huge antique four-posters (king-size upstairs, 2 queens downstairs)

Meals: Breakfast 8:00–10:00, lunch noon–2:30 (both al fresco on the terrace), complimentary afternoon tea 4:00, dinner 8:00 (in the indoor garden pavilion, fixed menu, $60 for 2); informal, but jackets not inappropriate (partly because of the elevation); room service for breakfast, lunch, and afternoon tea, no extra charge; lunch is also served at the beach bar

Entertainment: Bar-lounge, parlor games, billiards, darts, some taped music in bar ("never in the dining room"), live music Tuesdays (calypso) and Saturdays (native band), telescope for stargazing

Sports: Spring-fed pool, tennis (1 court, recently resurfaced but with constricted alleys) in the garden, transportation to the inn's private beach properties twice daily, snorkeling masks—all free; hikes through the rain forest; other water sports can be arranged nearby

P.S.:   "Not really suitable for children"; open all year

Hermitage Plantation

Nevis

| Atmosphere | Dining | Sports | Rates |

Alexander Hamilton found it to his liking, we're told. So did Horatio Nelson. And so today do bevies of contemporary knights and lawyers, actors and low-key rock singers. Certainly this place has been around long enough to have welcomed Nelson and Hamilton: The Great House is something like 250 years old, all shingles and rafters and in remarkably fine if somewhat fragile fettle for its age. Its book-laden foyer leads to a roomy, raftered lounge furnished with Victoriana and assorted period pieces, the setting for house party–style gatherings before the pumpkin fritters and shrimp in vodka sauce or after the last crumb of key lime pie has been plucked from the plate; the trellised dining veranda, just off the lounge, blends nicely with its venerable surroundings.

The Carriage House, in traditional Nevisian style, houses three of the guest rooms. The remaining lodgings are six new island-style villas in the garden, up the hill a few paces behind the stone-surrounded swimming pool. Decor features four-poster canopy beds (on wood and foam bases), Schumacher bedspreads with pastoral patterns, frilly pillowcases and sturdy wardrobes, and showers rather than tubs in the bathrooms. The newest quarters also have small kitchenettes.

Like so many Nevis plantations, Hermitage sits high in the hills, in a garden terraced by hand-cut stone, flowering shrubs, and tangerine, lime, tamarind, and soursop trees. Owners/managers Maureen and Richard Lupinacci built a reputation for fine cooking and cordial hospitality when they ran nearby Zetlands Plantation: Their infectious charm brings their guests back year after year, and they now have a loyal following, turning the Hermitage into the tropical cousin of a quiet little country inn in Vermont—or, I should say, Pennsylvania's Bucks County, the Lupinacci's original home. It's so peaceful here that movie producers have been known to settle in for a week or two to work on scripts and shooting schedules. It's moderately priced, too, a fact that wouldn't be lost on Scots-descended Alexander Hamilton if he were around today.

Name: Hermitage Plantation

Owners/Managers: Maureen and Richard Lupinacci

Address: Nevis, West Indies

Location: In the parish of St. John Figtree, in the hills about 30 minutes and $20 by taxi from the airfield

Telephone: 809/469-3477

Fax: 809/469-2481

Reservations: 800/682-4025

Credit Cards: American Express, MasterCard, Visa

Rooms: 12, all different, in 9 separate garden villas; all with showers, ceiling fans, balconies or patios, 4-poster canopy beds, antiques, electric kettles; 4 with pantries

Meals: Breakfast "anytime after 8," lunch noon–2:30, afternoon tea 4:00, dinner 8:00 in the covered veranda draped with flowering vines (approx. $70 for 2); informal dress; room service during meal hours; West Indian buffet with music on Wednesday evenings

Entertainment: Conversation around the bar, parlor games, TV room (alas, in the Great House), scores of paperbacks, rides along the back roads in an antique carriage hauled by a Belgian draft horse (for a fee)

Sports: Pool, walking, trips to the beach by shuttle van, tennis, stables/trail rides

P.S.: Some children but not many; open all year

Croney's Old Manor Estate
Nevis

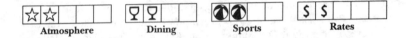

☆☆			
Atmosphere			

♀ ♀			
Dining			

◐ ◑			
Sports			

$ $			
Rates			

Here you wile away your hours among monkey-no-climb and gooseberry trees, surrounded by gardens that are almost an outdoor museum of colonial industry, dotted with antique pistons and gearwheels and other metal sculptures from another era. Mount Nevis itself looms above the garden swimming pool, and the island of Nevis slopes off to the distant sea.

The ground floors of the 200-year-old original cut-stone buildings—sugar mill, hospital, smokehouse, and sugar factory—are topped with wooden-sided plantation-style structures with steep roofs and wooden verandas. Longtime owner Vicky Knorr has now been joined by her sons Gregg and Glenn, and between them they're revitalizing the place, adding refinements like a Jacuzzi and a stable. They're also fixing up the guest rooms, in some cases adding dubious (in these times-gone-by surroundings) improvements like fitted carpeting. Still, the guest quarters are spacious, uncluttered, comfortable, and not at all pricey.

One thing hasn't changed: the reputation of Croney's Cooperage Dining Room. They take cuisine seriously here, growing their own spinach and lettuce in what used to be the settling tanks, serving tasty dishes like Jamaican jerk pork, local wahoo steak seasoned with lime and butter, breaded escalopes of Provimi veal sautéed in butter and served with a champagne morel sauce. Friday night is given over to a lobster and steak buffet—with steel-band accompaniment. It's about the only time you'll hear anything louder than the trade winds rustling the monkey-no-climb.

Name: Croney's Old Manor Estate

Address: P.O. Box 70, Charlestown, Nevis, West Indies

Location: 1,000 feet up the flank of Mount Nevis, 20 minutes and $20 from the airport

Telephone: 809/469-3445

Fax: 809/469-3388

Reservations: 800/892-7093 or International Travel & Resorts, Inc.

Credit Cards: All major cards

Rooms: 15 rooms and suites in 4 buildings, with balconies or patios

Meals: Breakfast 7:30–10:00, lunch noon–2:30, dinner 7:00–9:00 (approx. $60 for 2); informal dress; no room service; Friday buffet with steel band

Entertainment: Bar adjoining the restaurant, billiards, games room, library

Sports: Swimming pool, Jacuzzi, miles of hiking trails, shuttle to beach—all free; 5 horses for trail rides ($25 for 2 hours)

P.S.: "Not recommended for children under 12"; open all year

P.P.S.: *Please note*—As we go to press, new owners have taken over Croney's, renaming it Old Manor Estate & Hotel. They plan, under new manager Helen Kidd, to make a few alterations and additions—but slowly.

Jumby Bay Island
Antigua

Atmosphere

Dining

Sports

Rates

A private islet just off the northern coast of Antigua, Jumby Bay is one solution for escapists who want a resort that is at once secluded and accessible. Secluded because its 300 acres are shared by only 76 guests and a flock of wild sheep. Accessible because you take a taxi, 3 minutes, to the resort's dock, then, assuming schedules gel, a boat ride of 10 minutes to the island, with the crew dispensing rum punches and registration cards on the way. When you arrive, a mini-van or electric buggy takes you past trim lawns and the 200-year-old estate house directly to your room.

You have your pick of three styles of accommodations: the original octagonal rondavels, rectangular cottages—both of which are scattered around the cillamont-shaded lawns—or the two-story mission-style Pond

Bay House at the far end of Jumby Beach. The rondavels and cottages, two rooms to each, are draped in tropical foliage that screens the private porches from passersby and wafts the scent of tropical blossoms through the rooms; cathedral ceilings, anterooms with daybeds/sofas, and huge bathrooms with double sinks and lushly planted shower courtyards create a sense of space and comfort. The Pond Bay House lodgings are virtually minisuites, designed on a sumptuous scale with Brunelleschi terra-cotta tiles, fabrics that are custom designed and hand painted, outline quilted bedspreads ("eight ounces," as the proud decorator points out, "not the usual four ounces"), oversize showers, and louvered doors opening onto a private oceanfront patio or balcony.

All rooms have a few of those extra little touches that separate the memorable from the merely good: scads of big fluffy towels, cuddly terry-cloth robes, golf umbrellas, walking sticks, wall safes. (One minor gripe is the lack of hooks and conveniently placed towel racks in the bathrooms. The folded towels hang above a counter, and once you've used one, there's no place to hang it without refolding it and leaning uncomfortably over the counter.) The welcome includes a refreshment tray with a bottle of private-label rum, cans of Coke, and a bottle of Banfi sparkling wine. Banfi? Right, but let me back up a little. The resort, then known as Long Island, was started by the island's owner, Homer Williams, about a decade ago. In 1985, he sold 80% to New York's Mariani brothers, who had built a company called Banfi Vintners into the largest wine importers in the United States.

In addition to the cottages and Pond Bay House, a number of private, multi-million-dollar homes have gone up on the island, plus eight new villa complexes, called the Harbor Beach Villas. All the villas have two bedrooms, a living room, kitchen, two bathrooms, cathedral ceilings, and louvered doors that open out onto an oceanfront terrace. The older Pond Bay villas are clustered around a courtyard with a Roman-style swimming pool, while the Harbor Hill villas are taller triplexes, each with its own small pool.

To their credit, the owners have set aside a beach on Pasture Bay as a protected nesting site for hawksbill turtles, the endangered *Eretmochelys imbricata* (a cool $5 million worth of prime beachfront real estate, to put it in material terms), and sponsor two student biologists who patrol the beach every night during the nesting season to make sure all is well with the turtles. (Don't even think of asking your waiter for turtle soup—it's not considered funny.) Located on the windward side of the island, the beach is accessible only on foot or by bicycle, a real Robinson Crusoe place with hammocks strung between the sea grapes and a conveniently placed cooler with soft drinks, beer, rum, and ice. On the house.

Also on the house are cocktails from the bar, vintage wine with lunch and dinner, launch service, stamps for your postcards, most water sports, and tennis. And, of course, nature: several beaches, 5 miles of walking trails, and bike paths snaking through the box briar and pink cedar, through groves of turpentine and loblolly.

The new chef, Rex Hale, frequently alters the menu to emphasize island specialties. On Sunday there's a lunch buffet featuring all West Indian dishes—pepper pot, salt fish and doucana (a coconut and sweet-potato dumpling), rôti, seafood water (or stew), and conch fritters. Many of these are fresh updates on the standard fare—sea urchin flan with mango ginger sauce, for example. Free-range chickens, fed on organically grown grain, and New York beef, aged 2 weeks, are flown in. Pastries and desserts are made on the premises by pastry chef Kirk Parks, whose creations are delicious and exotic, such as ginger beer ice cream and mango tart.

But you pay a price for Jumby Bay's accessibility; once or twice a day jets leaving the airport lumber upward close to the island, intruding on the tranquility, and once or twice a week a military plane overflies Jumby late at night and has been known to awaken slumbering guests. (Earplugs are thoughtfully left on the bedside table, along with the obligatory chocolates.) Awakened myself one night, I decided I couldn't really give Jumby Bay five stars, but next morning, surrounded by its ravishing attraction, I opted for the top rating. One of the Caribbean's finest resorts, no question.

Name: Jumby Bay Island

Manager: William K. Anderson

Address: P.O. Box 243, St. John's, Antigua, West Indies

Location: On an offshore islet, 8 to 10 minutes by 48-foot boat from the mainland (no charge); if your flight misses the scheduled ferry, you can have drinks at the hotel beside the dock, but it's hardly a deluxe establishment

Telephone: 809/462-6000

Fax: 809/462-6020

Reservations: Direct, 800/421-9016

Credit Cards: American Express, MasterCard, Visa

Rooms: 38, in cottages and 2-story Pond Bay House, all with ceiling fans, louvered walls or windows, porches or lanais, wall safes, wet bars, bathrobes, hair dryers, showers only; plus 17 villas for rent

Meals: Breakfast 8:00–9:30, Continental breakfast until 10:00, lunch 12:30–2:00 (at the beachside terrace), afternoon tea 4:00 in the Great House, dinner 7:30–9:30 (in the arcaded patio of the Estate House); weekly barbecue dinner and Caribbean Night at beach terrace; dress informal but elegant; limited room service; box lunches for picnics on Pasture Beach

Entertainment: Bar/lounge, library, backgammon, cribbage, etc.

Sports: 2 beaches (1 leeward, 1 windward), windsurfing, Sunfish sailing,
waterskiing, snorkeling, safaris, putting, croquet, 100 bicycles, tennis (3
courts, 2 with lights, pro), nature trails, boat trips to mainland—all free;
scuba diving and sport fishing can be arranged (as can golf, but hardly
worth the effort)

P.S.: Children under 8 permitted only in July, August, and September;
some small seminar groups in the off-season

Blue Waters Beach Hotel
Antigua

| Atmosphere | Dining | Sports | Rates |

Before you catch your first sight of the blue waters, you'll be charmed by the
lovely botanical garden setting—down the steep hill, into the circular tree-
shaded driveway, through the open lobby to the flowering terrace, pool,
and beach, with two-story wings of rooms fanning off on either side.
Balconies are festooned with bougainvillea and plumbago and shaded by
Antigua palms and flamboyants. There are so many plants here, 10 gardeners toil full-time to keep everything spruce and dandy.

Guest rooms (all of them face the beach) have been enhanced with
stocked refrigerators, quieter split-unit air conditioners, and, in some
cases, more space by extending the original balconies. The new clusters of
one- and three-bedroom condos at the far end of the garden give guests
even more room to lounge around in (although some of the Hillside Suites
have views of other condos rather than the sea).

There's always been a friendly, congenial atmosphere at Blue Waters,
nurtured by senior staff, many of whom have been around for years. That's
still one of the resort's lures, but the confluence of sea and beach and
garden—the profusion of hibiscus and pink ixorra, white lantana and red
gingers, et al—may be what makes it so popular with the British. Even for
guests with no horticultural bent, there are plenty of opportunities to enjoy
the setting in romantic ways. Stroll past the plumbago and tamarinds to the
breakwater known as North Point. There's a tiny gazebo in this spot, just big
enough for two (except when corraled for a wedding), where you can get

away from the chatter and laughter, listen to the waves, marvel at the clear waters, maybe even discover another shade of blue.

Name: Blue Waters Beach Hotel

Manager: Keith Woodhouse

Address: P.O. Box 256, St. John's, Antigua, West Indies

Location: On the north shore, 15 minutes and $10 by taxi from the airport in one direction, from St. John's in the other

Telephone: 809/462-0290, 0292

Fax: 809/462-0293

Reservations: Direct

Credit Cards: All major cards

Rooms: 46 in 2-story wings, all with balconies or loggias facing the beach, all with air-conditioning and louvers, stocked refrigerators, closet safes, amenities trays, hair dryers, direct-dial telephones, clock radios, plus 21 deluxe rooms and suites in 8 2-story villas, some with kitchens, all with refrigerators-bars

Meals: Breakfast 7:30–10:00, lunch 12:30–3:00, afternoon tea 4:00–5:00, dinner 7:00–11:00 (approx. $75 for 2) on the veranda or in the air-conditioned Cacubi Room; barbecue Tuesdays, buffet Fridays, curry brunch Sundays; "elegantly casual" dress (no shorts after 7:00); room service during dining room hours, no extra charge

Entertainment: 2 bars, dancing, library, video room, dancing under the stars to live music 8:00–11:00 ("the bands have been chosen for how *quietly* they play")

Sports: 2 beaches and a human-made sandy terrace, freshwater pool, snorkeling, Sunfish sailing, kayaks, windsurfing, pedalos, tennis (1 court, with lights)—all free; waterskiing you pay for; scuba, yachting, golf nearby

P.S.:   Some children occasionally; open all year

Galley Bay
Antigua

   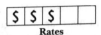

| Atmosphere | Dining | Sports | Rates |

Old Antigua hands may wonder about the name: Yes, it is the former Galley Bay Surf Club, but with a different owner (English) and manager (Canadian) and a million dollars in rehabbing it's better than ever. Relax, though, it still has the same laid-back, take-life-easy, get-away-from-it-all ambience.

You still enter along a bumpy dirt track, through a grove of coconut palms and sea-grape trees, with the gentle surf on one side and a placid lagoon on the other.

Guests who like to step from their rooms straight onto the sand (or nod off to the sound of the surf) check into the beachfront bungalows; romantics bed down beside the lagoon in thatch-roofed, Polynesian-style quarters called Gauguin Cottages. The beachfront bungalows are attractive but not very different from beachfront rooms elsewhere, so it's the Gauguin Cottages that put Galley Bay in a romantic class by itself. They're not exactly cottages, despite the name: Each consists of a pair of rondavels, neither of them very large but very sensibly arranged, one for sleeping, the other for showering and dressing, with a covered breezeway-cum-patio between the two. They're kooky and romantic but also very practical: You come in from the sea and sand, head for your shower hut without tracking sand all over your bedroom; then, all fresh and shiny, you can skip across your private breezeway to bed—or lounge around dishabille, since all the breezeways have neck-high lattices that screen out intruders but let the breezes waft through. But don't let the word *hut* fool you, either—they're neat little whitewashed rooms, dressed with lace curtains, floral bedspreads, and island wall hangings.

The beachside lodgings are one-story, flat-roofed bungalows, two guest rooms to each, now with swank white-tiled bathrooms and a few grace notes like cotton kimonos, hair dryers, mini refrigerators, and coffeemakers. A recent refining added new decorative touches with swathed fabrics and woven baskets. Number 18, one of the Executive Rooms with a private sundeck and hammock, is particularly attractive, with a handsome bamboo four-poster bed (a feature scheduled to appear in more rooms later in 1995).

Guests gather beneath a cone-shaped pavilion of local hardwoods and cedar shingle, which serves as the bar, lounge, dance floor, tearoom, and rendezvous. Old-timers are smart enough to arrive early to get first dibs on the traditional planters' chairs—wood and canvas armchairs with straps for putting your feet up and wide armrests for holding your rum punch and freshly baked coconut chips.

The adjoining restaurant, the Sea Grape Terrace, is likewise open to the sea breezes, part outdoors with market umbrellas set up beneath coco palms and sea grapes, part indoors in a newly restyled open-sided pavilion decorated with Antillean paintings, native pots, fans (the ladies' kind rather than the whirling coolers), and more of that decorative basketware. Even the menu has been revamped, and you can now fill the balmy evenings with island-accented dishes such as chilled butternut squash and ginger soup, coconut shrimp and mango *coulis*, spicy rare grilled yellowfin tuna with melon salsa.

Galley Bay is now run as an all-inclusive, with everything included in the rate, from the new water-sports gear to the Chilean house wine, but it's certainly a notch or two above the run-of-the-mill all-inclusive when it comes to a romantic setting.

Name: Galley Bay

Manager: Daniel Reid

Address: Five Islands, P.O. Box 305, St. John's, Antigua, West Indies

Location: About 10 minutes from the capital, at the end of an unpaved road that discourages casual sightseers; about 15 minutes and $20 by taxi from the airport

Telephone: 809/462-0302

Fax: 809/462-4551

Reservations: Robert Reid Associates

Credit Cards: American Express, Diners Club, MasterCard, Visa

Rooms: 30 rooms, including 5 deluxe beachfront suites (larger, but otherwise not much different from the regular rooms) and 13 Gauguin Cottages (all with new bathrooms and ceiling fans); all with showers, ceiling fans, bathrobes, hair dryers, coffeemakers, in-room safes, refrigerators, patios

Meals: Breakfast 7:30–10:00, Continental breakfast 9:30–10:00, lunch 12:30–2:30, afternoon tea 4:30–5:00, dinner 7:30–9:30, all in the beachside pavilion (5-course dinner, $100 for 2); informal dress ("but we do request that guests do not wear jeans, T-shirts, or shorts after 7:00 p.m. in our bar and restaurant"); room service for breakfast only, no extra charge

Entertainment: Bar, live music 3 evenings a week (unamplified), barbecues on Wednesdays and Saturdays, chess, backgammon, and other parlor games, small library

Sports: Half-mile beach (good swimming and snorkeling most of the time), hammocks, tennis (1 court, no lights), windsurfing, kayaks, Sunfish sailing, bicycles, 2 catamarans, snorkeling equipment—all free;

waterskiing nearby; the resort also operates a "Sail & Sea" option—4 days ashore, 3 days under sail cruising the beaches and bays of Antigua

P.S.:   Children 8 years and older are accepted during the peak season except in February and March; open all year

Curtain Bluff
Antigua

Atmosphere

Dining

Sports

Rates

Behold: one of the loveliest settings in the Caribbean. A 12-acre headland, lagoon-smooth beach on the leeward side, breezy surfy beach to windward, rocky bluff at the tip. The flowers are brilliant, the trees tall and stately, the lawns primped to the nearest millimeter. And with rooms for just 126 vacationers, there's more garden than guests.

Curtain Bluff also happens to be one of the most consistently dependable, top-drawer resorts in the islands, thanks largely to the personality of its owner, the inimitable Howard Hulford. Thirty-plus years ago, when he was piloting planes around the Caribbean for oil company executives, he used to fly over and lust after this south-coast headland, vowing that one day he would build a dream home there. In 1985, he and his wife, Chelle, moved into a *spectacular* dream home on the very tip of the bluff, but in the intervening 25 years he had opened, modified, perfected his stylish resort and welcomed people to Howard's Headland year after year, decade after decade.

For some people, though, Curtain Bluff seems to be too cultivated, too country-clubby. In the high season, you're expected to dress for dinner most evenings (except Wednesday and Sunday), and judging by the sartorial propriety, guests must send their togs ahead on container ships. Dinner is a serious affair, in an elegant garden pavilion surrounded by lawns, a gazebo, the Sugar Mill Bar, and a dance floor beneath a tamarind tree. Add to that a well-rounded wine cellar that wouldn't look out of place in Beaune and you may decide that dining here is the sort of event that makes all the dressing up worthwhile. Of course, you may also decide to forego the dining room and the combo tootling Gershwin and have your dinner shipped to your private balcony or patio.

The suites are located in villas built step-fashion up the leeward side of the bluff. Living rooms measure a generous 17 by 20 feet, bedrooms a few feet more; each room (not suite, room) comes with a comfy balcony overlooking the sea, and the suites with duplex configurations also have open dining terraces and secluded patios strung with hammocks. Everything in the suites seems to come in multiples. Two ceiling fans per room (again not suite, but room), plus another in the bathroom. His and her lighted closets and twin vanities. Three, sometimes four, telephones to a suite. The one-bedroom suites are fitted with 18 light switches—for fans, vanities, dimmers, terraces, and the track lighting that pinpoints gallery-caliber artwork, most of it commissioned for the Bluff. Fabrics and rugs are in delicate pastels, glass doors and screens positively *glide*, oversize rattan sofas and chairs billow with 18 cushions; Italian marble covers the walls and floors and separate shower stalls of the sumptuous bathrooms. Chelle Hulford designed and decorated these suites with great good taste—and has conjured up some of the grandest accommodations in the Caribbean. The grandest of these is probably the Terrace Room, at the top of the bluff, with a king-size four-poster bed and huge terrace.

The remaining rooms, all deluxe (six have connecting bedrooms), have more traditional proportions and accoutrements. They too have had their own dose of prettifying, and now look all spic-and-span with rattan end tables and chairs, jollier fabrics, circular headboards, and new tiled bathrooms and balcony screens. To celebrate the resort's 30th anniversary several years ago, the Hulfords added an international squash court and an exercise room. It's all very relaxed and genteel here (there are no room keys and no one ever asks for them), but despite its country-club flavor, Curtain Bluff is far from being a pasture for geriatrics.

It's actually one of the sportiest small hotels in the Caribbean (see listing below). And, into the bargain, one of the best values despite what at first glance might seem like stiff rates. All meals and all drinks are included; most sports facilities are available at no extra charge. Even waterskiing. Even scuba diving. You only pay extra for day or half-day sails on the resort's yacht *Tamarind*. From its decks, Curtain Bluff looks even more stunningly lovely than it did from the air all those 30 years ago.

Name: Curtain Bluff
Owner/Managers: Howard Hulford (owner), Robert Sherman (managing director), Calvert Roberts (general manager)
Address: P.O. Box 288, Antigua, West Indies
Location: On the south coast, next to the village of Old Road, 35 minutes from the airport ($22 by taxi)
Telephone: 809/462-8400, 8401, 8402
Fax: 809/462-8409

Reservations: Own office, 212/289-8888 or 800/672-5833
Credit Cards: American Express
Rooms: 63, in 2-story wings and the 6 1- and 2-bedroom suites, all beachfront with balconies or lanais, bathrooms (amenities trays, bathrobes,
and bathtubs), ceiling fans, louvers and screened glass doors, telephones, wall safes, refrigerators in suites
Meals: Breakfast 7:30–9:30, Continental 9:30–10:00, lunch 12:30–2:00
(in the open-sided garden pavilion or Beach Club), dinner 7:30–9:30
(for outside guests, approx. $60 per person) in garden pavilion; beach
barbecue buffet on Wednesday afternoon; "we do request jacket and tie
for the gentlemen after 7:00" from December 19 to April 15 (5 nights a
week); room service, no extra charge
Entertainment: Bar, lounge, library, parlor games, TV-video room, live
music for dancing every evening (combos, native bands, etc., amplified
but not loud), steel band with beachside buffet
Sports: 2 beaches (1 windward, 1 leeward), hammocks, snorkeling, scuba,
waterskiing, Sunfish sailing, seascopes (for fish watching), reef trips,
deep-sea fishing, tennis (4 lighted courts, pro shop), squash court,
exercise room, croquet, putting green—all free; day and half-day sails
on the resort's own 47-foot sailboat cost extra
P.S.:   "Please, no unaccompanied children in the bar after 7:00" and no
children under 12 between January 10 and March 10; mid-May features
a very popular pro-am tennis tournament; closed May 21 through mid-
October

The Copper & Lumber Store Hotel

Antigua

☆☆☆			🍷🍷					💲💲	
Atmosphere			**Dining**			**Sports**		**Rates**	

Four of the Caribbean's most stunning, most unusual suites can be found,
not beside a beach, but in a dockyard—Nelson's Dockyard.
  Don't let that faze you. No cranes and clatter, no grease and goo here—

this is the National Park kind of dockyard, the former headquarters of Britain's navy back in the days when Lord Nelson was still Captain Horatio.

The revered hero/admiral is commemorated in a wood-frame mansion (now a museum), between the engineers' workshop (now the Admiral's Inn) and the warehouse that is now the dockyard's second inn, the Copper & Lumber Store. On a hillside across English Harbour stands Clarence House, the home of Nelson's buddy, the duke of Clarence (Princess Margaret stayed here on her honeymoon); higher up the hill, on Shirley Heights, the former barracks have been restored as a museum, and on the battlements there's a pleasant pub/restaurant with panoramic views of mountains and yacht-filled harbor. For yachting buffs, Nelson's harbor is the Caribbean's most popular, best-equipped marina and revictualing base.

Throw open your shutters in the morning and you look out on a stunning setting of bollards and capstans, masts and rigging. The pride of the world's yacht builders spread out all around you—classic schooners from Maine, sleek 70-foot ocean cruisers from Cowes, mammoth powerboats laden with antennae, radar scanners, flying bridges, and unseamanlike names. Most of them are charter yachts, and many of the people staying or dining at either of the dockyard's inns are waiting to ship out—or have just returned from a cruise, unsteady of gait, getting back to normal before returning to the 20th century.

The Copper & Lumber Store Hotel, in its current incarnation, is a sturdy, two-story structure in Georgian/Admiralty style, built of native stone and hefty rough-hewn timbers that wouldn't have looked out of place on a ship of the line.

The "office" is a desk under the stairs. Not just any desk, but a sturdy 17th-century *escritorio* carted off as booty from a Spanish galleon. The lobby (weathered brick floor and walls, oriental rugs, beamed ceilings, buttoned red leather wing chairs, breezes fore and aft) serves as an informal lounge/ bar and opens onto the cloisterlike patio restaurant, its warehouse doors opening to the lawns and marina. Dinner, which features rôti, lobster, snapper creole, and other Caribbean specialties, is served here every night. In the adjoining pub—called the Mainbrace, it's open for breakfast, lunch, and dinner in the high season—the menu features traditional English items such as Scotch eggs, English bacon, sausages, mango chutney, pickled onions, and assorted cheeses. A welcome bargain, too, for these parts.

All the guest rooms have views of the harbor and yachts in one direction or another; all are furnished with antiques and period pieces accenting the basic decor of raw brick and ceiling beams, hand stenciling and classic fabrics, but there's nothing "homemade" about the interiors. Even Nelson didn't live in such style.

The pièces de résistance are the seven Georgian suites, each named after one of Nelson's ships. Africa, for example, a one-bedroom suite, is adorned with 200-year-old paintings, 400-year-old charts, and a display of antique Wedgwood. The floor sports hand-stenciled pineapple motifs, the paneling is Philippine oak, the wallpapers and fabrics are replicas of 200-year-old patterns, and the document chest is made of camphor wood on a steel frame. In the sleeping loft all the furnishings are authentic Chippendale, except for the double beds, which are replicas. What sets these seven suites apart, though, are their bathrooms—paneling of Honduras mahogany, washbasins of Argentine brass, shower stalls of Welsh slate. It's all done with a sympathetic feeling for authenticity.

Although most people who stay here are overnighting, before or after cruises, these are suites to settle into for several days. Take time to explore the battlements on foot, for the 5-minute boat trip to the beaches in the outer harbor, to visit Shirley Heights for lunch, to row among the yachts at sunset. English Harbour was a "hurricane hole" for sailing ships, but the fact that it's so sheltered doesn't necessarily mean it's going to be hot and sticky; you can spend time there even in the summer without feeling uncomfortable.

There are several restaurants within walking distance of the Copper & Lumber Store (none of them, frankly, outstanding, but at least they have some atmosphere); but there's less reason than hereto for eating out, now that the Copper & Lumber Store gives you the convenience of private pantries *and* a new restaurant.

Name: The Copper & Lumber Store Hotel

Manager: Alan Teyes

Address: P.O. Box 184, St. John's, Antigua, West Indies

Location: Anchored in the middle of Nelson's Dockyard in English Harbour, 25 minutes and $25 by taxi from the airport or St. John's

Telephone: 809/460-1058

Fax: 809/460-1529

Reservations: Caribbean Inns Ltd., or 800/275-0877

Credit Cards: American Express, MasterCard, Visa

Rooms: 14, all suites (including 3 studio suites and 7 deluxe Georgian suites), all different, all with private bathrooms (showers only), kitchens (refrigerators stocked on request, commissary nearby), ceiling fans, antiques

Meals: Breakfast 7:30–11:00, lunch 11:30–2:30, afternoon tea, dinner 7:00–9:30 in the courtyard restaurant, cooled by breezes and ceiling fans, 6:30–10:00 in the pub; from December 1 through April, the pub is open all day for meals and snacks (pub lunch for 2, approx. $16; dinner for 2, $20 to $30); informal dress (but no shorts in the evening); taped classical 18th-century music; room service for breakfast only

Entertainment: The bar/lounge of the inn is popular with visiting yacht people, and it's not unknown to have an erudite conversation on politics continue into the wee hours; parlor games (Scrabble, wari, chess, darts, cribbage, shoveha'penny, backgammon)

Sports: Beaches nearby (the inn will supply beach towels and arrange on request for a launch to 1 of 3 beaches in Freeman's Bay, 5 minutes away across the bay); boats for rent nearby, boat tours of harbor, scuba and snorkeling from the Dockyard, tennis/squash courts just outside the Dockyard

P.S.: "Not really suitable for children"; open all year; expect some ongoing renovations in 1995, including the restoration of an adjacent building to create 30 more suites

The Admiral's Inn

Antigua

☆					♟											$	$		
Atmosphere					**Dining**					**Sports**						**Rates**			

In Nelson's pre-admiral days as commander in chief of the dockyard, this two-story weathered brick structure was an unglamorous corner of his domain—the storehouse for turpentine and pitch. You'd never suspect it today. It's now a lovely 30-year-old inn in a most unusual setting. A well-worn stone patio, set with tables and chairs, shaded by sun umbrellas and casuarina trees, leads to a lawn that ends at the water's edge. Just off to the right, a row of sturdy but stunted stone pillars are all that remain of the former boathouse, decapitated in a long-ago earthquake, and just beyond that another section of the dockyard has become an annex with four more guest rooms. Yachts lie at their moorings a few oar strokes offshore, and somewhere behind you the market women of English Harbour have draped the old stone walls with batiks and T-shirts, necklaces and baubles.

 The inn's lobby is a tiny desk beneath the stairs in a beamed lounge, bar on one side facing French doors that lead to the dining terrace. A dart board adds the right Royal Navy touch; the burgees of 100 yachts and yacht clubs remind you that the Admiral's Inn is a favorite gathering place for sailing buffs. If the Flying Dutchman were to come ashore again one of these days, this would be a sensible place for him to come ashore and search for a latter-day Senta.

Being a gathering place for yachtspeople, the inn may not be the serenest of hideaways, but it has a lot of charm and camaraderie. Guest rooms are small, simply but tastefully furnished, with Williamsburg fabrics by Schumacher, cooled by ceiling fans or air conditioners. Some of the rooms have patios. The prime nest (indeed, one of the prettiest in all of Antigua) is number 1, a large corner chamber with lacy curtains, straw matting, and canopied four-poster king-size bed (two of the other rooms have queens, the others are twins). Since it's right at the head of the stairs, number 1 gets a certain amount of inn traffic outside its doors, and since it's directly above the bar it picks up some of the chatter and jollity from rendezvousing voyagers. But the carousing generally ends around midnight, and then all you hear when you throw open the window shutters is the clank of the rigging on the sailboats.

The four rooms across the pillared lawn are a shade quieter—smallish in floor space but with high ceilings, whitewashed stone walls, built-in dressers, modern plumbing, fans, and air conditioners. Room A is the biggest, and being at the harbor end of the row with louvered windows on three sides, it is also the brightest and breeziest.

Even if you don't have time to stay here, stop in for a drink on the broad terrace. Or a meal—indoors beneath iron chandeliers, outdoors beneath the lacy casuarinas. The inn is a popular spot for lunch, which always features delicately seasoned pumpkin soup and fresh fried fish; the cost, excluding wine, will run about $65 for two. The surroundings are delightful, the welcome friendly. It's another century. Even if the yachts have aluminum rather than wooden masts.

Name: The Admiral's Inn

Manager: Ethelyn Philip

Address: English Harbour, P.O. Box 713, St. John's, Antigua, West Indies

Location: In Nelson's Dockyard national park, on Antigua's south coast; 16 miles directly across the island from the airport (40 minutes and $22 by taxi) and 14 miles from St. John's (30 minutes, $21 by taxi)

Telephone: 809/460-1027

Fax: 809/460-1534

Reservations: American Wolfe International

Credit Cards: American Express, MasterCard, Visa

Rooms: 14, all with private bathrooms (showers only); 8 with air-conditioning, all others with ceiling fans, some with patios

Meals: Breakfast 7:30–10:00, lunch noon–2:30, dinner 7:30–9:00 (approx. $65 for 2) served indoors or on the terrace; casual dress (but not scruffy, despite the proximity of all those yachts); room service available

Entertainment: West Indian combo Thursdays (in season), steel band Saturdays, dancing, some taped music, darts

Sports: Snorkeling gear, Sunfish sailing—free; windsurfing, paddleboats, beach, water sports, boat trips, tennis, squash, scuba diving, and horseback riding, nearby, golf a half hour away

P.S.: Some (sometimes lots of) cruise ship passengers, since you're right in the middle of what tourists come all the way across the island to see; especially busy during Sailing Week (late April, early May) and charter yacht review week (early December); closed September 1 to mid-October

P.P.S.: The inn's sister establishment, Falmouth Harbour Beach Apartments, is located 10 minutes away on a small beach in the next bay; 28 twin-bedded apartments come with kitchenettes, private verandas, and maid service—and bargain rates (doubles $118 and $130, winter 1995). A larger beach is a 5-minute walk away

The Inn at English Harbour
Antigua

☆	☆	☆				🍷	🍷					◓	◓					$	$		
Atmosphere						**Dining**						**Sports**						**Rates**			

Rather than follow the low road to English Harbour, take the road to Shirley Heights. Just before the fortress restorations, you'll find a tiny sign with 18th-century script identifying the inn. Turn off and there among the flowering shrubs and fruits you come upon a lodge with a few cottages nestled among the trees, 150 feet above the outer anchorage of English Harbour. Actually, this is only the upper level of this upstairs-downstairs inn—the bulk of the rooms are all the way down the hillside beside the beach. No, you won't have to trek all the way up again for breakfast, lunch, or a drink—there's a bar-restaurant right there on the beach. And when it's time for dinner upstairs, just call the front desk and someone will send the Mercedes down to collect you.

Where you unpack, though, can make a difference. For breezes and a view, go hilltop, but if you want the sea to be a toe-skip away, choose the two-story beach wing. But as far as decor and amenities are concerned, all the rooms come with island-style rush rugs, wicker and contemporary furniture, ceiling fans, faux driftwood walls with white trimmed jalousie windows, and sliding glass doors to balconies or patios. Because the resort was recently bought by Paul Deeth, the son of the former owner and founder, much of the inn has been upgraded. The kitchenettes in the six rooms on the hill have been replaced with a vanity area; there are new curtains, bedspreads, mini-bars, wall safes, and hair dryers; and bathrooms have been enlarged, with a separate cubicle for the toilet and bidet.

The focal point of the inn is the sturdy, open-plan hilltop lodge, crafted from native stone, with quarry-tile floors and beamed ceilings. Chandeliers are fashioned from ships' wheels, and the bar has something of the air of an English pub, with high-backed booths, wooden tables, and a dart board. Edgar the bartender, who has been here since the inn opened 35 years ago, remembers actor Richard Burton (who spent two of his honeymoons here) and still greets everyone by name even when they haven't been back for a few years. In the adjoining lounge, the shelves and tables have enough copies of *Country Life* and the *Daily Mirror* lying around to remind you that this inn has always been a favorite of the English. Come here for cocktails and the accents might have you thinking you're in Cornwall rather than the Caribbean.

The dining pavilion and its broad tree-shaded terrace, much loved by the inn's habitués, hasn't changed (except in such subtleties as new paddle fans for the pavilion). But the chefs who come from the U.K. each season have refined the menus. No tampering, of course, with English standbys like roast beef and Yorkshire pudding, but guests now also have options such as avocado with passion-fruit dressing or garlic prawns with snow peas, farfalle pasta with a seafood and cream sauce, or baked dorado with tomato and onion salsa.

One of the Inn at English Harbour's special attractions is its 10-acre headland, part of the island's national park. A short walk from the entrance will bring you to the start of several nature trails through the forest, among an exotic collection of shrubs and trees, many of them planted by the British garrison hundreds of years ago. You'll find whip dagger and ram goat cherry, fishing rod or wild orchid.

But it's hard to stay at this inn and not think of going to sea. There are boats everywhere. Before taking over the inn, Deeth spent many years roaming the oceans as captain of luxury sloops and schooners. His love of the sea persists in the form of a classic wood-hulled ketch, the 50-foot *Flicka*, moored just a few yards offshore. It's available for half-day or full-day cruises along the western coast of Antigua. Looking at its lovely, sleek, graceful lines, it's hard to resist Deeth's invitation: "Relive the golden era of 1930s sailing! . . . Decide how you would like to spend your day, whether sailing, relaxing on deck, or picnicking on the beach."

Name: The Inn at English Harbour

Owner: Paul Deeth

Address: P.O. Box 187, St. John's, Antigua, West Indies

Location: On the bay called English Harbour, on the south coast, 16 miles, 40 minutes, and $24 by taxi from the airport, slightly less from St. John's

Telephone: 809/460-1014

Fax: 809/460-1603

Reservations: Robert Reid Associates

Credit Cards: American Express, MasterCard, Visa

Rooms: 28, 22 on the beach, 6 on the hill, ceiling fans and breezes; tiled bathrooms, balcony or patio

Meals: Breakfast 7:00–10:00, lunch noon–2:30, afternoon tea on the beach 4:00, dinner 7:30–9:30 (approx. $70 for 2 in season, $66 off-season, on the hilltop terrace, or indoors on breezy nights); beach bar open until 10:00 p.m.; informal dress (but no shorts at dinner); room service 7:30 a.m.–11:00 p.m., for a small extra charge

Entertainment: Taped music, beach barbecues on Wednesdays, live music Saturdays and Tuesdays

Sports: Beach, snorkeling, windsurfing, Sunfish sailing, dinghy to Nelson's Dockyard—all free; tennis, scuba, sailboat trips, deep-sea fishing, waterskiing, and horses nearby

P.S.:   No children under 12 in February; closed first Saturday in September to mid-October

St. James's Club

Antigua

Atmosphere

Dining

Sports

Rates

The St. James's Club opened with great fanfare in 1985 and the staff had a chance to polish their act in front of such inaugural celebrities as Joan Collins, Michael York, and Liza Minnelli. Elton John, David Frost, and the duke of Kent checked in shortly afterward, and ever since the glitzy flow has continued more or less unabated.

What's the big attraction? At first glance, it's hardly the physical plant, which started out in the 1960s as a formula two-story Holiday Inn resort, first class rather than deluxe. Hardly an architectural gem, it has little romantic character, except for the mildly Polynesian rooflines and 60,000 flowering shrubs, trees, and plants. The recently redecorated lobby is furnished with forest green wicker chairs and floral-print couches. Custom fabrics, bamboo étagères with bird figurines, bamboo four-posters, and Haitian paintings add a dash of distinction to the basically standard-size rooms, which even with new white-tiled floors, new decorative tilework in the bathrooms, and pastel fabrics, look frumpy (although the flimsy dark-wood armoires criticized in the last edition have now been painted white).

Of the St. James's three residential blocks, your best bet is probably Poinciana (rooms 180–190), if you want privacy, with balconies looking out to sea; Hibiscus (rooms 100–109), if you prefer to be close to the ocean beach and the tennis courts (but avoid the ground-floor rooms or you'll have a steady stream of sun worshipers trotting past your balcony); Bougainvillea (rooms 160–179), if you want a sea view but still like to be close to bars and restaurants. If you'd rather have breezes than air-conditioning, be warned that some of the lower rooms have a restricted flow of air. The quietest rooms of all are 14 and 15, in a string of villas known as the Frangipani Rooms, with none-too-private patios on a small peninsula facing a sheltered lagoon. The best quarters in the hotel, for anyone with moolah to spare, are in the Roof Garden Suite, on the upper floor of the Poinciana block—the terrace is as large as the suite itself, ideal for very private sunbathing.

Five years ago, the resort decked the hillside behind the lagoon with 73 new villas, all two-bedroom, full-kitchen units, more plushly furnished than the hotel rooms. Since these villas are priced for foursomes rather than twosomes (and since they're somewhat huddled together), you'll probably still prefer the hotel itself. But that still leaves the question: What do all these additional accommodations do to the overall ambience of the club? They don't help, that's for sure, unless you're interested in more action. With the additional rooms come more water-sports equipment, two more tennis courts (for a total of seven), and a striking multilevel bar-restaurant for dinner.

More recent changes include a sprucing up of the main dining room, which now has new planters, track lighting, and a peach canopy suspended over the ceiling. A tiered patio has been added around the pool, where guests enjoy afternoon tea at iron garden tables.

Drawbacks aside, few resorts offer guests so many diversions, so for vacationers who want more than a patch of sand and the shade of a palm, the St. James's hundred acres would seem to be as generous as they come—especially when you consider that most of the facilities come at no extra charge. Tennis champ Martina Navratilova came here to learn to scuba dive; she liked the diving and the resort so much that she bought one of the villas. Nevertheless, the St. James's Club is not, as it claims in its brochure, "the best resort in the world." Far from it. It's not even in the top 100 these days.

Name: St. James's Club

Manager: Milton Flueckinger

Address: P.O. Box 63, St. John's, Antigua, West Indies

Location: At Mamora Bay, on the south coast, 30 minutes and $21 by taxi from the airport (the club has a rep at the airport to meet guests)

Telephone: 809/460-5000

Fax: 809/460-3015

Reservations: Leading Hotels of the World

Credit Cards: All major cards

Rooms: 105, including 20 suites, plus the 73 2-bedroom hillside condominium villas in what's called the Village, all with balconies or patios, air-conditioning and ceiling fans, telephones, bathrobes, television, clock radios, safes, amenities trays; some also have hair dryers and scales; suites with mini-bars (stocked on request), villas with kitchenettes; also 4 3-bedroom homes, with private pools and cars, on the hill

Meals: Breakfast 7:30–10:00, lunch noon–2:30 (by the pool or beside the dock), dinner 7:00–10:30 (anywhere from $45 up, in 1 of 3 restaurants); no T-shirts or shorts allowed at dinner, jackets required in main dining room on Saturdays; on Thursdays, Caribbean buffet on beach with steel band or live calypso; 24-hour room service

Entertainment: Something every evening—cocktail piano or combo in the restaurant every evening, disco, casino (blackjack, roulette, 5 slot machines)

Sports: 2 beaches (1 ocean, 1 lagoon), 3 freshwater pools, Jacuzzi, gymnasium (Nautilus, weights, etc.), snorkeling, windsurfing (Mistral instruction), Sunfish and Hobiecat sailing, pedalos, waterskiing, tennis (5 Laykold courts and 2 Omni, 5 with lights, pro shop), putting green, croquet—all free; massage, horseback riding (with guides), scuba diving, sport fishing, and charter sailing extra

P.S.: Expect some parties of cruise ship passengers during the day—in the restaurant, in the pool, on the beach or tennis courts; some children year-round; closed September and October

K Club

Barbuda

| Atmosphere | Dining | Sports | Rates |

When the Milanese fashion mogul Mariuccia Mandelli, aka Krizia, got around to choosing her "personal eden," she opted for Barbuda.

Barbuda? That flat pancake of an island with a nondescript village and a bird preserve where ornithologists from far and wide come to study the frigate bird? That speck of island about 15 minutes by air north of Antigua?

The same. Because what Barbuda has (apart from no hassles) is a forever beach—one of those strands of softest sand that seem to go on and on, running along most of the island's west coast. At the south end of the beach there's a small, clubby resort called Coco Point Lodge, but otherwise there was virtually nothing here until Krizia came along. She and her husband, Aldo Pinto, used to vacation at Coco Point, but had a spat, so the story goes, with the owner; they were in a position to do what we'd all like to do in those circumstances—snap our fingers and say, "Fine! We'll go and build our own resort." Which, after several stops and starts and false alarms, they did.

Usually when an owner or spouse of an owner decides to design a hotel, the results can be a bit of a hodgepodge (there are, of course, some eminent exceptions); but when that owner happens to be a world-class modiste of impeccable taste and, moreover, someone answerable, apparently, only to herself and her husband/manager for the bottom line, then the ingredients are in place for something special. And something special this is.

Her $30-million, 241-acre country club comes with a wondrous sense of space and beachiness, with everything open to the trades and the sea. Her architect, Gianni Gamondi, has given the spread a contemporary flavor but (bless him) has kept within the Antillean vernacular—40 square white cottages with lots of louvers and high-pitched roofs widely strung out along the beach, no rooftop higher than the palm trees. Even the staff housing has more class than the guest rooms in many other hotels.

Everything here is a reflection of Krizia's tastes—down to the Krizia-designed doorknobs. Decor is awash in the house color, a delicate green somewhere between turquoise and aquamarine (turquamarine, perhaps?)—in fact, the place is so color coordinated that I suspect if an errant yellow-breasted bananaquit appeared on the breakfast table it would be shooed off pronto.

As well as being uncommonly stylish, the K Club's suites and villas are unusually spacious. The 20- by 20-foot bedrooms incorporate reading corners with armchairs and ottomans and still don't feel cluttered. Wooden cathedral ceilings 14 feet high and white ceramic-tile floors add to the sense of spaciousness. The walk-in closets could hold enough Krizia dresses to give her Milanese seamstresses carpal tunnel syndrome. The shower stalls are big enough to party in; I love them, but I suspect some folks will say, "With all this space, why no tub?"—the answer probably being, "We want to conserve water."

All this refined decor notwithstanding, I'd probably wrap myself in my *yukata* (Krizia's custom-designed cotton lounging robe) and spend most of the time outdoors on my spacious private deck. Each suite has a swank white on white al fresco kitchenette—an inexplicable luxury since all meals are included in the rate, but it's useful to have the refrigerator close at hand. For siestas, there are bamboo shades to block out the glare and big bamboo loungers that look vaguely like those litters once used to carry missionaries around Africa.

I could happily dine at K Club for a week without feeling deprived of having no other place to go. Even if there were, it wouldn't be half as attractive as this one. The dining pavilion is part of the main lodge, beside the beach, open to the breezes with damar shutters, its lofty ceiling supported by 146 white columns and cooled by a battery of paddle fans. As you might expect, the linens and place settings (Granito Tognana Porcellana) are impeccable. The staff—mostly villagers without any hotel experience— was well trained, helpful, and, on the whole, adept. I don't think I've ever seen a water glass recharged so carefully, so that the slightest droplet never reaches the table; when I asked for an extra wedge of lemon I got a whole saucerful; and the servers were so proud of getting guests' names correct that I felt guilty about using a nom de guerre.

Nor would I feel deprived by a lack of daytime bustle. There's that deck for starters. Oh, the reading I could do there (many of the books in the club library are in Italian—anyone for *Ultima Fermata a Brooklyn* or *Le Avventuri di Huckleberry Finn?*). The pool is a dazzler, with the Krizia logo fashioned in tiles on the bottom. One day I'd have the boatman zoom me along in his Boston Whaler to Spanish Point—a lagoon, a reef, a beach deserted except for the odd charter yacht, a picnic basket, and a two-way radio to let the boatman know when to come back and fetch me.

Moreover, if all goes according to plan, by the time you read this, Aldo Pinto will have attained *his* personal eden—a private nine-hole golf course.

Yet with all its attractions, I have to hesitate about recommending K Club because managers come and go and come and go. Aldo Pinto (whose name I misspelled in the previous edition—or, as he graciously phrased it, "Ponti is Sophia Loren's husband"—and to whom I apologize) took me to task for pointing this out, writing me a thoughtful, detailed letter on the subject, even taking the trouble to list the names to show that there were only five rather than the seven or eight I counted. Even as Pinto sat down and wrote me from Milan (September 1994), a new manager had just taken up residence on the island, but sad to report *that* gentleman too has since left and as of this writing (spring 1995), the resort is now on manager number—well, who cares anymore? Unless it's the guests who pay more than $1,000 a day and expect to say good-bye at the end of their stay to the manager who greeted them when they arrived.

Apparently the resort is doing quite well (lots of Europeans), and there are few complaints about the food and service. Because the new man, Jean-Luc Chomat, has survived 2 years at the club as assistant manager, let's hope that K Club is now settling down—because it *should* be one of the highest rated resorts in the Caribbean.

Name: K Club
Manager: Jean-Luc Chomat
Address: Barbuda, Antigua & Barbuda, West Indies
Location: On the island's leeward coast, about 20 rutted minutes from the airfield (the hotel sends a Nissan Patrol to meet you); the resort will also arrange the last leg of your trip from Antigua on a 7-passenger Islander for about $150 per passenger round-trip (but beware—the brochure promises a trip from New York of "only 3½ hours [plus 15 minutes]," but if I were you I'd count on an extra hour rather than 15 minutes because of immigration and customs on Antigua)
Telephone: 809/460-0300
Fax: 809/460-0305
Reservations: 800/628-8929
Credit Cards: All major cards
Rooms: 40 cottages in various configurations, all with ceiling fans and air-conditioning, huge bathrooms (showers only, *yukatas*, hair dryers, generous supplies of Krizia amenities), refrigerators and pantries on the terrace
Meals: Breakfast 7:15–10:15, lunch 12:30–2:30, dinner 7:30–10:00 (lunch $160, dinner $200 for 2 outside guests); informal but stylish dress ("no jackets required"); room service 7:00 a.m.–10:00 p.m.
Entertainment: Comfy bar/terrace, library, TV/VCR lounge, occasional steel band (but "no amplification ever, and no taped music in the restaurant"—hooray!)
Sports: A mile-long beach, heated seawater pool, Jacuzzi, tennis (2 courts

with lights), snorkeling gear, windsurfing, waterskiing, sailing, boat trips, golf (9 holes)—all free

P.S.:　No children under 12; closed September and October

Vue Pointe Hotel
Montserrat

☆					♀				◖◗◖◗				$			
Atmosphere					**Dining**				**Sports**				**Rates**			

The view of Vue Pointe is coastline, gray-sand beach, a golf course streaking through the coconut palms in the valley, a few private villas on the hillside across the valley, the green mountains beyond. The hotel itself consists mostly of hexagonal rondavels on a grassy slope above the sea, each individual unit with a sitting area and deck screened by flowering shrubs. The bright rooms have modern rattan furniture and jaunty pastel colors. The main lodge at the top of the hill houses a large bar/lounge/terrace alongside a swimming pool. The spacious dining room makes no pretense to grand cuisine, but it does offer a tasty selection of West Indian dishes and a Wednesday-evening barbecue that's popular with islanders as well as guests. There's a water-sport facility and a lively little bar on the beach, the golf course is never crowded (it's a private club, not the hotel's, but guests have privileges), and the two tennis courts are in better condition than you'll find in many so-called tennis resorts—the Osbornes are big tennis buffs.

The Osbornes are about as dedicated and gracious as any hoteliers in the islands, so their hotel is comfortable and welcoming—the Caribbean in all its unspoiled simplicity. And *so* relaxing.

Name:　Vue Pointe Hotel
Owners/Managers:　Cedric and Carol Osborne
Address:　P.O. Box 65, Montserrat, West Indies
Location:　On the western shore, about 10 minutes and $8 by taxi from Plymouth, 30 minutes and $16 by taxi from the airport; Montserrat is 15 minutes by air from Antigua
Telephone:　809/491-5711

Fax: 809/491-4813
Reservations: 800/235-0709
Credit Cards: American Express, MasterCard, Visa
Rooms: 28 hillside rondavels and 12 rooms, all with private bathrooms, terraces, direct-dial telephones, cable TV, hair dryers, refrigerators; some with air-conditioning
Dining: Breakfast 7:30–10:30, lunch noon–3:00, dinner 6:30–10:00, all in the breeze-and-fan-cooled dining pavilion (approx. $75 for 2); Wednesday-night barbecue with steel band; Sunday barbecue buffet lunch, 12:30–2:00; casual dress; room service breakfast only
Entertainment: Steel band on Wednesdays, cocktail party in the Osbornes's home on Mondays, live band on Saturday nights
Sports: Hilltop freshwater swimming pool, tennis (2 courts with lights); 9-hole golf course down the hill (free transportation to and fro), water sports on the beach
P.S.: Some children, open all year

Other Choices

Hurricane Cove Bungalows

Nevis

Great view (the humped outline of St. Kitts just a mile across the channel), quiet location (a steep rise above a cove—don't let the name deter you, it means it's sheltered *from* big blows), and come-hither rates (from $125 in winter) make this a valid alternative to the island's inns. The mini resort consists of 10 timber bungalows cantilevered out from the hill, looking, with their glassless shuttered windows, raftered ceilings, and wraparound verandas, perfectly natural in their island setting; but, in fact, they're prefab structures from, of all places, Finland. Each bungalow has a shower rather than a bathtub, a well-equipped kitchen, and mosquito netting to jazz up the country-style wood-framed bed. Three bungalows have private pools, there's a small pool on the grounds, plus water sports and a close-by beach. 10 bungalows. Doubles: $125, winter 1994–95. *Hurricane Cove Bungalows, Nevis, West Indies. Telephone and fax: 809/469-9462.*

Ocean Terrace Inn
St. Kitts

This is not exactly what you would call a romantic hideaway, but it has a lot of island atmosphere in its role as a crossroads for dedicated island-hoppers, traveling either for pleasure or on business. The Ocean Terrace overlooks the town of Basseterre and the sweep of South Friar's Bay, packing 30 comfortable guest rooms (all with double beds except for 6 rooms, which have twins), 6 two-bedroom and 2 one-bedroom apartments into a well-tended garden, with an additional 12 efficiency apartments across the street in the bayside Fisherman's Village. The multilevel garden has two freshwater pools, one of them with a swim-up bar and a grottolike Jacuzzi. The inn's dining room and terrace bars are popular spots for lunch with both sightseers and Kittitians, but in the evening they have strong competition from Fisherman's Wharf, the barbecue restaurant at the hotel dock. Another option is Turtle Beach Bar & Grill, located on the southeastern peninsula. Open for lunch and dinner, the restaurant is a 20-minute bus ride (free transportation is provided) from the hotel. Free snorkeling equipment and Windsurfers, Sailfish, and acqua eye boards are available on the beach. A concierge desk caters to guests at all hours. 30 rooms. Doubles: $116 to $346, winter 1994–95. *Ocean Terrace Inn, P.O. Box 65, St. Kitts, West Indies. Telephone: 800/524-0512; fax: 809/465-1057.*

Siboney Beach Club
Antigua

Owned and run by a friendly, outgoing Australian named Tony Johnson, who arrived on the island by yacht more than 25 years ago and never left, Siboney is a small, relaxed, all-suite hotel on Dickenson Bay where you can hang out in the thatch-roofed restaurant for hours chewing the fat and basking in the sea breezes. Johnson has transformed a formerly undis-tinguished block of rooms into a lush retreat by planting a veritable jungle on the grounds; it's as if you'd stumbled upon a miniature rain forest. There's a fair-size pool tucked away in the greenery, and after you've worked up an appetite swimming laps or windsurfing on the bay, you can sit down to a meal of local shrimp sautéed in garlic and lime, roast duckling in apple and cinnamon sauce, or other tasty, hearty fare. Bedrooms have king-size beds, ceiling fans, and air-conditioning, the refurbished sitting areas open onto patios or balconies, and each unit has a refrigerator. Nothing fancy and contemporary styling, but for those who prefer a homey escape and friendly staff, this may be the place. 12 suites. Doubles: $230 to $290, winter 1994–95. *Siboney Beach Club, P.O. Box 222, St. John's, Antigua, West Indies. Telephone: 809/462-0806; fax: 890/462-3356.*

Covecastles Villa Resort

Anguilla

So distinctive is its postmodern architecture that Covecastles leaps out at you as you fly over Anguilla. From the coastline of St. Martin, just across the channel, it looks like a battery of bunkers and you half expect antiaircraft guns to pop out and *ratatat*. The stark-white sculptural forms presumably make some kind of statement, but if the architecture is too un-Caribbean for these parts, even the most ardent traditionalist is likely to be seduced by Covecastles's secluded setting, dazzling half-mile beach, refined luxury, and attention to detail—from the champagne on ice awaiting your arrival and the exquisite hand-embroidered linens that caress you at night to the raw-silk upholstery on the rattan loungers and the inviting Pawleys Island hammocks on the oversize terra-cotta verandas. Originally, Covecastles consisted only of two- and three-bedroom villas, which always posed problems for lovers; now there are also villa suites, more suitable for twosomes, with ceiling fans and acres of louvers (some bedrooms with air-conditioning), cable television, radio, telephone, and kitchens that give new meaning to the words *fully equipped*. There is a small restaurant on the premises, too (for a resort with lodgings for fewer than 40 guests!), open for dinner only, but its kitchens are available for room service throughout the day. Sports facilities include two lighted tennis courts, snorkeling equipment, bicycles, and Sunfish sailboats. 12 villas and villa suites. Doubles: $590, winter 1994–95, room only. *Covecastles Villa Resort, P.O. Box 248, Shoal Bay West, Anguilla, British West Indies. Telephone: 809/497-6801; fax: 809/497-6051. Reservations: 800/348-4716.*

The Mariners

Anguilla

This hotel, bless its unprepossessing heart, strives to be true to its West Indian heritage: verandas trimmed with gingerbread, lattice screens and louvers, two-toned shutters, tray ceilings and wood moldings, showers rather than baths, ceiling fans and breezes rather than air conditioners. And the hotel dining room is just what you would hope to find in a backwater such as this—island-style, indoor-outdoor architecture, planter and driftwood decor, and a wooden beachside gallery with views of outlying islets—Dog and Prickly Pear. Located on 8 acres beside a crescent of beach adjoining the salt ponds and a sleepy-eyed, one-street hamlet called Sandy Ground, the Mariners has rooms and suites that are divided among cottages and two two-story buildings. They're arranged basically in an arc around the beach and sea-grape trees, with others closer to the cliff; the setup and rate roster are confusing—Beachfront, Beachfront Special, Cliffside, Cliffside Special. The first two categories are best. Forget the others. Each cottage is ingeniously arranged so guests can have simply a double room or a studio with kitchen or a one-bedroom suite or the entire cottage (a two-bedroom suite), each unit with its own entrance (interior double doors enhance privacy). You'll probably see more than your cottage mates in the split-level dining room—although the resort is theoretically all-inclusive, it's a popular spot for guests in other hotels because it's so moderately priced. 65 studios, rooms, and suites. Doubles: $210 to $380, winter 1994–95. *The Mariners, P.O. Box 139, Sandy Ground, Anguilla, British West Indies. Telephone: 809/497-2671; fax: 809/497-2901. Reservations: 800/848-7938.*

The French West Indies

St. Barthélemy

Guadeloupe

Martinique

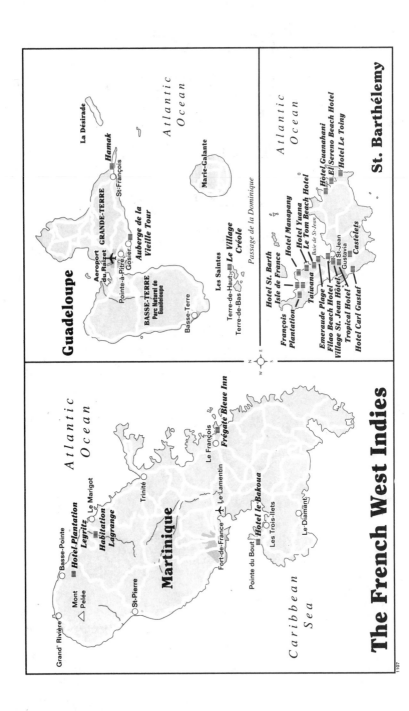

The French West Indies

The French West Indies

The *tricouleur* flutters above and microbikinis wiggle on Martinique, Guadeloupe, St. Martin (the French half of the island otherwise known as Sint Maarten), St. Barthélemy, and a few out-islands; French *savoir faire* and *joie de vivre* have been transplanted intact—in fact, they may even have gained from overlays of tropical sensuousness. You'll find some of the best eating in the Caribbean here, some of the sportiest highways, the most stylish dressers, and, on the nudist beaches, the most enthusiastic undressers. These are great islands, or integral political units, of *la belle France.*

The largest of the islands is Martinique (50 miles long and 22 miles wide), a lush, mountainous land with rain forests, plantations, fishing villages, and masses of wildflowers. It has enjoyed centuries of renown for its dusky maidens: Napoléon's Josephine is the most famous, but Martinique has also provided queens and consorts for a dozen other rulers— including Louis XIV and the Grand Turk of Stamboul. Fort-de-France, the capital, is an intriguing mishmash of West Indies seaport, the latest Peugeots, fishing boats, yachts, open-air markets, high fashion, and gourmet restaurants. But the most interesting part of the island for my money is the spectacular north around Mont Pelée, especially the town of St. Pierre, once known as the Paris of the Caribbean, before it was destroyed when Pelée erupted one Sunday morning in 1902. The highway/road/path along the rugged northeast coast to remote Grand'Rivière is also worth an excursion and picnic.

Guadeloupe (from the Spanish "Guadalupe" and the Arabic "Oued-el-Houb," meaning River of Love) is really two islands, Grande-Terre and Basse-Terre, linked by a short bridge. The capital is also known as Basse-Terre, away in the south, shut off from the rest of the island by the magnificent Natural Park of Guadeloupe. But the action is up around Pointe-à-Pitre, which is rapidly beginning to look like a suburb of Paris. When *les citoyens* of Pointe-à-Pitre want to get away from it all, they board a ferryboat for the 60-minute ride to Terre-de-Haut, one of the islets that make up the Les Saintes islands. It's about as quiet and unspoiled as they come, with an

---

Note: Hotels on St. Martin, the French half of the dual St. Maarten/ St. Martin, are listed under St. Maarten in the chapter on the Dutch Windward Islands.

atmosphere that's French Antillean to the last Gauloise. This is one place where you may need an acquaintance with French beyond *bonjour* and *merci*.

Technically, St. Barthélemy, or St. Barts, is part of the *département* of Guadeloupe, although it's closer to St. Martin, which is (at least on the French side) in the same geopolitical boat. St. Barts is the tiniest (about 8 square miles) of the French islands and something of a curiosity: It's the only island in the Caribbean with a predominantly white population (mostly descendants of the original Breton settlers), and its picture-postcard port of Gustavia was formerly an outpost of Sweden. Despite its modest size, St. Barts manages to accommodate something like 60 restaurants.

How to Get There   To get to Guadeloupe or Martinique, the most usual way is from San Juan on American Eagle, but there may also be direct service from New York with Minerve Airways, on weekends in winter only; from Miami, there's Air France service once a week. You can also make relatively easy connections via Antigua, St. Maarten, and Barbados.

For St. Barthélemy, you first fly to St. Maarten for connecting flights on Windward, Air St. Barthélemy, or some other local airline about 16 times a day, depending on the season. There are also scheduled flights on interisland airlines from San Juan and St. Thomas. For the fainthearted, who may prefer not to endure the modified kamikaze approach to St. Barts's airstrip, there are also several sea crossings (by launch or catamaran) from Philipsburg on the Dutch side or Marigot on the French side. Two upscale hotels on St. Barts—Carl Gustav and Guanahani—now have private launches that pick up and drop off more or less right at the airport on St. Maarten (this is a very pricey alternative). Since St. Barts cannot receive aircraft after dark, zealous trip planners may want to have some kind of backup option in mind in case they are stranded overnight on St. Maarten.

For information on the French West Indies, call 900/990-0040 (the call costs 50 cents a minute); Martinique, 800/391-4909. Information about Martinique is also available on the Internet at http://www.nyo.com/martinique

François Plantation

St. Barthélemy

☆☆☆			🍷🍷🍷		◑			$ $ $ $	
Atmosphere			**Dining**		**Sports**			**Rates**	

For 20 years or thereabouts, François Beret has been one of St. Barts's most esteemed restaurateurs, so his longtime fans have dutifully followed him to his new hillside inn. They applaud his restaurant, his cuisine, his wines, but his eyes really light up when you compliment him on his *garden*.

In this flowery minijungle you'll find lantana and mango, palmier and amandier, filao and caoutchou, "probably one of every type of tree that grows on the island," and 20 types of hibiscus in exquisite colorings, which M. Beret arranges in joyous bouquets to decorate his veranda. There are so many flowers and trees growing in this luxuriant garden that you barely see the inn and its dozen cottages until you're practically on the doorstep and walking beneath the whitewashed pergola into the lounge.

François Plantation sits on a cool hillside near the hamlet of Colombier (not far from where the Rockefellers built their private hideaway), with sweeping views from the veranda and most of the cottages, the grandest panorama reserved for the hilltop swimming pool with its sunbathing "island."

The pastel-colored cottages, too, are designed in traditional Antillean style—square wooden frames with steeply pitched roofs, raftered ceilings, terrazzo-tile floors, chunky pencil-post beds crafted of mahogany, with rattan stands to house refrigerators and television sets.

The veranda doubles as lounge and restaurant, the former furnished with cushioned rattan and plump sofas in shades that echo M. Beret's hibiscus, and the latter in Georgian-style mahogany tables and cane-seated chairs. Lavish greenery in pots and planters and the leafy garden just beyond the white balustrade give the place an authentic colonial look, while the fabrics and pastel prints add a dash of sophistication.

François Beret, although still the mastermind behind the menu and upholder of standards, now functions as boniface in chief, handing the kitchen brigade over to the talented Picard Christophe. The extensive à la carte menu includes fillet of red mullet scented with vanilla, *Legendus Boeuf de Coutancie* rib steak (the beef is organically raised—"they drink 3 litres of beer daily"—and aged slowly), rabbit spiced with sumac, and umpteen other meticulously seasoned entrées.

Name: François Plantation

Owners/Managers: François and Françoise Beret

Address: Colombier, 97133 St. Barthélemy, French West Indies

Location: In the hills, about 10 minutes and $12 from the airport or the main town of Gustavia

Telephone: 590/27-78-82

Fax: 590/27-61-26

Reservations: WIMCO

Credit Cards: American Express, MasterCard, Visa

Rooms: 12 colonial-style cottages, each with marble bathroom (twin vanities), air-conditioning and ceiling fan, direct-dial telephone, stocked mini-bar, cable television, wall safe

Meals: Breakfast 8:00–10:00 on the veranda; no lunch; dinner 7:00–10:00, also on the veranda (approx. $120 for 2), dress informal, some quiet background tapes; room service for breakfast only

Sports: Freshwater pool, sundeck; beaches nearby (within walking distance downhill, but you really need a car)

P.S.: Not suitable for children; closed August 15 to October 20

Castelets

St. Barthélemy

Atmosphere

Dining

Sports   **Rates**

Perch by the edge of the tiny triangular pool, feet dangling in the water, champagne glass dangling from your fingers, and take in the view. It's a breathtaking panorama: Far below (you're almost 1,000 feet up here), the Caribbean unfurls in a montage of silver beaches, rocky promontories, craggy islets, scudding sails. It's like watching a movie while sitting in the balcony (remember when movie theaters had balconies and big screens?) but without the in-your-face soundtrack.

Up here at Mont Lurin, all is peace and tranquility (well, maybe now and again the calm may be disturbed by diners arriving by Minimoke and grinding unfamiliar gears as they try to negotiate the almost perpendicular hill without running backward). That alone would be worth foregoing a resort by the edge of the beach. Castelets has always seemed to me like an Antillean version of one of those hill-town auberges back in France, a place where you stay overnight just to be close to a first-class kitchen.

New owners and a new chef have revamped the menu, so prepare for leisurely evenings devoted to *la bourride de poisson blanc, le tian de rouget de roche,* or *le mignon de veau griottines en noisette sauce légères aux épices,* desserts such as *nougat glace au gingembre*—gingered nougat with ice cream and jasmine-flavored tea.

Then after your demitasse and cognac you can slip off across the court-yard to your room or suite with its distinctive decor—Breton-style bed, rope balustrades, framed Hermès prints, and antique maps—throw open the louvered doors of Guyana greenheart, and take another long, lingering look at that view. Now the panorama is all twinkling lights. At times it may be a puzzle to tell where the lights on land become the shimmering of the sea become the twinkling of the stars.

Name: Castelets

Owner/Manager: Jean-Claud Laugeois

Address: 97133 St. Barthélemy, French West Indies

Location: On Mont Lurin, above Gustavia, about 15 minutes and $10 by taxi from the airport, less to town

Telephone: 590/27-61-73

Fax: 590/27-85-27

Reservations: Ralph Locke Islands

Credit Cards: None in the hotel; American Express, MasterCard, Visa for restaurant bills

Rooms: 7, 2 in the main house (above the kitchen, etc.) and 5 in garden villas, with ceiling fans, terraces, and tape decks

Meals: Breakfast 8:00–10:00, dinner 7:00–10:00, in the main dining room (approx. $80–$100 for 2); informal dress; room service for break-fast and dinner

Entertainment: Eating

Sports: Tiny plunge pool; beaches and water sports 7 minutes away

P.S.: "Not too suitable for children"; closed September and October

Hotel Carl Gustaf
St. Barthélemy

☆☆☆					♀♀♀			◐				S S S S S
Atmosphere					**Dining**			**Sports**				**Rates**

The 4-year-old Carl Gustaf is notched into a precipitous hillside on the edge of town, its suites cascading down from the lobby, just four suites on each level with an *escalier central* running down the middle.

Trouble is, there are 82 steps to the *escalier,* plus another score or so to reach the lobby and restaurant, so be sure to reserve a suite on the upper levels (rates are the same, regardless of location). Moreover, the lower the suite, the more the utility poles and power cables debase the view. But what a view!

Gustavia, with its rectangular yacht-filled port and red-roofed wooden houses, has to be one of the prettiest sights in the Caribbean, and the panorama from the Carl Gustaf is quintessential Gustavia. And so guests can enjoy the scene in uncrowded, scantily clad comfort, the architect has designed a living room with one wall removed, facing a broad wooden deck with wooden loungers—and a tiny plunge pool at the edge of each deck.

Carl Gustaf's cantaloupe-colored stucco cottages echo the style of the traditional St. Bart's home—trim squares with steeply pitched red roofs. One-bedroom suites consist of the terrace, adorned with a pergola; the three-walled open-air living room, measuring around 300 square feet; a small pantry with mini-bar and two-ring burner; and a bedroom with two sets of French doors opening to the deck and the living room—just as well it has so much glass, since it's quite small. Ditto the bathroom (which has a shower only). Two-bedroom suites have an identical bedroom on the other side of the living room, plus what the brochure calls a "cabin" with two bunks for kids. Cabin? Cubbyhole. It should be added, however, that the hefty rates bring many frills and refinements—Porthault bathrobes, Signoricci toiletries, two Matra fax machines, three telephones, three TVs, and a VCR. The one bedroomer ($950 with breakfast) rates only one fax, two phones, and two tellies.

The best view in the house is from the lobby/bar/restaurant level, a white on white terrace enclosed in frameless glass screens, with a few tables on a tiny terrace beside a bikini-size pool that's more decorative than swimmable. If you decide to eat here, let me point out that the view is best at lunchtime—in the evening the glass screens tend to reflect too much sparkle and glitter, dissipating the view. If the view is impressive, the cuisine is less so (surprisingly, since the chef's background is Château d'Artigny and the Hotel de Crillon).

There are, of course, lots of nice touches here. Blue-white-gold Haviland china for the filet of beef. Fretwork grills over the air-conditioning outlets (they look like they were done by one of the island's master carpenters; in fact, they were designed and worked by computers in Switzerland). The state-of-the-art halogen burners in the pantry. The fan-shaped headboards trimmed with Swiss fabrics. The paintings and lithographs of sailing ships in each suite. The flower-decked parking garage across the street. In fact, the Carl Gustaf would be a super-romantic hideaway if the rates were guillotined—say, by 50%. In that case, I could see myself very happily spending a couple of spellbinding nights here (the spellbinding part being the view, of course). As it is, for what you pay here you could have a lovely suite *and* all meals *and* all drinks *and* sports at Curtain Bluff on Antigua. Hell, you could rent Princess Margaret's five-bedroom villa on Mustique, with a private staff of four, for less than the cost of one of Carl Gustaf's two-bedroom suites.

Name: Hotel Carl Gustaf

Manager: Eric Tronconi

Address: Rue des Normands, Gustavia, 97133 St. Barthélemy, French West Indies

Location: In the foothills on the edge of town, about 5 minutes from the airport, easy walking distance to the cafés and restaurants of Gustavia; the hotel also has a high-speed launch which, for a stiff price, will meet guests in St. Maarten.

Telephone: 590/27-82-83

Fax: 590/27-82-37

Reservations: 800/932-3222 or 401/847-6290

Credit Cards: All major cards

Rooms: 6 1-bedroom and 6 2-bedroom suites, all with indoor-outdoor living rooms, broad wooden decks, private plunge pools, air-conditioned bedrooms, bathrobes, hair dryers, pantries, mini-bars, TV-VCR, direct-dial telephones, fax machines

Meals: Breakfast anytime, lunch noon–2:30, dinner 7:00–10:00 (approx. $120 for 2); informal but stylish dress; electronic piano in the evening; room service during dining-room hours

Entertainment: The bar, the view (a Yamaha Clavinova hardly rates as entertainment, does it?)

Sports: Plunge pools, exercise room—free; the nearest beach is a 5-minute drive away, water sports 10 minutes away

P.S.:   Some children; open all year

Hotel St. Barth Isle de France

St. Barthélemy

☆☆		
Atmosphere

♈ ♈ ♈	
Dining

◐ ◐	
Sports

$ $ $ $	
Rates

What this cumbrously named hotel has going for it is its beach—Anse des Flamands, one of the loveliest curves of sand on the island, enclosed by two low headlands, protected by reefs, with a pair of islets just offshore to make it picture postcard–perfect. Next door (well, 100 yards away, past a couple of junky backyards) is Taiwana, a nine-room ultraexclusive retreat for celebrities who don't mind paying ultra-top-dollar to sit around a pool with day-trippers who've just come for lunch and a swim.

The main clubhouse is a handsome, if concretey, echo of an old plantation house, with stairs sweeping up to a broad veranda, reception desk, and an antique-lined breezeway leading to the pool deck and beach.

The problem is that this lodge is the only part of the hotel adjoining the beach—the Hotel St. Barth Etcetera, to my mind, is really two hotels. Only 12 of the rooms and suites adjoin the beach; the others are strewn around a grove of latanier palms across the street. Each complex has its own swimming pool; the garden also has a squash court, exercise room, and tennis court.

Of the 12 beachfront lodgings in the clubhouse, 4 are suites, all with patios or balconies overlooking the pool and bay, but the patios on the lower floor are too close to the pool for comfort and privacy (unless you behave at all times in a very circumspect manner, you'd better keep the drapes drawn); verandas on the upper floor have too much concrete, which blocks much of the view. Suites and rooms alike blend light colors and fabrics with a smattering of Victorian and colonial furniture (they say every piece is antique, I say some are reproductions), interspersed with smart contemporary rattan and wicker. A couple of scatter rugs on the marble floors and a few extra decorations on the walls might make the lodgings feel more cozy.

Likewise, the garden cottages are pleasant enough, but they're designed for air-conditioning rather than breezes. Neither the French doors nor the windows have screens—try to get some fresh air and you're liable to get some bugs. But I know some people who prefer the garden's shade to the beach's glare.

What these rooms do have is space. The bathroom in my cottage was larger than the bedroom at the Carl Gustaf, and it was equipped with a large oval tub-for-two. The tub is positioned alongside a picture window with tinted glass; folks on the outside, I was assured, can't look in. Maybe yes, maybe no. I suspect most guests will keep the venetian blinds tightly shut, especially when the lights are on. (It's a dumb idea, anyway, since there's nothing much to look at.)

I stayed here shortly after the resort opened 3 years ago before the crew had gotten its act together, so I pointed out some of the shortcomings. Now the owner is furious with me and commands (with capital letters, double underscoring, lots of exclamation points) to remove his hotel from my guidebook. Well, of course, since no one pays to be in the guide no one can pay not to be in the guide, so here's a reevaluation.

Apparently I was right to criticize the cuisine because that chef was ousted soon after; apparently, too, I was right to carp about the location of the restaurant (in the garden, between the health club and the lit tennis courts), because that, too, is gone, replaced by a new dining pavilion beside the beach. Both changes add immeasurably to the pleasures of staying here, or even stopping off for a meal.

The new restaurant, La Case des Îles, is a variation on a traditional island house, or *case*, extended with a 30-seat pavilion, much more the sort of setting you expect to find in a location like this, with its views across the beach and bay to the whitecapped reef and the distant isles. My lunch— fresh salad, grilled espadon perfectly prepared and served with baby cour- gettes and carrots—held its own against any other meal I had on an island that's noted for its cuisine. Into the bargain, the staff is now much more personable and no longer treats guests and diners like intrusions, as they did in the early days.

Name: Hotel St. Barth Isle de France

Owner/Manager: Patric Pilzer

Address: Baie des Flamandes, P.O. Box 812, 97133 St. Barthélemy, French West Indies

Location: About 5 minutes from the airport, 6 minutes from Gustavia

Telephone: 590/27-61-81

Fax: 590/27-86-83

Reservations: 800/628-8929

Credit Cards: All major cards

Rooms: 28, including 8 rooms and 4 suites in the main lodge, the remain- der in cottages in the garden, all with air-conditioning, decks or ve- randas, cable TV with remote, stocked mini-bars, hair dryers, bathrobes

Meals: Breakfast 7:00–10:00, lunch noon–3:00, dinner 7:00–10:00 (approx. $100 for 2); informal but stylish dress; room service during dining-room hours, extra charge

Entertainment: Yourselves—but there's a wealth of nightlife a short drive away

Sports: Beach, freshwater pool, tennis (2 courts with lights), fitness center, squash

P.S.:   Some children; closed mid-September to November 1

Hotel Le Toiny

St. Barthélemy

Atmosphere	**Dining**	**Sports**	**Rates**

The birdsong tells you the sun is up. You scramble down from your oversize four-poster, pad across the floor, slide open the glass doors, blink in the light, then plop into your private swimming pool.

A few minutes later the sound of a Minimoke pulling up at the gate tells you it's time to slip into your embroidered bathrobe before the waitress appears with breakfast. Freshly baked croissants. Freshly squeezed fruit juice. Homemade yogurt. A platter of fresh fruit. A thermos of coffee. Bernardaud china, all carefully set on the patio dining table while you admire the view—across the flower borders to the beach and palms, with Caribbean all the way to the horizon. Try not to slurp your coffee—you'll disturb the peace.

Le Toiny is the third of a trio of small hotels that opened on St. Barts in 1992 and certainly the most romantic. It consists of 12 island-style cottages notched into a rise a few hundred yards from the shore, each cottage on a different level to ensure privacy, each with a 20- by 10-foot swimming pool—designed with admirable refinement.

Each 1,076-square-foot cottage can easily accommodate a large deck and covered terrace (with dining table, coffee table, chairs for each, and a pair of loungers); a living room with pantry, desk, fax, exercise machine, and a chunky armoire holding a VCR and 21-inch TV; a bedroom with a four-poster bed so high you almost have to hoist yourself aboard and a matching armoire with another TV; a bathroom with walk-in closets, separate toilet, separate tub, separate shower with a big window overlooking the bay. Granted, size is not everything. What is so impressive about these lodgings is the care that's gone into the decor and the spare-no-expense attention to detail—big decorative porcelain vases atop the armoires, the selection of hand-milled soaps in a small wooden box, the tissues wrapped in dainty white lace napkins handmade by women over in the village of Corossol, patio furniture that matches the lavender, mint, and peach hues of the drapes and bedspreads.

Each cottage has a view, though guests at the top of the hill see more of the Caribbean, and the *maison du directeur,* the owner's private aerie, comes with three bedrooms, a few additional refinements, and rents for $1,450 per night.

The main lodge houses a tiny lobby, furnished with oriental antiques and tastefully arrayed doodads; the bar/lounge has the air of a colonial plantation house, and the adjoining 30-seat restaurant, named La Gaiac for the distinctive native tree, spreads out behind sliding floor to ceiling windows. The terrace incorporates a swimming pool (outside lunch guests may use the pool and dressing rooms), but the breezes on this corner of the island often rule out al fresco dining. The cuisine is impressive, masterminded by a youthful Frenchman, Maxime Deschamps, who honed his skills at some of France's most honored hotels and restaurants. The wine list complements the French-Caribbean cuisine very nicely.

The few reservations you might have about Le Toiny are the price (even with a private pool, even with a self-contained cottage, steep compared with neighboring islands); the lack of sports facilities on the premises (tennis is 5 minutes away, water sports 10 minutes); and the nearby windward beach, which is better for surfboarding than for swimming. And given the breeze-cooled location, I would have preferred louvers rather than sliding glass doors.

But, for all those lovers whose idea of play is something other than tennis or waterskiing, Le Toiny is just about perfect.

Name: Hotel Le Toiny
Manager: Laurie Smith and David Henderson
Address: 97133 St. Barthélemy, French West Indies
Location: On the "far" side of the island, at Anse de Toiny, about 15 minutes by taxi from the airport (complimentary shuttle) or Gustavia
Telephone: 590/27-88-88
Fax: 590/27-89-30
Reservations: WIMCO
Credit Cards: All major cards
Rooms: 12 cottages, each a self-contained suite with private pool, pantry,

air-conditioning and ceiling fans, 3 direct-dial telephones, 2 TVs with VCR-cassette player, fax machine, gym equipment, veranda/deck, bathroom with tub and shower, bathrobes and hair dryer; the owner's suite also has a whirlpool tub and dining patio

Meals: Breakfast 7:00–11:00, lunch noon–2:30, dinner 7:00–11:00 (approx. $100 for 2) in the 30-seat La Gaiac, although lunch may be served on the terrace beside the pool, trade winds permitting; casual but stylish dress; 24-hour room service; some soft background music (mostly classic jazz)

Entertainment: Small bar adjoining the restaurant, in-room massage

Sports: Large freshwater pool, 12 private pools, snorkeling gear; beach (5-minute walk), tennis, and water sports nearby

P.S.:   Few children; closed September and October

Hotel Manapany
St. Barthélemy

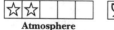
Atmosphere

Dining

Sports

Rates

The Manapany is tucked away on Anse des Cayes—among unkempt, typically Antillean landscape. Nonetheless, celebrities such as Mick Jagger, Peter Allen, Gianni Versace, and tennis ace Yannick Noah have sussed it out and local cognoscenti praise its Ballahou Restaurant as one of the island's finest. Given the competition, gourmet and otherwise, on St. Barthélemy, that's saying quite a bit.

The Manapany's cottages are designed in traditional island style with red-shingle roofs and gingerbread trim, and each consists of a suite with terrace and room with balcony. The rooms are small, but the suites are spacious and ideal for lounging and relaxing, with 20-foot screened terraces fitted with wicker sofas, armchairs, coffee table, dining table and chairs, and full kitchenette. Soothing pastel fabrics set off white on white walls, ceiling, and floors. Beachfront rooms cost more, of course, but since most of them tend to look out on other cottages (try to avoid the Lapis Lazuli and Chrysolite suites), you may want to opt for one of the upper cottages clinging to the steep, terraced hillside. They impose a bit of a hike down a somewhat precipitous path to get to the beach, pool, or restaurant, but they do afford more breezes and a stunning view. But the choice quarters are now the 12 Club Suites, with larger bathrooms and porches with refrigerators and two-ring burners (four beside the beach, eight on the hillside).

Whether you walk down the hill, Minimoke it, or just step over from your beach cottage, it's worth the effort when you're bound for dinner at the Ballahou (French nouvelle) or the glass-enclosed Ouanalou (Italian nouvelle). The Ballahou is attractive, with a bar at one end (equipped, alas, with a TV), its gingerbread trim fashioned from a single piece of timber about 40 feet long and decorated with lobsters, seahorses, and crabs. The Ouanalou curves around the big pool by the edge of the beach and seems to be one of the most congenial spots on St. Barts.

Name: Hotel Manapany

Owner/Manager: Guy Roy

Address: Box 114, 97133 St. Barthélemy, French West Indies

Location: On the bay known as Anse de Caye, about 5 minutes and $6 from the airstrip

Telephone: 590/27-66-55

Fax: 590/27-75-28

Reservations: Direct

Credit Cards: All major cards

Rooms: 52, including 20 rooms, 20 junior suites, 12 new Club Suites, all with air-conditioning and ceiling fans, balconies or patios, private bathrooms (showers only, baths in Club Suites, bathrobes, wall-mounted hair dryers), clock radios, color TV (in-house movies, English and French), direct-dial telephones, pantries in suites

Meals: Breakfast 7:30–9:30, lunch noon–3:00, dinner 7:00–10:00 (approx. $60–$90 for 2), in the Ballahou or the Ouanalou; informal dress; 24-hour room service (including full menu during restaurant hours), $2 per person extra charge; piano player or taped background music.

Entertainment: Bar/lounge/terrace with piano, taped music, and *quel horreur!* a big TV set "for Americans who want to watch football"; chess, Scrabble, backgammon; to say nothing of oodles of bars 10 to 15 minutes away by Minimoke

Sports: Beach (windswept, with coral, not especially good for swimming or windsurfing), large egg-shaped freshwater pool with island deck for sunbathing, whirlpool (solar heated, sometimes lukewarm), tennis (1 court, pro, lights), snorkeling masks, exercise room with Universal equipment—all free; boat trips (with hotel-prepared picnics), scuba diving, and sailing can be arranged

P.S.:   Closed September and October

Filao Beach Hotel
St. Barthélemy

 Atmosphere   **Dining**   **Sports**    **Rates**

The ambience around here is pure Côte d'Azur—but most resorts on the French Riviera would give an arm and a leg to have a beach like the Filao's.

This plush little hideaway is on one of the prime locations on St. Barthélemy, right on fashionable (and usually topless) St. Jean Bay, on that talcum-fine strand between the island's toy-town airstrip and the rocky promontory known as Eden Rock.

Hugging its plot of precious beach, the hotel meanders back along well-marked paths through gardens of sea-grape trees livened with white hibiscus, allamanda, and red cattail. Red-roofed bungalows house 30 guest rooms, each named for a château in France, with the name (Villandry, Montlouis, whatever) etched on a ceramic owl above the door. Each room is generously furnished with double bed, daybed/sofa, plenty of chairs and tables, television, refrigerator, both air-conditioning *and* ceiling fan. The roomy bath incorporates tub, shower, and bidet.

All 30 rooms have been recently restyled with new Italian floor tiles, but it's in the niceties that Filao scores—fresh flowers in all the rooms, a continually replenished supply of bottled water in the fridge, an electric hair dryer in the bathroom, and chaises covered with comfy cushions in green and white stripes on each private terrace. You'll probably do more snoozing than sunning on your terrace because of the copious shade from the sea grapes, but almost certainly you'll have breakfast there, seated at the glass-topped table decorated with an island chart, pouring over the topography of St. Barthélemy's, deciding which beach to visit once you've scooped up the last flakes of croissant.

After a morning's swim you can look forward to a pleasant lunch at the Filao's beachside bar/restaurant, a peak-ceilinged pavilion with lazily turning fans. It opens directly onto a raised wooden deck and an angular swimming pool, with the flags of France, Sweden, the United States, and Filao Beach fluttering fraternally in the trade winds above the topless sunworshipers. The Filao's light lunches (no, not the topless bathers, the lunches) draw a crowd from all over the island to nibble on the freshest lobster (the brother-in-law of one of the friendly, longtime staffers is a lobsterman), sip Sancerre, and look out across the sand to the sea breaking on the reefs.

Afterward, if you're feeling too sated for much else, you have to walk only a few steps to the beach and settle into a molded plastic lounger for a siesta. For something more active, the waters off St. Jean Bay, protected by those scenic reefs, are ideal for windsurfing—and there's a windsurfing concession on the beach to rent boards and offer instruction.

Name: Filao Beach Hotel
Manager: Pierre A. Verdier
Address: P.O. Box 667, 97133 St. Barthélemy, French West Indies
Location: On St. Jean Bay, about 1 mile from the airport, free shuttle for guests
Telephone: 590/27-64-84
Fax: 590/27-62-24
Reservations: 800/74-CHARMS
Credit Cards: American Express, Diners Club, Visa
Rooms: 30 (8 Deluxe Beachside, 10 Deluxe, 12 Garden), all with ceiling fans and air-conditioning, refrigerators, hair dryers, TV, video, and safe-deposit box
Dining: Breakfast and lunch only, and the bar closes at 8:00; room service for breakfast only; there are lots of restaurants within walking distance
Sports: Freshwater pool, beach swimming, snorkeling equipment and Windsurfers for rent
P.S.:   Closed September through mid-October

Hotel Guanahani
St. Barthélemy

Atmosphere

Dining

Sports

Rates

Sixteen swimming pools. A couple of tennis courts. A couple of restaurants. St. Barts has never had it so lavish.

Bay and beach, reef and islet, headlands and blue but breeze-whipped sea— few resorts have a setting so beautiful. Guanahani sprawls over several acres of landscaped hillside tucked into one corner of Grand Cul-de-Sac Bay, a reef-protected beach, with the low-profile but snazzy El Sereno Hotel on one side, a grove of coconut palms belonging to Edmond de Rothschild on the other.

The island's largest resort, the 9-year-old Guanahani got a little larger a couple of years ago when it added a new row of plank-walled bungalows facing a quiet bay above the Rothschild family compound (artfully concealed behind a bamboo fence). But it still has well under 100 rooms, deployed two or three to a cottage up and down the hillsides. The new rooms are eye-catchers, designed with a quirky Gallic flair—Citroëns instead of the average resort's Ford Taurus—dashing candy-shop colors setting off curvaceous rattan headboards and bedside lamps, custom-designed cabinets for TVs and mini-bars, custom-designed desks and chairs, lava-laminated washbasins. The spacious patios have wooden dining tables and slat-backed chairs, the bathrooms have marble shower stalls (no tubs), double vanities, waffle-weave robes, and Hermès toiletries.

The original rooms are currently being restyled, although more or less in the original style with pencil-post beds, so your choice of lodging may boil down to location: Whether or not you want to be next to the beach and a few paces from the sea, whether or not you want to be on the hillside to catch the views and breezes (all the guest rooms have air-conditioning and paddle fans anyway). Tennis buffs might enjoy rooms 10, 11, and 12, overlooking one of the resort's two courts and sharing a pool for après-match dunking (conversely, late sleepers may want to shun these rooms to avoid being awakened by the thunk-thunk of tennis balls rather than the coo-coo of morning doves). Rooms 39 and 41, newly renovated one-bedroom suites with private pools, are particularly attractive because they're at the edge of the property, overlooking the Rothschild's coconuts. And there are three new one-bedroom suites in the original part of the hotel, overlooking Marechal Beach and Anse de Grand Cul de Sac.

No one can hope to run a successful hotel on St. Barts without paying almost as much attention to the kitchen as the decor. Maybe even more. Chef Jean-Claude Buscaylet (from the Riviera's tony Eden Rock) is currently holding sway and upholding the Guanahani tradition. The Indigo Beach Restaurant, beside the beach and pool, is a Riviera-style café for casual lunches of grills and Chablis and three theme evenings a week— Caribbean, creole, South American. The main showpiece is the stylish 40-seat Bartoloméo Restaurant, at the top of the hill, with its soft candlelight, elegant Limoges, refined decor, and polished service. But whichever restaurant you decide to dine in, set aside an hour for apéritifs in Guanahani's new lobby/lounge, a charming plantation-style cottage with hardwood floors and raftered ceilings with hunter fans, antique chests and daybeds, Roman-style lamps and dugout canoes, and a pianist playing cool jazz.

If there were a special award for most improved resort on the island, it would go to Guanahani.

Name: Hotel Guanahani

Manager: Marc Theze

Address: Anse de Grand Cul-de-Sac, P.O. Box 609, 97098 St. Barthélemy, French West Indies

Location: On the Atlantic coast on Grand Cul-de-Sac Bay, about 15 minutes from the airport in courtesy air-conditioned mini-bus

Telephone: 590/27-66-60

Fax: 590/27-70-70

Reservations: Leading Hotels of the World

Credit Cards: All major cards

Rooms: 76 rooms and suites in 40 cottages, each with fans *and* air-conditioning, terrace/patio, mini-bar, satellite TV/VCR, radio, direct-dial telephone; some suites with private pools

Meals: Breakfast 7:00–10:00, lunch noon–6:00 in the Indigo Beach Restaurant, dinner 7:00–10:00 in the fan-cooled Bartoloméo Restaurant (approx. $100–$120 for 2); informal but stylish dress ("shorts, T-shirts, swimsuits, or other similarly casual clothing are inappropriate after dark in the dining room and bar"); 18-hour room service

Entertainment: Theme evenings at the beach with live music three evenings a week; live piano jazz in lounge

Sports: Beach (with a second swatch of sand on the other side of the Rothschild coconut grove), 11 individual swimming pools, 2 large pools and Jacuzzi beside the beach, snorkeling, tennis (2 courts, hard court, with lights), exercise room—all free; beach concession offering windsurfing (including Surf School), Hobiecats; deep-sea fishing, sailing by arrangement

P.S.: Some children; open all year

El Sereno Beach Hotel

St. Barthélemy

Atmosphere

Dining

Sports

Rates

Despite the attraction of a ribbon of white sand and a lagoonlike, reef-protected bay, despite the sexy blue-tiled swimming pool with sunbathing "islands," the high point of a stay at this Antillean cousin of a Côte d'Azur resort has always been eating. Now the resort has a brand-new restaurant to enhance the pleasures of the table, an oversize gazebo beside the beach and a few paces from the pool. Its new name, West Indies, will give you a clue to the drift of the menu.

Set among a cluster of low palm trees, El Sereno is a dazzle of free-form white stucco, royal blue lampposts, and the shimmering red and blue tiled pool. Guest rooms surround a sandy courtyard, each with a fragrant private patio-garden of hibiscus and latanier and laurier. Indoors, the rooms are more or less identical—white stucco walls with blue beams, cot-size beds, closets in the bathrooms, accents of bold colors, wicker furniture—but rather small. The terraces are equipped with chaises, hammocks that look like trampolines, tables and chairs for your morning croissants—and since the garden foliage and shoulder-high wall offer some privacy, you don't have to be too fussy about dressing for al fresco breakfasts.

What you may have to think about, though, is the lack of good cross-ventilation, despite the glass sliders that divide the rooms from the terraces. You may have the air conditioner running more often than you'd like (prime rooms 1, 2, and 6 get a few more riffles of breeze than the others since they face the bay). But this may not be much of a drawback, because most of the time you'll be skimpily attired—indoors or out, paddling in a bay so shallow the water is still no more than shoulder-high some 200 yards out, sunning yourself on those "islands," or lazing on a lounger while the boardsurfers strain and struggle as they go skimming across the wind-whipped lagoon.

This is about as close as you can get to the French Riviera without flying to Nice.

Name: El Sereno Beach Hotel

Owners/Managers: Jean-François Marinacce

Address: P.O. Box 19, 97133 St. Barthélemy, French West Indies

Location: On Grand Cul-de-Sac Bay, about 3 miles from the airport, about $12 by taxi

Telephone: 590/27-64-80

Fax: 590/27-75-47

Reservations: Robert Reid Associates

Credit Cards: American Express, MasterCard, Visa

Rooms: 20, each with patio-garden, showers only, satellite TV (VCR upon request), wall safe, air-conditioning, refrigerator, direct-dial-phone, hair dryer

Meals: Breakfast, lunch, and dinner in West Indies restaurant (approx. $100 for 2); dress code "elegantly casual" in the evening; room service for breakfast only

Entertainment: The bar, or video movies in your room

Sports: Swimming, freshwater pool; windsurfing, pedal boats, tennis nearby

P.S.: Closed September 1 through October 14

P.P.S.: Nearby, 9 peak-roofed villas with gingerbread trim are available for rent, each with a large living room, bedroom, kitchen, bathroom, and terrace; high-season rates range from $230–$265 a day, double occupancy

Hamak

Guadeloupe

Atmosphere

Dining

Sports

Rates

Hammocks, hammocks everywhere. One waiting on your front patio. Eight more swinging over the bar. And embossed on every towel, plate, and ashtray as well. The message here is clear: relax.

On an aquamarine lagoon where a perpetual ocean breeze cools the sunshine even at high noon, this is a place for doing everything or nothing in great style. A technicolor botanical garden of 10,000 (the gardener keeps count) exotic trees and flowers undulates around 56 cabana suites. The glass wall of your bedroom opens into a private walled garden with a locked gate to which only you and the maid have a key. Along with hummingbirds, bougainvillea, and beach chairs, each garden has a tiled open-air shower big enough for your own private splash party. But this is one of the few Caribbean resorts where you can do your topless tanning anywhere. For Hamak has both an openness and a privacy few other places have mastered.

A hundred other guests are here—somewhere. In their walled gardens. On a little scallop of private beach in front of their cabanas. Or out to sea waterskiing, pedal boating, Sunfish-sailing, windsurfing, etc. But the only spot where you're likely to encounter more than one body at a time is in the middle of Hamak's main beach, and most of them make very pleasant scenery. Even the adjoining sweeping Robert Trent Jones golf course is blessedly free of both crowds and the island's famous *yen-yens* (nasty gnats that make a buzzing sound just like their name as pronounced by a Frenchman).

As all good things usually do, Hamak's sophisticated simplicity emanates from an owner who runs the place strictly to his own tastes. What Jean-François likes *you* had better like, too. And why not?

Every last matchbox and dinner napkin has been chosen with bull's-eye taste. And there's not a polymer in sight. Creamy stucco and poured concrete, dark woods and terrazzo tiles are the stuff everything's made of. The cabanas are simply but thoughtfully done: a comfy sitting room (recently redecorated and refurbished), roomy bath, nearly silent air-conditioning, and refrigerator.

But the instant you want to get away from it all, the hotel provides jitney, powerboat, or private plane to take you where you want to go. With a landing strip right on the property, you can arrange to go on an island hop to St. Martin and St. Barthélemy (both in 1 day), to the nearby islets known as Les Saintes, or all the way to Mustique for lunch and a swim at the Cotton House.

Name: Hamak

Owner/Manager: Jean-François Rozan

Address: 97118 Saint-François, Guadeloupe, French West Indies

Location: On the beach, about 20 miles and $40 by taxi from Pointe-à-Pitre and the airport

Telephone: 590/88-59-99

Fax: 590/88-41-92

Reservations: Caribbean Inns Ltd.

Credit Cards: American Express, Diners Club, MasterCard, Visa

Rooms: 56, in garden bungalows, all suites, all with garden patio, extra shower on patio, terrace with hammock, air-conditioning, refrigerator, pantry, wall safe

Meals: Breakfast 7:00–10:00, lunch noon–3:00, dinner 7:30–11:00 (approx. $65–$75 for 2); informal dress; room service

Entertainment: Taped music, "mood music" combos; casinos and shopping nearby

Sports: 3 virtually private beaches, waterskiing, Sunfish sailing, windsurfing, tennis (2 courts, with lights, at nearby club); golf (Robert Trent Jones design, 18 holes, guaranteed starting times for Hamak guests *twice* a day); snorkeling gear for rent; excursions by boat and twin-engined plane can be arranged

P.S.: Closed September and October

Hotel Plantation Leyritz
Martinique

☆					♀				☀				$	$		
Atmosphere					**Dining**				**Sports**				**Rates**			

Born before Mozart, before the steamboat, before even the United States, Leyritz is a living, working banana plantation three centuries old and as close to unspoiled as a national treasure can be that's not locked behind glass. The guardhouse, the slave quarters, the grand manor house are all intact—but now instead of *planteurs* bedded down in them, you find guests. The former chapel and sugar factory have been transformed into beamed, stone-walled dining rooms with stenciled ceilings. And at the bottom of a long emerald lawn, a swimming pool with fountains sparkles like a big, cool sapphire.

Accommodations here are comfortable but far from luxurious. What wins Leyritz its rating is that overworked catchall word, *charm.* Everywhere you go, a miniature stone canal splashes fresh mountain water along your route. Through the garden, past the guest rooms of the carriage house, cascading over the walls. Engineered by the first French colonial owner to bring water down from the rain forests to the coffee and spices he grew here, the canal's role now is to provide water music for the guests.

The 14 tiny cottages that once housed the plantation's slaves provide the most privacy—snug little tile-roofed warrens with foot-thick stone walls and windows discreetly screened by tropical flowers and mango trees. Rooms in the carriage house all have sundecks and the easiest route to the swimming pool—just 250 grassy feet down the hill; the smallest rooms are the newest—in a one-time dormitory. But probably the two most unusual places to hang your sun hat at Leyritz are what once served as the guardhouse and the master's kitchen—each gives you your own stone cottage surrounded by guava trees and manicured lawn. The guardhouse cottage gives you the best of both worlds: inside a cool and shadowy stone-walled bedroom with slit windows just wide enough to poke a musket through, and outside your own tiled patio with nothing in sight but a few million banana trees.

The problem here is that Plantation Leyritz is a tourist attraction by day—carloads and busloads of people from other hotels and cruise ships come to admire the corn-husk doll in the Musée de Poupées Végétales, drink at the bar, nosh in the pavilion restaurant, and frolic in the pool—

your pool. After 4:00, of course, the day-trippers have gone and the hush returns, but it's not my idea of a secluded hideaway and nook.

Name: Hotel Plantation Leyritz

Manager: Cyril Mond

Address: 97218 Basse-Pointe, Martinique, French West Indies

Location: In the north, 35 miles from Fort-de-France, or $55 and an hour's drive by taxi from the airport; most people rent a car to get there, but if you will be arriving after dark, let the hotel know and they'll arrange to have a reliable taxi driver waiting for you at the airport (you pay the fare, of course)

Telephone: 596/78-53-92

Fax: 596/78-92-44

Reservations: International Travel & Resorts, Inc.

Credit Cards: MasterCard, Visa

Rooms: 68, in former plantation annexes, all with telephones, air-conditioning, color TV, hair dryer

Meals: Breakfast 7:30–10:00, lunch noon–2:00, dinner 7:30–9:00 in dining pavilion (approx. $50–$60 for 2); informal dress; no room service

Entertainment: Dancing to live music twice a week, some local folklore groups or bands

Sports: Pool, tennis, walks through the plantation; beaches 30 minutes away

P.S.: Tour groups for lunch almost daily (eat early or late or request seating in the smaller room adjoining the noisy main dining room); several staff members speak English, but you can expect a few verbal hitches; open all year

Habitation Lagrange

Martinique

Atmosphere

Dining

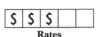
Sports

Rates

The jungly greenery practically sneaks through the shutters into your room, and if you're lodged in the main house you can reach out and pluck breakfast mangoes straight from the tree. Beyond the lawns and pool a

wooden bridge leads to a banana plantation that seems to go on forever up
the narrow valley.

Habitation Lagrange is the brainchild of local hotelier Jean-Louis de
Lucy, who used France's tax-shelter laws to restore a landmark rather than
build yet another formula hotel from scratch.

Although the plantation manor dates only from the turn of the century,
it looks as if it should have been around when de Lucy's ancestors fled the
French Revolution and settled on Martinique. The centerpiece of the
estate is a two-story plantation great house with a wraparound veranda and
gracefully curving corners. Tall mahogany doors lead into a hallway with
polished parquet and oriental bric-a-brac, a library on one side, a wood-
paneled bar on the other. The bar is the perfect spot for settling into one of
the antique planter-style rockers, the kind with big footrests, and sipping a
tì-punch.

The 17 guest rooms are deployed around a garden—4 in the great
house, 2 in a former stable wing, the remainder in new two-story structures
that blend in nicely with the others. Furnishings are country Caribbean
(cane and rattan, mahogany colonial-style pencil-post beds), but the designer telephones are dashingly modern. The big armoires were intended
for TVs and VCRs, but the sets were late arriving for the opening of the inn,
and the first guests persuaded de Lucy that TVs would be out of place. The
rehabbing of the estate was something of a family effort—de Lucy's wife
sewed the drapes and bedspreads and framed the pictures; an uncle came
down from Montreal to paint the murals in the main house; whoever
happens to be on hand mixes the traditional tì-punch in the bar.

Of special note is the cuisine, which is under the guidance of chef Jean-
Charles Bredas. The food is decidedly French, but seasoned with island
spices—nutmeg, cloves, cinnamon. The service is gracious and unobtrusive, and the meals are delicious.

Life among the bananas is probably not for everyone. Beach lovers may
be disappointed by the absence of talcum sand in these parts (the nearest
decent beach is at Trinite, a 30-minute drive away), but Lagrange is not so
remote that guests have to settle for an anchoritic existence. A drive of an
hour or so takes you to some of the most opulent scenery in the Caribbean.
My choices would be a morning trip to Grand'Rivière, or a day trip up the
flanks of Mont Pelée, across to the Caribbean coast and the dolorous town
of St. Pierre, snuffed out when Pelée erupted back in 1908. Another trip
down the center of the island. Another over to the Trinite Peninsula for a
swim and lunch at a waterside bistro.

On the other hand, the slow jouncing track back to the main road may
persuade many travelers to stay put, and there's no reason to leave anyway.
Lagrange rewards you with tranquility. Here there's time to sniff the jasmine. Time to listen to birdsong by day and cicadas after sundown.

But I like the garden best in the morning, with the rain pattering on the leaves, as I am admiring breakfast. Not eating, admiring: a bowl of freshly sliced bananas and mangoes from the garden, freshly baked croissants and toast wrapped in linen, a carafe of freshly squeezed fruit juice, all presented in a native basket artistically decorated with delicate ferns and red ixorra.

For connoisseurs of real island ambience, Habitation Lagrange is hard to beat.

Name: Habitation Lagrange

Manager: Geraldine Mur

Address: 97225 Le Marigot, Martinique, French West Indies

Location: On the Atlantic coast, about 1 hour and $40 by taxi from the airport; if you're driving yourself, it's just north of the village of Le Marigot, just past a sign announcing the *Bassin Ecrevisse Seguinneau* (a shrimp farm)

Telephone: 596/53-60-60

Fax: 596/53-50-58

Reservations: Caribbean Inns Ltd.

Credit Cards: All major cards

Rooms: 17, 4 in the great house (including a Junior Suite), 2 in a former stable wing, the remainder in new 2-story wings, all with air-conditioning and ceiling fans, verandas or porches, direct-dial telephones, stocked mini-bars, bathrobes

Meals: Breakfast 7:00–10:00, lunch noon–2:00, dinner 7:30–9:30 ($80 for 2), all served in the garden pavilion; casual dress; room service for breakfast only

Entertainment: Bar, billiards, parlor games, library of sorts

Sports: Curvaceous pool (not for laps), tennis (1 court with lights), miles of walks; beaches down the coast, day trips to Les Ilets de l'Imperatrice (an intriguing property owned by the de Lucy family, a 30-minute drive away)

P.S.:   Some children; open all year

Other Choices

Le Tom Beach Hotel
St. Barthélemy

It seems hard to believe that another hotel could be shoehorned into the strip beside St. Jean Beach, but here it is—just 12 rooms, most of them at right angles to the beach, facing a courtyard with a pool. A footbridge spans the pool and leads to an inviting bar-restaurant by the edge of the beach. What saves the day here is that the Tom has the island's only underground parking garage (fear not, it's so small it's hardly noticed, although it holds 24 cars). The Tom's rooms are pleasantly comfortable, with clay-tile floors, pencil-post beds, small patios or verandas, and such up-to-date amenities as TVs, direct-dial phones, and private safes. Windsurfing (1 free hour per day), sailing, and other water frolics are available right and left on St. Jean Beach. 12 rooms. Doubles: $190 to $360, summer 1994–95, room service breakfast included. *Le Tom Beach Hotel, 97133 St. Barthélemy, French West Indies. Telephone: 590/27-53-13; fax: 590/27-53-15.*

Tropical Hotel
St. Barthélemy

Located up on the hill next to Village St. Jean, Tropical Hotel is a huddled enclave of greenery and blossoms with just 20 rooms, some facing the sea, some facing the gardens. There's a bar that serves light snacks around a small pool. Guest rooms are small but nevertheless manage to squeeze in modern amenities such as a TV, radio, direct-dial telephone, refrigerator, and, in the bathroom, a hair dryer. Jot this down as a possibility for the off-season—to my mind, it's overpriced in winter, but just half the price during the remaining 8 months of the year (except June and the first half of July, when it's closed). 20 rooms. Doubles: $285 to $310, winter 1994–95, with breakfast. *Tropical Hotel, P.O. Box 147, 97095 St. Barthélemy, French West Indies. Telephone: 590/27-64-87; fax: 590/27-81-74.*

Village St. Jean Hotel

St. Barthélemy

Picture a hillside of blossoms and greenery with a handful of cottages tucked in among the hibiscus and bougainvillea. Add a blue-tiled pool with a terra-cotta deck and white sunshades, paint a backdrop of red roofs and blue sea, then anchor the garden with an indoor-outdoor restaurant serving acclaimed Italian food. Voilà: one of St. Barts's most inviting small hotels! Village St. Jean has been charming guests for more than 30 years (food guru Craig Claiborne came so often, he kept his personal pots and pans in his favorite cottage), always under the watchful, caring eye of the French American Charneau family. The Charneaus have just emerged from a major renovation of their inn. All 20 cottages (including 14 suites and 6 regular "hotel" rooms) have air-conditioning and paddle fans, terraces or gardens, refrigerators, telephones, and radios. The suites have kitchenettes with four-ring burners and family-size refrigerators. The deluxe cottages have been spiffed up with new tiled bathrooms, new fabrics, antique wood and cane furniture from India, and top-of-the-line patio furniture that's so inviting you may want to throw dinner parties every evening, even if you're not Craig Claiborne (fear not: Daily maid service includes dishwashing). Which cottage? Some are more private than others, but for views, none are grander than those from cottages 12 and 14. Take one look at those spacious decks and terraces with their plumply padded loungers and you might easily forget that the beach is just 5 minutes down the hill. Sample one of the $10 pizzas or $12 linguines in Le Patio and you might forget all about dashing around the island in your Minimoke looking for a great place to eat. Besides the pool, there's a Jacuzzi, commissary (basics only), and a library-TV room with parlor games. But maybe the most appealing feature of Chez Charneau is the cost: Even in winter (1994–95), doubles begin at just $135 (hotel rooms, with continental breakfast) rising to $295 for a deluxe cottage with terrace; summer equivalents are $85 to $190. 26 rooms and suites. *Village St. Jean Hotel, 97133 St. Barthélemy, French West Indies. Telephone: 590/27-61-39; fax: 590/27-77-96.*

 ⌒⌒

Emeraude Plage

St. Barthélemy

Another garden full of bungalows, this time by the edge of the beach in St. Jean. All 24 bungalows have kitchenettes, sundecks, and maid service; the atmosphere is totally beachcomber, and there are water-sports facilities on the doorstep. 24 bungalows, 3 suites, 1 villa. Rates are $184 to $560, winter 1994–95. *Emeraude Plage, P.O. Box 41, 97133 St. Barthélemy, French West Indies. Telephone: 590/27-64-78; fax: 590/27-83-08.*

Hotel Yuana

St. Barthélemy

This is a sort of poor man's François Plantation without the restaurant—in a positive way, I hastily add. Like François, it's on a hillside, in this case overlooking Anse des Cayes and a grove of coconuts, and it, too, is a collection of tiny island-style cottages around a small pool and terrace bar. Each cottage is outfitted with kitchenette, tiled showers, air-conditioning, and ceiling fans—and, despite its modest rates, refinements like hair dryers, VCR, and remote control for the air-conditioning. Ask for one of four corner rooms—they have the largest terraces. No meals except breakfast. 12 rooms. Doubles: $225 to $334, winter 1994–95. *Hotel Yuana, Anse des Cayes, 97133 St. Barthélemy, French West Indies. Telephone: 590/27-80-84 or 800/633-7411; fax: 803/686-7411.*

Auberge de la Vieille Tour

Guadeloupe

Some travelers choose great hotels with a decent restaurant attached. *French* travelers choose great restaurants with a decent hotel attached. Hence, the never-ending popularity of this fifties-style hotel. Yes, it has nice beaches, pool, tennis, boats, and refurbished guest rooms—but the real attraction here is what comes steaming out of the kitchen every night. Delicately prepared local fish in perfect sauces. Pink and tender lamb. A rolling silver cart of fresh Caribbean antipasto. Bries and camemberts. Rum cordials with a headiness inherited from the exotic fruits you find lurking at the bottom. So, although that handsome 18th-century sugar-mill tower at the entrance is what gives the *auberge* its name, as soon as you step into the lobby you sense that eating is the main sport here. If the 3 tiny beaches get too crowded for you, the hotel will send a boat around to take you to a nearby island where you can establish your own beachhead, break out a picnic lunch supplied by the hotel chef, and still be back in time for one of Vielle Tour's outstanding dinners. 80 rooms. Doubles: $231 to $407, winter 1994–95. *Auberge de la Vieille Tour, 97190 Gosier, Guadeloupe, French West Indies. Telephone: 590/84-23-23; fax: 590/84-33-43.*

Le Village Créole
Les Saintes

Look straight ahead and there's a bay, some yachts bobbing at anchor, an islet with a fort on top—Fort Josephine. Turn around, look up, and there, somewhere above you, is another fort—Napoleon. Opened in 1987, this hideaway sits on a 3½-acre waterfront site, but rather than a beach you have a garden with tropical flowers and lawns. The 11 cottages are designed in the island vernacular—small and square with pointed rooflines and garden patios. Interiors have separate bedrooms and living rooms with kitchens in a duplex arrangement, and one extraswank suite has a Courrèges bathroom in light blue. Furnishings are comfortable and practical, and if you're looking for someplace well off the beaten track, someplace quiet and uncrowded, someplace unpretentious, consider checking into this *domaine*. 11 cottages with 22 suites. Doubles: $128 to $198, winter 1994–95. *Le Village Créole, Pointe Coquelet, 97137 Terre-de-Haut, Les Saintes, French West Indies. Telephone: 590/99-53-83; fax: 590/99-55-55.*

Frégate Bleue Inn
Martinique

Two years ago Yveline de Lucy Fossarie, former owner of one of Martinique's most romantic inns, Plantation Leyritz, opened a small inn, Frégate Bleue, on the island's Atlantic shore. A simple modern house with gingerbread trim and much more modest than Leyritz, the seven-room hotel is nonetheless an enticing hideaway. Part of its appeal is the setting: on a hilltop overlooking the sea, dotted with islets and reefs where islanders like to wade in the morning while sipping a cool drink. Behind the building there's a swimming pool shaded by trees and perfumed by flowers. Each of the seven rooms is furnished in a tasteful assortment of antiques, with four-poster beds and Persian rugs. Each has a balcony with an ocean view, ceiling fan (with air conditioning as a backup), cable television, wet bar, and kitchenette. 7 rooms. Doubles: $200 to $225, winter 1994–95. *Frégate Bleue Inn, 97240 Le François, Martinique, West Indies. Telephone: 596/54-54-66; fax: 596/54-78-48. Reservations: Caribbean Inns Ltd.*

Hotel le Bakoua

Martinique

The distinctive feature of Le Bakoua is a cluster of orange conical rooftops representing the *bakoua*, or conical native hat, for which the hotel is named. They cap a colorful, open dining pavilion seating 500 (that is, two and a half times the guest count), where fresh anthuriums and crotons climb the columns, the table linen matches the anthuriums, and waitresses in local costume serve the Bakoua's French and Creole delicacies (Sunday is "lobster night," with island crustaceans cooked half a dozen different ways). But what are we to make of a restaurant that could sell me a white wine by the glass, but not a red? Expect distractions too—the dining area abuts a dance floor and a circular open bar. Le Bakoua, now a part of the Sofitel chain, is probably your best bet for a resort hotel in Martinique, a ravishing island short on refined lodgings (with the exception of Habitation Lagrange, above). The rooms are comfortable, amply equipped, recently refurbished with spanking new tiled bathrooms, although the owners are so chintzy with the wattage you may have to use the *bathroom* if you want to do lots of reading. The 20-odd compact *casitas* between the garden and the sea are probably the best buy, with modern fitted wall units, balconies, sliding screen doors, tiled floors, tiled showers, and double beds. Originally sole guardian of a quiet peninsula, Le Bakoua has managed to keep its calm and its distance through all the development on its doorstep and now offers the best of both worlds. If you want beach, you have a beach, of sorts, and lots of water sports and tennis; if you want a disco or casino, they're just a stroll away; and if you want the markets, shops, and nightlife of the city, they're just across the harbor, a 20-minute trip by *vedette*. And if you want a good dinner and a quiet drink on your private terrace, you can have that, too. 140 rooms and suites. Doubles: $267 to $515, winter 1994–95. *Hotel le Bakoua, Pointe du Bout, 97229 Martinique, French West Indies. Telephone: 596/66-02-02; fax: 596/66-00-41. Reservations: 800/221-4542.*

The Queen's Windwards

St. Lucia
Barbados
Tobago
Dominica

The Queen's Windwards

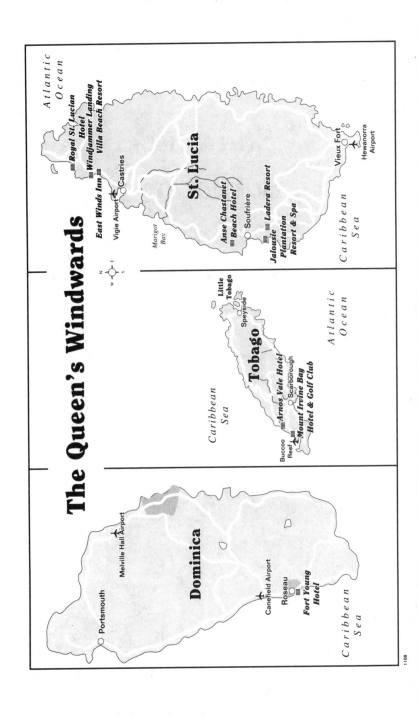

Dominica

Portsmouth

Melville Hall Airport

Canefield Airport
Roseau
Fort Young Hotel

Caribbean Sea

Tobago

Little Tobago
Speyside

Arnos Vale Hotel
Scarborough
Mount Irvine Bay Hotel & Golf Club
Buccoo Reef

Caribbean Sea

Atlantic Ocean

St. Lucia

Atlantic Ocean

Royal St. Lucian Hotel
Windjammer Landing Villa Beach Resort
East Winds Inn
Vigie Airport
Castries

Marigot Bay

Anse Chastanet Beach Hotel
Soufrière
Jalousie Plantation Resort & Spa
Ladera Resort

Vieux Fort
Hewanorra Airport

Caribbean Sea

N
W E
S

1108

The Queen's Windwards

Dominica, St. Lucia, Barbados, Trinidad, and Tobago are not, strictly speaking, a geographical entity, and any sailors who think of them as "windwards" may find themselves way off course; but for lovers and other romantics this is a convenient, if grab-bag, grouping. What these islands have in common is that they were all British dependencies at one time.

Of the group, Dominica is the most fascinating—the Caribbean as it must have been at the turn of the century, or, once you get into the mountains and rain forests, as it must have been when Columbus arrived here one *dominica* in 1493. This is an island for travelers rather than vacationers, with real me-Tarzan-you-Jane countryside—untamed, forbidding landscapes, mountains a mile high, primeval forests, waterfalls, sulphur springs, lava beaches, and communities of the original Carib Indians. But for lovers I haven't been able to find a suitable hideaway since my previous favorite was wiped out by a hurricane.

St. Lucia has much the same topography as Dominica, but somehow this one is a gentler island, its landscape softened by mile after mile of banana, spice, and coconut plantations, by bays and coves of white-sand beaches. The new road from the international jetport takes you along the windward Atlantic shore and across the mountains, but if you have time, return to the airport by the old road down the west coast. It winds and snakes and twists and writhes forever, but the scenery is impressive, and you pass Marigot Bay (good lunch stop), Soufrière, the famed Pitons, with possible side trips to volcanoes, sulphur springs, or rain forests. The problem with this idea is that you'd have to rent a car, trot round to the police station to get a local driving permit (I also got zapped for a donation to Police Week), and when you leave the car at the jetport, you may be asked to pay an outrageous drop-off charge. But I'm almost persuaded it's worth the effort and expense.

Barbados is hardly a St. Lucia or Dominica in terms of scenery (it's relatively flat and pastoral except for a hilly region in the northeast), but it has a cosmopolitan air that few other Caribbean islands have, maybe because it has always been a favorite with the English gentry. Its main attraction, of course, is its scalloped western coastline, each cove with a lagoonlike beach. It may be rather crowded these days, but it still shelters most of the island's finest resorts. When it's time to take a break from sunning and swimming, however, Barbados rewards the leisurely tourist with a variety of sights, from caves and flower forests to plantation houses and forts and venerable churches. There's even a house where George Washington slept when he visited his brother Lawrence.

Trinidad you can keep. At least as a lovers' hideaway. This island seems to get by on the strength of its carnival and, to some extent, the bustling, swinging, melting-pot qualities of its capital, Port of Spain. Its airport would be high on the list of places to avoid at all costs (although it is currently being upgraded), if it weren't for the fact that you have to transit there to get to a gem—Tobago.

Tobago is another story: 114 square miles of lush mountains, backwater fishing villages, beautiful beaches, and Buccoo Reef. It's certainly worth the trouble it takes to get there, if you want someplace offbeat and secluded.

How to Get There   Barbados's Grantley International is the only airport in the world—other than JFK and Dulles on this side of the ocean and Heathrow and De Gaulle on the other—that has scheduled service by the Concorde every weekend in winter from London. There's a strong possibility that there may also be scheduled charter flights by Concorde from New York to Barbados during the winter of 1995–96—keep it in mind for the grand gesture. Otherwise, American and BWIA from New York and Miami; American from San Juan; Air Canada and BWIA from Toronto and/or Montreal.

Getting to St. Lucia needs a little more attention because it has two

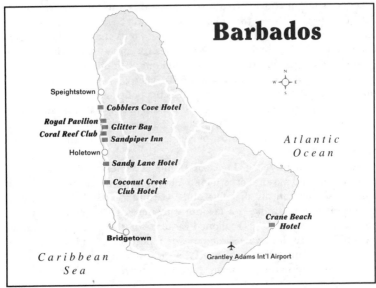

airports: Hewanorra International in the south for jets, Vigie in the north for interisland services. Choose carefully because otherwise there's a long, winding drive (at least an hour, possibly longer) between the two groups of hotels. To complicate matters further, airline schedules identify Hewanorra with a V. From New York to Hewanorra, American flies nonstop and BWIA makes one stop; from San Juan, American Eagle flies to both Hewanorra and Vigie, all nonstops.

For Tobago, you first fly to Port of Spain on Trinidad—nonstop from New York on BWIA, from Miami on American and BWIA. The connecting flights are on jets. Check with your travel agent about new direct flights to Tobago from the U.S. on BWIA.

For information on Dominica, call 212/599-8478; St. Lucia, 212/867-2950; Barbados, 800/221-9831.

Windjammer Landing Villa Beach Resort
St. Lucia

☆☆☆	🍷🍷	🌂🌂	$ $
Atmosphere	**Dining**	**Sports**	**Rates**

Here are some of the most appealing lodgings on St. Lucia, even if they are in a condo-style development and even if there have been several management changes since Windjammer opened in 1989.

The accommodations are all in dazzling white Mediterranean-style villas, spread over 55 acres of hillside, with lots of grace notes and refinements that set them apart from run-of-the-mill condos. Two- and three-bedroom villas come with their own private plunge pools, extraspacious terra-cotta tiled patios, and glorious views of the ocean and surrounding hills. Couples on a splurge can rent a suite with a private pool in one of the two-bedroom villas for less than the usual foursome rate (villas 1, 2, 7, and 8 are particularly appealing).

Dotted around elsewhere on this hillside estate are one-bedroom villas (a very few—such as 43B—have plunge pools) with their own large swimming pool and restaurant, Papa Don's. Each of these 1,300-square-foot villa suites comes with a complete kitchen (including microwave), TV, terrace, air-conditioning (bedrooms only), and ceiling fans. Some of the bathrooms have the same stunning views as the balconies.

In 1994, some of these villas were subdivided into smaller units, with only a bedroom and no living room or kitchen. All the new units have balconies, however, and those in the deluxe rooms have the same sweeping ocean views. The deluxe units even have a private rooftop sundeck in addition to the covered balconies. Although light filled and tastefully decorated, these rooms are a little small, with tiny bathrooms and inadequate closet space. Splurge on the villas.

The public areas, like the private quarters, are among the most attractive on the island. (The original designs were by Bajan architect Ian Morrison, who also did Barbados's Glitter Bay and Royal Pavilion hotels. Renovations were made by Hal Sorrenti.) A split-level lobby-lounge flows into a poolside bar and a multilevel thatched dining pavilion overhanging the sea, all done in pickle pine with designer fabrics in soothing pastel shades. The cuisine is varied and appetizing, with several restaurant choices. The staff is welcoming and eager to please. The beach is not the greatest, but it's par for the course on St. Lucia, with fine white sand imported from Barbuda and enough water sports and activities to fill your days. If anything, when the hotel's full, the beach can get a little crowded.

The drawback for visitors may be the terrain. The steep hills can be negotiated only by jitneys (no private cars are allowed on most roads). Because there are only seven electric carts to cover the entire estate, you may find yourself waiting around for transportation, even though they run around-the-clock. Another possible drawback is the private pools: Some of them are private only in the sense that you have one all to yourself, but they are sited in such a way that people walking up and down the pathways may look directly down on your frolics. Be warned!

Still, now that Cunard's splashy La Toc has been transformed into a Sandals all-inclusive, Windjammer is your best and most elegant bet on the north side of St. Lucia.

Name: Windjammer Landing Villa Beach Resort
Manager: Anthony Bowen
Address: P.O. Box 1504, La Brelotte Bay, Castries, St. Lucia, West Indies
Location: On the northwest coast, about 15 minutes and $14 by taxi from Vigie Airport, 20 minutes from Castries; 90 minutes and $60 from Hewanorra Airport (by helicopter, 20 minutes and about $90)
Telephone: 809/452-0913
Fax: 809/452-0907

Reservations: JDB Associates

Credit Cards: All major cards

Rooms: 94 villas (35 1-bedroom, 27 2-bedroom, 28 3-bedroom, 4 4-bedroom). Also 21 superior 1-bedroom units with garden view, 21 deluxe 1-bedroom units with ocean view. All villas and units have air-conditioning (bedrooms only) and ceiling fans. Villas have separate living rooms and kitchens or pantries; units have bedrooms only, with refrigerators and tea/coffeemakers. All have private patios or terraces, remote-control television, telephones, radios, hair dryers, and bathrobes. All 1-, 2-, and 3-bedroom villas have private plunge pools, as do a few 1-bedroom villas.

Meals: Breakfast 7:30–11:00, lunch 11:00–3:00, dinner 6:30–10:00 at Ernestine's (approx. $70 for 2), Jammer's Bar & Grill, or Papa Don's; casual dress; limited room service

Entertainment: 2 bars, some live music around the main pool 6 nights a week, special shows 2 nights a week; shuttle service into Castries ($8) twice weekly

Sports: 2 large freshwater pools, 56 private villa pools, humanmade sandy beach on a calm bay, with white sand imported from Barbuda, 2 Astroturf tennis courts (lit for night play, rackets available), windsurfing, waterskiing, volleyball, snorkeling, Sunfish sailing, volleyball—all free; boat trips (on the *Endless Summer*), scuba, golf (18 holes), horseback riding at extra charge

P.S.: Some children of all ages, especially holidays, with a full children's program (ages 4–14) available all year; some business groups; very hilly terrain and numerous steps necessitate jitney transportation, not suitable for people with disabilities or those not in shape; open all year

East Winds Inn

St. Lucia

☆☆				♀				☁				$	$	$	$	
Atmosphere				**Dining**				**Sports**				**Rates**				

Inns don't come more beachcomberish than this—on a virtually private bay with sea grape and coco palms separating the white sand from a peaceful garden of mango and pomegranate trees and colored with hibiscus and bougainvillea. You come upon this garden setting almost as a surprise, an oasis at the end of 800 yards or so of what feels like the most potholed road on an island of potholed roads, with a dinky turquoise chattel house guarding the entrance to a cluster of lime-green cottages. The birdsong tells you you're someplace special.

Beyond the lime-green cottages you come to a group of hexagonal cottages, then a free-form pool with a swim-up bar, then an open-sided clubhouse with a piano lounge and casual beachside dining pavilion with thatch roof and dark beams and pillars. Now the birdsong switches to squawks as Mac and Eric, the mascot parrots, hold forth in their giant cages.

The 10 hexagonal cottages are the originals, renovated in 1992, still with their trademark patio tables topped by palm-thatch shade; the 16 lime-green cottages, the deluxe lodgings, are only a few years old. They're not really luxurious (although the newcomers have TV-VCRs), but they are comfortable and well maintained (which wasn't always the case with the previous owners), with a welcome island-style flavor to the decor.

Nothing pretentious here. It's all very laid-back and relaxing. A real back-to-basics, lolling-around barefoot vacation. As one guest wrote in the visitors' book, "The most relaxing, friendly, good-value holiday we have ever enjoyed. We shall return."

Name: East Winds Inn

Manager: Gareth Leach

Address: P.O. Box 1477, La Brelotte Bay, Castries, St. Lucia, West Indies

Location: On the northwest coast, about 15 minutes and $14 by taxi from Vigie Airport and Castries; 90 minutes and $60 from Hewanorra Airport

Telephone: 809/452-8212

Fax: 809/452-9941

Reservations: 800/223-9832 or E&M Associates

Credit Cards: American Express, MasterCard, Visa

Rooms: 26 single-story cottages (10 superior hexagonal cottages, renovated in 1992, and 16 deluxe traditional cottages built in 1993, with television, VCR, and sunken-tile shower/tubs) with patios, ceiling fans (no air-conditioning), refrigerators, tea/coffeemakers, hair dryers; all rooms face the gardens, no water views

Meals: Breakfast 7:30–10:00, lunch 12:30–2:00, dinner 7:30–9:30 at informal open-air restaurant on the beach; limited room service

Entertainment: Local musicians play 3 times a week; videotapes available for loan (no charge)

Sports: 1 large free-form swimming pool with swim-up, self-service bar, small, pleasant white-sand beach, snorkeling, pedalos, straddle canoes—all free

P.S.:   Children welcome, but no special facilities; international, mainly European clientele; open all year

Anse Chastanet Beach Hotel
St. Lucia

   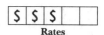

| Atmosphere | Dining | Sports | Rates |

Don't come here for three-speed showerheads and Porthault sheets. The luxuries at Anse Chastanet run deeper, and dearer. First, there's the Caribbean's most spectacular view, a Bali Ha'i of jagged mountains soaring out of the sea that would have sent Gauguin diving for his umbers and indigos. Then there's the hotel's simple good taste, from handmade mahogany bed tables to the twist of immaculate madras on every waitress's head.

But you find something else here that is all too rare in the Caribbean these days: a caring and a closeness not just between owner and guests or staff and guests, but with the whole tiny community—taxi drivers, schoolgirls, fishermen, banana cutters. Consider what happened to the guests here on Christmas Eve. As they sat sipping their after-dinner cognacs high above the darkened beach, suddenly a flaming torch appeared in the sea. Then another and another and another. The villagers had come to sing carols from their canoes. No hats were passed; no bows were taken. It was just to say Merry Christmas.

Artfully tucked away in a 5,000-acre estate in one of St. Lucia's remotest back pockets, Anse Chastanet proves hard to get to even once you get there. Its private roadway rocks and rolls you up and up and up until at the end of it all you discover the beginning of the hotel, spiraling down the other side of the mountain to the sea.

Octagonal, whitewashed guest cottages cantilever from the hibiscus like vacationers who can't get enough of that Gauguin view. The style is beach functional: wraparound windows and terraces, paddle fans, island-crafted furniture of local wood, crisp madras and muslin at the windows and on the beds, ingenious overdimensional burlap wall hangings, and wood-trimmed showers. All of it born of the theory that beach houses are for sleeping. (Best views, by the way, are from rooms 5, 6, and 7.) The prime lodgings are the 11 suites built in 1990, a notch or two up the hill, ranging from 900 to 1,600 square feet, some with ceilings soaring 20 feet, and some with bathrooms larger than most hotel rooms. Each of these suites has a breathtaking view, whether it's facing north across the luxuriant dell and beach and/or south to the Pitons. Among the new premium suites, 7B has a perfectly framed view of the peaks; 7E's bed has been set at an angle for a classic view of the Pitons; 7F has a 180-degree vista and a *shower* with a perfect Piton view; suite 14B, slightly futuristic in looks with soaring ceiling, sports a free-form stucco shower open to the breezes with a 30-foot-high St. Lucian fir tree in the middle; 15B suggests a sort of tree house with its wraparound louvers opening onto dense foliage. The 12 spacious rooms tucked behind the beach are handsome and luxurious (room 11 is best in terms of privacy) and some of them may, at some point in the future, compensate for what could be a breezeless location with private plunge pools. For the rest, there is a series of multilevel open-air terraces, dining rooms, and bars—and, at the bottom of a long hillside stairway, a graceful quarter-mile beach of fine volcanic sand the color of pussy willows.

But who says you have to be a stay-at-home? Take a picnic lunch to the hotel's private waterfall. Get a native guide to paddle you around the neighboring mountain islands. Give your camera a workout in Soufrière, a tumbledown fishing village as picture-perfect as a movie set. Tour an authentic French colonial banana plantation. Soak your weary bones in the hot mineral baths of a tropical rain forest. Visit a volcano.

Fortunately, you can do just about all of that in one day. Set aside another day for a trip to Castries. The resort's launch makes the trip five times a week. Have lunch at Jimmie's or the Green Parrot, and don't expect too much of Castries—the main point of this 40-minute trip is the breathtaking scenery there and back.

Name: Anse Chastanet Beach Hotel

Owners/Managers: Nick and Karolin Troubetzkoy

Address: P.O. Box 7000, Soufrière, St. Lucia, West Indies

Location: On the southwest coast, 75 minutes and $45 by taxi from Hewanorra airport, 2 hours and $80 from Vigie or Castries (the fare is included in the weekly scuba package or escape package); the hotel will have someone meet you at the airport if you let them know when you're arriving

Telephone: 809/459-7000

Fax: 809/459-7700

Reservations: Ralph Locke Islands

Credit Cards: American Express, Diners Club, MasterCard, Visa

Rooms: 48, 11 in spacious hillside villas, 25 in the hillside cottages (of which 5 are suites), 12 in 2 plantation-style villas at beach level, all with ceiling fans, balconies or patios

Meals: Breakfast 7:30–9:30, lunch 11:30–3:30 (at the beachside bar, Trou-au-Diable), dinner 7:30–9:30 (approx. $60 for 2), in one of two hillside terraces, the Treehouse; informal dress; coal-pot barbecues Friday evenings, Creole buffet Tuesdays; room service for breakfast only, $1 extra

Entertainment: Live entertainment most evenings—dancing, local "shak-shak" band, steel band, library

Sports: Beach (volcanic sand), snorkeling, windsurfing, Sunfish sailing, pirogue trips to the Pitons, tennis (1 court, no lights)—all free; complete scuba facility with 3 dive boats and photo lab extra (no spearguns—the sea around here is a designated marine reserve and the entire bay has been bouyed off to limit boat traffic)

P.S.: No children under 2, given the hilly terrain

Ladera Resort
St. Lucia

Atmosphere   Dining   Sports   Rates

Waking up here is like being present at the Creation. Immediately below, an amphitheater of hillside thick with tropical greenery drops off precipitously to a coconut plantation. Beyond it, the Caribbean glistens and glitters and shimmers all the way to the horizon. And framing the entire view, the famed Pitons, those postcard-perfect twin volcanic cones soaring straight from the sea to more than double the height of 1,000-foot-high Ladera.

And it's all right there before your bedazzled eyes without the effort of opening the windows or pushing back the shutters, because your hilltop aerie has no west wall. In fact, in some of the suites, you can ooh and aah at the panorama without even getting out from between the sheets. This most unusual inn, part Big Sur, part Bali Ha'i, sits atop the ridge of an extinct volcano (which you would never guess in a thousand nights was a volcano, given the dense foliage), a 4-acre plot in a 200-year-old working plantation that still produces cocoa, coffee, and copra. Conceived by an American designer/sculptor back in the days before people worried about the environment (say, the 1960s), Ladera's villas and public spaces are constructed of hardwoods and native stone, camouflaged by flowering shrubs, all with that "invisible" west wall. (Panic not—the villas are designed in such a way that no one can see in; but if you see a helicopter hovering around longer than usual, maybe you'd better slip into the kimono the resort provides for just such moments. Likewise, you don't have to worry about being rained upon because the roofs project far enough.)

The resort (at that time known as Dasheene) closed for several years in the 1980s because of some legal wrangling among the major shareholder and the people who own the individual suites; but late in 1992 it reopened with a single owner, $1 million worth of renovations, a new name, and a new team of eager beavers in charge. If all continues to go well, romantics once more can frolic in one of the loveliest, most idyllic spots in the Caribbean.

You enter via a gatehouse that still sports the former name, then go up a narrow steep driveway surrounded by more of that luxuriant foliage to the main building—a series of terraces and decks with a tiny rock pool that seems to be spilling over the side of the hill. (If it all seems familiar, it's probably because you saw *Superman II*—this is the spot, I'm told, where Christopher Reeves landed with flowers for the lovely Lois.)

Each of the wood-framed villas is different in layout and decor, each a designer's fantasy with splashes of color to enliven the stone and tile, wicker and bamboo. Some of the furniture is 19th-century French; some was crafted right there in Soufrière by local craftsmen. In one, a gallery bedroom with open shower, in another the bathroom is in the style of a Polynesian grass hut, while some of the bedrooms sport mahogany fourposters or double beds posed on platforms beneath clouds of mosquito netting ("no-see-ums," by the way, are not a problem at this altitude).

For sure, Ladera is not for everyone. The fitted carpet brigade and people who insist on air-conditioning will balk at the plank floors and missing wall; others may quibble about the absence of tubs or telephones and the trek to the beach. But I can't imagine that too many will complain about the sheer romance of the terrace restaurant by candlelight, or, after dinner, there's another pleasure waiting: lying in bed looking out beyond the Pitons to the moonlight shimmering and glistening and gleaming on the sea.

Name: Ladera Resort
Manager: Ivan Moyses
Address: P.O. Box 225, Soufrière, St. Lucia, West Indies
Location: In the hills south of Soufrière, about 40 minutes by taxi from Hewanorra International Airport (the hotel will pick up the tab) and 1 hour, 45 minutes by taxi from Vigie Airport (approx. $70)
Telephone: 809/459-7323
Fax: 809/459-5156
Reservations: Insignia Marketing, 800/467-4464
Credit Cards: All major cards
Rooms: 13 1- or 2-story suites and 6 3-story villas, all different, all open to the breezes, most with showers only (no phones or TV or other distractions). All villas have kitchenettes, some villas and suites have private plunge pools

Meals: Breakfast 8:00–10:00, lunch 11:30–2:30, dinner 6:00–10:00, in the covered but breeze-cooled Dasheene Restaurant (approx. $100 for 2); dress is "smart casual"; room service for breakfast only, $7 per person

Entertainment: Live reggae music Fridays, the bar, the guests, the lighted botanical garden, the view, the moon, and Venus; shuttle bus to Soufrière 3 times daily

Sports: Small pool; water sports and tennis nearby; hikes in the hills to sulfur springs and botanical gardens; shuttle buses twice daily to beach at Anse Chastanet

P.S.:   Because of the layout, not really suitable for young children; open all year

Jalousie Plantation Resort & Spa

St. Lucia

Atmosphere   **Dining**

Sports   **Rates**

In the last edition of *Caribbean Hideaways,* I suggested that you give this newcomer a couple of years to get its act together. Well, I'm happy to report, it has been moving in that direction, give or take a glitch or two.

For sure, settings don't come much more Edenic than this: a luxuriant coconut plantation on the outskirts of a rain forest, beside a curve of beach between the two glorious Pitons, Gros and Petit, which rise more than 2,600 feet practically from your doorstep. Many St. Lucians wanted the plantation to become a national park, and it certainly has all the attributes, but it became a resort instead, at the urging of Lord Glenconner, the former Colin Tennant, who put Mustique on the map (see next chapter). Disenchanted with that island, he turned his formidable powers of persuasion on St. Lucia, where he owned this large swatch of plantation on which he planned to build luxury homes for his aristocratic pals. But first he had to parcel out this 325-acre tract of land to an Iranian-born American entrepreneur to develop a resort-spa to accommodate would-be homeowners. Glenconner now lives on an estate adjacent to the resort, near his barefoot restaurant on the water, Bang Between the Pitons.

Jalousie is defined by its location, likewise Bang Between the Pitons. Hilly and lush, the property spreads out over acres of beachfront and then several hundred feet up the mountain. You enter through a gate at the top of a hill and spiral down a long, winding road, first passing the sports complex (spa, tennis, fairways) and then one by one the cottages, clustered into small groups, until eventually you reach the reception area in the so-called Lord's Great House. From there you can look down on the sweep of the beach, the manicured grounds, the swimming pool, the Sugar Mill complex, and, at the far end of the resort, the marina.

The 102 cottages are designed like mountain chalets, single-story with brown wooden exteriors to blend, apparently, into the wooded hillside, which they do nicely. But despite the topography this is not a mountain but a beach setting, and to my mind the architect missed a great opportunity in a glorious location to design something inspired (ah, if only the folks who put together Strawberry Hill Hotel in Jamaica could have had a crack at this spot!).

As it is, what we have are comfortable, pleasantly appointed lodgings with private patio plunge pools but poky windows that turn to take advantage of the view without a traditional louver in sight. Is this asking too much? After all, most of the public rooms are designed on an open plan to make the most of the setting, so why not the guest rooms? For the record, rooms 109, 501, 316, 614, and 301 have particularly private pools, while the others, especially those near the road, may be too public for comfort or your sense of modesty.

Because the cottages are so spread out and the hills so steep, it's difficult to navigate the distances from your room to the beach and restaurant and elsewhere without the ubiquitous jitneys that circulate seemingly nonstop. If you want a convenient location, the 12 Sugar Mill Suites, in two two-story cream-colored buildings, are closest to the beach. They don't have plunge pools, but they do have terraces with water views, and they're particularly nicely designed—here you feel you're really at a beach resort.

The beach is better than it was (but still not much to speak of given what's available on other islands)—mostly dark, volcanic sand augmented with imported white sand that is wont to wash away. Jalousie's public rooms are generally impressive, with breeze-cooled restaurants and sitting areas. The food can be excellent (try some of the innovative dishes, such as carrot orange soup with green shell mussels or fresh lobster fricassee with asparagus in passion-fruit sauce), and the service is invariably gracious. The main lodge is made to resemble a plantation great house, and its Lord's Great Room is filled with antiques and *objets* on loan from the personal collection of Lord Glenconner. I've been chided for calling this place a mishmash; apparently I should have said museum. You can decide when you get here. It certainly is unusual.

Jalousie also got off to a bad start with its early management, but it has now snared one of the Caribbean's most esteemed hoteliers, David Brewer, a longtime fixture at Little Dix Bay. As of this writing, it's too early for him to have put his stamp on the resort, but given his track record we may see Jalousie join the exalted ranks where its owner has always thought it belonged.

What sets this resort apart from others in this part of the island is a full-scale, professionally staffed spa with gym and beauty facilities. Because the resort operates as an all-inclusive, all meals, drinks, and most of the spa facilities are included in the rates. There are nature walks and aqua exercises, even a special spa menu for calorie counters.

But unlike some boot-camp spas, there is no pressure here to do anything other than revel in the lush scenery surrounded by the majesty of the Pitons.

Name: Jalousie Plantation Resort & Spa

Manager: E. David Brewer

Address: P.O. Box 251, Soufrière, St. Lucia, West Indies

Location: On the southwest coast, in the valley between the two Pitons, just outside Soufrière, about 45 minutes by taxi from Hewanorra Airport, 1¾ hours from Vigie Airport, near Castries. Taxi transfers from Hewanorra are included in the rates; helicopter transfers can be arranged ($75 per person one-way)

Telephone: 809/459-7666

Fax: 809/459-7667

Reservations: 800/392-2007

Credit Cards: All major cards

Rooms: 114 cottages and Sugar Mill rooms, all with patios or terraces, air-conditioning, ceiling fans, stocked refrigerators, remote-control television, FM radios, hair dryers, direct-dial telephones, bathrobes, in-room safes; all cottages have private plunge pools

Meals: Breakfast 7:30–10:30, lunch noon–3:00, tea 4:30–6:00, dinner 6:30–10:30 in alternating restaurants, including the elegant Plantation Room in the Great House overlooking the hotel grounds, and the informal, open-air Pier Restaurant on the water's edge; dress "casual elegant," no T-shirts or shorts at dinner; room service available during dining hours

Entertainment: 4 bars, Sunday afternoon jazz buffet in the Pier Restaurant, live music most evenings, carnival jump-up night Friday evenings

Sports: Beach (dark volcanic sand covered with imported white sand), large freshwater pool, waterskiing, snorkeling (protected reef just off the beach), sailing, windsurfing, aqua cycles, shore dives, tennis (4 Plexicushion courts, 3 lit for night play), squash court, supervised gym (no air-conditioning) with aerobics and other classes, 3-hole golf course—all free; full-scale spa facilities, including whirlpool and sauna (body massage included in rates); scuba, local excursions to the Pitons and other sites, horseback riding at extra charge

P.S.:   Children's program available; some groups, international clientele, predominantly European; special spa program includes computerized individual fitness and nutritional analysis and treatment programs; resort is spread over 325 hilly acres, so jitneys, which stop at designated locations, are required for transport; open all year

Crane Beach Hotel
Barbados

☆☆				♀♀			● ●			$ $ $	
Atmosphere				**Dining**			**Sports**			**Rates**	

Once the only thing that stood on this airy bluff was a gigantic wooden crane that handed down bales of sugarcane to British schooners bobbing in the sea below. By the turn of the 18th century, the gentleman who owned the crane had done so well that next to it he built himself a very small, very grand manor house. Close to 200 years later, that minimansion of gray white coral stone is the east wing of the Crane Beach Hotel.

You can usually count on a couple of centuries to take their toll, especially in a windswept, spume-swept spot like this. But the miraculous thing about the old Crane is that its original seigneur would probably still feel right at home—even with the addition of a new wing in the 19th century and a swimming pool in the 20th.

This pool, a spectacular Roman affair with Ionic columns, is scooped right out of the edge of the cliff with a backdrop of sea and beach and a full-blown coconut grove. It's the kind of vista that dreams are made of (although some purists might cringe at the columns). In fact, the view is so spectacular that it used to attract parties of sightseers, an annoying disruption. However, that problem has been alleviated somewhat since the hotel added a new, attractively landscaped entranceway with a booth where a staff member charges nonguests a $5 entrance fee. And a "residents only" sign has been erected on the fence surrounding the pool area.

The guest rooms may be outshone by the hotel's setting—but only just. They're closer to a country auberge than an Antillean resort. Floors of polished wide-plank pine or cooling quarry tiles. Canopy beds and 16-foot ceilings. Walls a foot thick, of coral stone or old brick. Antique chests and wardrobes. Tiled baths with both overhead and hand-held showers. All 14 suites have breezy terraces or balconies. The 9 deluxe suites are in the process of getting kitchens or pantries, complete with blenders and microwave ovens.

Some favorites: Room 3 may be the most intimate of all the Crane's romantic nooks and crannies; it has simple beachy furniture, a refrigerator and honor bar, and a flowery brick patio. Above, room 10A has a balcony that gives you a two-way view—along the picture-book beach and east out to the reef and sea. Rooms 1, 2, 8, and 11 have four-poster beds.

For going the whole hog, there's no place like suite 8. Beyond the gleaming foyer waits a sitting room worthy of a governor-general: a burnished wood ceiling, silken sofas, glass-doored bookcases imaginatively stocked. Beyond that is a functional pantry, and beyond *that* a bedroom full of splendid antiques. In the middle of it all, on a carpeted platform of blue, looms a huge canopied bed from which, on a clear day with the wooden louvered shutters pushed aside, you can view the same sunny sea-lane that those ancient sugar schooners followed home to Liverpool.

The Crane Beach dining rooms are not the most attractive in Barbados, but the kitchen has gotten its act together and has racked up several culinary awards.

Name: Crane Beach Hotel

Manager: Edwin Luke

Address: Crane Beach, St. Philip, Barbados, West Indies

Location: On the southeastern corner of the island, 15 minutes and $10 by taxi from the airport, 30 minutes and $18 from Bridgetown (bus to town)

Telephone: 809/423-6220

Fax: 809/423-4763

Reservations: Direct

Credit Cards: American Express, Diners Club, MasterCard, Visa

Rooms: 18, including 9 1-bedroom suites and 5 junior suites, all with ceiling fans (air-conditioning in 2 standard rooms only) and telephones, all suites have terrace or balcony, some with 4-poster beds and antiques

Meals: Breakfast 7:30–10:00, lunch noon–3:00 in the glass-enclosed terrace overlooking the beach and reef, afternoon tea 3:30–6:00, dinner 6:30–10:00 (approx. $70 for 2); informal dress (but no shorts at dinner); entertainment for lunch and dinner 7 days a week; full room service from 7:30 a.m.–10:00 p.m., no extra charge

Entertainment: Taped classical music in lounge, steel band with buffet lunch on Sundays

Sports: 1,000 feet of white-sand beach (down spiral steps), freshwater pool (with 160,000 gallons, every drop from a private well), snorkeling, tennis (4 courts, no lights)—free; horseback riding, sailing nearby

P.S.: "Not suitable for young children" because of the location; 3-night minimum in winter, 7 at Christmas/New Year's Day; open all year

Sandy Lane Hotel

Barbados

Atmosphere

Dining

Sports

Rates

Physically, Sandy Lane is one of the class acts. An imposing driveway curves beneath enormous mahogany and tamarind trees, past terraced gardens with cherub fountains and flowerbeds, down to the Palladian porte cochere and main lodge of pink gray, hand-cut coral stone. And you know you're in class surroundings when the resort's two vintage Rolls-Royces pull up beneath the porte cochere after shuttling to and from the airport with lords and ladies who have just arrived from London. The Mercedes station wagon tags along, too—for the luggage.

A recent history of the resort's first 30 years is peppered with the names of British aristocrats and American celebrities who have vacationed here. But even classics sometimes fade and there was a time in the 1980s when Sandy Lane was coasting along on its reputation. Then, just in time for the resort's 30th birthday, one of its most devoted guests, Lord Forte (whose hotel group just happens to own Sandy Lane), decided to treat it to a multi-million-dollar face-lift.

The project was a dream come true for Richard Williams, the personable, hands-on manager, whose ancestors came over to Barbados from the U.K. more than 200 years ago. Every room was spiffed up with new fabrics and furnishings, the famous al fresco dance floor had its art deco whirls restored, the golf course, tennis courts, and swimming pool were upgraded— and a new club for children was installed in a corner of the garden to keep the young Fauntleroys occupied (and, not coincidentally, out of the hair of the elder Fauntleroys).

The most striking improvement, though, was the creation of luxury ocean view rooms. At 670 square feet, they're half as large as the rooms they replaced, with 19 switches to handle all the lights and fans, door chimes that also buzz on the terrace so you can relax while waiting for breakfast, stocked mini-bars, phone extensions everywhere—bed, bath, toilet, desk, terrace. Ah, the terrace! For my money, what makes these 11- by 13-foot enclaves so appealing is that they're virtually full-scale indoor/outdoor living rooms, complete with plump upholstered chairs and sofas, reading lights, dining tables, and ceiling fans. The marble bathrooms are no less splendid: sunken corner tub, separate shower, bidet and toilet in their own cubicle, two sinks, and, of course, those two telephones.

These are some of the comfiest lodgings in the islands, I thought, until I stayed recently in a one-bedroom suite that is similar but more so—with a larger armoire for television, shelves for books (crisp, new hardcovers) and assorted bric-a-brac, two armchairs with ottomans, a wet bar. On the other hand, I also stayed in one of the regular oceanfront rooms and I can't say I was unhappy—and it just happened to be a few doors from Luciano Pavarotti's favorite room (no fancy suites for him when he and his entourage take their annual vacation at Sandy Lane).

A more recent innovation is the restyling of the beach-level dining pavilion, now transformed into the Seashell and specializing in Italian cuisine. Very pleasant, very tasteful, very comfortable (you certainly can't complain about too-close tables here), but I still prefer the classic Sandy Bay Terrace upstairs. It was designed by the great Oliver Messel and has remained virtually the same from day one: slender white iron columns and balustrades topped with pink and white striped awnings beneath a shingled roof.

The good news is that the resort now has its most distinguished chef in years, Hans Schweitzer, fresh from triumphs and Michelin stars in Bad Homburg and Cambridge (the English one), to say nothing of preparing banquets and buffets for Queen Elizabeth. Applying his classical training to local produce, he enlivens these candlelit tropical evenings by adding, say, a passion-fruit vinaigrette to escalopes of foie gras or cassava croquettes to accompany a flavorful *ballotin* of chicken. He brought with him a former colleague, sommelier John Gilchrist, who has refined an already outstanding *carte des vins* and instituted teatime wine tastings that tempt sun worshipers into leaving the beach an hour earlier than usual.

It should be noted, of course, that Sandy Lane is just as likely to take your breath away with its rates as with its elegant setting, although the tariffs are practically a bargain for people who want to play lots of golf or tennis or skim around on water skis, all of which come with the room. Fortunately, Williams and his team know their resort is pricey, so they go flat out in their effort to lavish everyone with personal service. There's always someone to open your car door, always someone to grab your luggage; the front-desk staff is on its toes day and night, the dining-room staff is ever alert to empty plates, the housekeeping people behave like doting grandmothers. Two tireless, smiling ladies are always at the airport to greet arriving passengers. In your room personal stationery is preprinted and waiting and a Black &

Decker toaster stands ready to make your morning toast crisp and fresh. When you go down to breakfast you'll find one table laid with a selection of newspapers, another with fresh fruit juices and a chilled bottle of champagne in case you feel like a revivifying mimosa. Minor perks, maybe, but they show that someone is thinking about the guests.

"I plan to make this one of the 10 best resorts in the world," Richard Williams told me a few years ago. I told him I'd settle for one of the 10 best in the Caribbean—but his boast is now closer to reality than mine.

Name: Sandy Lane Hotel

Manager: Richard Williams

Address: St. James, Barbados, West Indies

Location: On the west coast, 18 miles and 25 minutes from the airport (a concierge service meets you at the airport, takes care of immigration, and puts you in the complimentary Rolls); 20 minutes and $10 by taxi from Bridgetown

Telephone: 809/432-1311

Fax: 809/432-2954

Reservations: Leading Hotels of the World or Forte Hotels, 800/225-5843

Credit Cards: American Express, Diners Club, MasterCard, Visa

Rooms: 120 rooms and suites in 3 2-story and 4-story wings (even if you save a few dollars, avoid the garden view, since the beach views are so stunning); all with balconies or patios, bathrobes, hair dryers, refrigerators, toasters, wall safes, clock radios, direct-dial telephones, cable television

Meals: Breakfast 7:30–10:00, lunch 12:30–2:30 (to 5:00 in the poolside café), afternoon tea 2:30–6:00, dinner 7:30–10:00 (approx. $80–$90 for 2), in the beachside Sandy Bay, the Seashell, or Putters on the Green, at the golf club; informal but dressy most of the time, no jeans or shorts after 7:00; beach barbecue on Tuesdays, Sunday brunch buffet; 24-hour room service, no extra charge; member of Elegant Resorts' dine-around program

Entertainment: Terrace bars, lounge with big screen for VCR movies, live music every evening, dancing under the stars on the Starlight Terrace, some floor shows and folklore shows (including the inescapable limbo, which you'd think regular guests would be bored with by this time)

Sports: Long, long stretch of beach (public, of course, so sometimes bustling with folks from cruise ships), freshwater pool at the tennis club, tennis (5 courts, lights, pro), golf (18 championship holes, shared with local club members), weekly golf and tennis clinic, fitness center, snorkeling gear, waterskiing, windsurfing, Hobiecats, Sunfish sailing, mats, and floats—all free; on-property massage, scuba diving, yacht trips, and horseback riding can be arranged

P.S.: Children's "Tree House Club" for kids 2–12, also complimentary babysitting; some executive seminars in the off-season; open all year

Coral Reef Club

Barbados

Atmosphere	Dining	Sports	Rates

You stay in bungalows with names like Petrea and Allamanda and Cordia, and you walk to the beach past splashes of blue petrea and yellow allamanda and orange cordia.

You swim a few leisurely breast strokes to the coral reef offshore.

You dine off flying fish mousse and marlin pâté and tipsy trifle and coconut meringue pie.

Above all, you relax.

The Coral Reef Club is the sort of place where people go to wind down rather than dress up, where entertainers such as Engelbert Humperdinck and Tom Jones or Olympic skating stars Torvill and Dean go to find undisturbed seclusion. This clubby but unstuffy inn has been a standard-bearer among Barbados resorts for more than 35 years, a prototype of the small Barbados retreat built around a coral-stone villa. And because it was there before the others, it managed to snare more beachfront acreage— more than a dozen acres of tropical greenery. Space enough for most of the rooms to be in semiprivate bungalows, spread out among cannonball and mango and mahogany trees. From the open-air dining pavilion, the sea seems to extend around you on *three* sides.

The other attraction that sets Coral Reef apart is the O'Hara family. Budge and Cynthia O'Hara started the place all those years ago (after a stint at England's famed Lygon Arms), and they haven't missed a year since, greeting every guest, overseeing gardens and kitchens, buying gifts for everyone staying at the club at Christmas. (Question: What do you get Engelbert *and* Tom when they're *both* guests over the same holiday? Answer: Each other's records.)

Now the torch has passed to a new generation of equally dedicated O'Haras—sons Patrick and Mark—who, with the long-serving staff (some of whom have been there almost since day one), maintain a special, warm family feeling. (Breakfast, for example: No pressure—Continental breakfast is available anytime between 8:00 and noon.)

But the new regime has inaugurated a few changes in the past few seasons. Most noticeable was the addition in 1994 of a new two-story wing with 10 rooms and suites. It might have been a visual sore thumb, but it has been artfully designed in a harmonious plantation-house style with verandas and gingerbread trim. The new rooms are slightly larger, slightly plusher than the originals, with sumptuous rattan and wicker furniture, plumper fabrics; the sleek new bathrooms come with black-tile floors and white-tile tub-shower units adjoining white Barbados shutters that open to greenery.

Best of all are the new verandas, about 12-by-16-feet, furnished for indoor-outdoor living. Rooms and suites on the second floor will have an edge for some, with their cathedral ceilings of pickled pine and better (but only marginally) views. They all retain the usual homelike O'Hara touches—individual toasters so that you get your breakfast toast crisp and fresh, shelves of paperbacks in each room. The original cottages— Frangipani, Poinsettia, Cordia, Petrea, et al—are nothing to sneeze at, given their sense of spaciousness and privacy, but even they have been subtly upgraded without losing any of their casual, homespun flavor (although I still find the refrigerators on the patios something of an eyesore— apparently the guests do not). And my favorites would still be rooms 3 and 4 in the original Great House.

A few other refinements: Each year, a top chef from Europe spends time in the kitchen, coaching and encouraging the local cooks, a project that is paying off, judging by the flavorful and refreshingly original dishes on a recent 40-dish luncheon buffet—guava mousse, miniature pine-nut burgers, and sweet-potato cakes to complement the traditional roast beef and turkey. The bar, too, has been repositioned and restyled and seems to me an even more inviting venue than it was before. Now it's beside the beach and decorated with pleasant island flair (note the hanging planters/ lights—they did duty in another incarnation as farmers' dung baskets).

For some of Coral Reef's hatibués, the best news is that the grounds are as lovely as ever, with the usual brigade of 20 gardeners tending the lawns and every last petal of petrea, cordia, red acalypher, and yellow sage.

Name: Coral Reef Club
Owners/Managers: Patrick and Mark O'Hara
Address: St. James, Barbados, West Indies
Location: On the northwest coast, 25 minutes and $19 by taxi from the airport, 20 minutes and $20 from Bridgetown (free shuttle to town weekdays at 9:30 a.m.)
Telephone: 809/422-2372
Fax: 809/422-1776
Reservations: Ralph Locke Islands
Credit Cards: All major cards
Rooms: 69, in garden bungalows, the Clubhouse, or in a 2-story wing, all

with private bathrooms, refrigerators, hair dryers, patios or balconies, air-conditioning and ceiling fans, direct-dial telephones, toasters, wall safes, shelves of paperbacks

Meals: Breakfast 7:30–10:30, Continental breakfast until noon, lunch 1:00–2:30, afternoon tea 4:00–6:00, dinner 7:30–9:30 (approx. $120 for 2) in the breeze-cooled beachside pavilion; Monday evening Bajan buffet; Sunday brunch buffet; optional jacket and tie 3 evenings in winter, informal the remainder of the year; 24-hour service (but not always full meals) at no extra charge; member of Elegant Resorts' dine-around program

Entertainment: Live music and dancing 7 evenings a week year-round, 5 evenings in the off-season (amplified "but not loud"), weekly folklore show and beach barbecue, parlor games, TV room

Sports: Good beach, good swimming and snorkeling, freshwater pool, tennis (2 all-weather courts, no lights, across the street and a 5-minute walk), Sunfish sailing, windsurfing, cocktail cruises, snorkeling gear, Hobiecat—all free; catamaran cruises, scuba diving, waterskiing for a fee; golf at nearby Sandy Lane; horseback riding and deep-sea fishing can be arranged

P.S.: "Children welcome except during February, when those under 12 years cannot be accommodated"; closed June and July

Glitter Bay
Barbados

☆☆☆		🍷🍷		🎯🎯		$ $ $ $	
Atmosphere		**Dining**		**Sports**		**Rates**	

The glitter comes from the play of sun on sea, but when the Cunard family of steamship fame took over the estate in the 1930s, the *guests* were the glitter—Noël Coward and Anthony Eden, assorted lords and ladies and merchant princes. Oceangoing Cunarders putting into Bridgetown often found their ships' orchestras shanghaied to play for Sir Edward Cunard's garden parties. All very romantic.

Today, the sea still glitters, lords and ladies still winter here, and at least one Arab prince has settled in for 6 weeks on more than one occasion, accompanied by an entourage of 25. But Sir Edward's original coral-stone

Great House is now the centerpiece of a small resort, created 11 years ago by an Englishman, Michael Pemberton. He made his bundle in amusement arcades and real-estate development, but with his prime Caribbean estate he has opted to develop it in the style of Andalusia rather than the Antilles—white-stucco buildings rising three or four stories above the lawns, their ocher-tiled rooftops eye to eye with the coconut palms, their balconies and terraces angled for sea views. By confining the rooms to one side of the garden and by building up rather than out, Pemberton avoided that pitfall of so many of the newer beachside resorts in Barbados—rooms looking into rooms.

The decor is attractively tropical with Mediterranean overtones: scatter rugs to brighten the quarry-tile floors and (nice touch) cushioned banquettes on the stucco balconies. Since the resort was conceived originally as a condo operation, most of the accommodations are suites with kitchenettes, in versatile configurations of duplex suites, penthouse suites, and nests with one to three bedrooms.

But Glitter Bay is almost two distinct resorts, because the most appealing rooms, for my money, are located not in the Andalusian-style villas but in the beachside villas known as Beach House, a coral-stone replica of the Cunards' palazzo in Venice, with five luxury suites.

Glitter Bay also gives you a sense of space rare in Barbados—22 acres tended by a dozen gardeners, lawns shaded by royal palms and cannonball trees, pathways lined by frangipani and lady-of-the-night, sturdy saman trees embraced and entwined by traceries of wild orchids.

The old Great House sits well back from the beach, while the remaining structures are grouped around a split-level swimming pool with a wooden footbridge and waterfall. Down by the beach, the restaurant, Le Piperade, enjoys fresh sea breezes and lavishes attentive service on its diners (the young staff are forever checking if everything is fine, heating plates for entrées, whisking dishes away promptly). Prices are reasonable (for food *and* wine), and the menu runs the gamut from fillet of flying fish or jumbo coconut prawns to citrus roasted chicken or Maroon Town jerk pork loin.

Name: Glitter Bay

Manager: Andrew Humphries

Address: St. James, Barbados, West Indies

Location: On the northwest coast, 25 minutes and $25 by taxi from the airport (you can also arrange to have 1 of the resort's Mercedes collect you for $60), 20 minutes and $15 from Bridgetown

Telephone: 809/422-5555

Fax: 809/422-3940

Reservations: Direct, 800/283-8666

Credit Cards: All major cards

Rooms: 83, in 3- and 4-story wings or beachside villas, all with air-conditioning and fans, terraces or patios, refrigerators, direct-dial telephones, cotton bathrobes, hair dryers, radios; suites also have kitchenettes

Meals: Breakfast 7:30–11:00, lunch 12:30–6:30, dinner 7:00–10:00, in the breeze-cooled, beachside restaurant (approx. $100 for 2); afternoon tea 3:00–5:00 in the air-conditioned Great House lounge; informal dress (but no shorts or T-shirts in the evening); Monday buffet dinner, with live entertainment, open to nonguests; Friday-night barbecue; room service during dining-room hours; snacks around-the-clock; meals can also be charged at Royal Pavilion (see below)

Entertainment: Beachside bar, live amplified music for dancing, some folklore shows, TV-VCR in lounge (TV sets can also be rented)

Sports: Cove beach, raft, 2-tiered free-form freshwater pool, windsurfing, snorkeling masks, Hobie 16s, waterskiing, tennis (2 courts, with lights), fitness center—all free (shared with Royal Pavilion guests); sailboat and speedboat cruises and scuba can be arranged at the beach hut, horseback riding 10 minutes away; golf on the brand-new Royal Westmoreland course, 15 minutes away

P.S.: Expect lots of children during holidays (but they have their own planned activities) and a few seminar groups in the off-season; open all year

Royal Pavilion

Barbados

Atmosphere

Dining   **Sports**

Rates

When Mike Pemberton of Glitter Bay told me that he had bought the old Miramar Hotel, next door, and planned to turn it into a deluxe resort, I thought the midday sun had finally befuddled his English brain. How could anyone take that dumpy motel and transform it into anything remotely luxurious?

Well, Pemberton has shown us how.

First you call in Glitter Bay's landscape architect extraordinaire, Fernando Tabora, to work his green-thumb magic on the 7 acres of grounds. Next you summon Ian Morrison, the architect who designed Glitter Bay, to work his visual magic—adding a tower here, a turret there, primping the facades with fretwork motifs, knocking down a wall here, adding an archway there to create a pink palace out of motel-like squatness. Morrison's pièce de résistance is the resort's Palm Terrace, a capacious beachfront room for lounging, sipping, chatting, and dining—about as elegant, comfortable, and eye pleasing as any room in the islands. The two-story, vaulted ceiling of pickled pine is specially designed to let in the 20% of sunlight Tabora needs for the nourishment of 20-foot McCarthy palms and other plants that turn the terrace into a miniconservatory. Five pink stucco archways along the front of the room open to the sea, with graceful arches along the sides encasing Renaissance-paned windows. On the pink marble floors sit natural-stained wicker furniture plump with cushions and pillows covered in a striking water-splashed gray and pink fabric. Even the lighting is carefully contrived, with some bulbs reflecting up pink stucco columns, others focusing downward from the eaves. Ceiling fans add the right tropical touch and yet the overall elegance of the room allows the ebony grand piano to seem very much in its rightful place.

The entrance to all this elegance is equally impressive: several plant-filled patios with crested tiles on the walkways and gouaches by an Englishman named Adam Smith on the walls, with very fancy boutiques (but why, oh why, have they added taped music?).

The rooms (referred to as junior suites, but really just large rooms) come with oversize terraces with divans and breakfast tables facing the beach. They are plushly decorated, with king-size beds, small sofas, and coffee tables in the sitting areas, dressing areas beside the bathroom, and glass doors that open to each terrace. With the drapes pulled back and the doors wide open, your room feels bathed in space, Caribbean breezes, and gentle surf sounds. (It's a pity that the rooms don't have eiling fans in addition to the air conditioners.)

Since the guest rooms are essentially identical, the choice is in location. Those on the third floor are not only the most private but they also have pickled-pine ceilings with beams that add a nice sense of space and warmth. Those on the first floor, though, score by having a garden patio in addition to a large terrace—a semiprivate front yard, as it were, with a low wall separating it from the beach—but you'll probably have to lock your doors and therefore sleep with the air-conditioning on. Top or bottom, though, a room in the north wing offers the most privacy.

Fernando Tabora's landscaping is lush and often breathtaking. There's a gigantic travelers' palm beside the pool (artfully lit at night), an amazing bearded fig tree behind the north wing, and hardly a vista or nook that is not accented by flowering flourishes. No wonder Pemberton honored his gardener by naming one of the hotel's restaurants Tabora's. It serves light fare; at the more ambitious Palm Terrace, your best bet is to stick to simple preparations such as broiled fish or steaks, although the cuisine *has* improved in the past year.

Name: Royal Pavilion
Manager: Peter Bowling
Address: Porters, St. James, Barbados, West Indies
Location: On the northwest coast, 20 minutes and $15 by taxi from Bridgetown, 30 minutes and $20 by taxi from the airport (you can also have 1 of Pemberton's Mercedes meet you at the airport, about $60 1-way)
Telephone: 809/422-5555
Fax: 809/422-3940
Reservations: Direct, 800/283-8666
Credit Cards: All major cards
Rooms: 72 junior suites, all beachfront, all with balconies or patios, air-conditioning, direct-dial telephones, clock radios, cotton bathrobes, hair dryers, stocked mini-bars, toiletry amenities including English soaps; plus 1 beachfront penthouse and 1 villa for 6
Meals: Breakfast 7:30–11:00, lunch and dinner 12:30–10:00, both in Tabora's, the casual beachfront dining pavilion, afternoon tea 3:00–5:00, dinner 7:00–9:45 in the Palm Terrace (approx. $90 for 2); informal dress; room service; some live music most evenings, international buffet Wednesday in the Palm Terrace; guests can also charge bills at the Piperade in Glitter Bay or on the dine-around program with nearby resorts
Entertainment: Some form of live music most evenings, classical or light classical piano at teatime
Sports: Half-mile beach, pool, tennis courts (2 lit, 1 Astroturf), waterskiing, Hobiecats, windsurfing—all free; golf and horseback riding nearby
P.S.: No children under 12 during the high season; open all year

Cobblers Cove Hotel
Barbados

| Atmosphere | Dining | Sports | Rates |

Claudette Colbert lives two villas along the beach and when several years back, Ronald Reagan came a-calling and a-swimming, quiet little Cobblers Cove found itself awash with paparazzi and a perspiring Secret Service.

Next day, it was back to being its cozy, relaxed self. Just 39 suites, 76 guests. A stately drawing room. A charmer of a wood-framed dining pavilion beside the beach. A mini-swimming pool and a quarter-mile of unspoiled palm-fringed cove—with just the resort at one end, a fleet of fishing boats at the other, and Claudette Colbert in the middle, screened by a mass of sea grape.

The most northerly of Barbados's small hideaways, Cobblers is a world apart, the unsung rendezvous of actors from the U.K., CEOs from the United States, professionals and romantics from hither and yon. For some it may be too small—3 acres of garden with 10 two-story shingle-roofed cottages, 4 suites to a cottage, arranged in a V around a 50-year-old castellated folly that looks like a setting for a Gilbert and Sullivan opera.

If the property is a tad cramped, the suites are not—big hardwood balcony or patio with loungers, living room with a wall of louvered shutters that folds right back to make the room and balcony one large space, air-conditioned bedroom, and bathrooms that have just been restyled and spiffed up. All the suites come with small pantries, but they, too, are being redesigned to create even more space. The prime locations are those facing the beach (suites numbered 1 through 8 and 33 through 36), but try for one of the upper-level suites—they have higher ceilings, more ventilation, more privacy (and you don't have the security patrol asking you to close and lock your shutters and windows).

Suites located at the bottom of the V may have less privacy than you prefer and some of them may pick up too much traffic noise from the main road just beyond the fence. So 2 years ago the owners came up with an ingenious sound baffle in the form of a coral stone enclosing wall, which is already being decorated and disguised with vines and foliage. The enclosing wall now incorporates the reception area, with a pathway winding through the garden to the Great House, where the former reception desk has been commandeered by the concierge, just in case any guests happen to think of something urgent while they're in the water and need an answer without having to (heaven forbid) traipse through the garden to the front desk.

A few years ago the upper level of the Great House was converted into the very spacious, very private Camelot Suite, with a king-size four-poster bed, a whirlpool bath, a 14- by 16-foot lounge with wet bar, and a spiral stairway leading up to a totally secluded rooftop deck, private plunge pool, and a second wet bar. Camelot indeed! At $1,200 a night in winter you might think it had few takers. On the contrary, sometime during 1995, manager Hamish Watson plans to vacate his second-floor office overlooking the sea to conjure up a second luxurious penthouse suite, the Colerton, to satisfy the pent-up demand for romance and fantasy.

But whatever your suite, you'll find a welcoming, instantly at-home feeling to Cobblers Cove, from the genial Watson to the maids and busboys. And an unusual attention to detail. When Watson invited master chef Pierre Gleize of La Bonne Etape, the two-star Michelin restaurant in Provence, to spend the winter months at Cobblers Cove to tune up the kitchen staff, he may not have known how much of a perfectionist he was getting. Because fowl cannot be imported into Barbados, Gleize brought in fertilized eggs so that he could serve his guests the freshest quail and pheasant. Now, with the kitchen preparing the tempting dishes you might expect to find on St. Barts rather than Barbados—*rillette de canard et papaye marinée, langouste à la vanille au rhum, rosette d'agneau aïolli à la menthé*—Cobblers Cove's tiny beachside dining pavilion is one of the most esteemed dining spots on the island. Where once there was a nice little hotel with a fine kitchen, now there's this outstanding restaurant with a nice little hotel attached.

Name: Cobblers Cove Hotel

Owner/Manager: Hamish Watson

Address: St. Peter, Barbados, West Indies

Location: On the sheltered northwest coast, adjoining the village of Speightstown (pronounced "spiteston"), 45 minutes and $28 by taxi from the airport, 15 minutes from Bridgetown (free shuttle/mini-bus daily or $20 by taxi)

Telephone: 809/422-2291

Fax: 809/422-1460

Reservations: Robert Reid Associates

Credit Cards: American Express, MasterCard, Visa

Rooms: 38, all suites, with private bathrooms, air-conditioning and ceiling fans, louvered doors, kitchenettes, stocked mini-bars, hair dryers, English bath amenities, bathrobes, mini-safes, balconies or patios, direct-dial telephones; plus the stunning Camelot Suite

Meals: Breakfast 8:00–10:00, lunch 12:30–2:30, snack menu 2:30–4:00, afternoon tea 4:00–5:00, dinner 7:00–9:00 (approx. $120 for 2), in the beachside pavilion; Sunday brunch buffet, open to nonguests; barbecue buffet Tuesday, "elegantly casual" dress; room service from 8:00 a.m.– 9:00 p.m., no extra charge; dine-around plan with nearby resorts

Entertainment: Lounge/bar, occasional live music (not too loud, not exactly pianissimo either), radio or TV for rooms available.

Sports: Lovely beach and lagoon-smooth bay, small freshwater pool, snorkeling gear, waterskiing, windsurfing, Sunfish sailing, new Omni tennis court across the street (with lights)—all free; scuba diving, picnic sails, tennis and golf can be arranged, at extra charge

P.S.:   Some families with small children; no children from mid-January to mid-March; closed September 1 through mid-October

Sandpiper Inn
Barbados

☆☆					🍷🍷					🌑🌑					$ $				
Atmosphere					**Dining**					**Sports**					**Rates**				

Owned by the O'Hara family of the esteemed Coral Reef Club and located beachside just a few miles south, the Sandpiper is run by daughter Karen Capaldi and her husband, Wayne, with the same kind of dedication. Its 45 rooms, suites, and apartments embrace a trim and tidy garden with an inviting thatch roofed bar-restaurant and swimming pool. The newer lodgings have large living rooms and bedrooms with floors of white ceramic tiles, pastel colors, and rattan and wicker furniture, a kitchen with a four-ring burner and a refrigerator (better note that dishwashing is not part of the maids' regular duties), and spacious balconies or patios.

These rooms are very comfortable and relaxing, but I think I prefer the two wings of older lodgings, which have more of an island flavor (louvers rather than sliding glass doors, for example) and happen to be closer to the relatively uncrowded white-sand beach. Wednesday night is the managers' cocktail party and buffet, Sunday is barbecue day, but other days of the week the restaurant is busy with people from other hotels—and the food consistently earns kudos from local gourmets.

Name: Sandpiper Inn

Managers: Karen and Wayne Capaldi

Address: St. James, Barbados, West Indies

Location: On St. James Beach, 20 minutes from the capital and $19 from the airport

Telephone and Fax: 809/422-2251

Reservations: Ralph Locke Islands

Credit Cards: American Express, MasterCard, Visa

Rooms: 45 rooms, including 1- and 2-bedroom suites with living rooms and kitchens, all with terrace, air-conditioning, ceiling fans, hair dryer, wall safe, refrigerator

Meals: Breakfast 7:30–10:30, Continental breakfast 7:00–noon, lunch noon–2:30, afternoon tea 3:00–5:00, dinner 7:00–9:30; dress is "elegantly informal," but no T-shirts or shorts in the bar or restaurant after 7:00; room service available during restaurant hours

Entertainment: Bar, low-key live entertainment every night in season, manager's cocktail party and Sunday barbecue

Sports: White-sand beach, tennis (2 courts with lights), windsurfing, snorkeling, sailing—all free; waterskiing, 2 golf courses within walking distance, scuba-diving school at nearby Coral Reef resort

P.S.: Children under 12 not allowed in February

Arnos Vale Hotel
Tobago

☆ Atmosphere   ♀ Dining   ◐ Sports $ Rates

When you sit down for afternoon tea, a giant flamboyant shades you from the sun, and a sprawling sea-grape tree cools you when you sip a punch on the beachside terrace. You stroll to and from your room along pathways hugged by oleander and frangipani. Bananaquits come to filch tidbits from your breakfast, and you lunch to the cries of parrots and jacamars, mockingbirds and motmots.

"We wanted the place to look as little like a hotel as possible," said the original owners. They certainly succeeded. What you see when you step through the lobby is an arena-shaped botanical garden, solid greenery accented with splashes of color, the sea glittering beyond the foliage. Look more carefully and you notice a building or two here and there at different levels, up there on the hillside, down there by the cove. The shingled, cut-coral cottage housing the lobby, lounge, and dining veranda is perched at the 100-foot level. Follow the footpath 20 feet higher and you come to six rooms in three cottages, including an aerie called the Crow's Nest Suite. The remaining rooms are by the beach and pool, each different, but simply furnished with few frills, even though they come in two categories, standard and superior.

The most romantic suites are right on the beach, with local fishermen's dugout canoes hauled up at the foot of the tiny stone stairway that leads to a small private terrace. Back in the days when Arnos Vale was a sugar plantation, this was part of the storehouse where the cane was stacked before being shipped to England. What makes a real difference between the rooms is location—whether you want to be close to the beach and pool, or up in the hills with the birds and breezes.

There are plenty of paths to follow through virtually unspoiled tropical forest. Your best plan would be to ask the bartender to make up a flask of rum punch, then follow the path up the hill to Sunset Point, where you'll find a bench for two, strategically placed to face the sun.

Since the original owners left, so has much of the tender loving care a place like this needs to keep it spic-and-span, but it's still a place for true solitude. Maybe too much so—I met an Englishman there once who claimed, in impeccably clipped accents, that he could actually talk to the motmots.

Nowadays you'll hear fewer English accents since the resort has been taken over by an Italian tour operator, who usually fills the place in winter.

Name: Arnos Vale Hotel

Manager: Vittorio de Felice

Address: P.O. Box 208, Scarborough, Tobago, Trinidad & Tobago, West Indies

Location: In a tropical vale beside a quiet cove on the southwest coast, 20 minutes and $18 by taxi from Crown Point Airport

Telephone: 809/639-2881, 2882, 3247

Fax: 809/639-4629

Reservations: Direct

Credit Cards: American Express, Diners Club, Visa

Rooms: 30, divided between the hilltop main lodge, hilltop cottages, and beachside wings, all with balconies or terraces, telephones, air-conditioning, and showers

Meals: Breakfast 8:00–10:00 and lunch 1:00–2:00 on the beachside terrace, dinner 8:00–9:00 (on the veranda of the main lodge, approx. $40

for 2); barbecues at lunchtime; informal dress (but trousers rather than shorts for men after 6:00)

Entertainment: Taped music in the dining room, local entertainment nightly, TV on terrace adjoining the dining room (spewing forth "Down by the River Side" in the middle of the afternoon, with not even a bananaquit watching it)

Sports: Sheltered beach, freshwater pool, tennis (1 court)—free; snorkeling gear for rent, fishing, scuba diving, golf, excursions to Buccoo Reef and bird sanctuaries can be arranged

P.S.: Open all year

Mount Irvine Bay Hotel & Golf Club

Tobago

Atmosphere

Dining

Sports

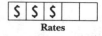
Rates

It's constructed around an old sugar mill, fitted with a shingle-roofed ramada and stylishly transformed into an open bar and dining terrace.

A two-story wing of balconied guest rooms forms a protective around a big blue-tiled swimming pool with a swim-up bar in one corner. Other rooms (46 out of 105) are housed in little square bungalows engulfed in heliconia and thumbergia. But what makes this 1970s resort so attractive is the setting—27 acres of tropical flora surrounded by 130 acres of fairways and coconut palms, laid out on a bluff above the curve of Mount Irvine Bay, with the famed Buccoo Reef breaking the sea just beyond the headland.

Most of the balconies and loggias are sited to make the most of the gardens and the views, and without the views the rooms would be fairly conventional. Nice views can also be found at the restaurant, Le Beau Rivage, which overlooks the 18th hole.

With the exception of the standards, the rooms are quite large, with double the usual closet space. The bungalows, the priciest accommodations, have large loggias that are virtually breezy outdoor living rooms with terrazzo floors and khuskhus rugs; the bedrooms, with beige-plum wall-to-wall carpeting, are smaller and probably need the air-conditioning units stuck in the walls.

The pièce de résistance of Mount Irvine is its newly restored Sugar Mill Restaurant, especially in the evening with the candlelight flickering, its raftered ceiling, its gray stone walls softly lighted, the scent of jasmine wafting in from the garden. (There's also a second air-conditioned restaurant for, quote, gourmet dining, unquote, but my bet is you'll prefer the open terrace.)

For guests who enjoy a round of golf, earnest or casual, the Mount Irvine might rate high there. Not because its lovely, rolling fairways are a challenge for players of all handicaps, but because any time I've been there I had the fairways and greens (and, alas, traps) almost to myself. Even if you're not a golfer, take a walk or bike ride along the course's winding pathways to enjoy the views of the bay and the reef and the tropical greenery.

Name: Mount Irvine Bay Hotel & Golf Club

Manager: Giobata Pescio

Address: P.O. Box 222, Scarborough, Tobago, Trinidad and Tobago, West Indies

Location: 10 minutes and $14 by taxi from the airport

Telephone: 809/639-8871, 8872, 8873

Fax: 809/639-8800

Reservations: Utell International, 800/448-8355; Robert Reid Associates; Golden Tulip Reservations system, 800/344-1212

Credit Cards: American Express, Diners Club, MasterCard, Visa

Rooms: 105, including 52 superior rooms and 6 suites in the main building; the remainder in 2-room bungalows; all with private bathrooms (tub and showers), air-conditioning (cross-ventilation in bungalows only), balconies or loggias, telephones, wet bars and refrigerators in bungalows

Dining: Breakfast 7:00–10:00 (Continental breakfast to 10:30), lunch noon–3:00 (the quietest spot is the golf course clubhouse), snacks at the beach pavilion all afternoon, dinner 7:00–10:00, at the open-air Sugar Mill Restaurant or the air-conditioned Jacaranda Room or Le Beau Rivage at the Golf Club (dinner approx. $60 for 2); jacket and tie in the Jacaranda and Le Beau Rivage, informal on the terrace, but "we do believe that informality has its acceptable limits within a hotel and house rules do not permit T-shirts or sleeveless vests in the public areas after 6:00 p.m."; room service 7:00 a.m.–10:00 p.m., $2 extra; taped music or radio on terrace, possibly live music in the Jacaranda Room

Entertainment: Steel bands, calypso and limbo shows, live entertainment in the Jacaranda Room and Le Beau Rivage

Sports: So-so beach across the road, with beach bar, snack bar, chaise longues, changing rooms, and local fishermen and their boats (there are better beaches nearby), freshwater pool with swim-up bar, tennis (2 courts, with lights), sauna—all free; snorkeling gear, bikes and scooters for rent, golf (18 holes, reduced fees for guests); excursions (to Buccoo Reef to watch the fish, to Grafton's estate to watch the birds) can be arranged

P.S.:   The hotel can handle groups of up to 200, but they are usually low-key

Other Choices

Coconut Creek Club Hotel

Barbados

There are two small coves and just enough palms to justify the name, but the architecture—white free-form stucco with tile roofs—may remind you more of the Greek islands than Barbados. Most of the 50 rooms and suites are clustered around a central garden and pool, but the choice lodgings are the 10 rooms that perch on the coral cliffs above the sea, while a dozen of the newer rooms—the most attractive and luxurious—are done in Moorish style with tiles and columns, walled flower gardens, and posh rattan furniture (but avoid the rooms beside the restaurant). The most striking feature of Coconut Creek Club, however, is the drinking-dining enclave, a cross between a Greek taverna and an English pub, its whitewashed walls decorated with Britannic nostalgia—pewter mugs, dart boards, cricket bats, and photographs of ships of Her Majesty's Royal Navy. You will be regaled with music most evenings (steel bands, guitarists, combos) while you dine on callaloo soup or chilled cream of christophene or roast shoulder of pork. At lunchtime there are some attractive island dishes, such as shrimp rôti or crunch vegetable sticks. 50 rooms and suites. Doubles: $295 to $345 with breakfast and dinner, winter 1994–95. *Coconut Creek Club Hotel, St. James, Barbados, West Indies. Telephone: 809/432-0804; fax: 809/422-1726.* Note: *Coconut Creek is one of a group of resorts known as St. James Beach Hotels, the most recent addition being the Crystal Cove, a restyled 18-room version of the former Barbados Beach Hotel, with an inviting palapa-shaded dining room a few steps from the beach. Rates at these hotels (the others are Tamarind Cove and Colony Club) are a notch or two below most West Coast resorts and, give or take a service or two, are generally good value.*

The Royal St. Lucian Hotel
St. Lucia

Yet another luxury resort with acres of marble, fountains, satellite television, air-conditioning, bathrobes, lavish pool—everything but personality (even lavish landscaping is unlikely to disguise the cookie-cutter, three-story architecture). It happens to be on the island's grandest expanse of beach, which it shares with its sister hotel, the St. Lucian (popular with package groups), but only a few of its suites—your best bet—actually face directly across the beach to the sea and some of them have enormous terraces. All the rooms are comfortable and thoughtfully designed. The Royal St. Lucian could be anywhere, and when it names its coffee shop La Nautique and its dining room L'Epicure, someone is sticking a neck out further than this resort can afford to go. 98 suites. Doubles: $355 to $615, winter 1994–95. *The Royal St. Lucian Hotel, P.O. Box 977, Castries, St. Lucia, West Indies. Telephone: 809/452-9999; fax: 809/452-9639. Reservations: 800/255-5859.*

Fort Young Hotel
Dominica

The guest rooms face directly out to sea atop a curving parapet of foot-thick stone, the swimming pool takes up much of the former parade ground, and the restaurant fills the former guardroom. Fort Young was built in the 1700s to ward off invaders with a view to ransacking the island capital, Roseau; sometime in the 1960s it was converted into a hotel, then battered by a hurricane in the 1980s before being rebuilt. The latest version is an improvement on the one I stayed in back in 1974, although even then it was kind of funky. Guest rooms now have fancy gadgetry like direct-dial telephones and satellite TV with nine channels, ceiling fans, and air-conditioning. But avoid the rooms at the far left—they're too close to a schoolyard for lay-in-beds or siesta lovers. The restaurant is fine for breakfast but a bit gloomy for dinner. 33 rooms. Doubles: $125–$160, winter 1994–95. *Fort Young Hotel, P.O. Box 519, Roseau, Dominica, West Indies. Telephone: 809/448-5000; fax: 809/448-5006.*

St. Vincent–Grenadines & Grenada

Bequia
Mustique
Canouan
Palm Island
Mayreau
Petit St. Vincent

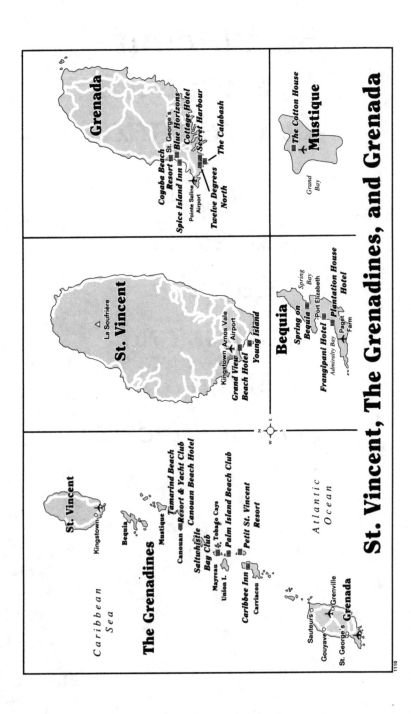

St. Vincent, The Grenadines, and Grenada

St. Vincent–Grenadines & Grenada

The most desirable islands, like the most desirable lovers, make extra demands. That's how it is with the Grenadines; they'll reward you with seclusion, serenity, and privacy, but you first have to get there, switching planes at least once, maybe twice. These islands are really part of the British Windwards, but they're so special, so totally Caribbean, that they deserve a category all to themselves.

They are, in fact, two quite separate and independent nations—St. Vincent–Grenadines (consisting of, for the purposes of this guide, St. Vincent, Young Island, Bequia, Mustique, Canouan, Mayreau, Palm Island, Petit St. Vincent, and Union, which is the transit airstrip for Mayreau, Palm, and PSV) and Grenada.

St. Vincent is a mountainous island, lushly forested, incredibly fertile, brimming with papaws, mangoes, and breadfruit. The bustling capital, Kingstown, is in the south, surrounded by towering hills, but the main scenic attractions are day-long excursions along the Leeward Highway to the foothills of 4,000-plus-foot Mount Soufrière or via the Windward Highway to Mesopotamia and Montreal—all very picturesque.

Bequia is a dream. The only way to get there is by boat. Not a big, powerful cabin cruiser or twin-hulled ferry, but by cargo/passenger ferryboat or island sloop stacked with chickens, toilet paper, kerosene, Guinness stout, Heineken beer, bags of cement, a carburetor, more Guinness, more Heineken. If you see a man get aboard carrying bags of money accompanied by a guard with a discreet gun, you know you're on the "bank boat." The trip takes about an hour, and you arrive in one of the most beautiful and most sheltered harbors in the Caribbees, in the town of Port Elizabeth. There's not much more to Bequia than the hills you pass on the way into the harbor, but it's one of the most charming, most idyllic islands of all. Nothing much happens here, except once or twice a year when whales are spotted, and the men go out in their small boats armed only with hand harpoons—the only remaining fleet of hand harpooners in the world. Of course, the island acquired an airfield in 1993 or thereabouts, but for true Bequia lovers the only way is by boat.

Mustique, Palm Island, and Petit St. Vincent are privately owned, and when you read about their hotels you're reading about the islands them-selves. Canouan, to the north of Union, is, of course, part of St. Vincent, while Carriacou (a constant source of confusion) is to the south and part of Grenada.

Grenada, like St. Vincent a lush volcanic island, is the largest of the group (21 miles long, 12 miles wide) and scenically one of the most beautiful of all the Antilles. Still—despite the efforts of modern firepower to wipe the island off the charts. You remember the events of October 1983? Some people called it an invasion, others a rescue mission. The official island description is a diplomatic "United States/Eastern Caribbean Interven-tion." Whatever, not much has changed, give or take a pockmarked wall or two. The Grenadians are pro-American (they always have been); some of the roads have been resurfaced, mostly those between Government House and the new airport. The major improvement these days is the airport that started it all, Point Salines International. It's located in the southwest, near the hotels, thus eliminating the hour-long drive from the old Pearls Airport. Does this mean cheaper taxi fares? No. Taxis serving the airport belong to a special association, most of whose members still live in villages near the *old* airport, and since they now have to drive all the way across the island to the *new* airport, visitors—aka you—have to pay through the nose. Why, you might ask, don't they use taxi drivers who live near the *new* airport? Because those taxis belong to another, ineligible association—either the "hotel" association or the "cruise ship" association. It's all very simple. If you're a taxi driver. But these are inconsequential matters if you're simply planning to find a great little hideaway and flake out—and Grenada has plenty of pleasant, friendly places for doing just that. Into the bargain, to try to lure back their old North American clientele (the British kept on coming), the local hotels have been raising their rates by minuscule smidgens, so you may find your vacation dollars will go further here.

How to Get There   To get to any of these islands you have to switch planes at Barbados or Antigua or San Juan. Except for Grenada, Barbados is the simplest route—nonstop or direct on American, Air Canada, and BWIA from Boston, Miami, Montreal, New York, and Toronto. From there you can catch a scheduled LIAT or Caribbean Express flight to St. Vincent, Union, and Grenada. But, as mentioned in the introduction to the guide, your best bet is to allow your hotel to arrange seats on a shared charter, probably on Mustique Airways, most likely a nine-seater Islander or a five-seater Beach Baron. This arrangement costs a few dollars more but can save a lot of aggravation for flights to Mustique, Canouan, and Union Island.

Bequia now has its own brand-new airstrip, but air service is so erratic (shared charter on Mustique Airways is your safest bet) that getting there may still involve a trip across the waters—either by charter launch (which your hotel can probably arrange, but it's expensive) or by the *Admiral I* or *Admiral II,* the ungainly but efficient Danish coasters that shuttle back and forth between St. Vincent and Bequia two times a day on weekends and four times a day during the week. The last departure from St. Vincent is 7:00 p.m. on Saturdays and weekdays, which allows at least some passengers from North America to get to Bequia the same day. If you find you have to spend the night in St. Vincent, Grand View Hotel is a convenient address. In town, the Heron Hotel has local color and tends to be rather noisy but is within walking distance of the jetty, if you're not carrying too much luggage.

> For information on St. Vincent–Grenadines, call 212/687-4981; Grenada, 212/687-9554.

Young Island
St. Vincent

Atmosphere

Dining

Sports

Rates

A Carib Indian chieftain, they say, once kept his harem on this islet, and generations of Vincentians used it as their vacation escape from the "mainland," a couple of hundred yards away across the lagoon. Now Young Island is 35 acres of petaled Polynesia. Half a million plants clamber up the hillsides. It took almost as long to landscape the grounds as it did to build the cottages and pavilions, but that was almost 30 years ago and now the island garden luxuriates. White ginger and giant almond trees soften the sun's rays as you stroll along stone pathways to quiet benches where twosomes can enjoy the breezes and sunsets. Swimming in the free-form pool, canopied by bamboo and fern and mango, you half expect Lamour and Hope to go floating by. And you're still shrouded by shrubbery and flowers when you rinse the sand off, because each room has an open patio shower screened by neck-high bamboo fences.

Two hundred yards may not sound like much of a journey, but once you board the dinky water taxis for the 3-minute voyage, you could be on your way to Bali Ha'i. Once guests step ashore and sip the zingy Hibiscus Special that's waiting for them on the dock, they usually find there's no compelling reason—not even the 200-year-old botanical garden, not the oddball 150-year-old cathedral—to board that dinky taxi again until it's time to head for home. (Actually, if they sip more than half of their Special they probably *will* see Lamour and Hope.)

Why escape tranquility? There are so many ways to enjoy the barefoot euphoria of Young when you put what's left of your mind to it. At the Coconut Bar, a thatched *bohio* on stilts about six strokes from the shore. Curled in a *bohio*-shaded hammock, within semaphore distance of the shore-bound bar. Flat out on the sand. Climbing the hundred-odd steps to the peak of the island for an isolated stroll in one direction or the tennis court in another. For any guest who finds a 35-acre islet and some 50 guests claustrophobic after a while, manager David Settle and his boatmen whisk the guests over to the most romantic manager's cocktail party in the Caribbean—on the nearby chimney rock known as Fort Duvernette, complete with native bamboo band, barbecue, and flickering torchères.

But maybe the most sensuous way to enjoy the serenity of Young Island is to stay put in your own wicker wonderland: Guest rooms feature lots of rush matting, native fabrics, terrazzo and shell floors, screened windows with jalousies, and hardwood louvers. For anyone who has been to Young Island in the past, the rooms were refurbished, and although the overall Polynesian ambience remains, they're brighter, more inviting. The cottages are located on the beach and at various elevations up the jungly hillside, accessible by stone steps; the higher the cottage, the cooler the air but the wider the panorama. Of the beachside cottages, number 10 still has the fairest breezes and the most private of patios.

While the original rooms were being prettified, the management was installing three hilltop cottages, each a spacious luxury suite (a first for Young Island) with huge semicircular deck/terrace with loungers and hammock, living room with rattan sofa and swivel chairs, wet bar and stocked refrigerator, toaster, kettle, and the makings for a pot of coffee or tea. Each louvered bedroom, recently refurbished, has two queen-size beds, separate dressing room paneled with greenheart, with bathrobes and amenities, twin vanities, and open-to-the-breezes shower stall with its own water heater. The views are eye filling, the breezes rejuvenating, the solitude complete. Just *how* far you've gotten away from it all is brought home to you when, thumbing through the welcome booklet, you come upon this sentence: "Keys for the cottages are available at the front desk, if this is considered necessary."

Name: Young Island
Owner/Manager: David Settle
Address: P.O. Box 211, St. Vincent, West Indies

Location: Just east of Kingstown, 200 yards offshore, about 10 minutes and $7 by taxi from the airport, shuttle launch to the resort free at all times; the hotel can arrange a "shared seat" charter flight from Barbados to St. Vincent for about $10 more than the scheduled 1-way fare

Telephone: 809/458-4826

Fax: 809/457-4567

Reservations: Ralph Locke Islands

Credit Cards: American Express, MasterCard, Visa

Rooms: 29, all cottages, some beside the beach, others on the hillside, 1 with air-conditioning, all with ceiling fans, patios or verandas, indoor/outdoor showers, some with wet bars and refrigerators

Meals: Breakfast 7:30–9:30, lunch 1:00–2:30, dinner 7:30–9:30 (approx. $70 for 2) in one of the breeze-cooled beachside pavilions; informal dress; room service for breakfast only, no extra charge

Entertainment: Live music 3 nights a week—steel band on Saturday, Bamboo Melodion Band 2 other nights

Sports: Beach with offshore Coconut Bar, saltwater lagoon pool in the garden, snorkeling, Sunfish sailing, windsurfing, glass-bottom boat trips—all free; tennis (1 court, free by day, $5 per hour with lights); scuba, waterskiing, and cruises (to Bequia, Mustique) on the resort's 44-foot yacht by arrangement

P.S.: A few (very few) cruise ship passengers and day-trippers on weekends; open all year

Grand View Beach Hotel
St. Vincent

☆☆			♇			◑◑			$ $		
Atmosphere			**Dining**			**Sports**			**Rates**		

Your Grand View grand view is made up of islands, lagoons, bays, sailboats, Young Island, a fort, mountains, headlands, and dazzling sea that turns into dazzling sky somewhere beyond Bequia. The hotel itself is a big, white, rather ungainly two-story mansion on top of a bluff (not on the beach, despite its name) between two bays and surrounded by 8 acres of bougainvillea, frangipani, palms, and terraced gardens. It's a beautiful location (breezes, flowers, birds, trees) if you don't mind climbing up and down to the beach. About 150 years ago it was a cotton-drying house, the private home of the Sardines, whose ancestors came over from Portugal; Frank Sardine, Sr., converted it into a hotel almost 20 years ago, and despite its longevity, it's in spanking fresh condition. It's homey, pleasant, and very relaxed, like the sort of small hotel Europeans would flock to on the Riviera (and, in fact, the hotel gets lots of visitors from Europe); the guest rooms are plain and unadorned—but who needs decor when you have a view like this? Seven additional rooms, including two suites with whirlpool baths, are located above the lobby, each equipped with TV and mini-bar. An added bonus is the Grand View Club, a racket and fitness center that opened several years ago and offers aerobics classes and equipment, a sauna, and massage.

Name: Grand View Beach Hotel

Owner/Manager: Tony Sardine

Address: P.O. Box 173, Villa Point, St. Vincent–Grenadines, West Indies

Location: At Villa Point, 5 minutes and $7 by taxi from the airport, 10 minutes from town

Telephone: 809/458-4811

Fax: 809/457-4174

Reservations: Robert Reid Associates and Caribbean Inns Ltd.

Credit Cards: American Express, MasterCard, Visa

Rooms: 20 rooms, with air-conditioning, TV, direct-dial phone, some with mini-bars; 2 suites with whirlpools

Meals: Breakfast 7:15–9:00, lunch noon–3:00, afternoon tea 4:30–5:30, dinner 7:00–8:30 (approx. $45 for 2); casual dress; room service (no extra charge)

Entertainment: Pleasant lounge with wicker armchairs, a vintage radio, a few books; maybe a cocktail party once a week in season, depending on the guests

Sports: Beach at the base of the cliff, swimming pool; snorkeling gear for rent; tennis court ($20 an hour with lights), 31-foot fishing boat, squash court, windsurfing, plus exercise classes, aerobic machines, sauna, and massage at the fitness center (membership available to locals); sailing and scuba by arrangement

P.S.: Open all year

Spring on Bequia
Bequia

Atmosphere

Dining

Sports

Rates

You're sitting on the terrace of your room, maybe lounging in a hammock, and looking across a valley of coconut palms toward a bay, a pair of headlands, and a sheltering reef. What you see is a working plantation that produces mangoes and avocados and plums and melons—to say nothing of all those coconuts; and what you are staying in is a 10-room jewel on a very quiet hillside in a very quiet corner of a very quiet island.

The 250-year-old Spring Plantation was bought up about 20 years ago by an Iowa lawyer, who planned to build a few unobtrusive homes among the trees of the hillsides (they're there, but you may not see them!) and a small inn to house prospective buyers and visitors. Part Japanese, part Finnish, part Caribbean, the hotel's clean, contemporary lines enclose open-plan rooms with native stone walls, stone floors, furniture fashioned from wood right there on the plantation, khuskhus rugs, whole walls of purpleheart louvers that push back to bring the outdoors right inside. Spring now has electricity, so the stone-floored, stone-walled shower stalls gush hot water.

All the guest rooms are charmingly rustic. The four rooms in the old plantation Great House, draped in frangipani and cordia, are close to the swimming pool and tennis court, but since they're also next to the kitchen some guests prefer to be higher up the hill in one of two cantilevered wings: Gull, with four rooms, halfway up the hill, or the Fort, with two and higher still. They're a stiff climb from the dining room, even more so from the beach; but if you've come here for seclusion, this is *seclusion*—with a beautiful view thrown in for good measure.

Spring's lobby/bar/dining room attached to the old Great House is open on two sides and overlooks the old syrup mill and slave quarters, a pleasant, breezy gathering place, with a rustic roof of beams and planks, walls of canvas, and matted bamboo screens. The bar stools are the stumps of coconut palms with purpleheart seats; the native stone walls are covered with vines and planters, decorated with turtle shells and anchor chains. But mostly the decor is the trees and the flowers, and you're more aware of plantation than inn. Having dinner here is a bit like dining out in a cage of tree frogs and crickets—real Caribbean flavor. The home-cooked meals are no letdown, either.

The good news, of course, is that Spring is still there and receiving guests. Closed for a few years, it is now the pride of the Rudolf family from Minnesota (who attribute their fascination with inns to an earlier edition of this guidebook); daughter Candace may be the only innkeeper in the Caribbean who speaks fluent Chinese. Wish them well, since Spring is still one of the most romantic tiny inns in the islands—even with its new electricity and solar-heated hot water.

Name: Spring on Bequia

Manager: Candace Leslie

Address: Bequia, St. Vincent–Grenadines, West Indies

Location: On the southeast coast, but just 1 mile over the hill from Port Elizabeth; the inn will pick you up at the dock; for some guests, the inn is a pleasant 30-minute *walk* from town

Telephone: 809/458-3414

Reservations: Own U.S. office, 612/823-1202

Credit Cards: All major cards

Rooms: 10, 4 in the main lodge, 6 in 2 hillside units with private bathrooms (showers only), breeze cooled (now with electricity and hot water), most with balconies

Meals: Breakfast 7:30–9:00, lunch noon–2:00, dinner 7:00 (approx. $50 for 2); informal; no room service

Entertainment: Parlor games, conversation

Sports: 500 feet of virtually solitary sandy beach (with beach bar), about 5 minutes away along a pathway through the coconut palms and Pride of Barbados, freshwater pool, tennis (1 court, rackets available), walking and hiking trails, snorkeling—all free; sailing trips to Mustique and the Tobago Cays

P.S.: "Not really suitable for children"; closed mid-June through October

Plantation House Hotel

Bequia

☆☆☆		🍷🍷		🏖🏖		$ $	
Atmosphere		**Dining**		**Sports**		**Rates**	

If you make landfall on Bequia by boat and you're toting just one carryall (all you ever need on this island unless you bring your own dive gear), you can walk to the hotel from the dock. Along the main street beside the beach where they build wooden schooners. Past the big tree with the wooden benches. Through the garden of the Frangipani Hotel. Past Gingerbread House and a couple of private homes until you arrive at this two-story, plantation-style house with a broad veranda on three sides, framed by sea-grape trees and clumps of bougainvillea.

If you've ever been to Bequia before, you'll recognize it as the old Sunny Caribee. Now the main house has been rebuilt (concrete rather than wood, after the original burned down) and modernized; the once-gloomy wooden cabins have been freshly painted, enlarged, and primped up with brighter colors on the walls and decorative netting over the beds. Very attractive. They've now been augmented with a three-bedroom cottage by the edge of the beach, which has been extended. And the 10 acres of garden are in better shape than ever—trim lawns, splashes of oleander and hibiscus and fragrant frangipani.

The main lodge is a pleasant surprise, just the right balance between tradition and sophisticated comfort. There's that shady wraparound veranda, one side of it the dining terrace. The semisunken lounge/bar has a coffered ceiling, paddle fans, and local art decorating its coral-pink and pickle-pine walls. Its comfy upholstered armchairs and sofas are perfect for relaxing and reading at teatime. The kitchen is under the watch of a new chef, and the owners promise West Indian cuisine.

There's a pleasant, beachy laid-back feel to the place, but with just the right touch of sophistication. Because the roadway winds into the foothills before dipping down to the hotel, there's little traffic and no crowds. But otherwise in the evening you can just sit there and watch the occasional dinghy drifting ashore with thirsty voyagers—or you can amble back along that beachside path to see what the rest of the world is up to. Fortunately, not much. Bequia is about as slowpoke as an island can be, even if someone did tack on a landing strip.

Name: Plantation House Hotel

Owner/Manager: Marcel van Lieshout

Address: P.O. Box 16, Bequia, St. Vincent, West Indies

Location: On the edge of town, about 5 minutes by taxi from the ferry dock, 10 minutes from the airport

Telephone: 809/458-3425

Fax: 809/458-3612

Reservations: E&M Associates

Credit Cards: All major cards

Rooms: 25 rooms, 3 upstairs in the main lodge, 17 in individual guest bungalows, 3 in a 3-room cottage, all with air-conditioning, mini-bars, showers only; ceiling fans and mosquito nets in cottages

Meals: Breakfast 7:30–10:00, lunch noon–2:30, afternoon tea 3:00–4:00 in the sunken living room, dinner 7:30–9:30 on the veranda or beside the beach (approx. $60 for 2); informal dress; no room service

Entertainment: Veranda bar, live music nightly and barbecue every Saturday at Greenflash, the new beach bar, other bars and restaurants a short walk away along the beachside path

Sports: Freshwater pool, tennis (1 court with lights), windsurfing—free; waterskiing extra; 4-instructor, 4-boat dive shop on the premises; Sail-Away package with crewed CSY 44-foot yacht; water taxi to Lower Bay, about $10 round-trip

P.S.:   "We love children"; some small groups from cruise ships; closed September and October; expect some construction in 1995 as 10 double rooms are added

Frangipani Hotel
Bequia

☆						♀					◐					$			
Atmosphere						**Dining**					**Sports**					**Rates**			

They used to build island schooners in the front yard here, the lounge was a ships' chandlery back in the 1930s, and the sea captain who built it disappeared with his crew in the Bermuda Triangle—while his schooner sailed on. His son, currently prime minister of St. Vincent and the Grenadines, turned this white-walled red-roofed family home into an inn back in the 1960s, and it's now one of the most popular watering places in the Grenadines. It hasn't lost touch with its nautical heritage, either: Antique charts and seascapes decorate the lounge; the jetty at the bottom of the garden welcomes fleets of dinghies from the yachts moored just offshore; and sooner or later everyone who sails the Grenadines stops off at the Frangipani beach bar to greet old friends they last saw beating toward the Tobago Cays.

The Frangipani is a real wicker-decked West Indies inn. The rooms upstairs are scantily furnished, with mosquito nets, partition walls, and a couple of shared bathrooms down the hall—like the deck of a schooner, functional rather than frilly. The exception is also upstairs, where two rooms have been blended into one charming, plank-floored nest with four-poster canopy bed and private, if tiny, toilet/shower. If you prefer bunking down in something more substantial, ask for one of the rooms in the stone and timber garden cottages—big comfortable cabins with big bathrooms, dressing rooms, grass mats, and louvers. Each of these 10 rooms has beams and furniture crafted from local hardwood; each has its own sundeck or covered veranda.

There's absolutely nothing to do here, nothing but unwind. Evenings, you can nibble fresh seafood on the veranda or sit on the seawall and listen to rigging; you can swap a few fancy tales with yachters or listen to a folksinger or have another beer and watch the last sailors row off zigzaggedly to their yachts. In the morning, grab a cup of coffee and settle into a large, purpleheart armchair beside the beach. Watch the schooners and ketches weigh anchor for the Tobago Cays or Martinique. Don't even bother waving good-bye—they'll soon be back at Frangipani.

Name: Frangipani Hotel
Owners/Managers: Marie Kingston and Lou Keane
Address: Bequia, St. Vincent–Grenadines, West Indies
Location: On the waterfront, a 3-minute walk from the schooner jetty, 15 minutes from the airport by taxi
Telephone: 809/458-3255
Fax: 809/458-3824
Reservations: Direct
Credit Cards: American Express, Discover, MasterCard, Visa
Rooms: 10 with private baths and balconies in the garden cottages; 4 in main house, 1 with private bath, 3 with washbasins but sharing bath and toilets; mosquito nets, ceiling fans
Meals: Breakfast 7:30–10:00 (served on verandas of the garden units), lunch anytime, coffee, wine, snacks, dinner 7:00–9:30 (approx. $30–

$40 for 2), served in the beachside patio bar/restaurant with harbor view; casual dress

Entertainment: Barbecue and "jump-up" every Thursday, string band every Monday in season

Sports: "Along the bayside" at the Gingerbread complex is the Sunsports center—Mistral Windsurfers, NAUI and PADI scuba, tennis (1 hard court), Sunfish sailing, waterskiing—all extra, with a discount for guests; 45-foot yacht available for day trips or special 3-day charters to Tobago Cays

P.S.:   Lots of yachters, castaways, and beachcombers; closed September and first half of October; some remodeling of the main house and upstairs rooms may be going on in 1995

The Cotton House
Mustique

Atmosphere

Dining

Sports

Rates

It's that rare combination of informality and elegance, of pristine (well, relatively pristine) surroundings and civilization. Here you are, on a private tropical island with a permanent population of 300, a few coconut groves, a few citrus groves, a dozen deserted beaches.

You can spend an entire day here without meeting anyone other than your maid or waiter or gardener; you can disappear to a beach for a picnic lunch—not another soul in sight; you can spend hours snorkeling among fish that rarely if ever encounter *homo sapiens*. Then in the evening you mingle with escapists who turn out to be cosmopolitan, urbane, and sophisticated—maybe even celebrated. And, at the end of the day, you hop into bed in a dreamy boudoir designed by no less a talent than the late Oliver Messel.

Mustique, unique Mustique, is small (3 miles long, ½-mile wide) and flat (about 400 feet at its highest point); you arrive by air in a seven seater that sweeps in between a pair of breastlike hills, to touch down in a pasture with a runway and thatch and bamboo terminal. When Reynolds, alias Snaky, the hotel's effervescent porter/majordomo/greeter/chauffeur/

guide, sees the plane coming in, he jumps into his mini-bus, and by the time you've taxied to the toy terminal and cleared customs, he's there waiting to convey you to the hotel.

And what a hotel! The Cotton House itself is an 18th-century storage house of handsome proportions—two floors of mellowed stone and coral rimmed by deep verandas accented by louver doors. A few yards away, on the peak of a knoll, Oliver Messel created a swimming pool surrounded by "Roman ruins," the sort of setting he might have designed for a Gluck opera at Covent Garden. Beyond the stone stump of the mill (now a boutique) a pair of handsome two-story Georgian-style villas house half the guest rooms, each room with a different decor and furnishings, but all with custom-designed bedspreads and matching drapes, plank floors with rush mats, ceiling fans, breezy balconies, or patios. Color schemes are restrained and cool, with antiques and doodads adding delightful little touches of neo-Messel charm. Other guest rooms are in three cottages fashioned in vaguely "island hut" style; in a new two-story wing in vaguely Motel Georgian style; and the newest of all, five guest rooms and suites in a villa formerly owned by the Guinness family (smaller bedrooms, but with a big open-to-the-breezes common room lounge-terrace), with decor and furniture that doesn't quite do credit to the memory of Messel.

But none of the guest rooms ever quite matched the exquisiteness of the main lounge in the Cotton House itself—with its raftered ceiling, its hand-carved bar, and masses of antiques—once one of the most beautiful rooms in the Caribbean. In the hemisphere. Alas, each "refurbishing" has detracted from some of the refinement.

The veranda facing the sunset is given over to comfy armchairs and loungers; another corner, shaded by shutters and foliage, is the dining room, where candles flicker on rustic tables and straw-seated chairs and the air is filled with the sound of tree frogs. In a setting as romantic as this, who cares if the cuisine is not quite three-star or if the managers come and go too frequently?

Mustique may be too quiet for some, no doubt. Yet, for all its isolation, it can, on occasion, plunge its guests into nightlife that larger islands envy. For a start, there's Basil's Bar, a lively, sometimes raucous wood and wicker deck on Britannia Beach, blaring rock and roll even at noontime, positively hopping at the Wednesday barbecue, popular with homeowners and yachters, so you might find yourselves at 3:00 some morning, beneath a full moon and myriad stars, listening to bamboo flute and "shak-shak," mingling with princesses, viscounts, rock stars, fishermen, and CEOs masquerading as swingers.

Name: The Cotton House
Manager: Warren W. Francis
Address: Mustique, St. Vincent–Grenadines, West Indies

Location: On a private island, 45 minutes by twin-engined plane from Barbados (the hotel will arrange space on a charter flight, approx. $200 per person, round-trip); there is also frequent scheduled service from Martinique, St. Vincent, and Grenada; the hotel, 4 minutes from the airstrip, will collect you by mini-bus, free of charge

Telephone: 809/456-4777

Fax: 809/456-4777

Reservations: Ralph Locke Islands

Credit Cards: All major cards

Rooms: 22 rooms and 5 suites, in villas, cottages, and a 2-story wing, all with balconies or patios, ceiling fans (some with air conditioners), telephones, some with showers only

Meals: Breakfast 7:30–10:00 and buffet lunch 12:30–2:30 served poolside, afternoon tea 4:00, dinner 8:00 (approx. $90 for 2) on the candle-lit veranda of the Great House; informal but "island elegant" dress; room service for all meals, no extra charge; some taped music, not always appropriate

Entertainment: Bar-lounge, parlor games, taped music, "Flambeaux" beach barbecue Saturdays (with native band—and perhaps some of the island's other celebrity homeowners), weekly managers' cocktail party for hotel and villa guests, Caribbean buffet every Thursday, piano bar twice a week; "jump-up" at Basil's Bar every Wednesday

Sports: 12 beaches (free transportation, with picnic lunch), freshwater pool, tennis (2 courts, no lights), snorkeling, windsurfing, Sunfish sailing—all free; horseback riding, scuba, and cruises to Tobago Cays or Bequia can be arranged

P.S.: "No cruise ships with more than 100 passengers"; open all year

P.P.S.: In addition to the Cotton House, Mustique has 40-odd one-of-a-kind luxury villas for rent, some perched on hillsides, some beside the beach. None of them are designed specifically for twosomes, but if you decide to junket with friends, this could be a memorable way to spend a vacation à la jet set. Mick Jagger's wood and bamboo home may or may not be on the list of rentals, but Princess Margaret's is (although it's quite modest compared to some of the others). Among the most attractive 2-bedroom villas: Blue Waters, Ultramarine, Jacaranda, and Pelican Beach House (all on the water), Yellowbird and Marienlyst (in the hills). Current rates are no longer outlandish compared with some of the Caribbean's new hotels: in 1994–95 2 bedroom villas cost approximately $2,750–$4,950 a week in winter, $2,750–$3,960 in summer, in each case with full staff, Jeep, and laundry. Or, in other words, less than $200 per day for 2 couples sharing. For details, write to Mustique Villas, c/o Resorts Management, Inc.; 201½ E. 29th St., New York, NY 10016. Telephone: 800/225-4255 or 212/696-4566; fax: 212/689-1598.

Tamarind Beach Resort & Yacht Club

Canouan

☆☆			
Atmosphere

| ♉ | | | |
Dining

| ◐ | | | |
Sports

| $ $ | | | |
Rates

Two things happened recently to help put Canouan, all 3 square miles of it, on the map of the Grenadines: Electricity arrived in 1994 and this sprightly new 44 roomer arrived at the beginning of 1995. The Tamarind's timber and gingerbread architecture with multipeaked roofline is an odd combination of plantation great house and South American Indian architecture, yet it somehow sits nicely in its setting—a quiet corner of Grand Bay—and will look even prettier a year from now when the bougainvillea has twined itself around the treillage that trims the facades. The resort's centerpiece is a dramatic Amazon-style pavilion, with a palapa-thatch roof soaring to 30 feet or so above eight ocher columns. The adjoining lobby is a smaller open pavilion huddling beneath a less soaring palapa canopy and furnished with comfy rattan chairs and sofas.

Guest rooms are deployed in three two-story wings, built from Brazilian ipe hardwood, with carved wooden balustrades and white gingerbread trim framing the balconies. These rooms remind me in a way of large staterooms on a classic yacht—paneled and trimmed in two tones of hardwood, with rush rugs on hardwood floors and white wicker furniture adding a brighter touch here and there. The wall adjoining the balcony consists of six panels of floor to ceiling hardwood louvers, two of them opening out to the view of the bay and its bobbing sailboats.

Despite the simplicity of style and the modest rates, the Tamarind's rooms come with extras such as mini-bars and private safes (both in one neat little cabinet) and bathrooms with wall-mounted hair dryers, hardwood floors, plenty of room for drying off with the big fluffy towels, but—we can't have everything—molded plastic shower stalls.

The two palapa pavilions are given over to dining—breakfast, lunch, and dinner beside the beach, cooled by the breezes, comfortably furnished with tubular café tables and cushioned chairs. Waitresses are garbed in traditional gowns designed specially for the Tamarind by the prime minister's daughter over on St. Vincent. For lunch, there's a choice of a cold buffet with a couple of island entrées, as you might expect in a small resort, but the surprise is a decorative wood-fired pizza oven and barbecue grill just beyond the tables.

Dinner presents a more ambitious menu, part Caribbean, part Continental, but guests are expected to order by number—on an island with a population of less than 1,000, there's hardly a reservoir of expert waiters familiar with dishes such as carpaccio of beef and vitello alla pizzaiola. And there's the rub. The personable managers, a young French couple named Alain and Natasha Jomeau, had to start from scratch, setting up their own hotel school (both of them are not long out of that other hotel school in Lausanne, which hardly prepared them for Canouan) to train the islanders how to make beds, greet guests, take drink orders, pour coffee.

In a way, though, this gives the place a certain unpolished, naive charm, and even if the service may not pass muster with impatient yuppies, at least everyone is trying hard, everyone is smiling, and the welcome is warm. In any case, you can always admire the yachts, listen to the surf, or order another piña colada.

Name: Tamarind Beach Resort & Yacht Club

Managers: Alain and Natasha Jomeau

Address: Charlestown, Canouan, St. Vincent–Grenadines

Location: About 7 minutes from the airstrip (the hotel will pick you up); the most dependable way to get to Canouan is Mustique Airways from Barbados, $200 round-trip per person (the Mustique Airways people will meet you at Barbados and take you directly to your twin-engine plane—it helps to take along only carry-on luggage)

Telephone: 809/458-8044

Fax: 809/458-8851

Reservations: Ralph Locke Islands

Credit Cards: All major cards

Rooms: 42 rooms and 2 suites, all with mini-bar, safe, ceiling fans, hair dryers, balconies

Meals: Breakfast 7:30–10:00, lunch noon–2:00, dinner 7:30–10:00 (approx. $80 for 2); casual dress; quiet taped music; no room service

Entertainment: The bar, the yachties, occasional live music

Sports: Beach, windsurfers, snorkeling gear, Sunfishes—all free; day trips (Mustique, Bequia, Tobago Cays) on the resort's private 58-foot catamaran; scuba diving nearby

P.S.:   Closed September and October

Palm Island Beach Club
Palm Island

☆☆☆		Y		◑◑		$ $ $	
Atmosphere		**Dining**		**Sports**		**Rates**	

The beach curves on and on for a mile and a half, and you get so spoiled for space here that if half a dozen other sun worshipers get to the strand before you tumble out of bed in the morning, you'll probably walk around the next bend to yet another uncrowded spot.

Not too many tides ago there weren't even half a dozen people here—and the island was no more than a ring of beach around a swamp, on the charts identified prosaically as Prune. Then along came John Caldwell. Alias "Coconut Johnny." "Tree planting is my hobby. . . . There's hardly an island in these parts where I can't go ashore and look at some trees I've planted." At Palm he can look at somewhere between two and three *thousand.*

Caldwell, now in his seventies, is a Texan who grew up in California, short, wiry, a mizzenmast of a man who bought a pair of shoes 15 years ago and has been seen wearing them once ("I've lived for 24 years on $1,200 a year"). Over 20 years ago he set out to sail single-handed across the Pacific and ended up on a reef off Fiji; somehow he continued to Australia, where he built a 45-foot ketch, loaded his wife and two young sons aboard, and set off again—this time smack into a hurricane in the Indian Ocean and then through the Suez Canal and across the Atlantic to the Grenadines. He spent 5 years there chartering; on each trip he came ashore on Palm/Prune Island with his charterers, and while they were having a picnic or swim he was planting his coconut palms. Before long, the swamp was a grove, the Prune was a Palm, and John Caldwell had started to plant a hotel. He and his sons designed and built the entire place from scratch, putting in power, water, roads, an airstrip, a dock—and 18 months later, in December 1967, they were ready to open Palm Island Beach Club.

The club (it's a club in name only—you don't have to join anything) at first sight appears to be a white beach sprinkled with coconut palms, casuarina, sea grape, and almond trees, dotted with brightly colored plastic loungers; a second look and you'll find that there are bungalows strung along free-form stone paths rambling through lanes of sun-dappled greenery, a few steps from the edge of Casuarina Beach. "It's small because we want to enjoy it ourselves." The dozen two-room bungalows are half stone, half hardwood, with two walls of wooden-slat vertical louvers, a third of sliding glass doors facing a patio. Some have open-air shower stalls, where you wash out the sand with water heated by solar power. John Caldwell designed and built his own furniture—in the no-nonsense, shipshape manner of a man who's fitted out a 45-foot ketch (although a recent restyling has added rattan furniture and television).

You spend your days at Palm Island Beach Club shuffling from your louvered room to the beach to the circular beach bar to the big open-air timber Polynesian longhouse for an informal Creole-dish dinner (note the ceiling, a superb piece of carpentry). Maybe at some point you'll grab your snorkeling mask and sneakers and go for a walk on the coral garden on the front beach, a hundred yards north of the yacht club's beach bar. Maybe tomorrow you'll sail over to the Tobago Cays. Maybe you'll go diving. Maybe you'll join the visitors from the yachts at the beach bar for a tall, cool drink and a tall, salty tale. More likely you'll just lounge around in a couple of chaises and look at Union Island—one of those enticing mirages whose contours change with the passage of the sun, revealing unsuspected hamlets or coconut groves sparkling in the afternoon light.

By sundown, the loudest sound on Palm Island is the rigging of visiting yachts.

By 9:00, you're in bed—flicking flecks of sand from each other's cheeks.

Name: Palm Island Beach Club

Owners/Managers: John and Mary Caldwell and family

Address: Palm Island, St. Vincent–Grenadines, West Indies

Location: The Club *is* the island, and the island is 15–20 minutes by a 36-foot launch (free) from Union Island; Union, in turn, can be reached by scheduled flight from St. Vincent by LIAT, from Martinique, St. Lucia, and St. Vincent by Martinique Airways, or by charter flight from Barbados (about $103 per person, and the hotel can help arrange the flight if you give them plenty of warning)

Telephone: 809/458-8824

Fax: 809/458-8804

Reservations: Paradise Found Inc., 800/776-PALM; fax: 301/762-7283

Credit Cards: American Express, Visa

Rooms: 24, in bungalows, breeze cooled, refrigerators

Meals: Breakfast 7:30–9:30, lunch 1:00–2:00 (buffet), afternoon tea 4:00–4:30 on your patio, dinner 7:30–8:30 (family style, barbecues Wednesday and Saturday), light meals are also served at the yacht club; casual dress, barefoot if you wish; room service for breakfast, lunch, dinner at no extra charge

Entertainment: Barbecues twice a week, calypso night on Wednesday, Saturday evening "jump-up"; TV, video

Sports: 5 beaches, paddle tennis (1 untended court), games room, snorkeling gear, Sunfish sailing, windsurfing and "Highway 90," John's own aerobic fitness trail—all free; sailboats for rent; scuba equipment, diving off Palm or at nearby Tobago Cays; day sails to Tobago Cays and Mayreau on an Irwin 52 ketch

Saltwhistle Bay Club
Mayreau

☆☆ Atmosphere   ♀♀ Dining   ◑ Sports $ $ $ Rates

Real barefoot, flake-out, crash territory—an unspoiled bay on an unspoiled cay in the unspoiled Grenadines. To get there you first fly to Union Island, where you'll be met by the resort's launch, which will skim you across the channel past Saline Bay, then finally around a headland and into Saltwhistle Bay.

Tom and Undine Potter, a young Canadian/German couple, settled here almost a decade ago and built a beachside restaurant catering to passing yachts, then 4 years ago opened their hotel. When you sail into the bay, with its glistening semicircle of sand, and beyond the beach, where dwarf palms and sea-grape trees part to reveal glimpses of another shining sea beyond, you may well wonder where *did* they build their hotel?

Go in a bit farther; it's all there nestled into 22 acres of coconut palms, more sea grapes, that great curve of soft white sand, and a windward beach that's pure Robinson Crusoe.

Though the landscape may be lush, there's nothing plush or luxurious about the Saltwhistle's accommodations—but there's nothing uncomfortable about them either. The guest quarters are in sturdy native stone and timber cottages at one end of the beach, each with hardwood louvers, handcrafted furniture, ceiling fans, and showers supplied with water heated by the noonday sun. At the other end of the beach, there's a sprinkling of circular gazebos in matching stone with stone banquettes and palm-thatched shades. The two-room cottages share a spacious rooftop gallery with loungers, tables, and chairs. The Potters' dining room is an ingenious collection of circular stone booths topped by thatched canopies where you can stuff yourselves with local delicacies like curried conch, turtle steaks, and lobster, all fresh from the surrounding reefs.

There's not much to do at Saltwhistle—delightfully so. Of course, for the truly ambitious there's snorkeling gear, picnics to the wild and windswept beach with views of Palm Island and Tobago, fishing with the locals in their gaff-rigged sloops, a walk up the hill to the village for a warm beer and a sweeping view of all those cays and reefs, or a hike down to Saline Bay to watch the mail boat come in. And if any or all of these possibilities (or just the thought of them) exhaust you, there's always the lure of a good book, a rum punch, and a nice big hammock.

Name: Saltwhistle Bay Club

Owners/Managers: Tom and Undine Potter

Address: Mayreau, St. Vincent–Grenadines, West Indies

Location: South of St. Vincent, a few miles from the islands of Union, Petit St. Vincent, and Palm; to get there, you fly from Barbados to Union, where the hotel collects you by boat ($50 per person, round-trip), but since the Club (with advance notice) will make all the arrangements, all you have to do is get to Barbados

Telephone: 809/458-8444

Fax: 809/458-8944

Reservations: North American office, 800/561-7258 (in Toronto, 613/634-7108); fax, 613/384-6300

Credit Cards: American Express, MasterCard, Visa

Rooms: 21, including 7 standard, 10 superior, 4 junior suites; all with sun-warmed showers, ceiling fans (and steady cross-ventilation); superior rooms also have shared rooftop decks

Meals: Breakfast 8:00–10:00, lunch noon–2:00, dinner 7:00–9:00 (approx. $60 for 2), all served in beachside booths; occasional beach barbecues; casual dress; taped music; room service on request

Entertainment: Hammocks strung between the palm trees, conversation in the bar, darts, backgammon, a moonlit stroll on the beach

Sports: 300–400 yards of beautiful beach, snorkeling, windsurfing—all free; scuba diving, boat trips to Tobago Cays, island picnics, excursions with local fishermen at extra charge

P.S.: Closed September and October

Petit St. Vincent Resort

Petit St. Vincent

☆☆☆☆☆	♀♀♀	◑◑◑	S S S S S
Atmosphere	**Dining**	**Sports**	**Rates**

"Some of our guests never put on any clothes until dinnertime." Not in public, perhaps, but on their private terraces, because all but half a dozen of the rooms here are self-contained cottages, widely dispersed around this 113-acre private out-island. It may well be the most secluded, most private of the Caribbean's luxury hideaways.

It's certainly one of the most consistently dependable. PSV has no problems of revolving-door management. Any good resort manager knows where the pipes and power cables are, but in the case of Haze Richardson, he not only knows where they are—he put them there in the first place. He helped lay the cables and the pipes, helped quarry the stones for the cottages, installed the refrigeration in the kitchen, built a desalination plant, planted the fruit trees. Now the resort even makes its own fiberglass Jeep-like Minimokes. Richardson came to the island by way of a 77-foot staysail schooner, *Jacinta*, which he skippered. One of his charterers was the late H. W. Nichols, Jr., then the top man at a big corporation in Cincinnati, who bought this dinky Grenadine from a little old lady in Petit Martinique, the island just across the channel. They started building in 1966 and slaved for 3 years, working with whatever was available (mostly bluebitch stone and hardwood), planning the location of the individual cottages to make the most of the breezes and vistas.

It may sound simple and rustic, but it's really quite lavish in terms of solitude and seclusion—all that space for only 44 guests. And a staff of 75 to boot. The cottages follow a basic U-shaped pattern: big open sundeck, big shaded breakfast patio, big glass-enclosed lounge separated by a wall of bluebitch from a big sleeping area with twin queen-size beds, separated in turn from a stone-walled dressing room and bathroom with curtain-enclosed shower. There are no newfangled gadgets such as television or telephone. For room service there's the unique PSV semaphore system: a bamboo pole with a notch for written messages (e.g., "Two piña coladas fast," "afternoon tea for two") and two flags—red for "Do Not Disturb," yellow for "Come In." But the tactful maids and room-service waiters first ring the little brass bell at the entrance—just in case you want to slip into your fluffy PSV-crested bathrobes.

Guest-room interiors follow a basic style of bluebitch walls, purpleheart louvers, khuskhus rugs on red tile floors, new bathrobes, new fabrics—in soft islandy shades of yellow, turquoise, and terra-cotta.

Where the rooms differ is in location: up on the bluff for the best breezes and views, down on the beach by the lagoon, or on the beach beyond the dock. Cottage 1, on the bluff, is one of the most secluded, with a big deck overlooking a dazzling sea and the craggy silhouette of Union Island. For a beach right on your doorstep, cottages 6 through 11 look out on unspoiled castaway beach. For total detachment, turn your back on the entire resort and check into cottage 18, where a few stone steps lead to a private patch of beach, and beyond that nothing but ocean—all the way to Guinea-Bissau or thereabouts. Some of the cottages are what passes in these lazy climes as a stiff hike (all of 5 minutes) to the dining pavilion, but you can always arrange to be picked up by one of the ubiquitous "mokes."

This hilltop bar/dining pavilion is the focal point of the resort, with soaring hardwood roof and indoor/outdoor patios overlooking the anchorage and Petit Martinique. The owner has added two additional open-air dining gazebos, with panoramic views of the bay and boats. Beautiful place to sit and savor the twilight while sipping a Banana Touch or mango daiquiri. PSV meals are above average for these parts (meats, for example, are personally selected by Julia Child's butcher, a regular PSV guest, and flown in specially for the resort); the dining room staff is particularly attentive.

Indeed, one of the main attractions of PSV, a feature that sets it apart from many of its peers, is its long-serving staff. They seem to care genuinely about making your vacation perfect. More often than not, Haze Richardson is at the dock to greet you with a piña colada when you arrive. The *Wakiva* skipper, Maurice, is solicitous about getting you back to Union on time for your plane. There are totable beach chairs in your room in case you want to sample a nearby beach, but if you want to cart your *lounger* along, one of the roving stewards will pick you up in his Minimoke and transport you to whichever beach you choose (the one at the west end is particularly tranquil, with hammocks strung beneath thatch *bohios*). If you're bored with *that,* you can even have one of the boatmen transport you to PSR—Petit St. Richardson, a minuscule offshore cay with lots of sand and a solitary palm.

But why quit your own private deck in the first place—with or without swimsuits?

PSV may not be for everyone. You have to be your own entertainment. You have to forego the plushest amenities. You have to dine in the same dining room every evening, except one. But for anyone who genuinely wants a castaway setting with civilized comforts, who wants to get as far as possible from the everyday world without spending forever getting there, Petit St. Vincent is one beautiful, enchanting hideaway.

Name: Petit St. Vincent Resort

Owner/Manager: Haze Richardson

Address: Petit St. Vincent, St. Vincent–Grenadines, West Indies

Location: An inkblot on the charts, just 40 miles south of St. Vincent and 20 minutes from Union Island, the nearest airstrip, by PSV's 42-foot Grand Banks yacht, *Wakiva* (the ride is free); the easiest way to get to Union is by shared-seat charter from Barbados (about $113 each way per passenger), which can be arranged by PSV; there are also scheduled flights to Union by LIAT and Mustique Airways, from Grenada, Barbados, St. Vincent, and Martinique

Telephone: 809/458-8801

Fax: 809/458-8428

Reservations: Own U.S. office (513/242-1333 or 800/654-9326, fax 513/242-6951), or Leading Hotels of the World

Credit Cards: None

Rooms: 22 cottages, all with bedrooms and sitting rooms, open *and* shaded patios or terraces, showers only, amenities trays, bathrobes, hammocks, some with ceiling fans (otherwise acres of louvers take care of the cooling)

Meals: Breakfast 7:30–10:00, buffet lunch 12:30–2:00, afternoon tea 4:00–5:00, dinner 7:30–9:30 (all in the hilltop dining pavilion); Saturday beach barbecue, with Grenadine flute band; dress—informal but stylish (cover-ups required at lunchtime); room service all meals (including early-morning coffee service), no extra charge

Entertainment: Quiet taped music in bar, occasional live music (guitar, folk), backgammon and other parlor pastimes

Sports: Virtually continuous beach (plus the offshore cay), snorkeling, Sunfish sailing, Hobiecats, windsurfing (with instruction by shore simulator), tennis (1 court with lights), croquet, fitness trail, footpath up 275-foot Mount Marni (great view), snorkeling on 20-foot island boat built from island cedar—all free; waterskiing, scuba diving and day trips on Chester's high-speed powerboat or sailboat trips to Tobago Cays and Mayreau at extra charge

P.S.: Few children, no groups except maybe the crew from a passing yacht who stop by the bar for a drink; closed September and October

The Calabash
Grenada

☆☆☆			🍷🍷🍷			🌓🌓			$ $ $		
Atmosphere			**Dining**			**Sports**			**Rates**		

You never have to worry about making it to the dining room in time for breakfast because you have a kitchenette and maid (who has her own entrance to let herself in without disturbing you). So leave your order in writing the night before, or wake up and whenever you feel like breakfast, just tell the maid. She'll serve it to you in bed, in the sitting room, or on your private patio. Eating, in fact, is one of the prime pleasures at the Calabash. Lunch is served in a breezy new gazebo a few paces from the lagoonlike waters of l'Anse aux Epines. Dinner is served in the main dining pavilion, one of the island's most acclaimed restaurants, an open terrace fashioned from native stone and furnished with chairs and tables of polished saman. Flowering *Thunbergia grandiflora* dangles from overhead vines, threatening, it seems, to reach down and gobble up your lambis or swordfish pie creole, prepared by a chef who once served aboard the royal yacht *Britannia* and cooked for the Prince and Princess of Wales when they were still talking.

The Calabash is an old Grenada favorite—the British in particular have been wintering here loyally for more than a quarter of a century. The intimate little resort circles 8 beachside acres, a "village green" dotted with lofty trees and fragrant shrubbery. The 28 suites perfectly capture island atmosphere, comfortable but not plush, rustic but snug. For my money, the best buys are the suites in the two-story cottages on the west side of the lawn, and preferably the higher-ceilinged units on the second floor: each suite subdivided with kitchenette, indoor sitting room, lazy breeze-cooled porch, small fan-cooled bedroom (showers only in the bathrooms). Room 1 is listed as a Honeymoon Suite, close to the beach, with a big hand-carved mahogany four-poster bed.

Three years ago six rooms were knocked down and replaced with six rooms with private plunge pools and six with bathrooms equipped with whirlpool tubs. These enhancements are welcome, but what brings the British and others back year after year to the Calabash is the long-serving staff—friendly, willing, attentive but unobtrusive. They make the Calabash an inviting, relaxed hideaway.

Name: The Calabash
Manager: Clive Barnes
Address: P.O. Box 382, St. George's, Grenada, West Indies
Location: At L'Anse aux Epines (Prickly Bay) on the south coast, about 10 minutes and $10 by taxi from the airport, $12 from St. George's
Telephone: 809/444-4234, 4334
Fax: 809/444-4804
Reservations: GHA, 800/322-1753, or International Travel & Resorts, Inc.
Credit Cards: American Express, MasterCard, Visa
Rooms: 30 suites, most with baths and showers, most with kitchenettes and porches, ground-floor rooms with air-conditioning, mini-bars, safes, tea or coffeemakers, ceiling fans throughout, telephones, 12 with whirlpools, 8 with private plunge pools
Meals: Breakfast anytime, lunch 1:00–2:30 in the new beach bar (with taped music), dinner 7:30–10:00 in the arbor-covered dining terrace (approx. $70 for 2); informal (but preferably trousers, rather than shorts, for men in the evening); room service at no extra charge
Entertainment: Some taped (or radio) music, occasional live piano music, steel band or country trio several times a week in winter, less frequently in the off-season, TV room, library
Sports: Beach, tennis (1 court, with lights), billiard room, fitness room—all free; snorkeling, scuba, waterskiing, sailing can be arranged
P.S.: Occasional din of planes, rarely after 10:00 p.m.; some cruise ship passengers come to enjoy the dining and the beach

Secret Harbour

Grenada

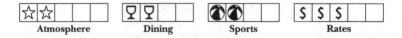

☆☆	🍷🍷	◕◕	$ $ $
Atmosphere	**Dining**	**Sports**	**Rates**

For lovers, the secret harbors at Secret Harbour may be the bathtubs—sunken, free-form, masses of colorful Italian tiles surrounded by colorful Italian tiles, matching towels, potted plants, and an unglazed "wagon wheel" window that lets you listen to the lapping of the water below as you lazily lap the water on each other's backs.

Secret Harbour is the dream come true of an expatriate Englishwoman, Barbara Stevens, a chartered accountant, who closed her books one day about 25 years ago and set sail with her first husband to cross the Atlantic in a 45-foot ketch; after spending 4 years chartering in the Grenadines, she decided Grenada was her island and Musquetta Bay her mooring. This is where she built her dream hotel back in 1970.

It's more like a Spanish-Mediterranean village on a terraced hillside of gardens and greenery: a splash of red-tiled roofs, white stucco arches, and hand-hewn beams among lime and papaw trees, frangipani, and triple bougainvilla. At the top of the hill are the lobby-lounge and restaurant; the guest bungalows are a few feet above the water, and between top and bottom there's a big, tiled free-form pool as colorful as your bathtub.

Secret Harbour, now owned by the Moorings, a yacht-charter company, welcomes you with low-key luxury—but luxury in keeping with the Spanish-Mediterranean theme: a big, semicircular balcony overlooking the bay, with padded loungers and enough room for a dinner party; arched glass-paneled doors leading into a small sunny lounge foyer with bright two-toned banquettes; a pair of authentic four-poster double beds from island plantations; stained-glass windows to cast spangled light for just the right romantic mood. To say nothing of your tasteful bathroom.

Name: Secret Harbour

Manager: Lin Nelson

Address: P.O. Box 11, St. George's, Grenada, West Indies

Location: On a quiet bay (Mount Hartman) on the south shore of the island, a few miles from the resort hotels along Grand Anse Beach, 10–15 minutes from St. George's ($12 by taxi), 10 minutes from the airport ($10 by taxi)

Telephone: 809/440-4548

Fax: 809/444-4819

Reservations: 800/334-2435; fax 813/530-9747

Credit Cards: American Express, Discover, MasterCard, Visa

Rooms: 20 suites in 10 cottages, all with air-conditioning, ceiling fans, verandas, refrigerators, hair dryers, and radios

Meals: Breakfast 7:30–10:30, lunch noon–2:00, afternoon tea 4:00, dinner 7:30–10:00 (approx. $60 for 2); room service at no extra charge; informal dress (but slacks rather than shorts at dinner)

Entertainment: Piped music, amplified combos, steel bands occasionally

Sports: Small (private) beach, sunbathing terrace, pool; Sunfish sailing, windsurfing, waterskiing, snorkeling; trips by speedboat to nearby Hog and Calivigny Islands

P.S.: Open all year

Spice Island Inn
Grenada

☆☆☆☆	♀♀		$ $ $
Atmosphere	**Dining**	**Sports**	**Rates**

Begin the day by slipping out of bed, sliding back the screens, and plopping straight into your private plunge pool. When the bell by the garden gate rings, it means the waiter has arrived with your breakfast, which he'll set up on your private, shaded breakfast patio. Dawdle over the fresh island fruits and nutmeg muffins—the hot plate will keep your coffee piping hot. After breakfast, step down onto your private sunning patio and spread out on a lounger—the garden wall screens you from passersby, the doorbell guards you against maids and waiters, so you can shuck your bikini or robe or whatever you have half on, half off. Spend the entire day here— sunning, dipping, eating, loving, dipping, sunning, all in your own private little sun-bright world.

Your suite, if you take time to notice, is craftily designed: The sundeck is in the sun all day; the breakfast patio is in the shade all day. In addition to your tiny garden and freshwater pool, your suite has tiled floors with soft scatter rugs, wicker chairs, and fitted dressers crafted from local hardwoods; the bathrooms are like locker rooms (but swank locker rooms)— big tiled sunken shower stalls, whirlpool baths, and, in some suites, double washbasins. The 20 beach suites, the original 20-year-old accommodations, are less opulent, with a hot tub separating the sleeping quarters from the bathroom. All Spice Island's suites, beach or pool, have louvers and air-conditioning for cooling and individual solar water heaters to give you reliable supplies of hot water. A recent $2-million renovation added 14 suites, 7 with private pools, and all the rooms have been redone in Spanish tile and bright tropical fabrics.

When you get curious about the rest of the world, stroll a few yards across the lawn, among the coconut palms and flowering shrubs, to Grand Anse Beach—2½ miles of fine white sand. Jog. Walk. Work up an appetite or thirst, both of which you can satisfy in pleasant surroundings under the inn's beach canopy. But no matter how tasty the breadfruit vichyssoise or nutmeg ice cream, no matter how jolly the music of the folk trio that serenades you, it's always a delight to slip off to your private patio and your private pool for a midnight swim beneath your private stars.

Name: Spice Island Inn

Manager: Augustus Cruickshank

Address: P.O. Box 6, Grand Anse, St. George's, Grenada, West Indies

Location: On Grand Anse Beach, 10 minutes and $15 by taxi from St. George's, 15 minutes and $15 by taxi from the new airport

Telephone: 809/444-4258, 4423

Fax: 809/444-4807

Reservations: International Travel & Resorts, Inc. in the United States, Robert Reid Associates in Canada, GHA, 800/322-1753

Credit Cards: American Express, Discover, MasterCard, Visa

Rooms: 56, including 17 pool suites, all with whirlpools, air-conditioning, ceiling fans, louvers, patios or lanais, safes, mini-bars, clock radios, telephones

Meals: Breakfast from 7:30, lunch 12:30–2:30, afternoon tea 4, dinner at 7:30 (approx. $70 for 2); full complimentary room service; elegantly casual dress

Entertainment: Barbecues and steel bands, local bands 3 nights a week; new open-air dance floor

Sports: 2½ mile beach (hotel's frontage about ½ mile), 17 private freshwater pools; fitness center, bicycling, tennis (1 court with lights), snorkeling gear, and Sunfish sailing—all free, a short walk along the beach; scuba diving, waterskiing, and water sports nearby, at extra charge

P.S.: Children under 5 not allowed in season; open all year

Other Choices

Twelve Degrees North

Grenada

Another spot worth looking into, although it's not a hotel: Twelve Degrees North, a group of eight self-contained apartments (six with one bedroom), each with its own maid, who prepares breakfast, lunch, fixes the beds, tidies up, and does your personal laundry. The apartments are immaculate, attractively decorated with simple island-style furnishings, and each has a large balcony or patio overlooking L'Anse aux Epines. On the beach, at the foot of the hill, you'll find two Sunfishes, a 23-foot launch, two Windsurfers, and a freshwater pool; up top there's a Plexi-Pave tennis court in tiptop condition (but bring your own rackets and balls). Twelve Degrees North, owned and operated by Joe Gaylord, the American who built it and keeps everything running like clockwork, is in the residential area of L'Anse aux Epines, a short taxi ride from several good restaurants. No children under 15 years old. 8 apartments. Doubles: $175 EP, winter 1994–95. *Twelve Degrees North, P.O. Box 241, St. George's, Grenada, West Indies. Telephone: 809/ 440-4580; fax: same as phone number*

Blue Horizons Cottage Hotel
Grenada

For many visitors to Grenada, this is the garden they pass through on the way to one of the island's finest restaurants, La Belle Créole. Diners have a hillside view over the bay as they sit down to conch scram, Grenadian caviar, and deviled langouste; beneath the newly decorated La Belle Créole, hidden among the saman and cassia trees and coral plants, are the cottages housing the guest rooms. The 32 suites, including 22 deluxe, have all been recently spiffed up with new mahogany furniture, new kitchenettes, new beds, and even new hair dryers; all have air-conditioning, ceiling fans, and patios. Communal areas include a pavilion lounge beside a freshwater pool, shaded by a tall Barringtonia that blossoms for 2 hours every evening at twilight. A short walk from Grand Anse Beach and the sports facilities at Spice Island Inn, a sister hotel, Blue Horizons, is ideal for lovers on a tight budget, although the restaurant, of course, is not inexpensive. 32 suites. Doubles: $145 to $165 EP, winter 1994–95. *Blue Horizons, P.O. Box 41, St. George's, Grenada, West Indies. Telephone: 809/444-4316; fax: 809/444-2815.*

Coyaba Beach Resort
Grenada

What this moderately priced resort has going for it is Grand Anse, that grand expanse of powdery beach that's Grenada's trademark. Spice Island Resort, costing twice as much, is a short jog down the beach. First impressions are not, fortunately, everything, because Coyaba's motel-like two-story wings with faux thatch roofs may not reach out and grab you. But once you walk through the lobby to the gardens, things perk up—a cane and bamboo dining pavilion, bar, inviting swimming pool with a swim-up bar, lawns and flowers running all the way to the water-sports shack and the palm trees on the beach. The 40 guest rooms are comfortable and functional, each with color TV and a patio or balcony angled to overlook the gardens and the sea. Tennis is free (1 court, no lights). 40 rooms. Doubles: $165, winter 1994–95. *Coyaba Beach Resort, P.O. Box 336, St. George's, Grenada, West Indies. Telephone: 809/444-4129; fax: 809/444-4808.*

The Caribbee Inn

Carriacou, Grenada

Carriacou is one of the last of the unknowns—although now that the landing strip has had a lighting implant for after-dark landings, the island may get more than a couple dozen visitors a day. But it's not likely to boom: This is the sort of place where the main road crosses the landing strip and cars have to line up behind a gate, like a railroad crossing, when a plane lands or takes off (not a lengthy process, because the strip can handle only small twin-engine planes). But drive north from the tumbledown Hillsborough and 20 minutes later there's this 6-acre oasis of refinement, a large villa that's been converted into a small inn—just seven rooms and suites set on a bluff with a tricky pathway down to a secluded beach 300 feet below. There's a sunset bench at the end of the promontory, a few remains of 18th-century structures, a cageful of macaws that squawk and squawk at the slightest provocation—and that's it. Owners Robert and Wendy Cooper, with backgrounds in theater and country-house hotels back in the U.K., have fashioned each guest room for tropical living—lots of louvers to catch every wisp of trade wind, mosquito netting draped decoratively around the four-poster beds, lamps fashioned from driftwood, hammocks slung across the patios. The lounge-bar-dining room is whimsically decorated with everything from an antique cash register to a stylish contemporary leather sofa on a gray pink "superb South American ceramic floor." Alas, the floor is so superb guests are instructed (not requested, instructed) to remove their shoes and sandals before stepping inside. Thus, the Caribbee's convivial evenings of candlelight dining with a French Creole flavor can only be enjoyed barefoot. Not that going barefoot is so much of a price to pay for staying at such a Caribbean curio, it's just that things might have been done a little more graciously. Then again, look at the prices. 7 rooms and suites. Doubles: $120 to $170, winter 1994–95 (add just $70 per couple for breakfast and barefoot dinner). *The Caribbee Inn, Prospect, Carriacou, Grenada, West Indies. Telephone: 809/443-7380.*

Canouan Beach Hotel

Canouan

The beach is the grabber here: about a quarter mile of white palm trees sprouting up at strategic spots for shade, loungers awaiting beneath the fronds, and beyond the gently rolling surf and reef the kind of view that dreams are made of. A grab bag of Grenadines is on the horizon—Mayreau, Union, Palm, the Tobago Cays, even Carriacou, neatly arranged by the hand of some master landscaper. There's another beach to windward on the other side of the property, perfect for long walks at sunset. The inn itself has just the right castaway feel to it—low bungalows with pairs of rooms, simply furnished in French style with wood-framed cot beds, desk-dresser, and chair. There's only air-conditioning, alas, except in the three "Privilege" rooms, which also have paddle fans. For active guests there's a water-sports shack (windsurfing, Hobiecats, snorkeling, day trips to the Cays aboard the resort's catamaran), a tennis court with lights, and, for some inexplicable reason, a golf driving range. I didn't see too many active guests, though, and I suspect that most people who come here spend most of their days lounging around on their patios or on the beach, their evenings lounging around drinking one of the bartender's ominous specialties—sex on the beach, earthquake, or Long Island iced tea (vodka, rum, tequila, and triple sec in unspecified quantities). The joy of dining on freshly caught grilled snapper and the castaway ambience of the beachside dining pavilion are flawed by the blaring music—nothing that a couple of Long Island iced teas won't solve. 18 rooms. Doubles: $156 to $210, winter 1994–95, with all meals. *Canouan Beach Hotel, South Glossy Bay, Canouan, St. Vincent–Grenadines, West Indies. Telephone: 809/458-8901; fax: 809/458-8875.*

The Dutch Leewards

Curaçao

Bonaire

The Dutch Leewards

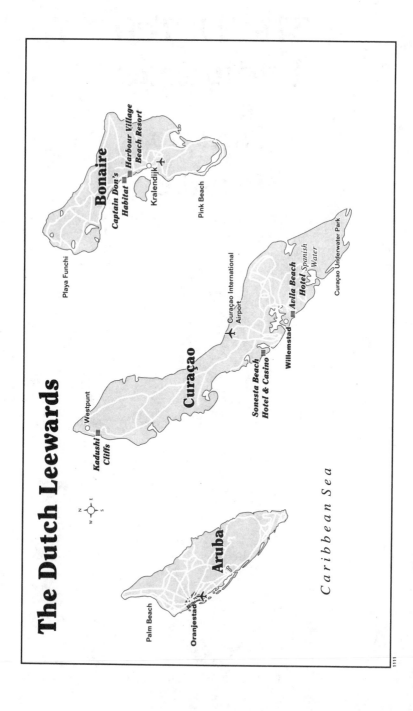

Bonaire

Playa Funchi

Captain Don's
Habitat

Harbour Village
Beach Resort

Kralendijk

Pink Beach

Curaçao

Westpunt

Kadushi
Cliffs

Curaçao International
Airport

Sonesta Beach
Hotel & Casino

Willemstad

Avila Beach
Hotel

Spanish
Water

Curaçao Underwater Park

N
W — E
S

Aruba

Palm Beach

Oranjestad

Caribbean Sea

The Dutch Leewards

They're ledges of coral rather than volcanic peaks, they're covered with cactus rather than jungle, and they have a personality all their own—part Dutch, part Indian, part Spanish, part just about everything else. They even have their own language, *Papiamento,* which grabs a few words from any language that happens to come along, shakes them around like a rum punch, and comes up with something as infectiously charming as the people themselves. Thus, *Carne ta camna cabes abou, ma e sa cuant' or tin* means, "He is as innocent as the babe unborn," although the literal translation is, "The sheep walks with its head down, but it knows what time it is"; or *stropi cacalaca,* which means "sweetheart" or "darling," although its literal translation means something quite unsuspected.

Bonaire is the loveliest of the trio, a coral boomerang 24 miles long and 5 miles wide, a world all its own, a world so bright, so luminous from coral and sand that you practically get a suntan crossing the street. It has more goats than cars, and almost as many flamingos as people; one-third of the island is national park, and another large chunk is salt flats cultivated by Dutch seafarers a couple of centuries ago.

Curaçao is the largest of the three, and its main city, Willemstad, is the capital of all the Netherlands Antilles. Willemstad is utterly unique, almost a miniature Caribbean Amsterdam with gingerbread houses the colors of a coral reef. Of late, it has become a bit grungy and slightly overcommercial, so maybe you'd better skip town and head out to the *cunucu,* or country-side, to find yourselves a quiet cove for the afternoon.

Aruba is all beach, but a beach unsurpassed by any other island, with mile after mile of some of the whitest sand in the Caribbean. It's the smallest but the liveliest of the Dutch Leewards, with high-rise hotels, nightclubs, ca-sinos, and lots of restaurants to keep you from enjoying the moon and the stars—but, alas, no romantic hideways.

How to Get There Since Aruba is the biggy here, most flights head there first—from Miami (American, Air Aruba, and ALM), Atlanta (ALM), Baltimore/Washington (Air Aruba), Houston (Viasa), and San Juan (American). Curaçao rates nonstops from Miami (American and ALM). Bonaire has hitherto been the poor relative that always involved a change of plane, but you can now go direct on one-stop flights from New York via Aruba on Air Aruba; otherwise, fly to Curaçao and catch one of the commuter flights on the new Cats Air (with 19-seater EMB 110s) and you can switch aircraft without standing in line for customs and immigration in Curaçao—that is, you avoid lining up with the hundreds of passengers on a big jet and instead clear customs and immigration with only 17 others.

For information on Aruba, call 800/862-7822; Bonaire, 800/826-6247; Curaçao, 800/270-3350.

Avila Beach Hotel
Curaçao

☆☆☆			𝒴			◑			$		
Atmosphere			**Dining**			**Sports**			**Rates**		

With its jungle greenery and glimpses of sun-dappled patio, this driveway spells "tropics" even before you step inside. "I like to give my guests a feeling of the tropics; I like to find things to make it interesting," says owner Nic Møller. "It" being a four-story colonial governor's mansion built in a time (early 19th century) when ships had to fire gun salutes for the mansion as they bobbed and tacked down the coast to the great harbor of Curaçao. The impeccably kept mansion, sunburst yellow with white trim and a red-tiled roof, stands next to the octagon-shaped home where Simón Bolívar used to visit his sisters (it could still receive a liberator or governor at a moment's notice). And it certainly is interesting.

The lobby area has been brightened with a cultivated Euro-Caribbean air—pastel colors replacing the heavy wood paneling, Oriental rugs blending with smart cane furniture, a grand piano standing ready for the occasional recital. Wood beams decorate the ceilings, large mirrors are guarded by life-size ceramic hounds.

Follow the sun through this pleasant lobby and you come to a breezy patio-terrace with flagstones and ceramic lamps, a sunshade of twining palms and flamboyant trees, cacti and rubber plants, with white wooden chairs grouped around tables. Farther down, there's a second arbor shading rustic lounging chairs and the inn's signature Schooner Bar, shaped like a ship's prow with a sail projecting from the mast.

Then comes the beach. And here's where a little ingenuity came in: The Avila is indeed on the seafront, but on this stretch of the coastline there's precious little natural beach, so someone fashioned two breakwaters to create two small lagoons, each with a sandy beach. Between the lagoons, a pier leads out to the "Blues" restaurant and cocktail lounge, perched on stilts over the water. It's a great place to watch sunsets and listen to live jazz. One beach is ringed by a sunbathing terrace and shaded by half-a-dozen bohios; the other is bordered by a promenade lined with benches and tall, iron-poled, orange-capped lanterns that guide you to the edge of the property—perfect for private stargazing and surf listening.

The Danish-descended Møller family, owners of the Avila since 1977, doubled the size of their inn in 1992 with the opening of a completely new wing, the Governor, that dramatically upgraded the personality of the hotel without destroying the style of the original, now known as Classic Avila. Classic Avila's rooms were refurbished around the same time with striped fabric blinds, wooden beds and couches, framed antique maps, or pretty watercolors. The 40 "standard" rooms in the Classic Avila are fairly small and sunless, in traditional island style; favorite rooms here are the "preferred" rooms on the upper floors, such as rooms 344 and 345, which have terraces for afternoon sunning. In the new wing, all the rooms and suites have terraces facing the water and are simply but pleasantly designed in tropical fabrics and rattan furniture, and they catch cross breezes (at least on the upper floors). A few of the one- and two-bedroom suites also have kitchenettes.

The Avila in either of its incarnations is by no means a plush hotel, but it's lovely and welcoming, with more colonial charm than any other hotel on the island. Especially in the evening, when you sit around the Schooner Bar sipping an Amstel and the pelicans dive for their suppers or a cruise ship passes like a wall of lights. You'll soon be sitting down to a dinner of fresh fish smoked in the kitchen's own spice room, topped off by homemade sorbet, all beneath the twining palms and flamboyants.

Name: Avila Beach Hotel
Manager: Tone Møller
Address: P.O. Box 791, Willemstad, Curaçao, Netherlands Antilles
Location: On the outskirts of Willemstad, approximately 15 minutes and $15 from the airport.
Telephone: 5999/614-377
Fax: 5999/611-493
Reservations: Direct
Credit Cards: All major cards
Rooms: 80 rooms and 7 suites. 40 rooms in the Classic Avila, all with air-conditioning, direct-dial telephones, television. Only 2 rooms have

terraces (344 and 345). 40 rooms in the new wing, all with air-conditioning, balconies, refrigerators, television, direct-dial telephones, some with kitchenettes and king-size beds

Meals: Breakfast 7:00–10:00, lunch noon–2:00, dinner 7:00–10:00 at the Belle Terrace restaurant near the beach (approx. $60 for 2) or at the Blues restaurant on the pier; casual dress; no room service

Entertainment: Schooner Bar near the beach, Antillean night on Wednesdays, barbecue on Saturdays with mariachi or steel band, blues band on Tuesdays; free shuttle bus to Willemstad on weekdays

Sports: 2 small, pleasant beaches, tennis (1 night-lit court)—all free. Snorkeling off the beach (bring your own equipment)

P.S.:   The Avila gets a good mix of clients and is popular with businesspeople and families, the latter especially on weekends. Music on Saturday nights can be heard in the guest rooms and on terraces and might spoil your reverie.

Sonesta Beach Hotel & Casino

Curaçao

☆☆	𝅝𝅝	●●	$ $ $
Atmosphere	**Dining**	**Sports**	**Rates**

On an island where cacti and gravel are more common than palms and bougainvillea, the manicured lawns and fountains make this Sonesta as welcome as an oasis. A curving driveway winds round the lawns toward a large, open-sided reception hall, ringed by the usual facilities you expect in this kind of resort—boutiques, casino, lounge, and restaurants. Curving steps lead past a cooling waterfall to an informal, open-air café, then to a large, sometimes crowded pool area, and finally to a welcome if gravelly beach lined with palm trees and dotted with chiki huts. Lined up parallel to the beach and sprawled over several acres are the Sonesta's three-storied buildings, designed in Dutch-Caribbean style with ocher-yellow stucco and red-tiled roofs.

Sonesta is not usually the kind of place that appears in *Caribbean Hide-*

aways: This 4-year-old is big (248 rooms and suites); it thrives on groups and conventions; it's run by a chain; and its interior decor is that style best described as Deluxe Anywhere. But the exteriors of Sonesta Beach have been designed with unusual sensitivity to blend with the island character, its kitchens offer an unusually high level of cuisine and service, and the best of its rooms afford an uncommon level of comfort and luxury. In any case, it has one of the best beaches on the island—so here it is.

Many of guests rooms, though, are short on privacy: The beach-level, ocean-view studio suites, for example, are spacious and attractive but their glass sliders (no screen, alas) lead directly to private patches of grass furnished with chairs and a table. But anyone can walk past those rooms and peek in—which means I'd have to keep my curtains drawn and air conditioner switched on to avoid being a potential exhibit. These rooms are, of course, the most convenient to the sand and the sea, but some guests might sacrifice a little convenience (and pay a few dollars more) for a deluxe oceanfront room on the second or third floor, with private balconies and lovely views.

Better yet, splurge on one of the eight terrace suites—third floor, corner—each with a separate bedroom and living room and huge terraces (of these, suites 384, 350, 334, and 337 are especially attractive). The bathrooms not only have whirlpools, but you can also step from your whirlpool, slide open the glass doors, and dry off on your second terrace, just big enough for a chaise longue.

There's a temptation, in pampering quarters like these, just to call down for room service, but the Sonesta happens to have three fine restaurants, each with its own chef and own style of cuisine. In the evening, when the bustle quiets down and the conventioneers have trooped to the casino, the Sonesta's beach is positively romantic—dozens of small iron lanterns dot the paths, spotlights illuminate the copse of palm trees, steady trade winds cool the balmy air. You can easily forget how many people you're sharing with and pretend it's all your own.

Name: Sonesta Beach Hotel & Casino
Manager: Danilo Checcucci
Address: Piscadera Bay, P.O. Box 6003, Curaçao, Netherlands Antilles
Location: On the southern coast, 3 miles from Willemstad and the airport
Telephone: 5999/368-800
Fax: 5999/627-502
Reservations: Own U.S. office, 800/766-3782
Credit Cards: All major cards
Rooms: 248 rooms and suites, all with balcony or patio, mini-bar, remote-control TV, clock radio, air-conditioning, direct-dial telephone, some with king-size bed, hair dryer

Meals: Breakfast from 6:00 at the al fresco Palm Café, lunch 11:00–3:00, dinner 6:00–11:00 at Portofino or Emerald Bar & Grill (with soft music); casual dress; room service (extra charge) 6:00 a.m.–midnight

Entertainment: Trio 10:00–midnight, casino, sunset cruises, shopping arcade

Sports: Beach, free-form swimming pool with swim-up bar, 2 whirlpools, wading pool—all free; nearby 9-hole golf course, Jet-Ski, deep-sea fishing charters, scuba diving, windsurfing, waterskiing, horseback riding

P.S.:   Counselor-supervised program for children ages 5–12; open all year

Harbour Village Beach Resort

Bonaire

☆ ☆					🏆					🏖🏖				S S S		
Atmosphere					**Dining**					**Sports**				**Rates**		

Harbour Village Beach Resort is sort of a work in progress, with potential for becoming a top-caliber destination. It's not quite there yet, but it's aiming high, and you'll enjoy the ride.

The resort has a lot going for it, not the least of which is the laid-back island of Bonaire itself. The island's incredibly clear water and protected coral reefs are world famous dive destinations, and even if you're not a diver you need only to *walk out* from the hotel's private beach, snorkeling gear in hand, to glimpse some of that precious beauty.

Harbour Village is situated on the western side of the island, facing the tiny islet of Klein Bonaire and the nightly tropical sunsets, only a few minutes' walk from the small capital town of Kralendijk. Surprisingly, this side of the island—the entire island, in fact—lacks long, beautiful, sandy beaches. Harbour Village has solved this by creating its own horseshoe-shaped stretch of cool white coral sand lined with palm trees. At one end of the horseshoe is a fully staffed and equipped dive shop; at the other end sits La Balandra Beach Bar and Grill, its terrace jutting out over the water just far enough to catch the trade winds that cool the Bonaire coast.

The resort is laid out village style, with two-story cantaloupe-colored stucco buildings and sloping Spanish-tile roofs. Some buildings face the ocean, others the marina or gardens. Try for one of the oceanfront rooms; for privacy and view, they're worth it.

Rooms are light, comfortable, and spacious. No. 325, for example, is a one-bedroom oceanfront suite just a few steps from the beach. The full living room had a nicely designed sofa, chairs, dining area, and remote control cable television. The bedroom had a king-size bed and a second television. In addition there were two large bathrooms, each with tub and abundant towels, and plenty of closet space stocked with more than enough wooden hangers (a rarity in itself). The room also had a terrace overlooking the plam trees and the beach beyond.

Unfortunately, despite a lovely view and privacy, the rooms lack cross-ventilation or an "islandy" feel, and terraces don't capture any of those pleasant offshore breezes just a few feet away. So you really do need either the ceiling fans or the air-conditioning.

The guest rooms are undergoing remodeling in several stages. Still to come (as of February 1995) are mini-bars, screens for the terrace doors, and new bathroom amenities (I hope that includes at least one full-length mirror). Four hard-surface, night-lit courts are in the works, scheduled for completion in spring 1995. They'll be located at the far end of the property, on the other side of a 60-slip marina, a long 10-minute walk from the reception desk. A full spa center is also planned for mid-1995 to augment the well-equipped (free weights, treadmills, Stairmaster, Nautilus) but not very used fitness center.

The food is surprisingly good, and the service pleasant if slow. Lunch at the Balandra Beach Bar and Grill is informal and delightful; dinner at the Kasa Coral restaurant, a semiopen terrace overlooking the swimming pool, is more formal (although jackets for men are not required).

Service throughout the hotel is attentive, gracious, and unpretentious. How many hotels give you not one but three house staff members to turn down the bed at night and place chocolates on the pillow, and then, a half hour later, send a superviser to make sure everything was done properly? Service can still be uneven, but it will no doubt be perfected under the watchful eye of the current manager, Jurgen Dinger, a real pro.

Name: Harbour Village Beach Resort
Manager: Jurgen Dinger
Address: P.O. Box 312, Kralendijk, Bonaire, Netherlands Antilles
Location: At Playa Lechi, on the edge of town, about 10 minutes and $10 from the airport
Telephone: 5997/7500
Fax: 5997/7507

Reservations: 800/424-0004

Credit Cards: American Express, Diners Club, MasterCard, Visa

Rooms: 70, including 1-bedroom suites, all with balcony or terrace, air-conditioning, ceiling fan, telephones, hair dryers, terry-cloth robes, remote cable television

Meals: Breakfast 7:30–11:00, lunch noon–4:00, dinner (in Kasa Coral) 6:30–10:00 (approx. $60–$100 for 2); informal dress; room service 7:30 a.m.–10:00 p.m.

Entertainment: Lounge/bar, island buffet with local music Fridays

Sports: Small beach, freshwater pool, fitness center and new spa, snorkeling, windsurfing, kayaking, tennis (4 lit courts), waterskiing, small-boat sailing—all free; scuba diving (fully equipped dive shop, lessons, 2 scheduled dives daily), deep-sea fishing, powerboat rides, bicycles

P.S.: Small children welcome, but there are no special facilities for them

Captain Don's Habitat

Bonaire

☆					♡				●				$	$			
Atmosphere					**Dining**				**Sports**				**Rates**				

Captain Don's is, first and foremost, top to bottom, a dive resort, and since it happens to be on one of the best dive islands in the world, diving diving diving is what all the other guests will be talking about in the bar. But that doesn't mean nondivers will find nothing to divert them.

On the contrary, since the first dive boat leaves at sunup, nondiving guests will have the pool, vest-pocket beach, and terrace all to themselves for much of the day, and since the main form of nightlife here is night diving, you may well also have the bar and dining terrace to yourself in the evening. If the cuisine is relatively undistinguished, the same can't be said of the lodgings (except for the original Habitat rooms, which should be avoided). Most of the rooms are in contemporary, white stucco two-story villas spread out along the coral seafront. The best of the bunch are the villa deluxe studios and suites (ground floor, ocean view, with large patios facing the water) and villa superior doubles (second floor, ocean view, many with balconies). Although they lack TV and phones, the rooms do have space, privacy, and views; the suites and studios have fully equipped kitchens. Room no. 601 is particularly appealing: A villa deluxe suite, it has a large bedroom with king-size bed, full living room, dinette, and kitchenette, plus a lovely patio a few steps from the water but set back just far enough to give you some privacy.

The Captain Don of the title is Don Stewart, a Californian who sailed into Bonaire back in the 1960s. I first met him in the early 1970s when he was moonlighting as bartender at the old Flamingo Beach Hotel. This was no ordinary bar (the Flamingo had functioned as a prisoner-of-war camp during World War II), and Don was the island's leading dive master and raconteur. And conservationist: Long before it was the fashionable thing to do, Don was lobbying Caribbean governments and fellow divers to ban spearguns and the chipping of coral for souvenirs. That Bonaire still has some of the finest reefs and a pacesetting conservation policy is largely due to Don. If you're a diver you probably know that; if you're not, go ask Captain Don.

Name: Captain Don's Habitat

Manager: Albert Romijn

Address: P.O. Box 88, Kralendijk, Bonaire, Netherlands Antilles

Location: On the leeward side of the island, approximately 10 minutes and $10 from the airport

Telephone: 5997/8290

Fax: 5997/8240

Reservations: Own United States office, 800/327-6709

Credit Cards: American Express, Diners Club, MasterCard, Visa

Rooms: 68 rooms and suites, plus full villas, all with air-conditioning, some with balconies or patios, kitchenettes. No phones or televisions in rooms

Meals: Because 7:00–10:00, lunch 11:00–2:00, dinner 7:00–10:00 at Rum Runners, overlooking the water (approx. $25–$35 for 2); casual dress; no room service

Entertainment: Recorded music at dinner, slide shows, theme buffets, and special entertainment nights during the week

Sports: Small beach, pool—all free; fully equipped dive facility with scuba and snorkeling equipment for rent or sale, dive certification courses available, fishing charters

P.S.: This hotel is primarily a dive facility that attracts serious divers

Other Choices

Kadushi Cliffs

Curaçao

Although time-shares are usually off limits for *Caribbean Hideaways*, I'm including Kadushi Cliffs by virtue of its scenic, dramatic locations, intelligent and sensitive design, and romantic ambience. Located about 45 minutes from Willemstad, at the northernmost tip of the island near Mt. Christoffel National Park on a dramatic bluff overlooking the sea, Kadushi currently consists of 12 two-story villas, each with an unobstructed view of the sea. Ten more villas are planned for fall 1995; eventually there will be 36. The villas are available for rent for a minimum of 2 days, and daily maid service can be arranged. Each air-conditioned villa has a living room, dining room, patio, bathroom, and fully equipped kitchen downstairs, plus another large terrace, bathroom, and two large bedrooms upstairs, one with a full Jacuzzi, so that you can indulge your body without missing one minute of the ravishing ocean view. Kadushi Cliffs is still being developed, and a large complex—with additional buildings, tennis, and golf—is ultimately planned. But for now there is peace and privacy, and an inviting open-air thatched-roof restaurant, the Cliff House, serving three meals daily (except Mondays). 12 villas, rooms for two to four people: $295, winter 1994–95. *Kadushi Cliffs, P.O. Box 3673, Curaçao, Netherlands Antilles. Telephone: 5999/640-200; fax: 5999/640-282. Reservations: 800/523-8744.*

All-Inclusive Resorts

A Quick Rundown of Some of the Places You Won't Be Embarrassed to Stay In

When I set out to research the first edition of this guidebook back in 1972 or thereabouts, I went to Negril in Jamaica to check out the recently launched Hedonism all-inclusive resort. Mistake. It was midday on a Sunday, but it might as well have been midnight, with music blasting and skimpily clad couples gyrating and whooping and nobody paying the slightest attention to the gorgeous beach. Dante's Inferno meets Spring Break. I reeled out and swore off all-inclusives evermore.

But raucous Hedonism wasn't the sole reason I shunned all-inclusives (nothing wrong with a little bit of hedonism now and then). They seemed to me to contradict one of the main reasons for going to the Caribbean in the first place—to get out and about and see something of other peoples and other cultures. Since guests pay for everything up front, there is little incentive to leave the compound. That would mean paying extra for drinks and meals already paid for.

But in recent years the all-inclusive concept has spread briskly ("all-inclusive" meaning resorts that throw in everything, including wines and liquor for one price), both geographically and demographically. The idea took root in Jamaica, but you'll find them now throughout most of the islands; they began for couples only, but they now offer special facilities for families, singles, and senior citizens. And some of them now do, indeed, encourage guests to get out and see something of the islands by organizing complimentary sightseeing tours, supplying bikes and picnics, or arranging dine-around plans that allow guests to eat in local restaurants at no extra cost.

Because the basic concept—everything for a fixed price with no surprises, no fussing, no tipping, etc.—seems to have wide appeal, I herewith pass along a few observations on some of the all-inclusives that readers of this guide might like to consider should they decide to sample this kind of vacation. I should also mention that several of the Caribbean's traditional resorts have decided either to offer all-inclusive plans along with their regular rates or to go whole hog and eliminate a lot of bookkeeping by offering guests wine, liquor, and sports facilities—in some cases, even laundry. This makes them, in essence, all-inclusive resorts, although they do not necessarily identify themselves with that tag. A few of them are in this guide: Jumby Bay Island, Galley Bay, and Curtain Bluff on Antigua, Jalousie Plantation on St. Lucia, to name four.

Note: In the following listings, all rates are for peak season, winter 1994–95, for 1 night unless specified otherwise. Most of the resorts also have package plans that include airfare, which may reduce the actual rates listed here.

Grand Lido, Negril, Jamaica. Probably the poshest of the all-inclusives, a member of SuperClubs, the outfit that started it all. One of its two beaches is reserved for nude sunbathing; hot tubs with bars-cafés are dotted among the trees; air-conditioned guest rooms come with TV and VCR; guests can take a sundown cruise on the 150-foot yacht on which Prince Rainier and Princess Grace honeymooned. Grand Lido was conceived for today's hard-working, hard-playing go-getters, so it also offers fax machines, personal computers, and other instant-communication gizmos with the folks back in the office. 200 rooms. Doubles from $560. *Grand Lido, Norman Manley Boulevard, Negril, Jamaica, West Indies. Telephone: 800/859-7873; fax: 809/957-4317.*

Swept Away, Negril, Jamaica. Swept Away is Grand Lido's next-door neighbor—for some guests its more appealing neighbor—because its guest rooms are designed for the breezes, with fans and lots of louvers as well as air-conditioning. The tennis center across the road is considered one of the finest in the Caribbean (it comes with a fitness center and racket ball and squash courts). Two restaurants, five bars, water sports. 134 rooms. Doubles from $425. *Swept Away, P.O. Box 37, Long Bay, Negril, Jamaica, West Indies. Telephone: 800/545-7937; fax: 809/957-4060.*

The Enchanted Garden, Ocho Rios, Jamaica. This was for many years a botanical garden and still is, but now it has 112 guest rooms and all the amenities of a resort tucked in among its 20 acres of saman and mango trees, waterfalls and koi ponds, and a walk-in aviary. There's also an al fresco massage and a "Trimnasium" for health buffs, plus a private beach club—but you have to drive 5 or 10 minutes to get there. The guest rooms are, given the unique setting, uninspired (they should have called in the architect from Swept Away), but 40 of them are suites with private plunge pools. When I tell you that one of the day's highlights is feeding the birds at 4:30, you get some idea of how relaxed and laid-back this place is. 112 rooms and suites. Doubles from $300. *The Enchanted Garden, P.O. Box 284, Ocho Rios, Jamaica, West Indies. Telephone: 809/974-1400; fax: 809/974-5823.*

Sans Souci Lido, Ocho Rios, Jamaica. There's a Riviera-like quality to this coral and white resort set among terraced gardens rising above the beach, with a mineral pool at one level, freshwater pool at another, dining terrace up top. Charlie's Spa offers, among other pamperings, al fresco massage in a gazebo beside the sea. Facilities include two restaurants, tennis, and water sports. Now operated by SuperClubs. 111 rooms and suites. Doubles from $610. *Sans Souci Lido, P.O. Box 103, Ocho Rios, Jamaica, West Indies. Telephone: 800/203-7456; fax: 809/974-2544.*

Casablanca Resort, Anguilla. An eye-boggling lobby with fountains, ponds, and elaborate Moroccan tile work leads guests to a windswept pool and beach. Fine cuisine is available in the main dining room (with a choice of 40 wines), which adjoins a bar inevitably called Café Americain; the minibars are stocked to suit the guests. Water sports, tennis, so-so fitness room. 87 rooms and suites. Doubles from $750. *Casablanca Resort, P.O. Box 444, The Valley, Anguilla, British West Indies. Telephone: 800/231-1945; fax: 809/497-6899.*

Le Sport, St. Lucia. Located at Cap Estates on the northern tip of the island in a secluded bay, Le Sport is primarily for the Body Holiday, as they put it, with an imposing hilltop spa for treatments. But for spouses and companions who don't want to be structured, slapped around, or dunked in seaweed, there are also tennis, water sports, and archery. Golf and horseback riding are available nearby (but not included in the rate). 102 rooms and suites. Doubles from $480. *Le Sport, P.O. Box 437, Castries, St. Lucia, West Indies. Telephone: 800/544-2883; fax: 809/450-0368.*

Sandals St. Lucia. La Toc, the former Cunard flagship, is now operated by the largest of the all-inclusive groups, Sandals of Jamaica. Amenities include an enormous swimming pool (swim-up bar, stage for floor shows), a 9-hole golf course, tennis, water sports, fitness center, and several restaurants. Sandals resorts can get really revved up at times, but the advantage of this one is that you can pay for the top-of-the-line lodgings—suites in cliffside villas—and get away from it all—especially if you go whole hog and check into one of the villas out on the bluff with private plunge pools. 273 rooms and suites. Doubles from $1,775 for 7 nights. *Sandals St. Lucia, P.O. Box 399, Castries, St. Lucia, West Indies. Telephone: 800/726-3257.*

LaSource, Grenada. This is one of the newest of the health and fitness spa resorts, a cousin of Le Sport in St. Lucia, but for my money it's more attractive (although I wish they'd turn down the air-conditioning in the reflexology cubicles). Lovely cove setting, stylish rooms, great views, two restaurants, upbeat service, 9-hole pitch-and-putt golf, tennis, water sports, and a Cadillac to meet you at the airport (just 3 minutes away, but aircraft noise is no problem). 100 rooms and suites. Doubles from $480. *LaSource, P.O. Box 852, St. George's, Grenada, West Indies. Telephone: 800/544-2883; fax: 809/444-2561.*

Caribbean Cruises: The Small Ships

I know, I know. It says in the introduction that *Caribbean Hideaways* features only inns and resorts where you will not be overrun by hordes of unleashed cruise ship passengers. So what am I doing with a section on cruise ships? Well, these are *small* cruise ships: The largest carries 204 passengers, the smallest no more than 100. I have sailed on five of them and my experience is that when they hit a port only a dozen or so of the passengers head for a beach (except when the ships organize beach parties, which are usually on deserted or isolated beaches, far from resorts).

These ships are really oversize luxury yachts, the seagoing equivalents of, say, Malliouhana or Curtain Bluff, offering the camaraderie of an *intime* inn and the privacy of an exclusive resort plus the opportunity to visit *several* islands on one vacation without the hassles of unpacking and repacking every other day.

In the case of the *Wind Star,* and its sister ship the *Wind Spirit,* or the *Star Clipper* and *Star Flyer,* the comparison is more accurately with tall ships since they are four-masters with sails. With the Windstar vessels, the sails furl and unfurl automatically at the behest of the ships' computers. Moreover, the computers ensure that the ships will never list more than 4 degrees, so from the point of view of comfort they function like regular cruise ships. You rarely have even the slightest sense of *sailing.* It is an interesting experience, nevertheless.

Otherwise, how do the five ships stack up? Since the Star clipper ships are really in a different category from the others, I'll treat them separately.

THE STATISTICS

These basic facts and figures give you a quick profile of each ship, arranged by fare, most expensive first. The fares are for comparison purposes only, a *daily* rate based on the ships' basic 7-day cruises; they have been culled from the cruise lines' brochures, but they can almost certainly be reduced by a few hundred dollars by talking to the right travel agents (in any case, you might want to check on special rates that include airfares and hotels before or after the cruises, like the *Sea Goddess* linkup with La Samanna on St. Martin).

Sea Goddess I/Sea Goddess II:

4,250 tons; 344 feet; 17.5 knots; 116 passengers; 86 crew. Daily rates for two, from $1,000 (including all drinks and tips). *Telephone: 800/458-9000 (U.S.) or 800/268-3702 (Canada).*

Renaissance I/Renaissance II:

4,500 tons; 290 feet; 16 knots; 100 passengers; 65 crew. Daily rates for two, $550 to $800. *Telephone: 800/525-5350.*

Wind Star I/Wind Star II:

5,350 tons; 440 feet; about 10 to 15 knots (under power); 148 passengers; 91 crew. Daily rates for two, $442 to $456. *Telephone: 800/258-7245 (U.S.) or 800/663-5384 (Canada).*

STATEROOMS

All staterooms on these ships are outside cabins. Cunard's Sea Goddess ships were the first of these yachtlike vessels and set the pace in cabin design, amenities, and comforts. Each stateroom (or suite-room, as Cunard calls it) is the equivalent of, say, a junior suite ashore, although a tad smaller, with a sitting area, mini-bar, television and VCR, and four-channel radio. With windows rather than portholes, the room is that much brighter, in addition to letting you see where you're going or where you've been; but the bed rather than the sitting area is next to the window, which is the wrong way round for my taste. The cabins on the Windstar ships are similar in format (but with large portholes rather than windows).

The other ships learned from their predecessors: In each case, the sitting area is next to the window, although on the Renaissance ships the furniture is arranged in such a way that both the sofa *and* the bed are next to the window. The Italian designers have used a laminate resembling highly polished mahogany, with lots of brass trim and mirrors, giving the stateroom a true yachtlike appearance (and its lighting was not merely functional—with the proper adjustment of spotlights and dimmers it could be downright sexy).

As for bathrooms, the Renaissance and Windstar ships have showers only (the latter in an ingenious space-saving tube, the former a sensibly designed saunalike stall); the Sea Goddesses have squeezed a tub/shower into a space that should have been tub only.

DINING

One attraction all these ships have in common is open seating in the dining rooms. In fact, their dining rooms function like regular restaurants, with passengers free to choose their times, tables, and table companions. No first and second seatings, here; no assigned tables; no risk of being stuck with bores for an entire voyage.

Open seating also encourages a higher caliber of cuisine, since dishes can be prepared à la minute rather than en masse. The cuisine in each case tends to be nouvelle continental with delicate accents from exotic lands that the ships and chefs have visited—Indonesian, Indian, Japanese, Polynesian.

The food was outstanding on my cruise on the *Sea Goddess II,* which actually had one of America's star chefs on board to prepare a couple of special dinners, but whose efforts, it seemed to me (and several of my fellow passengers) were outshone by the ship's own chef. The *Renaissance II,* although significantly less expensive, came close to being on par with the others; the *Wind Star* now has cuisine designed by Joachim Splichal of the acclaimed Patina Restaurant and Café Pinot in Los Angeles.

In terms of service, the restaurant of the *Sea Goddess II* had the most polished staff. (It should be noted that the Sea Goddesses serve complimentary wines with all meals—not great vintages, obviously, but a well-chosen variety from the prominent vineyards of France and California; if you're not impressed by their selections, you can always sip their complimentary champagne—or order other vintages from the ships' *cartes des vins.*)

On the Sea Goddesses passengers are expected to dress for dinner every evening, with black-tie affairs two evenings a week; the dress code is more casual on the other two (just as well in the case of the Star Clippers and the Windstars, where closet space is, well, yachtlike). The alternative to dressing up is to dine in your stateroom. All except the Star Clippers have around-the-clock room service menus, but the Sea Goddesses allow you to order from the restaurant menu during regular dining hours; in each case, the coffee table in your stateroom is converted to a dinner table, set with fine china and crystal, and your meal is served course by course.

ENTERTAINMENT

Except for the Star Clippers, each of these ships has at least one small lounge that doubles as a disco/theater/nightclub/boîte/casino; the Sea Goddesses also have piano bars. Live entertainment consists of a small combo for dancing (usually electronic keyboard and rhythm synthesizers, usually with the volume turned up higher than the acoustics warrant). They may be augmented by vocalists, talented people, all of them, and an hour or two of Gershwin or Sondheim before or after dinner is certainly more welcome than a pseudo-Vegas pseudoextravaganza.

These ships are blessedly free of talent shows and costume balls, and that blight known as the ship's photographer, who always wants everyone at the table to pose when I'm getting to the punch line.

Chalk up a point for the Windstar ships: While the others may organize an occasional buffet or postdinner dance on deck, only the *Wind Star* had a topside bar open after 6:00 every evening. Granted, because of its sails, it had more reason to entertain its passengers on deck than the others, but I'd happily settle for the moon and stars, sails or no sails.

SERVICE

In each case, overall service was above average for cruise ships, and well above the norm at Caribbean resorts. The top prize goes to Sea Goddess, by a short neck: You know you're dealing with a classy group from the minute your documents arrive in a burgundy leather wallet with matching luggage tags; and when you get to your cabin, the card key for your cabin and your ID pass are waiting in a matching leather card case. Moreover, the staff members seem to memorize names instantly and anticipate requests faster, which is not to downplay the other crews—but the Sea Goddess people have been around longer and their ratio of crew to passengers, 89 to 116, is probably the highest in the industry.

SHORE EXCURSIONS

The Renaissance ships have snappy, custom-designed launches for tendering passengers to shore; the Sea Goddesses use their lifeboats—real old-fashioned lifeboats, not the last word in convenience or comfort but adequate since the ships are never farther than 5 minutes from shore. On the other hand, the Sea Goddesses offered the best tendering service, by lifeboat or inflatable dinghy, with the boats leaving whenever anyone wanted to leave, rather than operating half-hourly shuttles.

The cruise directors were, for my money, the weak links in the service of all four ships I cruised on: This is not to say that they are not willing attendants or congenial traveling companions, but you'll probably find you know more about the islands than they do. Too often they seem to be captives of the shore agents who actually arrange the excursions; thus, your ship may go into Marigot on the French side of St. Martin/St. Maarten, but since the shore agents have to do something and have to earn some revenue they arrange for buses into Philipsburg on the Dutch side, a wasted half hour each way since the shopping there is only marginally better and Marigot offers more charm, more cafés, and more fine restaurants just a few minutes from the dock.

However, there are some out-of-the-ordinary highlights among the shore excursions: Renaissance organizes Minimoke car "rallies" for its passengers on St. Barthélemy, a jolly event that everyone seems to enjoy; Sea Goddess and Windstar arrange for passengers to race aboard twin America's Cup yachts (the real thing!) off St. Maarten.

Where these ships score with shore excursions is their beach parties—perhaps on an uninhabited island in the Tobago Cays, probably in the British Virgin Islands. The Sea Goddesses have the most famous of these outings—on the BVI's Jost van Dyke, complete with a dining tent, full buffet lunch, and waiters dressed up in proper uniforms and shorts who wade into the sea to serve your complimentary caviar and champagne.

SPORTS FACILITIES

Several of these ships have water-level platforms aft and carry their own equipment for windsurfing, waterskiing, and small-boat sailing. The Clippers, the Windstars, and the Renaissance ships carry scuba-diving gear and certified instructors. In the case of the *Renaissance II,* scuba-diving facilities include instruction videos, compressors, 21 tanks and regulators. In addition, each ship has a small pool and whirlpool on deck; all of them have exercise rooms, the most spacious and best equipped being on the Sea Goddesses (operated by Golden Door at Sea Spas).

ITINERARIES

All these ships have unusually shallow drafts (as little as 12 feet in the case of the Renaissance ships), allowing them to negotiate channels and moorings where larger ships never venture. Nevertheless, they seem to spend much of their time cruising to and from routine ports of call like St. Martin/St. Maarten, Barbados, St. Thomas, and Antigua. Among the out-of-the-way destinations are places like Bequia, the Tobago Cays, Jost van Dyke, Montserrat, and the Îles des Saintes; on islands like Antigua they may stop in Falmouth Harbour rather than St. Johns, and on St. Lucia, Rodney Bay, rather than Castries.

My problem with most of the itineraries is not the routine destinations but the fact that they have you in a different port (sometimes two ports) every day instead of treating you to one or two days at sea. It seems odd to provide ships with everything needed to keep passengers comfortable and amused at sea, then tie up in a harbor. For details of the specific itineraries, call the numbers listed above, in the section "The Statistics."

THE TALL SHIPS

Star Flyer/Star Clipper

3,025 tons; 360 feet; 10 to 17 knots (under sail); 170 passengers; 72 crew. Daily rates for two, $332 to $736. *Telephone: 800/442-0551.*

They're straight out of 19th-century engravings—long, graceful hulls topped by four masts, with yardarms, no less, on the foremast. At 360 feet from the tip of their bowsprits to their transoms, these lovely barquentines are longer than the classic clipper ship, *Cutty Sark,* and with their mainmast antennae topping out at 226 feet they claim to be the "tallest of the tall ships." Passengers lounge on teak decks beneath naves of rigging and 36,000 square feet of sails when all the canvas is flying; dark-paneled, brass-trimmed public rooms have the feel of a classic luxury yacht à la Vanderbilt.

The cabins average 120 square feet, smaller than the others in this chapter, but come equipped with amenities like air-conditioning, video, telephones, individual safes, hair dryers and private showers (the kind with timers that require a push every 30 seconds or so).

Unlike the computerized Windstar vessels, the Star clippers are authentic sailing ships and for that reason their passengers are prepared to sacrifice a few of the refinements of the more luxurious vessels in this roundup. Dining, for example, is less of an "experience," given the size of the galley, but on the basis of trips on both ships I can report that most passengers seemed to be enjoying themselves so much they were willing to overlook any inconsistencies in the cuisine or service.

For my money, the entertainment on a vessel like this should be the sails and the wind and the stars, but the Clipper people seem to feel obliged to provide an electronic piano, which is tolerable in its own little niche in the bar but less acceptable when the keyboardist sets up his device on the open deck.

Given the rates, vis-à-vis the luxury vessels, and the nature of these ships, there is less call for polished service. No room service, for example. But the staff is attentive, cabins get made up promptly, and tendering is rarely a problem; the tour directors sometimes left something to be desired (on early cruises—they have more experience in the Caribbean by this time so those shortcomings have probably been straightened out). Onboard sports facilities include snorkeling gear, windsurfing, scuba diving, etc.—all free except for a $40 charge for scuba. There are also two tiny pools, one fore, one aft, not much larger than plunge pools.

I know I'm not alone in hoping that these ships' itineraries will change to steer clear of routine ports of call and explore more backwaters—but, above all, incorporate more full days at sea, under sail. On a *Star Clipper* cruise south from Antigua, the skipper hoisted the canvas and *sailed away* from the tight little anchorage in Terres des Haut—a memorable experience, the sort of thing people want from such a cruise.

The great thing about *Star Clipper* and *Star Flyer* is to have the experience of sailing aboard a tall ship—without the Spartan comforts of the clipper ships of old.

The Rates—and How to Figure Them Out

Before you go any further: *All the room rates quoted in this guidebook are for two people.*

Islands have different ways of establishing their rates, and individual hotels have their own little methods. The variables include twin beds versus double beds, rooms with bath or without bath, rooms on the beach or near the beach, facing the front or facing the back, upper floors versus lower floors, cubic feet of space. Some rooms may cost more because they have air-conditioning, others because they have small refrigerators, and so on. It would be a lifetime's work to figure out all the odds. If you have any special preferences, let the hotel know when you make your reservations.

DIFFERENT TYPES OF RATES

Hotels in the Caribbean quote four different types of rates:

EP	European Plan	You pay for the room only. No meals.
CP	Continental Plan	You get the room and breakfast (usually a Continental breakfast of juice, rolls, and coffee)
MAP	Modified American Plan	You get the room with breakfast plus *one* meal—usually dinner
FAP*	Full American Plan	You get everything—room, breakfast, lunch, afternoon tea (where served), and dinner
FAP+	Full American Plan with extras	You get the room, all meals, afternoon tea, and items like table wines, drinks, laundry, and/or postage stamps—virtually all-inclusive resorts

* Sometimes known as American Plan and abbreviated to AP.

FAP and MAP rates may mean that you order your meals from a fixed menu, rather than from the à la carte menu; in some Caribbean hotels this is a racket because the choice you're offered is so limited or unpromising you're almost obligated to order the items that cost a few dollars more. That happens in only a few of the hotels in *this* guide; although in many of the smaller inns you will be offered a fixed menu for dinner, served at a fixed hour, often at communal tables.

Which rate should you choose? They all have their advantages. Usually you're better off having the EP or CP rate, because this gives you the flexibility to eat wherever you want to eat—for instance, to sample a rijstaffel in Curaçao or dine in some of the bistros on Martinique. On the other hand, in many cases the hotel dining room may be the best eating spot on the island (in some cases the *only* spot), and you'd want to eat there anyway; or the nearest restaurant may be a $10 or $15 cab ride away on the other side of the island and not worth the fare.

On some islands, as in Barbados, some hotels have wisely banded together to arrange an exchange program—in other words, you tell your hotel that you want to dine in hotel B, in which case they arrange to have hotel B send the bill to them. On other islands, you encounter a tiresome attitude among hotel managers in which each one claims to have the best restaurant on the island and therefore "everyone wants to dine in my place anyway."

REBATES ON MEALS

Many hotels allow you a rebate on the dinner portion of your MAP or FAP rate—probably not a full rebate, but most of it, and only if you let them know before lunchtime that you're not going to dine there that evening.

The reason why hotels put you through this hassle is that their supplies are limited, and they have to know in advance how many dinners they must prepare (in the case of steaks, for example, how many they have to thaw), without entailing a lot of waste.

In the hotel listings elsewhere in this guide, I've included the price of dinner where a hotel offers a choice of EP or MAP/FAP rates. Usually, the cost of dinners on a one-shot deal is more expensive (a couple of dollars or so) than the MAP/FAP rates.

TAXES

Most islands entice you to their island and then clobber you with a tax, sometimes two. These taxes may go under any of several euphemisms—room tax, government tax, airport tax, departure tax, energy tax—but what it boils down to is that you're going to pay more than the advertised hotel rates. Some are as high as 8% on your total bill; some are 3% on your room only. If you're on a tight budget, or if you simply don't feel like being taken for a ride, choose an island with no tax. In any case, check out such things if you're watching your pennies. If you *are* concerned about your dollars, note that on the French Islands, taxes and service charge are almost always *included* in the rate.

SERVICE CHARGE

Most hotels in the Caribbean now add a service charge to your bill, usually 10%, 12½%, or 15%, ostensibly in lieu of tipping. In some hotels you may tip in addition to the service charge; in others it's positively forbidden to tip and any member of the staff caught taking a *pourboire* is fired on the spot. The system has its pros and cons: From your point of view, it means you can relax and not have to bother about figuring out percentages, sometimes in funny currencies; on the other hand, a flat fee doesn't reward individual feats of activity, initiative, and personal attention, and without that incentive service can be lethargic. But the chances are service will be lethargic either way. If tipping is included, don't encourage layabouts who hover around looking for an additional tip—send them on their way; and if service overall is so bad it almost ruined your sex life, just refuse to pay the service charge.

ADDITIONAL NOTES ON RATES

In the list of rates that follows, please remember that "off-season" is spring, summer, *and* fall: In other words, these seemingly horrendous peak-season rates are in effect only 4 months of the year, the lower rates the remaining *8 months*.

For most hotels, the peak season runs from December 15 through Easter Day, but this may vary by a few days; if you check into the matter carefully, you may find that in some hotels the higher rates do not begin until Christmas, or even until late January, and you can grab a few unexpected "peak" season bargains. Still others will give you a reduced rate during the *first two weeks in January*. A few of the hotels listed here have three or four seasons; keeping track of them for this guide would be a round-the-year vocation, so the range of rates for those hotels represents the lowest and highest for the two winter and two summer seasons *combined*.

REMEMBER

The figures quoted are not the full story—to get a more accurate comparison of rates between hotels you should also check out the paragraph marked "sports" in the individual hotel listings, to determine what activities are *included* in the rates at no extra charge. For instance, Sandy Lane Hotel on Barbados includes free golf; Bitter End Yacht Club on Virgin Gorda includes virtually unlimited sailing.

SPECIAL PACKAGES

As I mentioned in the introduction, and remind you here, your wallet may benefit by looking into special packages offered by individual hotels and airlines to independent travelers. For example, Young Island in the Grenadines treats "Lovers" to their own special off-season rate that includes everything but drinks and postage stamps. American has an extensive selection of "Flyaway Vacations" that includes 3-night or 7-night stays (often including round-trip airport transfers, which can be costly otherwise). Continental's tours are detailed in a brochure called "Grand Destinations Caribbean." Check with your travel agent for details.

BEWARE

In the best of times, it's difficult for a hotel keeper to estimate rates for two seasons hence; in these inflationary times it's virtually impossible. Since most innkeepers wait until the last minute to publish their rates, I have used the winter rates for 1994–95. Add 5% and you won't be far wrong. So, alas and alack, some of these rates will be wrong by the time you get around to escaping. It's not my fault. It's not my publisher's fault. Blame it on oil sheiks, bankers, gold speculators, trade unions, fishermen, and the sailors who pilot the island schooners. In any case, the prices will still be valid as a *comparison* between hotels and resorts, even between islands. The differences shouldn't be more than a few percentage points, but always double-check the rates before you go.

The rates are arranged alphabetically by island and are quoted in U.S. dollars.

HOTELS	RATE/TYPE (U.S. $)	PEAK SEASON	SERVICE CHARGE	OFF-SEASON DISCOUNT
Anguilla (8% tax)				
CAP JULUCA	$435–1,630 CP	12/16–3/31	10%	20%
COCCOLOBA	$285–575 CP	12/15–4/15	10%	20%
CINNAMON REEF RESORT	$250–350 CP	12/21–4/3	10%	40%
MALLIOUHANA	$480–810 EP	12/18–3/31	10%	50%
LA SIRENA HOTEL	$210–280 EP	12/15–3/31	10%	40%

HOTELS	RATE/TYPE (U.S. $)	PEAK SEASON	SERVICE CHARGE	OFF-SEASON DISCOUNT
Antigua (7% tax)				
THE ADMIRAL'S INN	$104–128 EP	12/15–4/15	10%	30%
BLUE WATERS BEACH HOTEL	$245–455 EP	12/16–4/16	10%	40%
THE COPPER & LUMBER STORE HOTEL	$195–325 EP	12/16–5/7	10%	55%
CURTAIN BLUFF	$595–855 FAP+	12/19–4/14	10%	20%
GALLEY BAY	$445–$660 FAP+	12/16–4/23	(included)	20%
THE INN AT ENGLISH HARBOUR	$250–360 EP	12/21–3/15	10%	50%
JUMBY BAY ISLAND	$975 FAP+	12/16–4/16	10%	25%
ST. JAMES'S CLUB	$520–770 MAP	12/20–4/19	10%	30%
Barbados (5% tax)				
COBBLERS COVE HOTEL	$490–1,300 MAP	12/18–4/8	10%	40%
CORAL REEF CLUB	$310–575 MAP	12/15–4/21	10%	50%
CRANE BEACH HOTEL	$160–295 EP	12/22–3/31	10%	40%
GLITTER BAY	$395–555 EP	12/17–3/31	10%	50%
ROYAL PAVILION	$475–995 EP	12/17–3/31	10%	50%
SANDPIPER INN	$295–485 EP	12/15–4/21	10%	40%
SANDY LANE HOTEL	$720–1,600 MAP	12/16–4/6	10%	25%
Barbuda (7% tax)				
K CLUB	$950–2,700 FAP	12/16–4/14	10%	20%
Bequia (7% tax)				
FRANGIPANI HOTEL	$55–130 EP	12/15–4/14	10%	30%
PLANTATION HOUSE HOTEL	$320–350 MAP	12/15–4/14	10%	30%
SPRING ON BEQUIA	$200–265 MAP	12/15–4/14	10%	30%
Bonaire (5% tax)				
CAPTAIN DON'S HABITAT	$175–260 EP	year-round	10%	n/a

HOTELS	RATE/TYPE (U.S. $)	PEAK SEASON	SERVICE CHARGE	OFF-SEASON DISCOUNT
HARBOUR VILLAGE BEACH RESORT	$265–695 CP	12/19–4/6	10%	25%

Canouan (7% tax)

TAMARIND BEACH RESORT & YACHT CLUB	$250 EP	1/15–4/15	10%	25%

Cayman Islands (10% tax)

HYATT REGENCY GRAND CAYMAN	$295–500 EP	12/20–4/20	10%	40%

Curaçao (7% tax)

AVILA BEACH HOTEL	$100–240 EP	12/16–4/30	12%	5%
SONESTA BEACH HOTEL & CASINO	$230–450 EP	1/2–4/16	12%	30%

The Dominican Republic (13% tax)

CASA DE CAMPO	$180–650 EP	12/21–4/16	10%	30%

Grenada (8% tax)

THE CALABASH	$365–495 MAP	12/19–4/15	10%	30%
SECRET HARBOUR	$225 EP	12/20–4/14	10%	40%
SPICE ISLAND INN	$340–495 MAP	12/15–4/15	10%	20%

Guadeloupe (tax included in rates)

HAMAK	$300–400 CP	12/17–4/18	15%	30%

Guana Island (7% tax)

GUANA ISLAND	$595 FAP	12/16–3/31	12%	30%

Jamaica (tax included in rates)

GOOD HOPE GREAT HOUSE	$200–250 MAP	12/15–4/15	10%	25%
HALF MOON GOLF, TENNIS & BEACH CLUB	$150–450 EP	12/15–4/15	(included)	35%
JAMAICA INN	$385–475 FAP	12/16–3/15	10%	25%
HOTEL MOCKING BIRD HILL	$120–$140 EP	12/15–4/30	(optional)	25%

HOTELS	RATE/TYPE (U.S. $)	PEAK SEASON	SERVICE CHARGE	OFF-SEASON DISCOUNT
PLANTATION INN	$195–485 MAP	12/15–4/14	10%	30%
ROUND HILL	$300–690 EP	12/15–4/15	(included)	35%
STRAWBERRY HILL	$250–775 CP	12/15–4/15	10%	30%
TRIDENT VILLAS & HOTEL	$350–800 EP	12/15–4/15	(included)	40%
TRYALL GOLF, TENNIS & BEACH RESORT	$295–490 EP	12/15–4/10	(included)	35%

Martinique (tax included in rates)

HABITATION LAGRANGE	$380–440 CP	12/20–4/30	(included)	25%
HOTEL PLANTATION LEYRITZ	$102–158 CP	12/15–4/15	(included)	10%

Mayreau (5% tax)

SALTWHISTLE BAY CLUB	$490 MAP	12/16–3/31	10%	40%

Montserrat (10% tax)

VUE POINTE HOTEL	$126–166 EP	12/15–4/14	10%	30%

Mustique (7% tax)

THE COTTON HOUSE	$475–660 FAP	12/16–4/15	10%	30%

Nevis (7% tax)

CRONEY'S OLD MANOR ESTATE	$175 EP	12/15–4/14	10%	30%
FOUR SEASONS NEVIS RESORT	$500–2,200 EP	12/21–3/31	10%	60%
GOLDEN ROCK	$255 MAP	12/20–4/14	10%	15%
HERMITAGE PLANTATION	$325–425 MAP	12/15–4/15	10%	35%
MONTPELIER PLANTATION INN	$280 CP	12/15–4/15	10%	35%
NISBET PLANTATION BEACH CLUB	$355–455 MAP	12/21–4/14	10%	30%

Palm Island (7% tax)

PALM ISLAND BEACH CLUB	$265–345 FAP	12/21–4/14	10%	10%

HOTELS	RATE/TYPE (U.S. $)	PEAK SEASON	SERVICE CHARGE	OFF-SEASON DISCOUNT
Petit St. Vincent (5% tax)				
PETIT ST. VINCENT RESORT	$680 FAP	12/19–3/12	10%	35%
Puerto Rico (7% tax)				
THE HORNED DORSET PRIMAVERA HOTEL	$162.50–220 EP	12/15–4/15	3%	40%
HYATT DORADO BEACH RESORT & CASINO	$345–610 EP	12/20–3/31	(included)	40–50%
PALMAS DEL MAR	$205–325 EP	12/21–4/15	7%–9%	40%
Saba (5% tax)				
CAPTAIN'S QUARTERS	$125–150 CP	12/21–4/15	15%	20%
WILLARD'S OF SABA	$180–300 EP	12/15–4/14	(included)	20%
St. Barthélemy (tax included in rates)				
CASTELETS	$150–490 CP	12/18–4/19	10%	40%
EL SERENO BEACH HOTEL	$265–340 EP	12/15–4/15	15%	40%
FILAO BEACH HOTEL	$350–640 CP	12/20–3/1	(included)	25%
FRANÇOIS PLANTATION	$300–480 CP	12/21–4/14	(included)	50%
HOTEL CARL GUSTAF	$770–950 CP	12/20–4/14	(included)	25%
HOTEL GUANAHANI	$390–780 CP	12/22–4/18	(included)	45%
HOTEL MANAPANY	$413–628 CP	1/7–4/15	(included)	30%
HOTEL ST. BARTH ISLE DE FRANCE	$350–700 CP	12/15–4/15	(included)	15%
HOTEL LE TOINY	$720 CP	12/17–4/17	(included)	40%
St. Croix (8% tax)				
THE BUCCANEER HOTEL	$195–390 CP	12/20–4/1	(optional)	20%
CORMORANT BEACH CLUB	$210–295 EP	12/21–4/14	(optional)	40%
VILLA MADELEINE	$425 EP	12/15–4/14	10%	30%
St. John (8% tax)				
CANEEL BAY	$335–615 EP	1/1–3/31	(optional)	30%

HOTELS	RATE/TYPE (U.S. $)	PEAK SEASON	SERVICE CHARGE	OFF-SEASON DISCOUNT
St. Kitts (7% tax)				
THE GOLDEN LEMON	$350–495 MAP	12/16–4/15	10%	20%
OTTLEY'S PLANTATION				
INN	$300–385 MAP	12/15–4/15	10%	20%
RAWLINS PLANTATION	$390 MAP	12/15–4/15	10%	35%
THE WHITE HOUSE	$375 MAP	12/15–4/15	10%	30%
St. Lucia (8% tax)				
ANSE CHASTANET				
BEACH HOTEL	$330–550 MAP	12/20–4/16	10%	40%
EAST WINDS INN	$450–520 FAP+	12/18–4/16	(included)	35%
JALOUSIE PLANTATION				
RESORT & SPA	$350–475 FAP+	12/20–4/16	(included)	20%
LADERA RESORT	$330–650 CP	12/18–4/15	10%	40%
WINDJAMMER LANDING				
VILLA BEACH RESORT	$230–375 EP	12/18–4/18	10%	35%
St. Maarten/St. Martin (5% tax on Dutch side, $4 per person per day on French side)				
LA BELLE CRÉOLE	$315–1,045 CP	12/22–4/2	(optional)	35%
LE MERIDIEN				
L'HABITATION AND				
LE DOMAINE	$260–730 EP	12/18–4/9	(included)	40%
MARY'S BOON	$150 EP	12/15–4/31	15%	50%
THE OYSTER POND BEACH				
HOTEL, A COLONY				
RESORT	$170–310 CP	12/20–3/31	15%	30%
LA SAMANNA	$490–860 CP	12/16–4/16	(included)	35%
St. Thomas (8% tax)				
GRAND PALAZZO HOTEL	$470–865 EP	1/2–4/2	(optional)	50%
PAVILIONS & POOLS				
HOTEL	$235–255 CP	12/21–3/31	(optional)	25%
POINT PLEASANT	$275–380 EP	12/23–3/31	(included)	15%
St. Vincent (7% tax)				
GRAND VIEW BEACH				
HOTEL	$210–270 CP	12/15–4/14	10%	40%
YOUNG ISLAND	$430–590 MAP	12/18–2/28	10%	35%

HOTELS	RATE/TYPE (U.S. $)	PEAK SEASON	SERVICE CHARGE	OFF-SEASON DISCOUNT
Tobago (15% tax)				
ARNOS VALE HOTEL	$160 EP	12/15–5/2	10%	20%
MOUNT IRVINE BAY				
HOTEL & GOLF CLUB	$215–360 EP	12/17–4/15	10%	30%
Tortola (7% tax)				
LONG BAY BEACH RESORT	$195–295 EP	12/16–4/15	10%	40%
PETER ISLAND	$395–525 EP	12/23–3/31	10%	30%
THE SUGAR MILL	$250 EP	12/21–4/14	10%	30%
Virgin Gorda (7% tax)				
BIRAS CREEK	$465–685 FAP	12/17–3/31	10%	25%
BITTER END				
YACHT CLUB	$420–515 MAP	12/15–4/15	$12 per person per day	25%
DRAKE'S ANCHORAGE				
RESORT INN	$412–595 FAP	12/18–4/17	15%	20%
LITTLE DIX BAY	$480–675 EP	12/20–3/31	(optional)	25%

Reservations & Tourist Information

THE REPS

Hotel representatives keep tabs on the availability of rooms in the hotels they represent, and handle reservations and confirmations at no extra charge to you (unless you wait until the last minute and they have to send faxes or make phone calls back and forth, in which case you'll be charged). The reps who have appeared most frequently in these pages are listed below; in the interests of simplicity, only the main offices are listed for each one.

American Wolfe International
1890 Palmer Avenue
Larchmont, NY 10538
914/833-3303, 800/223-5695
Fax 914/833-3308

Caribbean Inns Ltd.
P.O. Box 7411
Hilton Head Island, SC 29938
803/785-7411, 800/633-7411
Fax 803/686-7411

Divi Resorts
6340 Quadrangle Drive, Suite 300
Chapel Hill, NC 27514
919/419-3484, 800/367-3484
Fax 919/419-2075

E&M Associates
211 E. 43rd St.
New York, NY 10017
212/599-8280, 800/223-9832
Fax 212/599-1755

International Travel & Resorts, Inc.
4 Park Avenue
New York, NY 10016
212/251-1800, 800/223-9815
Fax 212/251-1767

JDB Associates
P.O. Box 16086
Alexandria, VA 22302-6086
800/346-5358
Fax 703/548-5825

Leading Hotels of the World
747 Third Ave.
New York, NY 10017-2803
212/838-3110, 800/223-6800
Fax 212/758-7367

Loews Representation International
1 Park Ave.
New York, NY 10016
800/223-0888
Fax 212/545-2714

Mondotels
1500 Broadway, Suite 1101
New York, NY 10036
212/719-5750, 800/847-4249
Fax 212/719-5763

Preferred Hotels
1901 South Meyers Road
Oakbrook Terrace, IL 60181
800/323-7500
Fax 708/290-6172

Ralph Locke Islands
P.O. Box 492477
Los Angeles, CA 90049-8477
800/223-1108
Fax 310/440-4220

Robert Reid Associates
810 North 96th Street
Omaha, NE 68114-2594
402/398-3218, 800/223-6510
Fax 402/398-5484

WIMCO
Box 1461
Newport, RI 02840
401/849-8012, 800/932-3222
Fax 401/847-6290

TOURIST INFORMATION

The function of this guide is to give you facts and tips on where to stay, rather than what to see; there just isn't time or space to do both. In any case, with the exceptions of islands like Puerto Rico, Jamaica, and a few others, there really isn't much to see—a fort, a volcano, a native market or two. Many of the major sightseeing attractions (and a few offbeat sights) are mentioned in these pages; if you want more information on topics like shopping and sightseeing, I suggest you get in touch with the tourist office of the islands that interest you. The other possibility is to write to the Caribbean Tourism Organization (20 E. 46th St., New York, NY 10017, 212/682-0435) for information on most of the islands.

If you wait until you get to the island, you'll find no shortage of publications and notice boards with up-to-the-minute details on shops, restaurants, sights, and tours.

Index